CW01151452

DÉODAT DE SÉVERAC

to Evelyn and Robert Waters Sr. for their friendship and support

Déodat de Séverac
Musical Identity in *Fin de Siècle* France

ROBERT F. WATERS
Seton Hall University, USA

ASHGATE

© Robert F. Waters 2008

All rights reserved. No part of this publication may be reproduced, stored in a retrieval system or transmitted in any form or by any means, electronic, mechanical, photocopying, recording or otherwise without the prior permission of the publisher.

Robert F. Waters has asserted his moral right under the Copyright, Designs and Patents Act, 1988, to be identified as the author of this work.

Published by
Ashgate Publishing Limited
Gower House
Croft Road
Aldershot
Hampshire GU11 3HR
England

Ashgate Publishing Company
Suite 420
101 Cherry Street
Burlington, VT 05401-4405
USA

www.ashgate.com

British Library Cataloguing in Publication Data
Waters, Robert
 Déodat de Séverac : musical identity in fin de siecle France 1. Séverac, Déodat de, 1872–1921 – Criticism and interpretation 2. Regionalism in music 3. Regionalism – France – History 4. Folk music – France – Languedoc – History and criticism 5. Folk music – Spain – Catalonia – History and criticism
 I. Title
 780.9'2

Library of Congress Cataloging-in-Publication Data
Waters, Robert (Robert Francis)
 Déodat de Séverac : musical identity in fin de siècle France / Robert Waters.
   p. cm.
 Includes bibliographical references and index.
 ISBN 978-0-7546-4105-6 (alk. paper)
  1. Séverac, Déodat de, 1872–1921–Criticism and interpretation. 2. Music–France–History and criticism. I. Title.

ML410.S48W37 2008
780.92--dc22
[B]

2008014279

ISBN 978 0 7546 4105 6

Mixed Sources
Product group from well-managed forests and other controlled sources
www.fsc.org Cert no. SA-COC-1565
© 1996 Forest Stewardship Council
FSC

Printed and bound in Great Britain by
MPG Books Ltd, Bodmin, Cornwall.

Contents

List of Figures and Illustrations	*vii*
List of Music Examples	*ix*
Preface	*xiii*

PART I   Introduction, Biography, and Regionalist Philosophy

1	Introduction	3
2	Biography	17
3	*Le Régionalisme*	41

PART II   Compositions from the Paris Years, 1896–1909

4	Severac, Christianity, and Organ Music	81
5	Songs	97
6	Opera: *Le Coeur du Moulin* (The Heart of the Mill)	113
7	Piano Music	123
8	Unpublished, Unfinished, Lost, and Recently Published Works	153

PART III   Catalan Music, 1910–1921

9	Catalan Regionalism: Politics and Music	167
10	Severac's Catalan Works	197
11	Conclusion	243

Appendix: Selective Compilation of Severac's Work List	*247*
Bibliography	*255*
Index	*271*

List of Figures and Illustrations

Figures

3.1	Status of Regional Conservatories in France (1907). Conservatory Branches, Nationalized Conservatories, and Municipal Schools	60
3.2	Events during the 1906 *Congrès des chants populaires*	68
7.1	Sonata-Allegro Form in *Sonate*, 1st Movement	126
9.1	Sardana Structure and Score Format for Cobla	177
9.2	Catalan and Spanish Musicians at the Schola Cantorum between 1894 and 1925	183
9.3	Catalan and Spanish Musicians at the Paris Conservatoire between 1894 and 1925	184
10.1	Joseph Canteloube's Description of the Five Movements to *Cerdaña*	212
10.2	Text to *Lo cant del Vallespir*	222
10.3	Ten Sections in Séverac's one movement suite, *Sous les lauriers-roses*	233

Illustrations

3.1	Jean-François Millet, *L'angélus*. Permission courtesy of Réunion des Musées Nationaux/Art Resource, NY	77
9.1	*Sardana Dancers in Saint-Félix de Lauragais*. Permission courtesy of the Bibliothèque Festival Déodat de Séverac, Toulouse, France	170

List of Music Examples

4.1	Measures 1–5 of "Prélude," from *Suite en mi*	89
4.2	Measures 1–5 of "Fugue," from *Suite en mi*	90
4.3	Measures 42–52 of "Fantaisie pastorale," from *Suite en mi*	91
4.4	*Carillon languedocien* theme	92
4.5	Measures 1–3 of "Prélude," from *Petite suite scholastique*	92
4.6a	Measure 3 to "Cantilène mélancolique," from *Petite suite scholastique*, and Measures 192–195 of "Vers le mas en fête," from *En Languedoc*	93
4.6b	Measures 192–195 of "Vers le mas en fête," from *En Languedoc*	94
4.7a	Measures 49–53 of "Prélude," from *Suite en mi*	94
4.7b	Measures 101–109 from "Sur l'étang, le soir," from *En Languedoc*	95
5.1a	Measures 1–6 of Berlioz' "Villanelle"	99
5.1b	Measures 1–5 of Séverac's "Ritournelle"	99
5.2	Measures 1–7 of "Renouveau"	101
5.3	Beginning of "Paysages tristes" ("Soleils couchants")	102
5.4a	Measures 32–34 of Séverac's "A l'aube dans la montagne"	107
5.4b	6 Measures at Rehearsal 35 of Act IV, Scene 4 of Debussy's *Pelléas et Mélisande* (piano-vocal score)	108
6.1	Measure 3 of Act I, Scene 7 to *Le coeur du moulin* (piano-vocal score)	119
6.2	Excerpt from Act II, Scene 5 to *Le coeur du moulin* (piano-vocal score)	119
6.3	Excerpt from Act I, Scene 1 to *Le coeur du moulin* (piano-vocal score)	120
7.1a	Measures 1–2, *Sonate*, first movement	125
7.1b	Measures 1–2, *Sonate*, second movement	126
7.2a	Measure 256, *Sonate*, fourth movement, descending octave line	127
7.2b	Measure 305, *Sonate*, first movement, descending octave line	127
7.3a	Measures 349–352, *Sonate*, first movement, rhythmic pattern and major 2nd interval motion	127
7.3b	Measures 265–266, *Sonate*, fourth movement	128
7.4a	Measures 60–73, *Sonate*, third movement, Melody and Parallelism	128
7.4b	Measures 106–110, *Sonate*, fourth movement	128
7.5	Conjunct Modal Construction, Measures 1–7 of *Le chant de la terre* for piano, second movement ("Les semailles")	132
7.6	Measures 1-8 of the "Intermezzo" section of *Le chant de la terre*	132
7.7	Opening Prologue to *Le chant de la terre*	133
7.8	"Les moissons," Measures 1–8, *Le chant de la terre*	134
7.9	Interval structure in 'Halte à la fontaine' section, Measures 94–95, *En Languedoc*, first movement ("Vers le mas en fête")	145
7.10	Interval structure, Measures 183–190, *En Languedoc*, first movement, "Vers le mas en fête"	145
7.11	Interval structure, Measures 3–5, *En Languedoc*, second movement (Sur l'étang, le soir)	146

7.12	Interval structure, Measures 108–111 of *En Languedoc*, third movement ("A cheval dans la prairie")	146
7.13	Interval structure within augmentation in *En Languedoc*, third movement ("A cheval dans la prairie")	146
7.14	Rapid Arpeggios in Measures 128–129 in "Vers le mas en fête," from *En Languedoc*	147
8.1a	Measures 13–15 (Faun Theme) from *Nymphes au crépuscule*	156
8.1b	Measures 1–3 (Faun Theme) from Claude Debussy's *Prélude à "L'après-midi d'un faune"*	157
9.1	Metrical Variants within Sardana Structure	175
9.2	Typical Fluviol Introductory Solo	177
9.3	Isaac Albéniz, *Catalonia*, Measures 127–143	190
10.1	"Danse du soleil," *Héliogabale*, Act III, no. 1, mm. 1–9 (piano-vocal score)	208
10.2	Bugle Calls of Carabiniers, *Suite Cerdaña*, second movement ("Les fêtes: souvenir de Puigcerda")	214
10.3	Sardana Theme Embedded in Measures 1–6, *Suite Cerdaña*, third movement ("Ménétriers et glaneuses")	214
10.4	Goig Theme Embedded in Measure 64–70, *Suite Cerdaña*, third movement ("Ménétriers et glaneuses")	215
10.5	'Esperanza' Section, *Suite Cerdaña*, first movement ("En tartane: l'arrivée en Cerdagne")	217
10.6	Variation in B minor, 'Esperanza' theme in Measures 211–216, *Suite Cerdaña*, first movement ("En tartane: l'arrivée en Cerdagne")	217
10.7	'Esperanza' Theme, 'Charmante recontre' section, *Suite Cerdaña*, second movement ("Les fêtes: souvenir de Puigcerda")	218
10.8	Variation of 'Esperanza' Theme in G minor, Measures 226–243, *Suite Cerdaña*, second movement ("Les fêtes: souvenir de Puigcerda")	218
10.9	Stretto-like Variation on 'Esperanza' theme, Measures 46–53, *Suite Cerdaña*, fifth movement ("Le retour des muletiers")	219
10.10	'Esperanza' Theme in B minor, Measures 52–63, *Suite Cerdaña*, fifth movement ("Le retour des muletiers")	220
10.11	Hidden 'Esperanza' Theme, Measures 79–82, *Suite Cerdaña*, fifth movement ("Le retour des muletiers")	221
10.12	Variation of 'Esperanza' Theme in Sextuple Meter, Measures 117–123, *Suite Cerdaña*, fifth movement ("Le retour des muletiers")	221
10.13	Introduction, *Hélène de Sparte* (Facsimile)	227
10.14	Opening to *El divino de l'hort* (Facsimile)	229
10.15	*Minyoneta*, Measures 1–14	231
10.16	Fluviol Solo Followed by "Quasi sardana," *Sous les lauriers-roses*, Measures 149–211	234
10.17	"Quasi sardana," *Sous les lauriers-roses*, Measures 45–93	236
10.18	Comparison of Fluviol Solos in Séverac's *Sous les lauriers-roses* and Canteloube's *Lo pardal*	238
10.19	Sardana Section of Canteloube's *Lo pardal*, Measures 83–142	239

10.20	Comparison of Sardana Section in Séverac's *Sous les lauriers-roses* and Canteloube's *Lo pardal*	241
10.21	Funeral Sardana in Joseph Canteloube's *Lauriers*, Measures 70–107, second movement ("A la mémoire d'un ami")	241

Preface

I first became interested in French music as a young pianist studying with the French virtuoso Daniel Ericourt, a former pupil of Roger Ducasse at the Paris Conservatoire. Ericourt won the 1924 Diémer Prize, having earlier performed in the same benefit concert for prisoners of war as had Debussy directly before the composer's death in 1918. Ericourt's directions regarding phrasing, his approach to technique, and his overall temperament seemed to be thoroughly Gallic and helped to stimulate in me an embryonic interest in fin de siècle French music.

My specific interest in Déodat de Séverac's music began with the International Piano Competition at the University of Maryland, College Park, in 1981, when pianist Margaret Otwell performed "Les muletiers devant le Christ de Llivia," one of five movements from Séverac's then comparatively unknown piano suite *Cerdaña*. I proceeded to research and discover other piano compositions by Séverac and later performed many of these works in recitals myself.

My information about Séverac's later works came primarily from four sources: the Library of Congress in Washington, DC, the Bibliothèque Nationale in Paris, manuscripts and letters I uncovered in Séverac's baronial birthplace home in St Félix de Lauragais, and information acquired in the Catalan town of Céret, France, regarding Séverac's interest in cobla and sardana rhythmic structures.

I am profoundly indebted to members of the staff at the Library of Congress in Washington, DC, and the Bibliothèque Nationale in Paris for their help and patience during my period of stay. I also wish to acknowledge Jean-Jacques Cubaynes, director of the Séverac Festival in Toulouse, France, for guiding me in my quest for specific Séverac manuscripts and for clarifying various issues regarding Séverac; to French writer Jean-Bernard Cahours d'Aspry, for providing me with biographical information about Séverac's last years in Céret and for allowing me to consult his manuscript regarding Séverac's compositions;[1] to Catherine Blacque-Belair, for allowing me to reside at the Séverac home in St Félix de Lauragais and analyze the composer's manuscripts and letters; and to Max Havart, Professor of Music at the Perpignan Conservatory in Roussillon, for providing me with most valuable information during my stay in the Pyrénées as to Séverac's relationship with the cobla and sardana.

I also wish to express my appreciation to Shelley G. Davis at the University of Maryland, College Park, for his guidance on organizational issues with regard to chapters dealing with Séverac and Barrès, as well as those discussing Séverac's Catalan music. I would like to show thanks to Carlo Caballero, at the University of Colorado, Boulder, Steven Huebner, from McGill University, Jann Pasler, at the University of California, San Diego, and Brian Hart, at Northern Illinois University, for their detailed and significant suggestions concerning the chapter on French

---

1 Jean-Bernard Cahours d'Aspry, "Déodat de Séverac" (unpublished manuscript).

regionalism, as well as Steve Huebner's additional advice on the chapter discussing Séverac's opera *Le coeur du moulin*, and Carlo Caballero's further suggestions with respect to the chapter on Séverac's biography. Keith Waters at the University of Colorado, Boulder, offered invaluable ideas with respect to my music analysis of Séverac's songs, piano music, and Catalan works, and I also thank Eleanor McCrickard at the University of North Carolina, Greensboro, for her comments on Séverac's organ music. One cannot complete this work without thanking French organist and musicologist Pierre Guillot for clarifying certain questions about Séverac's political affiliations, and acknowledge his contribution in compiling many of Séverac's letters in his 2002 publication *Déodat de Séverac: la musique et les lettres*, and some of Séverac's articles in *Déodat de Séverac: écrits sur la musique*.[2] I am also most grateful to Ann Baptiste of Washington, DC and Scott Kusher of Duke University for their aid in the proofreading of my translations of French into English, and also thank Manel Lacorte at the University of Maryland, College Park, for help in translating Spanish into English and proofreading my Catalan into English translations. I would finally like to express my gratitude to Keith Waters and Robert and Evelyn Waters for their unending emotional support during this entire process.

***

Procedures in this book include the presenting of dates of composers, when available. References to terms and names of individuals are listed as they appear in the documents themselves. The primary sources of statements made by others will be listed unless unavailable to me. I have not italicized French terms and associations, except when introducing these terms, due to the voluminous entries within the book, which would render the pages cluttered. Composition, book, and publication titles are nonetheless italicized. I have capitalized the first word of all periodical titles and all proper nouns within these titles and my source for foreign capitalization comes from: Joseph Gibaldi, *MLA Handbook for Writers of Research Papers*, 5th ed. (New York: The Modern Language Association of America), 1999. This work is based on publications of the Modern Language Association.

---

2   Pierre Guillot, *Déodat de Séverac: la musique et les lettres* (Liège, Belgium: Pierre Mardaga, 2002); Pierre Guillot, *Déodat de Séverac: écrits sur la musique* (Liège, Belgium: Pierre Mardaga, 1993).

PART I
Introduction, Biography, and Regionalist Philosophy

Chapter 1

Introduction

The results of the Industrial Revolution were not unique to France. Increasing industrialization helped improve medicine throughout much of Europe, which subsequently led to a decrease in child mortality and greater longevity among the general population. From 1870 to 1914, the population of Europe increased by half, from 290 to 435 million people. However, the population growth in France was small when compared to the rest of Europe—9.7%, as compared to 57.8% within the German Empire, 42.8% in Great Britain, 38.3% in Austria-Hungary, 29.5% in Italy, and 20% in Spain.[1] This industrialization led to mechanized factory production, which, in turn, produced a demand for more workers within urban areas. Specialized agricultural production in the provinces also became important, which then resulted in a reduced demand for farm laborers. This rapid industrialization within Western Europe was coupled with an economic depression that lasted from 1873 to 1895. The slump resulted in falling agricultural prices, rural poverty, and unemployment within provincial areas.

Industrialization and poverty forced many rural peasants to migrate to urban areas. According to some historians, however, this urban migration did not preclude migrants from remaining in contact with their rural origins. In France, for example, many industrial workers returned to their villages yearly to help with annual harvests. In Russia, migrants to cities were forced by the state to maintain legal ties to their rural commune because of their continuous responsibility to the tax quota of their particular provincial region.[2] This trend towards urban migration, coupled with a regard for the provinces, led to an increased fascination with political and cultural regionalism.[3]

Cultural identity in France became an awareness of regional diversity among various provinces. The idea of living in the rural provinces was, in part, an escape from the tensions of an increasingly industrial age. This idea of escape was inspired by the idealization of rural provinces in literature and poetry.[4]

---

1 John Merriman, *A History of Modern Europe* (New York: W.W. Norton and Company, 1996), 857.

2 Ibid., 863.

3 The interest was further intensified by the perception among many that the centralized Third Republic government was becoming increasingly stagnant by the end of the century, and this belief prompted many regionalists to propose different forms of administrative reform.

4 See James R. Lehning, *Peasant and French Cultural Contact in Rural France During the Nineteenth Century* (Cambridge University Press, 1995); Xavier de Planhol, *An Historical Geography of France*, translated by Janet Lloyd (Cambridge: Cambridge University Press, 1994).

Yet many writer-philosophers and politicians promoted regionalism in order to inspire national cohesion. Regional identity could be a tool to persuade the population to pay homage to one's local pays in order to provide a sense of heritage and therefore nationalist feelings towards the patrie.[5] Carl Dahlhaus suggests this in *Between Romanticism and Modernism*, when he asserts the so-called volksgeist hypotheses, which stipulates that regionalism was appropriated by the bourgeoisie in order to reassure themselves that their national feelings had roots, which would then validate their own existence.[6]

Despite these arguments, including those made by Dahlhaus, regional styles within the arts nonetheless did develop, especially with regard to so-called folk music, a term primarily characterized as a communal and anonymous form of composition handed down from one generation to another. This oral tradition is thought to have taken place without academic elaboration and involves a continual process of transformation, so that a folk song becomes a collective rather than a personal creation. It is then the community which determines the form in which the music survives.[7]

Certain philosophers argue that the "discovery" of folk music consists of recycling the philosophy of primitivism, the belief that a technologically backward or chronologically earlier culture is in some respects purer than contemporary civilization; that those qualities that are least socialized and civilized are closest to the truth—characteristics such as "raw emotion" and "plain speech."[8] This concept

---

5 The term *pays* alludes to one's native village or region or place where one's ancestors lived, with the region's inherent folk traditions, dialects, customs, and other modes of local survival and ritual, including agricultural farming, love of nature, and dedication towards religion and local tradition. The word *patrie* implies a patriotic affinity for one's country.

6 Carl Dahlhaus, *Between Romanticism and Modernism: Four Studies in the Music of the Later Nineteenth Century*, translated by Mary Whittall (Berkeley, CA: University of California Press, 1980), 87–93; originally published as *Zwischen romantik und moderne: vier studien zur musikgeschichte des späteren 19. jahrhunderts*, as part of the following series: Carl Dahlhaus and Rudolf Stephan, ed., *Berliner musikwissenschaftliche arbeiten* (Munich: Musikverlag Emil Katzbichter, 1974). According to Dahlhaus, however, it was not until the age of nineteenth-century nationalism that folk art became viewed partly as a national rather than a purely regional or social phenomenon. The term *nationalisme* reflects an expression of shared history and ethnicity, but the term did not appear in any French dictionary until 1874, when the *Larousse grand dictionnaire universel* defined the word as chauvinism, or described it in relation to nationalist movements of subjugated peoples in nineteenth-century Europe. Carlo Caballero makes this distinction while differentiating between nationalism and patriotism, citing that the latter refers to feelings of loyalty or affection for one's homeland, or patrie, and that shared history and cultural characteristics of a group are emphasized, but without regard to the ethnicity of its members. He then concludes that patriotism is a loyalty to the state rather than nation-state, which would therefore be politically but not ethnically defined. Carlo Caballero, "Patriotism or Nationalism? Fauré and the Great War," *Journal of the American Musicological Society* (vol. 52, no. 3, 1999), 595–6.

7 Maud Korpeles, "Definition of Folk Music," *Journal of the International Folk Music Council*, vol. 7 (January, 1955), 6–7.

8 Richard Taruskin, "Nationalism," *The New Grove Dictionary of Music and Musicians*, second edition, volume 17 (London: Macmillan Publishers Limited, 2001), 692.

echoes Jean-Jacques Rousseau's *Le contrat social* of 1762, wherein Rousseau writes of a longing for unspoiled nature in preference to what he perceived as decadent culture.

Other scholars have characterized folk music as having evolved within cities, courts, and churches, and then had simplified; the music existed while cultural centers changed. It is because cities were small and close to rural areas during the Middle Ages that it becomes difficult to identify the roots of this so-called European folk music. It was not until the growth of cities during the Renaissance that provincial life became more isolated and folk music became more easily identifiable.[9] Because much folk music evolved within churches, many folk melodies are thought to have been derived from chant and some scholars therefore claim that most Western folk melodies are of relatively recent origin.[10]

Many nineteenth-century French writers idealized rural culture and its folk music, including François-René de Chateaubriand (1768–1848), Amandine Aurore Lucie Dupin, Baronne Dudevant (pseud. George Sand, 1804–76), Gérard de Nerval (1808–55), and Théodore Hersart de la Villemarqué (1815–95). Nerval collected folk songs, particularly those that he remembered from his childhood in Valois, and some of these songs are documented in *Chansons et légendes du Valois* of 1852.[11] Chateaubriand discussed folk song from his native Brittany in *Mémoires d'outre-tombe* of 1849, and George Sand highlighted indigenous music in *La mare au diable* of 1846.[12] Villemarqué wrote *Barzas-Breiz: chants populaires de Bretagne* in 1839, the first known publication exclusively devoted to French indigenous music.[13] The French government subsequently commissioned scholars to collect French folk songs, one such work being Julien Tiersot's *Chansons populaires recueillies dans les Alpes françaises* of 1903.[14] Many musicians also harmonized French folk songs and included these harmonizations in publications.

Romanticized theories regarding peasant culture and folk music were also echoed by French writers during the early twentieth century, including the philosopher-writer Maurice Barrès (1862–1923), who used these ideas in defense of regionalism. Barrès argued for the importance of rural culture by alluding to provincial peasants

---

9 Bruno Nettl, "Folk Music," *The New Harvard Dictionary of Music*, ed. Don Michael Randel (Cambridge, MA: Harvard University Press, 1986), 318.

10 Willi Apel, "Folk Music," *The Harvard Dictionary of Music*, 2nd edition (Cambridge, MA: Belknap Press of Harvard University Press, 1969), 324.

11 Gérard de Nerval, *Chansons et légendes du Valois* (Portland, Maine: T.B. Moscher, 1896).

12 See François-René de Chateaubriand, *Mémoires d'outre-tombe* (Paris: E. et V. Penaud frères, 1849); George Sand, *La mare au diable* (Paris: Larousse, 1977).

13 Théodore Hersart de la Villemarqué, *Barzaz-Breiz: chants populaires de la Bretagne* (Paris: Perrin et Cie., 1893).

14 Julien Tiersot, *Chansons populaires recueillies dans les Alpes françaises* (Paris: Grenoble H. Falque et F. Perrin, 1903). Julien Tiersot (1857–1936) was a librarian and musicologist and collected folk songs from various regions and cultures.

Harmonizations by other musicians include Vincent d'Indy's *Chansons du Vivarais* (Paris: A. Durand, 1900), Déodat de Séverac's *Chansons du XVIIIème siècle* (Paris: Rouart, Lerolle et Cie, 1906) and *Les vieilles chansons de France* (Paris: Rouart, Lerolle et Cie, 1906).

possessing qualities of honesty, seriousness, simplicity, fidelity, and sincerity, and people who live in regions with "unspoiled nature." Yet, Barrès's regionalist philosophies were intertwined with nationalism, and this was later echoed by those in Germany's Third Reich, which associated rural peasantry and ancestry with race. Barrès stipulated that those who felt pride in their native region must also pay allegiance to the nation, and foreigners were suspect.[15] Proponents in the Third Reich later used this philosophy in order to mobilize a politically fragmented, economically backward, and militarily weak society.[16] Nationalism in Germany then became a way of bringing together a diverse group of people into a single nation. The Third Reich accomplished this through criteria such as origin, descent, history, language, and culture, together with a historical territory, common myths, historical memories, public culture, a shared economy, and communal legal rights and duties.[17]

The Industrial Revolution further subjected folk music to the influence of popular music, which has often been associated with urban culture and the bourgeoisie that emerged toward the end of the nineteenth century. This new label was, in part, stimulated by the mass dissemination of sheet music, and music styles subsequently developed that were not indigenous to a specific region or ethnic group, but instead the property of the composer. Therefore, the term folk has been traditionally applied to communities uninfluenced by urban popular music.[18]

Determining the roots of so-called indigenous music also varies depending upon the location. Spanish composers often stressed regional characteristics in music, an emphasis apparent to many fin de siècle French composers on hearing Andalusian compositions. According to Gilbert Chase, this music was easily attributable to

---

15 Benedict Anderson suggests that nations were not the product of these characteristics, but were "imagined into existence through print-capitalism." See Benedict Anderson, *Imagined Communities: Reflections on the Origin and Spread of Nationalism* (London and New York: Verso, 1991), cited by Andrea Musk, "Aspects of Regionalism in French Music during the Third Republic: the Schola Cantorum, d'Indy, Séverac and Canteloube" (PhD Dissertation, Oxford University, 1999), 3. For additional studies on French nationalism, see Robert Tombs, ed., *Nationhood and Nationalism from Boulangism to the Great War, 1889–1914* (Cambridge: Cambridge University Press, 1980); Eugen Weber, *The Nationalist Revival in France, 1905–1914* (Berkeley, CA: Berkeley Press, 1959); Anthony Smith, *National Identity* (Reno: University of Nevada Press, 1991); Ernest Gellner, *Nations and Nationalism* (Oxford: Oxford University Press, 1983); Eric Hobsbawm, *Nations and Nationalism Since 1780: Programme, Myth, Reality* (Cambridge: Cambridge University Press, 1990).

16 Taruskin, "Nationalism," 692.

17 Ibid. Folk music has been linked with this criteria, but was not the only type of music to have been associated with nationalist sentiment. Taruskin states that sacred music is also indebted to nationalism, as Gregorian chant was a byproduct of a political alliance between Frankish kings and the Roman Church, the objective being to consolidate the Carolingian empire; see Taruskin, "Nationalism," 690.

18 It has also been argued by some historians that most French folk songs came from uneducated urban street singers during the eighteenth century, who migrated to rural areas and established the musical basis on which rural singers proceeded to produce variants. More than half of the folk songs from Séverac's birthplace in Languedoc are thought to have been created during the Industrial Revolution. See Planhol, *An Historical Geography of France*, 276–7.

Spanish composers, because this region of Spain was most highly influenced by Arab elements. The melodic augmented second was one characteristic in Spanish music that was in large part influenced by the Islamic invasion, as well as from Gypsy music, a musical culture with a genesis in northern India.[19] Gypsies settled in Andalusia as early as the fifteenth century. The use of modes from Byzantine and Hebraic chant also had an important influence on Andalusian music through ancient Spanish churches and synagogues.[20]

For this reason, it is much easier to classify Andalusian music when compared to regional music from the French provinces, including music from the region of Languedoc, French composer Déodat de Séverac's birthplace. Music from this area is more problematic to identify because of various dominions over time within that locale. Troubadours and seamen traveled through Provence and Languedoc and this changed the cultural landscape considerably. Albigenses also flourished in Languedoc during the thirteenth century, and the province was integrated into the royal domain at this time.[21]

Music from Languedoc was therefore the result of much cross-pollination. The music was nonetheless associated with specific characteristics during Séverac's lifetime, including modal harmonies, particularly the use of the Dorian mode, a prominent use of minor keys, slow lyrical vocal music, and rhythmic dances in sextuple meter. Joseph Canteloube, composer and contemporary of Séverac, in *Anthologie des chants populaires français*, declared Languedoc music to contain "vivacious rhythms and finesse [and a] profound expression," and included in his anthology rounds, noëls, a berceuse, a chant de labour (a genre used by Séverac in his piano suite *Le chant de la terre*), a chanson de mariage, and a chanson de bergère, or song intoned by a shepherdess.[22] Also included in Canteloube's anthology with regard to music from Languedoc is the chanson "O up! As-tu entendu," which was also heard in the regions of Gascogne and Quercy during the late nineteenth and early twentieth centuries, but interestingly placed by Canteloube into his collection *Chants d'Auvergne*.[23] Specific instruments also became associated with Languedoc, such as the fourteenth-century bodega, or type of bagpipe made out of goatskin.

It is also relatively difficult to identify Catalan folk music because of the close relationship between Catalan folk and art music since the Middle Ages. Catalan songs often have melodic shapes and cadential figures that suggest plainsong, and "indigenous" melodies therefore frequently bear characteristics found in ecclesiastical

---

19 Gilbert Chase, *The Music of Spain* (New York: Dover Publication, Inc., 1941), 223.
20 Ibid.
21 The Albigenses were a collective denomination of members of a Catharist religious sect that flourished in southern France in the twelfth and thirteenth centuries. They adopted Albigensianism, which was a heretical teaching that espoused a form of Manichean dualism. The Albigenses were exterminated by the Inquisition under Pope Innocent III, following the French conquest of Languedoc led by Simon de Montfort. Albi was the town in southern France in which the sect was dominant.
22 Joseph Canteloube, *Anthologie des chants populaires français groupés par provinces*, 4 vols. (Paris, 1951), 75. "vivacité des rythmes et la finesse ... profondeur de l'expression."
23 Ibid., 85.

modes.[24] In addition, the Islamic invasion of Catalonia was brief and therefore had little influence on Catalan music. As a result, the use of the melodic augmented second in Catalan music is rare, thus making identification even more difficult.

The sardana is easier to recognize than other forms of Catalan music because of its rhythm. This genre has roots in ancient Greek round dances, and more recent precursors include rondes (Catalan ballads that accompany round dances) and the contrapàs llarch, a genre in which words, music, and dance are incorporated into a popular liturgical representation of a Christian Passion drama. Yet the sardana is not, strictly speaking, a folk dance, because sardana music and choreography have been largely created by known individuals during the nineteenth century. The genre, however, is strongly rooted in older folk traditions and is therefore considered to be of a folk aesthetic.[25]

***

Séverac's interest in régionalisme and folk music was reflected in his 1907 graduating thesis from the Schola Cantorum, in which he accused the relatively centralized Paris Conservatoire and its administration of emphasizing compositions within too narrow a range of genres and styles.[26] His regionalist theories regarding education in France made him a partisan in the debate taking place over the relative merits of administrative centralization versus regionalism. The opposing perspective was espoused by France's Minister of Education, Jules Ferry (1832–93), who set in motion a nationalized educational system.[27] As Minister of Education from 1881 to 1882, Ferry made primary education free, compulsory, and secular, and proposed that no citizen be eligible for state employment unless educated in state schools. He also abolished the teaching of catechism in secondary schools while helping to suppress the power of Catholic universities, which was accomplished under the reforms of the Conseil supérieur de l'instruction publique. According to Ferry, the Catholic faith was often coupled with Legitimism, and his bourgeois republican ideals were diametrically opposed to this philosophy.[28] He also asserted that the

---

24 Ibid.

25 I will refer to the word *folk* when making specific points, while being fully aware of the strictly limited usage of the term involved. The main purpose of using the term folk in various contexts is to reflect the ways in which Séverac and his contemporaries would have understood the term. I will also limit this discussion primarily to French, Catalonian, and Spanish cultural influences, the three that had a most significant impact on Séverac's music.

26 Figures implied include Théodore Dubois, who accumulated power as the director of the Paris Conservatoire between 1896 and 1905. Dubois intensely disliked the symphony as well as other forms of instrumental music.

27 Ferry was also a Deputy from 1869 to 1889, Prime Minister from 1880 to 1881, and Senator from 1891 to 1893. As Minister of Education, Ferry introduced military training in the secondary school system and established secondary state schools for girls and training colleges for women.

28 Legitimism was one of three primary conservative factions in France opposed to the overthrow of the Bourbon dynasty in the 1830 July Revolution. This event sent many aristocrats back to their estates in the countryside and to private life. The other two factions

church taught students within the French school system to oppose various intellectual ideas, including the separation of church and state, which subsequently became law in 1905.

Séverac and other regionalists, including Barrès, objected to these proposals among other changes instituted by Ferry. Both disapproved of the centralized French government and the Paris Conservatoire, and they shared a mutual philosophy regarding regionalism in education and a common interest in régionalisme and its ties with nature, peasantry and ancestral roots.[29] Barrès called for new administrative and geographical boundaries, local democracy, and the devolution of centralized legislative and governmental authority. Séverac then expanded these regionalist ideas to include the politicization of the fine arts, wherein the music counterpart to the centralized bureaucracy of the French government was found in the bylaws of the Paris Conservatoire and in its relationship with provincial institutions.

Although Séverac's interest in folk music was primarily a way of expressing regional identity within France to counter styles sanctioned by the Paris Conservatoire and promoted throughout France, most composers living in Paris when Séverac was a student at the Schola Cantorum did not stress regional music in any form. Nationalist sentiment more often inspired composers to include folk music in their works as a patriotic gesture in order to escape from the dominance of German musical style.

Séverac therefore championed the importance of individuality within various regions of France in his 1907 thesis, and suggested that other composers emphasize regional identity in their own music. As a result of Séverac's influence, for example, Joseph Canteloube subsequently created works that included folk music, and also gathered indigenous music by means of written and oral sources from various regions within France, and placed these songs into collections.

Séverac's interest in cultural regionalism was largely inspired by the philosophies of Frédéric Mistral (1830–1914), the Provençal poet and leader of the Félibrige movement (1876–88).[30] Séverac's fascination with southern France and its peasantry, nature, and folk music paralleled Mistral's pan-Latin aesthetic, and it is in many of Mistral's poems that Séverac found a spiritual kinship. Just as Barrès's philosophy was influenced by witnessing the German occupation of his native Lorraine as a child following the Franco-Prussian War, Séverac's southern French upbringing helped foster this spiritual kinship with Mistral and his Mediterranean poetry and philosophy.[31]

---

were the Orléanists and the Bonapartists. Legitimists were opposed to the constitutional monarchy of Louis XVIII and to the limitation of the sovereign's power.

29 Barrès felt that attending Catholic churches reinforced tradition in the home within rural areas and directly or inadvertently promoted régionalisme as a result.

30 The Félibrige was an organization dedicated to promoting southern French culture.

31 Mistral's ideas were adopted by numerous southern French regionalists, including those from the Catalan province of Roussillon. This group includes the Roussillon writer and journalist Xavier Ricard (1843–1911), who was an intense admirer of Mistral's ideas and later became a member of the Félibrige, a group discussed in Chapter III. Ricard later organized the Félibre rouge of Montpellier in 1874. In 1876, Ricard formed La Cigale, a southern French academy designed to unite southern French peoples, and in 1900, he was named President of Honor of Charles-Brun's La fédéralist régionaliste française (FRF), a modern geographical

Séverac's compositions were most influential at the beginning of the twentieth century. During this time, he was regarded as one of the more creative composers in fin de siècle France. His composition teacher, Vincent d'Indy, described him as "one of the great figures in our music," and Gabriel Fauré called attention to the fact that "Séverac has something to say and says it quite simply."[32] Debussy characterized his works as "exquisitely orchestrated and rich with ideas," while further noting that Séverac "composes great music that feels good and one breathes with a full heart."[33]

In fact, Séverac's works inspired much acclaim from various factions within Paris, including two competing groups that he described in his 1907 thesis: those who believed in stressing contrapuntal devices and linear lines within compositions, or d'Indyists, most of whom taught or studied at the Schola Cantorum; and those who stressed harmony over the aforementioned characteristics, or Debussyists, largely from the Paris Conservatoire. Although Séverac studied at the Schola Cantorum, he did not sanction either group, and one of the more unusual aspects regarding Séverac's reputation in Paris was that he and his music simultaneously appealed to both camps. This was, in part, due to Séverac's ability to take different approaches within a single work and his predilection to use specific music characteristics at different stages during his career. D'Indy was also lenient as a pedagogue regarding compositional style, and therefore approved of Séverac's works regardless of the techniques employed. This is coupled with the fact that many at the Schola Cantorum felt a sense of pride in Séverac being their colleague, since his compositions were receiving more recognition in Paris than those by any other student at their school during the opening decade of the twentieth century.

Yet despite the popularity of Déodat de Séverac and his music, the influence of his compositions on other musicians began to wane gradually during the second half of the twentieth century.[34] Part of the reason for a decline in interest in Séverac's

---

and economic regionalist publication dedicated to encouraging the joining together of various factions of French regionalists. Ricard also argued for the pan-Latin idea in *Le fédéralisme* in 1877. Ricard was a friend of Mistral and corresponded with the poet in 27 letters dated between 1876 and 1911. Ricard was in favor of a federalist solution to the pan-Latin concept. The pan-Latin concept stressed the fact that troubadours originated in Provence, but also flourished in the regions of Languedoc, Catalonia, and the Auvergne. This sentiment led to Mistral's pan-Latin concept, which considered the south of France a federation of provinces.

32 Joseph Canteloube, *Déodat de Séverac* [1st Edition, Paris, 1929] (Béziers, France: Société de musicologie de Languedoc, 1984), 80, 69. Vincent d'Indy comments on Séverac: "Ses qualités laissaient présager une des grandes figures de notre art." Gabriel Fauré comments on Séverac: "Séverac a quelque chose à dire, et le dit tout simplement."

33 Ibid., 73. Debussy's first comment refers to Séverac's orchestral work *Nymphes au crépuscule* while the second remark concerns Séverac's piano suite *En Languedoc*: "Ce numéro est tout à fait exquis, d'un dessin précis et impressionniste à la fois, savoureusement orchestré et riche d'idées. Sa musique créé un sentiment de bien-être." "Il fait de la musique qui sent bon, et l'on y respire à plein coeur."

34 Articles and books on Séverac diminished following the publication of Blanche Selva's book *Déodat de Séverac* in 1930. It was not until Elaine Brody's dissertation in 1964

music was that many of his compositions were lost or withheld from publication as a result of legal battles over ownership rights.[35]

Another reason for Séverac's declining reputation is that composers in fin de siècle Paris were pressured to adopt either the philosophies and compositional styles espoused by the Paris Conservatoire administration, or choose those opinions voiced by the leadership within the Schola Cantorum; any composer who did not take sides in this battle was ostracized by powerful figures who were otherwise able to arrange performances of the composer's works.[36] Because Séverac reproved both institutions in his 1907 thesis, this could be one reason why the number of performances of Séverac's music would have gradually declined.[37]

Séverac's reputation also degenerated, in part, because a general interest in regionalism and regionalist compositions decreased between the World Wars.[38] Séverac died three years after the conclusion of the "Great War," which was a catalyst that unified France under the Third Republic government and helped to diminish regional differences. In addition, ensuing advancements in technology unified much of France. People from various regions became less isolated as a result of more rapid communication systems and an increasing number of roads and railways, together with significant improvements in ones that already existed.[39]

---

followed by additional articles on Séverac that attention again began to be paid to Séverac's music.

35 See Gabriel Boissy, *Comoedia* (Paris, August 2, 1936). A conflict developed between Séverac and Dr Joseph Charry, an investor in the Béziers première of Séverac's opera *Héliogabale*. Charry subsequently seized the orchestral score when Séverac and other participants felt cheated out of royalties and initiated a lawsuit. Charles Guéret, the poet of the prologue to the work, had initially insisted that his poetry be included in all performances, and because he felt cheated out of royalties, subsequently prevented *Héliogabale* from being performed once Séverac acquired the score from Charry. The work was therefore presented twice before going into hibernation. Two decades later, Joseph Canteloube requested that the orchestral score be made public, at which time Charry still refused.

36 Jane Fulcher, *French Cultural Politics and Music* (Oxford: Oxford University Press, 1999), 65.

37 More performances of Séverac's music might have encouraged even more attention from other well-known composers, potentially leading to greater visibility for later generations.

38 Exceptions exist, including Charles Koechlin's *Vingt chansons bretonnes* for cello and piano, op. 115 (1931), *Les chants de Kervelean*, op. 197 (1944), and *Quinze duos pour deux clarinettes (Souvenirs de Bretagne)*, op. 195 (1944). All three compositions are of Breton inspiration. *Vingt chansons bretonnes*, op. 115 is a compilation of 20 Breton folk songs arranged for cello and piano, and was Koechlin's first deliberate use of folk song. *Souvenirs de Bretagne* was inspired by Koechlin's 1940 visit to Brittany and includes programmatic titles. *Rapsodie sur des chansons françaises*, op. 62 consists of a popular compilation of Breton tunes and legends. Other musicians composed works that contained French folk music, including the composer Darius Milhaud in *Suite provençale*, op. 152 (1937; Paris: Editions Salabert), and *Suite française* for concert band (1944; New York: MCA Music, 1946).

39 Eugen Weber, *Peasants Into Frenchmen* (Stanford: Stanford University Press, 1976), 195.

It is also likely, however, that Séverac's own regionalist attitudes helped undercut his career and eventually his place for posterity. Because Séverac left Paris permanently for the south of France in 1907 as a way of living out his philosophy, many later compositions were not performed in Paris.[40] Although Barrès and many other regionalists spent their adult lives in Paris in order to expand their careers, Séverac was critical of those who spoke of the importance of rural life and regional identity while residing within urban areas.

***

Nationalism in Paris among writer-philosophers as well as composers was far more prominent than regional identity. Barrès, for example, often debated the relative merits of individual rights versus collective responsibility, an argument exacerbated by the Dreyfus Affair with Barrès and his nationalist sentiments at the center of this scandal. One historical contribution in this book, however, will be in emphasizing his less discussed regionalist ideas and their relationship with those philosophies espoused by Séverac, and in illustrating how these attitudes fit into the national culture.

This book will therefore explore the ways in which Séverac's earlier French regionalist philosophy echoed the writings of regionalist authors Maurice Barrès and Frédéric Mistral and paralleled his own use of approximations of modes and meters common to French folk music. However, these interests were later overshadowed by Séverac's increased fascination with Catalan rhythms and instruments, elements he incorporated in his later compositions. This stylistic evolution was prompted by Séverac's exposure to Catalan music and musicians in Paris, and by his later interest in the cobla and sardana of his newly adopted Catalan home in the village of Céret.

This book will also discuss composers who had an influence on Séverac's musical style. It is nonetheless consequential to recognize pitfalls when discussing these and other types of influences, as historians are frequently known to misread impressions. In addition, artists often misrepresent to themselves and to the public various influences when comparing themselves to contemporaries, progenitors, and cultural styles. Richard Taruskin cites Harold Bloom's idea that artists conceal their influences through repression, sublimation, and defense mechanisms, and therefore the critical task for historians is to penetrate the artist's defenses by analyzing the artist's misreadings.[41] As Bloom states:

---

40 Arthur Honegger made a similar remark about Guy Ropartz, a regionalist composer who spent much of his adult life in Nancy and Strasbourg following his studies in Paris. Ropartz often composed works with Breton themes. See Arthur Honegger, *Je suis compositeur* (Paris: Editions du Conquistador, 1951), 35.

41 Richard Taruskin, "Revising Revision," *Journal of the American Musicological Society*, vol. 46, no. 1 (Spring, 1993), 118. Taruskin is citing Harold Bloom, *A Map of Misreading* (Oxford: Oxford University Press, 1975), and *The Anxiety of Influence: A Theory of Poetry* (Oxford: Oxford University Press, 1973). Taruskin reviews the following two works that appropriate Bloom's theories: Joseph N. Straus, *Remaking the Past: Musical Modernism and the Influence of the Tonal Tradition* (Cambridge, MA: Harvard University Press, 1990),

More than ever, contemporary poets insist that they are telling the truth in their work, and more than ever they tell continuous lies, particularly about their relations to one another, and most consistently about their relations to their precursors.[42]

Bloom's thoughts here present an Oedipal viewpoint regarding human nature with what Taruskin views as its ties to jealousy, territoriality, resentment, and rivalry, so that artistic strength comes from shaking off progenitors in what becomes primarily an adversarial relationship. Taruskin continues to characterize Bloom's theories as to why artists unconsciously misrepresent themselves:

What influences an artist is not what he loves but what he fears; his engagement with his ancestor is a compulsion born of an envious antagonism so strong that it is unconscious or masked as the love it may once have been ... Artists are thus in no position even to know, much less acknowledge, who or what has influenced them.[43]

Regardless of these so-called unconscious reasons as to why artists falsely portray who they emulate, historical narrative does exist, and even Bloom admits the inescapability of influence for this reason alone. This is why I will discuss Séverac's music with regard to influence, while realizing the hazards of this process and asserting that this in no way denies the uniqueness of Séverac's compositions.

Séverac's music underwent various stylistic changes during his lifetime that can be fundamentally categorized into three compositional periods: beginning with his arrival in Paris in 1896, his music includes elements stressed by Schola Cantorum professors and mentors, chiefly choral director Charles Bordes, composition teacher Vincent d'Indy, and organ professor Alexandre Guilmant. These characteristics are found primarily in Séverac's organ music, as well as certain mélodies and early piano music. These include conjunct melodies, modality, comparatively stark harmonies, cyclic technique, and religious or regionalist references marked within the score.

The second period dates from 1901 up to his departure for Catalonia in 1910, and pieces written during this period are primarily Impressionist, including major second intervals employed as colorist devices, non-tension chords in the form of unresolved parallel sixth, ninth, eleventh, and dominant seventh chords, pentatonic and whole tone scales, echo effects, unprepared and unresolved appoggiaturas, secondary dominants which postpone resolution, chord alterations, and enharmonic spellings. These are primarily found in Séverac's piano suite *En Languedoc*, his opera *Le coeur du moulin*, and in a handful of mélodies.

Finally, music composed from 1910 up until his death in 1921 contains primarily Catalan elements, in part, inspired by his subsequent move to his newly adopted home of Céret in the French Catalan province of Roussillon. These characteristics are found primarily in the form of sardana dance rhythms and cobla instrumentation

---

and Kevin Korsyn, "Towards a New Poetics of Musical Influence," *Music Analysis* 10 (1991), 3–72.
  42 Bloom, *A Map of Misreading*, 114.
  43 Taruskin, "Revising Revision," 117.

that accompanied these dances.[44] Stylistically, Catalan sardanas resemble more closely music of Provence than of Spain.[45] Séverac's sardanas are different than those by his Catalan contemporaries, however, who largely created practical works designed to accompany social dances. Séverac's more adventurous and complex modulations within Catalan sardanas, his change of traditional sardana form from typical binary structures to works in ternary and rondo form, as well as his unusual choice of keys became a departure from the traditional model designed for cobla ensembles. Imitation of cobla instruments in Séverac's works is achieved through the employment of cobla harmonies, primarily harmonic fourths and fifths, as well as melodic configurations characteristic of fluviol writing.[46] Séverac also composed music based on a type of Catalan hymn, or goig, and often paid homage to these goigs through programmatic references.[47]

While some scholars have studied Séverac's earlier piano music, composed between 1896 and 1907 when Séverac was a Schola Cantorum student, little attention has been given to the later Catalan-based vocal and orchestral works.[48] These compositions include Séverac's piano suite *Cerdaña* of 1908–11, the tragédie lyrique *Héliogabale* of 1910, his cantata *Lo cant del Vallespir* of 1911, incidental music to Emile Verhaeren's *Hélène de Sparte*, composed in 1912, *Souvenirs de Céret* for violin and piano of 1919, *Minyoneta: souvenir de Figueras* for violin and piano, composed in 1919, and the one-movement piano work *Sous les lauriers-roses*, also completed in 1919.[49] Séverac's Catalan-based compositions merit attention because these works represent an important compositional style during a transitory decade. It must be remembered that Séverac was 11 years younger than Debussy, and died before the French neo-classicists of the 1920s became popular, and Séverac's late works were largely created during this transitional period. We must therefore not evaluate this music based on paradigms established by Debussy and Ravel, or those decreed by Les six, but judge Séverac's compositions on their own merit.

The discussion within this book is essentially divided into three parts. Part One provides a biography of Séverac from his childhood in Languedoc to his years in

---

44 The cobla is a Catalan ensemble in which during Séverac's lifetime members played two shawm variants, the tiple and tenor, as well as the fluviol, a piccolo-like wooden flute. These cobla ensembles often accompanied the sardana, a Catalan round dance.

45 See Véronique Nelson, "Sardana," *The New Grove Dictionary of Music and Musicians, Musical Instruments*, vol. 16, (London: Macmillan, 2001), 497

46 The fluviol is a Catalan flute included in the cobla ensemble and was traditionally played by goat herders.

47 Goigs are Catalan hymns reminiscent of plainchant.

48 Studies of Séverac's piano works include Elaine Brody, "The Piano Works of Déodat de Séverac: A Stylistic Analysis" (PhD Dissertation, New York University, 1964); Margaret Otwell, "The Piano Works of Déodat de Séverac: A Complete Recording" (DMA Dissertation, University of Maryland at College Park, 1981); Robert F. Waters, "Regionalism and Catalan Folk Elements in the Compositions of Déodat de Séverac, 1910–1919" (PhD Dissertation, University of Maryland at College Park, 2002); Blanche Selva, *Déodat de Séverac*; Joseph Canteloube, *Déodat de Séverac*.

49 Other works composed during this final period include those with neoclassical gestures and harmonies, as well as patriotic songs composed during World War I.

Paris at the Schola Cantorum, and finally to the last decade of his life spent in French Catalonia. I then address administrative and cultural regionalism in fin de siècle France, together with a discussion of the regionalist philosophies of five figures who had a profound influence on Séverac in this regard—Jean Charles-Brun, Charles Maurras, Maurice Barrès, Frédéric Mistral, and Vincent d'Indy. This section also compares and contrasts Séverac's regionalist philosophy, first espoused in his 1907 thesis, with the philosophies of these five figures.

Part Two provides an analysis of Séverac's works not based on Catalan music, most of which were composed while he was in Paris. These chapters are separated by genre, and include his organ works, songs, opera *Le coeur du moulin*, piano music, and unpublished, unfinished, and recently published works composed mostly during his years in Paris.

Part Three then discusses Catalan regionalism in music as well as Séverac's contact in Paris with Catalan music and musicians. A history and analysis of individual Catalan elements in Séverac's later works composed in French Catalonia will then enable a direct comparison with his earlier compositions.

Chapter 2

Biography

Marie Joseph Alexandre Déodat de Sévérac, Baron de Sévérac, Baron de Beauville, was born on July 20, 1872, in Saint-Félix-Caraman (now Saint-Félix de Lauragais), a small village east of Toulouse in the southern province of Languedoc, or region of Haute-Garonne.[1] Some biographers claim that the surname Séverac can be historically traced to an ancient Roman lieutenant named Severus.[2] The family then migrated to the province of Languedoc during the ninth century and moved to the village of Saint-Félix-Caraman six centuries later.[3]

Séverac's roots on his mother's side have been traced back to the Aragon family of Spain, and subsequently to his great-grandfather Bertrand Molleville, who was a naval minister under Louis XVI. Séverac's mother was privy to this heritage as she maintained discipline in the household; she nonetheless encouraged the children in their creative talents.[4]

Participation in the arts within the Séverac household was vital, as Séverac's father Gilbert was a prominent Toulousain painter. Gilbert, together with his brother Henry, frequented L'Ecole des beaux-arts in Toulouse, and then went on to study at L'Ecole impériale des beaux-arts in Paris.[5] Gilbert first exhibited his paintings

---

  1   Séverac spelled his name with two accents (Sévérac) while in Paris, as can be seen in the three installments of his thesis in "La centralisation et les petites chapelles musicales," *Le courrier musical*, 11e année, nos. 1, 3, 5 (January 1, 15, March 1, 1908), 1–6, 37–43, 142–4. He spelled his last name with one accent later in life. Except for the beginning of this chapter, this book will contain his name with one accent only. See Elaine Brody, "The Piano Works of Déodat de Séverac: A Stylistic Analysis" (PhD Dissertation, New York University, 1964), 25.

  2   Joseph Canteloube, *Déodat de Séverac* [1st Edition, Paris, 1929] (Beziers, France: Société de musicologie de Languedoc, 1984), 10. It has also been conjectured by Canteloube that there is a common origin between the King of Aragon and the Severus family and this becomes apparent in that they hold the same coat of arms. The composer was therefore a member of an ancient baronial family who distinguished themselves in the arts. Despite Séverac's heritage, however, it was reported that he rarely used his title of Baron de Séverac.

  3   Saint-Félix-Caraman became Saint-Félix de Lauragais in 1921, the year of Séverac's death. I will refer to Saint-Félix-Caraman when discussing Séverac and will only refer to Saint-Félix de Lauragais when discussing manuscripts currently found in the village.

  4   Séverac had four sisters, Marie Thérèse, who died in infancy (1864–65), Marthe Eugénie (or Maria Pia, 1878–98), who died at 19 when Séverac was studying at the Schola Cantorum, and two who survived Séverac, Marie Henriette (Alix, 1870–1949), and Marie Louisa (Jeanne, 1875–1965).

  5   Gilbert studied with Léon Cogniet (1794–1890), Tony Robert-Fleury (1797–1890), and Jules Garipuy (1817–93), who was the pupil of Delacroix. Garipuy became the director of L'Ecole impériale des beaux-arts in 1885.

in Paris in 1859 and subsequently presented his works there on a regular basis; he later studied with Jean-Auguste-Dominique Ingres (1780–1867). Although Gilbert's paintings were initially influenced by Eugène Delacroix as well as by Impressionist painters, he later studied in Italy where he became enamored of Neapolitan and Roman classicism.[6] His works at this time often depicted mythological topics, religious scenes, and Roman ruins, the latter predilection partly the result of his southern French regionalist heritage, since the architectural consequence of ancient Roman incursions are found throughout southern France. But most important for Séverac were Gilbert's idealistic reflections of local peasants and servants, which influenced Séverac's later regionalist aesthetic and resultant compositions. Séverac himself, together with his sister Alix, began to paint in childhood, and they soon became art students at L'Ecole des beaux-arts in Toulouse where their father had previously studied.[7]

Gilbert was also a musician and taught Séverac flute, piano, and harmonium, which continued until Séverac began tutelage with Louis Amile, the local church organist. He studied organ, piano, and solfège with Amile, who was a political regionalist and introduced Séverac to the chanson populaire, which later became a significant influence on Séverac's music.[8]

Séverac subsequently attended the Dominican Collège de Sorèze in Toulouse. From 1886 to 1890, he studied piano, oboe, and organ at this institution while accompanying singers in the college chapel. He also participated in the school chorus, played oboe in the orchestra, and composed marches for the school band, an ensemble in which he learned trumpet, bugle, and drums. Upon graduation and upon his father's insistence, Séverac enrolled in law at the University of Toulouse. However, he immediately withdrew after hearing a performance of Wagner's *Lohengrin* and transferred to the Toulouse Conservatory. From 1893 to 1896, he studied piano at this institution with Georges Sizes and harmony with Jean Hougenenc. He also accompanied a group of student dancers who called themselves Les joyeaux escholiers. Séverac would often paraphrase popular waltzes for the group and improvise his own compositions. Full-scale works thus began to appear in the last two years in which he attended the Conservatory.[9]

---

6   Eugène Delacroix (1798–1863) was an important French painter during the early Romantic period. Gilbert Séverac also knew Claude Monet and Monet's portrait of Gilbert de Séverac hangs in the Séverac house in Saint-Félix de Lauragais. Gilbert's paintings still hang in the Musée des Augustins and the Musée de Vieux-Toulouse in Toulouse.

7   In 1895, Séverac won a grand prize for painting in water colors. Séverac's mother maintained that Alix was a fine painter but was lazy.

8   Louis Amile taught Séverac organ in the local church. The Séverac family was a major benefactor of the church, and portraits of Séverac's parents still appear in stained glass windows facing the altar.

9   Jean-Bernard Cahours d'Aspry, "Déodat de Séverac" (unpublished manuscript), 26. These works include *Sérénade au clair de lune* and the unpublished *Promenade en mer également* for piano, as well as the *Preludio* and *Air de ballet*. Séverac composed many works before this time, but because he was a fluent improviser on the organ and piano, his mother and friends would often chastise him for neglecting to notate many of his compositions; see Brody, "The Piano Works of Déodat de Séverac: A Stylistic Analysis," 28. Letters written by

During this period, Séverac also began writing as a music critic in journals such as *Le mercure musical, La renaissance latine, Messager de Toulouse, La dépêche*, and *L'occident*, often under the pseudonyms A.C. Sever, C. Verac, Verasec, and Jean du Moulin.[10] In addition, he participated in a Toulouse choral organization that performed primarily Renaissance motets and masses. It was while in this ensemble that Dr Ernest Boyer, who also sang in the group, introduced the young composer to Charles Bordes, the choirmaster at the Saint-Gervais church in Paris. Bordes was making intermittent visits to the provinces in order to recruit and raise funds for his singers, the Chanteurs de Saint-Gervais. He immediately recognized Séverac's talent and quickly recommended him for acceptance as a composition student at the newly formed Schola Cantorum, as evident in a letter from Bordes to Paul Poujaud:

> I have just recruited an exceptional subject presented to me by Dr. Boyer of the Chanteurs de Saint Gervais. A quiet young boy, village aristocrat, natural, artless and alert, full of natural distinction and of sounds. [He is a] musician, artist, poet—a shepherd. You will see, and like me, you will love him.[11]

Despite Bordes' overtures, Séverac decided to study at the Paris Conservatoire and enrolled in the autumn of 1896. Théodore Dubois welcomed him and arranged for him to study composition with Charles Lenepveu.[12] However, Séverac quickly became disillusioned with what he perceived to be a centralized bureaucracy, and after attending only one class, felt that there was nothing of value to learn from this institution. Despite Dubois' letter to Séverac's father in a futile attempt to keep his son at the Paris Conservatoire, Séverac immediately transferred to the Schola Cantorum.

The Schola Cantorum was initially inspired by the Association des chanteurs de Saint-Gervais—which was founded in 1892 by Bordes and emphasized religious music, especially Gregorian chant. The singers numbered approximately thirty, and traveled to various provinces within France with works by the likes of Giovanni Pierluigi da Palestrina (1525–94), Orlandus Lassus (1530–94), Giacomo Carissimi (1605–74), and Heinrich Schütz (1585–1672). Two years later, Bordes founded the Société de la Schola Cantorum, which, among other things, performed a series of annual concerts of Bach's cantatas. The journal *La tribune de Saint-Gervais* was

---

Alfred Cortot and Paul Le Flem cite that some of Séverac's best music went with him to the grave. Cortot's letter was written to author Marc Lafargue (April 13, 1962); see Alfred Cortot, *La musique française de piano*, II, (1930–48; Paris: Presses Universitaires France; nouv. éd., 1981), 201–23, which cites that Séverac seemed unconcerned about preserving many of his compositions. Marc Lafargue also maintained this fact in "Souvenirs mêlés," *Les marges*, later reprinted in *Le coq catalan* (March 24 and 31, 1923).

10 See Brody, "The Piano Works of Déodat de Séverac: A Stylistic Analysis," 29.

11 Blanche Selva, *Déodat de Séverac* (Paris: Librairie Delagrave, 1930), 13. Paul Poujaud (1856–1936) was a lawyer who was often asked to participate on thesis committees at the Schola Cantorum. He was on Séverac's thesis committee. "Je viens de lever un sujet exceptionnel présenté par le Docteur Boyer, des Chanteurs de Saint-Gervais; un tout jeune garçon, petit noble de village, naturel, ingénu et éveillé, plein de race, de sons, musicien, artiste, poète, un pâtre. Tu verras, et comme moi, tu l'aimeras."

12 Louis Combes, *Le télégramme* (November 30, 1909).

created to further the interests of the organization, with the first issue published in June 1894, announcing the principles of the new society. Among these new principles included a return to the tradition of singing Gregorian chant, as well as placing Palestrina in a place of honor as a model figure whose music was to be associated with roots in plainchant. Another objective of the Schola Cantorum was to promote modern religious music respectful of texts and rules of the liturgy, as inspired by Palestrina and medieval chant. Finally, the organization was dedicated to improving the organ repertoire and uniting organ music with melodic ideals found in vocal incantation.

Bordes soon founded the Schola Cantorum, or Ecole de chant liturgique et de musique religieuse in 1896, which corresponded to the goals of the society. He accomplished this in partnership with composer Vincent d'Indy and organist Alexandre Guilmant, with Bordes essentially the choir director and spiritual backer of the Schola Cantorum, as d'Indy taught composition and later assumed most of the administrative and financial responsibilities.[13]

The Schola Cantorum was to be free from the perceived dogmatism and secular spirit of the Paris Conservatoire. The premise of the school was to study great composers of the distant past, a philosophy echoed by Alexandre Guilmant, who in the inaugural address for the Schola Cantorum, recommended that students have "faith" in art and remain unselfish within the music profession. He further insinuated that the administration, faculty, and students at the Paris Conservatoire were altogether too concerned with earning money. As Guilmant remarked, "rather than teaching students to be workshop painters, we should have them endeavor to love music like a holy mission."[14]

Schola Cantorum faculty initially included pianist Edouard Risler, who taught in 1897 and was subsequently replaced by Isaac Albéniz after leaving the institution for a concert career. Amédée Gastoué (1873–1943) became head of the musicology department in 1898 with a specialty in Gregorian chant, and also directed the medieval vocal ensemble from 1900 to 1901. Pierre de Bréville (1861–1949) taught counterpoint from 1898 to 1902. André Pirro (1869–1943) initially assisted Guilmant in organ classes and was soon granted the title of Director of Historical, Paleographical, and Bibliographical Studies (1895), and Louis d'Arnal de Serres (1864–1942) taught accompanying, improvisation, and chamber music between 1900 and 1905. He also taught a course in lyric declamation upon Bordes' departure from the Schola in 1905. Composer Albéric Magnard taught briefly at the Schola, as did organist Abel Decaux.[15]

---

13 For more information on this subject, see Catrina M. Flint de Médicis, "The Schola Cantorum, Early Music, and French Nationalism from 1894 to 1914" (PhD Dissertation, McGill University, 2006).

14 This inaugural address by Guilmant on October 15, 1896, was included in: *La tribune de Saint-Gervais* (1901), 52. Two years later, new students included Paul Le Flem, Armande de Polignac, Auguste Sérieyx, J.M. Gaillardo, Francisco de Lacerda, René Poire, and Gustave Samazeuilh.

15 Gastoué catalogued many works at the Bibliothèque nationale. He subsequently became president of the Société française de musicologie in 1934 and remained president for

Pianist and pedagogue Blanche Selva, who taught piano at the Schola Cantorum beginning in 1901, became acquainted with Séverac during the years in which the composer attended the institution.[16] She described the composer's personality and character in the following way:

> He was a sensual and spirited dreamer. An artist without the least jealousy, a man without any vanity, seemingly unaware of his talent for pleasing people which gained him their hearts—often more than that. He was neither intransigent nor intriguing, nor partisan. Liking neither theories nor systems, he remained an independent [thinker]. With very personable characteristics, he was open to all beauty.[17]

***

Séverac was undecided about what his emphasis within music would be upon first entering the Schola Cantorum. His initial primary interest was to study oboe, an instrument he had practiced since childhood and which reminded him of his rustic origins.[18] He nonetheless decided to place emphasis on composition, and spent 11 years at the school, from 1896 to 1907, learning composition under Vincent d'Indy, organ and harmonium with Alexandre Guilmant, and piano with Blanche Selva and Isaac Albéniz. Séverac led the Schola Cantorum orchestra in conducting class, while directing, among other works, the first movement of Beethoven's *Symphony no. 6 in F, op. 68* ("Pastoral"). Séverac also studied choral conducting with Charles Bordes, who entrusted his protégé with choral performances of music by Palestrina and Spanish Renaissance composer Tomás Luis de Victoria (1548–1611).[19] Bordes himself brought these two composers to public notice. Séverac held Palestrina in high regard as a result of the French composer's collaboration with Bordes, and his interest in other Renaissance composers was also greatly stimulated. As Séverac

---

two years. Bréville studied composition with Théodore Dubois at the Paris Conservatoire and later with César Franck, with whom Vincent d'Indy studied.

16 Blanche Selva (1884–1942) was a French pianist and teacher who studied at the Paris Conservatoire and eventually taught at the Schola Cantorum from 1901 to 1922.

17 Selva, *Déodat de Séverac*, 14. "C'était un rêveur sensuel et un distrait plein d'esprit. L'artiste sans la moindre jalousie, l'homme sans aucune vanité, paraissant ignorer ce don de plaire qui lui gagnait tous les coeurs, souvent même plus que les coeurs. Il n'était ni intransigeant, ni intrigant, ni partisan. Il n'aimait pas les théories, les systèmes, libre penseur qu'il était. Avec des tendances très personnelles, il était ouvert à toute beauté."

18 Amédée Gastoué, "Notes et souvenirs sur Déodat de Séverac," *La tribune de Saint-Gervais* (June, 1921), 199–200; reprinted by Aspry, "Déodat de Séverac", 33–4. The oboe reminded Séverac of his rustic origins because of the similarity between the oboe and the shawms Séverac heard in southern France.

19 Bordes also had Séverac prepare the choir for a performance of Berlioz's *Requiem*, as well as several oratorios by Handel. In fact, Séverac was exposed to various works of the baroque period at this time, including Monteverdi's *L'orfeo* and *L'incoronazione di Poppea*.

commented: "[At the Schola], each course is for me a true revelation ... about the great masters of the sixteenth and seventeenth centuries."[20]

Bordes also taught Séverac the notation system of Gregorian chant, as well as scholarly approaches to phrasing within this music. Séverac's compositions from these early years in Paris demonstrate the influence of chant, especially in modal tendencies within several organ works, sacred choral compositions, and songs.[21] Bordes taught additional classes attended by Séverac, including one on expression and rhythm and another on lyric declamation. Bordes' involvement with southern French folk music was also evident in his love of folk songs and dances from his native Basque region, which he collected and published in *Archives de la tradition basque*, inspired by a commission from the Ministère de l'instruction publique.[22] Séverac was therefore not only influenced by Bordes' interest in Medieval and Renaissance works, but also by this fascination with folk music.[23]

Séverac's primary mentor, however, was his composition teacher, Vincent d'Indy. Like Bordes, d'Indy believed that art was not a trade and a music conservatory should not be a professional school designed strictly for the purpose of finding students employment, as he felt was the case with the Paris Conservatoire before Gabriel Fauré took over as director in 1905. Instead, he felt that music study at the Schola Cantorum should provide a spiritual education—in essence, to promote a quasi-metaphysical approach to composing music. D'Indy refused a professorship in composition at the Paris Conservatoire in 1892, in part, because of his desire to maintain these ideals.[24]

Séverac considered d'Indy a mentor:[25]

---

20 Pierre Guillot, *Déodat de Séverac: la musique et les lettres* (Liège, Belgium: Pierre Mardaga, 2002), 24. [Letter to Alix Séverac, 1896.] "Chaque cours est pour moi une vraie révélation ... par les grands maîtres des XVIe et XVIIe siècles."

21 Charles Bordes was involved in asceticism, remained an anti-Wagnerian, and maintained an interest in religious as well as folk music from his native Basque region. As a pupil of Franck, who invited the young 22-year-old composer to play organ in mass, Bordes later became interested in restoring an emphasis on what he considered to be "true" French music at a time when Wagner's music had grown increasingly popular among Parisians.

22 Bordes also proposed a class for vocal students at the Schola Cantorum on the chant populaire; the class only lasted a few months. Bordes' compositions that contain Basque folk elements include *Suite basque* (1887) and *Rapsodie basque* (1889).

23 Séverac briefly replaced Bordes in the Schola Cantorum administration in 1899, and often informally submitted compositions to Bordes for advice. Séverac wrote: "I am preparing a cantata and fugue. My last fugue, in Bordes' opinion, was very admissible, despite 'modern' formulas." ("Je prépare une cantate et fugue. Ma dernière fugue, de l'avis de Bordes, était très admissible malgré bien des formules 'modernes.'") Guillot, *Déodat de Séverac: la musique et les lettres*, 83. [Letter to Mme. Séverac, 1899.]

24 Andrew Thomson, *Vincent d'Indy and His World* (Oxford: Clarendon Press, 1996), 83–4.

25 There are similarities between Séverac and d'Indy with regards to background in that both were from southern French families of minor nobility who distinguished themselves in the arts. D'Indy was a Viscount and Séverac a Baron. Like Séverac, d'Indy was an aristocrat who lived in Paris, but spent his summers in his native southern rural region. He often invited Séverac to Château des Faugs, his ancestral home.

D'Indy, who is, without contest, the premier symphony composer of our times, paid a friendly visit to me yesterday for a solid hour as a friend—laughing and chatting with unprecedented charm about art and a thousand other things ... All of the other professors here are similar. Next Sunday, Guilmant will take me to the Lamoureux Concert Hall where they'll play an admirable symphony by d'Indy, a cantata by Franck, and something by Saint-Saëns.[26]

As revealed in his statement, Séverac had the opportunity to hear much of d'Indy's music, which he respected. The feeling was mutual:

In d'Indy's course, I brought [my *Ave Maria* and] a variation on a chorale by Bach to the master. He examined it for a long moment and said to me: "I am delighted by your musical intelligence and the facility with which you assimilate the principles of the [Schola Cantorum], while always maintaining a distinct personality ... I predict good things for you ... " I was moved to hear myself described this way, and in front of all my friends. One needs to feel encouragement, especially from a master like d'Indy.[27]

D'Indy's high regard for Séverac is corroborated by his own words regarding Séverac's music:

Déodat *truly* loved music, a very rare quality among present-day musicians. When I was absent for three months for a series of performances of *Fervaal* in Brussels, I had my composition class taught by Magnard ... whose harsh frankness had the effect of discouraging all the students in the course ... Only one of them remained: Déodat, who made it to the end of the year without being bothered by Magnard's reprimands, which proves his strong constitution and his desire to learn.[28]

---

26 Guillot, *Déodat de Séverac: la musique et les lettres*, 52. [Séverac letter to sister Marthe, 1897.] "D'Indy, qui sans conteste est le premier symphoniste du jour, est venu hier se 'ballader' avec moi pendant une bonne heure, comme un 'copain,' riant, causant avec un charme inouï d'art et de mille autres choses ... Tous les autres profs. sont pareils. Demain dimanche Guilmant me prend au concert Lamoureux où l'on doit jouer une adorable symphonie de d'Indy, une cantate de C. Franck, quelque chose de Saint-Saëns."

27 Guillot, *Déodat de Séverac: la musique et les lettres*, 57. [Letter to the Séverac family, 1898.] Other references to d'Indy occur in an 1899 letter to his sister Alix, stating that d'Indy has given him an exam about aesthetic subjects, and that Séverac had been required to compose a symphonic piece, a lyric piece, and a fugue. A 1900 letter from Séverac to his sister Jeanne states that d'Indy confided to Sérieyx that Séverac's composition for the exam was excellent. "Au cours de d'Indy, j'avais apporté au maître une variation sur un choral de Bach. Il l'a examinée un long moment et m'a dit ceci: 'je suis ravi de vos tendances et de votre intelligence musicale. Je suis émerveillé de la facilité avec laquelle vous vous assimilez les principes d'école, gardant toujours une personnalité évidente ... Je vous predis de belles choses ...'j'ai été un peu ému de m'entendre ainsi prendre à partie devant tous mes camarades ... On a besoin de se sentir encouragé ... surtout par un maître tel que d'Indy."

28 Selva, *Déodat de Séverac*, 33. [Statement made after Séverac's death, date unknown.] "Déodat aimait *véritablement* la musique, qualité bien rare chez les musiciens actuels. Lorsque je m'absentai pendant trois mois pour les répétitions de Fervaal à Bruxelles, je confiai le Cours de composition musicale à Magnard ... qui eut la particularité de décourager par sa franchise un peu *rêche* tous les élèves de ce cours ... Il n'en resta qu'un: Déodat, qui suivit jusqu'à la fin

Although many regarded d'Indy as a polemicist with strong opinions on the relative value of various French compositions, numerous students viewed him as a supportive and flexible pedagogue. In one of his classes, he gave a detailed analysis of Richard Strauss's *Salome*, despite the fact that he personally deplored the work. According to Andrew Thomson, d'Indy disliked the composition because he perceived Oscar Wilde's play "Salome," the basis for Strauss's opera, as vulgar and morally corrupt.[29]

The pedagogical image of d'Indy letting each student be free to find his own style and encouraging them in finding their own way is confirmed by composer Joseph Canteloube, who describes his own experience with the teacher:

> One asserts that by his strict authoritarianism and his formalist doctrine, that his students would be obliged to think as he does, and to compose in the same manner that he does. [However] ... one day, I became perplexed by the composer on the subject of a dramatic work on which I was working, and I told him I intended to take one of his works as a model. He interrupted me by shouting "But no! Why? ... Just look for what is in yourself and listen to no one [but yourself]."[30]

Séverac himself encountered a similar experience with the director. When Séverac composed his tone poem *Nymphes au crépuscule* within a style similar to that of Debussy, d'Indy accepted it, despite its "new" form. D'Indy then strongly

---

de l'année sans se laisser troubler par les incartades grogneuses de Magnard, ce qui prouve sa force de résistance et son désir d'apprendre."

In a letter to Séverac's mother, d'Indy echoed these views concerning Séverac's talent: "[Séverac is] one of the most intellectual students [at the Schola Cantorum] and is one of my best students ... [he] is capable of doing solid work here and learning his trade very well." ("Un des plus intellectuels et des meilleurs de mes élèves ... est capable de faire de solides études et d'arriver à posséder sérieusement son métier.") Aspry, 'Déodat de Séverac,' 84. [Letter from d'Indy to Mme Séverac, October 5, 1897.]

Two years later, Magnard saw the score of a symphonic poem composed by Séverac, and commented that he was dumbfounded at the progress Séverac made in the two years since he had worked with him. See Guillot, *Déodat de Séverac: la musique et les lettres*, 87. [Séverac letter to his sister Alix, 1899.]

Unlike professors at the Schola Cantorum, Magnard did not like plainchant and believed in Debussy's harmonic system, despite the fact that he did not incorporate this system into his own works. Because of Magnard's austere approach, however, students were often timid in his presence.

29 Thomson, *Vincent d'Indy and His World*, 132.

30 Françoise Raginel Cougniaud, *Joseph Canteloube* (Béziers, France: Société de musicologie de Languedoc, 1988), 29. The text is a reprint of Joseph Canteloube, *Vincent d'Indy* (Paris, 1951), 95–6. "On a affirmé que, par son autoritarisme étroit et son formalisme doctrinal, [d'Indy] obligerait ses élèves à penser comme lui, et à écrire de la même manière que lui ... un jour le maître ma perplexité [sic] au sujet du final d'une oeuvre dramatique à laquelle je travaillais et je lui faisais part de mon intention de prendre comme modèle l'un de ses actes à lui. Il m'interrompit vivement en s'écriant: 'Mais non! Pourquoi? ... Cherchez donc simplement ce qui est en vous et n'écoutez personne!'"

encouraged Séverac to continue composing other works within that style.[31] This comment contradicts d'Indy's previous remarks regarding emulation, but nonetheless demonstrates his ability to accept from his students new styles not officially sanctioned by the Schola Cantorum. Since d'Indy emphasized form, which he considered the principal element of composition, he therefore placed linearity and counterpoint above Debussy's emphasis on harmony in terms of status, the latter considered by d'Indy to be a "false science."[32] Therefore although d'Indy's emphasis on rigorous counterpoint was part of Séverac's training, Séverac would nonetheless often employ Debussy's harmonic style, but within these more linear constructions, thereby providing ambiance and ornamentation to horizontal lines.

***

Séverac's first year at the Schola Cantorum was successful; however, he did not immediately return to the institution at the beginning of the second school year, in 1897, when his father became seriously ill. His mother feared that her only son lived too far from home, since he would be obliged to assume responsibilities within the household should his father not survive. Precedents had already taken place with regard to Séverac's uncle, Henry, who abandoned his artistic career to take care of agricultural tasks and responsibilities regarding Séverac's family property. It was at this time that Séverac's mother became concerned over whether music was a profitable livelihood for her son, and whether he had enough talent to warrant pursuing a musical career in Paris. His mother, therefore, wrote a letter to d'Indy asking about Séverac's future, to which d'Indy replied in the letter included earlier in this chapter.[33]

Séverac's father died in November 1897, and his sister Marthe one month later.[34] Séverac soon returned to Paris, where letters to his family reveal his persistent nostalgia for the southern countryside and perhaps guilt for having abandoned his native pays and family. In one such letter, Séverac reflects, "never had I felt nostalgia for my countryside and the house as this year!"[35] Séverac composed a plethora of regionalist songs at this time, including "Le ciel est par-dessus le toit," "Ritournelle," "Pastourelle," "Les huns," "Renouveau," "Les cors," and "Le chevrier."

Séverac's financial situation at this time was relatively unstable, and he was therefore obliged to earn spending money. Séverac himself spoke of the difficulties of maintaining financial stability:

---

31 Guillot, *Déodat de Séverac: la musique et les lettres*, 154. [Séverac letter to Séverac family, February, 1902.]

32 Thomson, *Vincent d'Indy and His World*, 133.

33 See footnote 28.

34 It was at this time that Séverac composed one of his most ethereal piano compositions, "Coin de cimetière au printemps," later inserted into his piano suite *En Languedoc* (1905).

35 Guillot, *Déodat de Séverac: la musique et les lettres*, 107. [Séverac letter to sister Jeanne, 1900.] "Jamais je n'avais senti la nostalgie du pays et de la maison comme cette année!"

When, like me, you have no fortune, you have to "get by" ... It is obviously very unfortunate not to have the considerable fortune of a d'Indy, which allows him to compose meticulous and well-thought out works. I don't have a wealthy wife, like Debussy ... My dear friends, the Castéra brothers, whom I love as my brothers, know nothing of the sadness of going without [money] ... They don't know what it's like to "save one's pennies"... even just to buy staff paper! I believe that I can succeed, as God has graciously granted me musical talents. But I do wish that my livelihood were secure.[36]

Séverac's share of his father's estate gave him a modest income, and he supplemented this salary by playing organ in church on Sundays in the outskirts of Paris, as well as by giving private lessons in harmony, solfège, and music appreciation.[37] Additional remuneration came by continuing to write as a music critic.

Sociétés

Séverac participated in various societies in Paris, including the Association Toulousaine de Paris, a philanthropic society founded in 1893 and dedicated to assisting fellow Toulousaines in need of financial support.

More significant, however, was the Société nationale de musique, created in 1871 by Camille Saint-Saëns and Romaine Bussine in an attempt to promote works by French composers, with its motto "Ars gallica." Participants in this organization included composers Edouard Lalo, Jules Massenet, Georges Bizet, Henri Duparc, Isaac Albéniz, Charles Bordes, Alfred Bruneau, Pierre de Bréville, Emmanuel Chabrier, Ernest Chausson, Claude Debussy, Julien Tiersot, and Alexis de Castillon. The first president was Romain Bussine, and Vincent d'Indy subsequently became secretary in 1876, when he dramatically increased the number of symphonic works performed. These compositions were not always French, which caused animosity between d'Indy and Saint-Saëns, and subsequently the splintering of the Société nationale de musique.[38] D'Indy also highlighted compositions written by Schola Cantorum faculty and students by having many of their works performed. Most of these pieces were instrumental symphonic and chamber compositions, both genres considered inferior by many at the time, as opera was more popular with the Parisian public.

---

36 Letter to editor Alexis Rouart (1904), reprinted by Aspry, "Déodat de Séverac," 182–3. "Lorsque comme moi, on n'a pas de fortune, on est obligé de se 'debrouiller' ... C'est évidemment fort malheureux de n'avoir pas la fortune considérable d'un d'Indy, qui lui permet de donner des oeuvres 'soignées' et 'réfléchies'! Je n'ai pas, comme Debussy, une femme dorée sur tranche ... Mes bons et chers amis Castéra, que j'aime d'ailleurs, comme des frères, ignorent l'ennui ou les ennuis des privations ... Ils ne se doutent pas de ce que c'est de 'compter' ... même pour acheter du papier à musique! ... je crois que je pourrais les réussir, le Bon Dieu m'ayant fait la grâce de quelques dons musicaux, mais je voudrais que ma vie soit assurée."

37 Brody, "The Piano Works of Déodat de Séverac: A Stylistic Analysis," 33.

38 For more information on this topic, see Michael Creasman Strasser, "*Ars Gallica*: The Société Nationale de Musique and Its Role in French Musical Life, 1871–1891" (PhD Dissertation, University of Illinois at Champaign-Urbana, 1998).

Many of Séverac's works were supported by and performed for this organization, beginning in 1899 with two songs, "Prends mon âme" (on a round by Georges Audiger) and "Les cors" (Paul Rey, text).[39] Séverac's song "L'éveil de Pâques," written in 1899, was performed two years later, as was "L'ouvrier qui pleure," "Infidèle," "Soleils couchants," and "Le ciel est par-dessus le toit." Séverac's piano suite *Le chant de la terre* was also sponsored by the society in 1903. His symphonic poem *Nymphes au crépuscule* was also performed by the organization, with d'Indy himself as conductor.[40]

Other groups with which Séverac met included Le nouveaux jeune-France, where Séverac and composers Maurice Ravel, Florent Schmitt, and Maurice Delage would play their compositions for each other, and the Apaches, a group formed in 1900 in an attempt to advertise the members as artistic outcasts who defended certain contemporary musics against the perceived onslaught of criticism from the general Parisian public.[41]

A society that Séverac joined in 1909 was the Société musicale indépendante, an organization founded in reaction to perceived injustices within the Société nationale

---

39 In 1906, Pierre Lalo noted that almost all important French musicians had stopped taking part in the Société nationale de musique. Séverac later referred to those in the organization in his 1907 thesis as "Les Indépendants;" see Pierre Lalo, "La musique: à la societé nationale de musique—son rôle ancient et son rôle actuel," *Le temps* (January 30, 1906), 3.

40 Séverac himself was elected to a committee within the organization in 1899. In a letter to his sister Lily, he stated: "I am happy to write you of the honor that came to me at the Société nationale de musique. Today, what took place was [voting among] the General Assembly ... After the election from the committee, I was voted in almost unanimously. I was a little surprised, for I am still a young musician and it is a great honor for me to be named in this way ... This proves to me that my artistic efforts have been appreciated and I know that this will please you." ("Je suis heureux de vous écrire tout de suite l'honneur que vient de me faire la Société nationale de musique. Aujourd'hui avait lieu l'assemblée générale ... Après l'élection du comité, quel n'a pas été mon étonnement d'être élu membre du comité à la presque unamité. J'ai été un peu ému, mais très fier car c'est pour moi, encore jeune musicien, un grand honneur d'être nommé à cet emploi à côté ... Cela me prouve que mes efforts artistiques ont été appréciés de la jeunesse musicale et je sais que cela vous fera plaisir.") See Guillot, *Déodat de Séverac: la musique et les lettres*, 91.

41 Aspry, "Déodat de Séverac," 243–4. The name was coined by Ricardo Viñes and referred to their self-perceived underworld status. They supported Debussy's *Pelléas et Mélisande* at its inception and attended innumerable performances of other contemporary compositions. The group usually met at the home of Tristan Klingsor and had their own secret theme song, the opening of Borodin's *Symphony No. 2*. They often discussed late into the evening painting, poetry, and music, including Chinese art, Mallarmé, Verlaine, Rimbaud, Corbière, Cézanne, Van Gogh, Rameau, Chopin, Whistler, Valéry, Russian composers, and Debussy. The group met regularly until World War I. Members of the group included poets Tristan Klingsor and Léon-Paul Fargue, painters Paul Sordes and Abbé Léonce Petit, conductor Désiré-Emile Inghelbrecht, decorator Georges Mouveau, pianists Marcel Chadeigne and Ricardo Viñes, critics Emile Vuillermoz and Michel D. Calvocoressi, and composers André Caplet, Maurice Delage, Manuel de Falla, Paul Ladmirault, Florent Schmitt, and Séverac. Séverac met with this group about two years after it was founded.

de musique.[42] The first director of the Société musicale indépendante was Gabriel Fauré, and other members included composers Roger Ducasse, Charles Koechlin, Maurice Ravel, Jean Huré, André Caplet, Louis Aubert, Florent Schmitt, and Emile Vuillermoz.

Séverac avoided numerous social events in Paris and his reluctance to participate in many of these soirées arguably had career repercussions, as attending these occasions might have led to more performances of his works. Nonetheless, Séverac frequented several music salons where fellow musicians would perform for each other. They were most often headed by women of taste with knowledge of art and literature, including, at times, technical forms within music, such as canon, fugue, and other contrapuntal forms. These parties were given by the likes of Princesse de Faucigny-Cystria, who invited not only musicians, but also painters and writers such as Odilon Redon and Colette.[43] More intimate gatherings took place at pianist Blanche Selva's home, where Séverac performed his music.[44] Séverac also attended parties at the home of painter Edouard Benedictus (1878–1920), and events hosted by Louis de Serres, where Séverac would often play the piano.[45] Additional gatherings took place at the home of Princesse de Polignac, as well as concerts at the Châtelet and Salle Pleyel, the latter often attended by Séverac together with Joseph Canteloube.[46] Séverac was introduced to Ravel in 1902 at the salon of Cipa and Ida

---

42 Ravel wrote the following critique of the Société nationale de musique: "Societies, even national, do not escape from the laws of evolution. But one is free to withdraw from them. This is what I am doing now by sending in my resignation as a member. I presented three works of my pupils, of which one was particularly interesting. Like the others, it too was refused. It didn't offer those solid qualities of incoherence and boredom, which the Schola Cantorum baptizes as structure and profundity ... I am undertaking to form a new society, more independent, at least in the beginning. This idea has delighted many people." As Orenstein notes, the Société nationale de musique did not disband until the late 1930s and remained a competitor to the new Société musicale indépendante. See letter from Ravel to Charles Koechlin, January 16, 1909 in Arbie Orenstein, *A Ravel Reader* (New York: Columbia University Press, 1990), translated by Orenstein, 102–3.

43 Parties given by Princesse de Faucigny-Cystria took place in 1901 and pianist Ricardo Viñes also frequented these events. Séverac met both Viñes and Redon in 1900 and subsequently became close friends with the two figures. In 1902, Séverac invited Viñes to perform his piano suite *Le chant de la terre*.

44 Robert F. Waters, "Regionalism and Catalan Folk Elements in the Compositions of Déodat de Séverac, 1910–1919" (PhD Dissertation, University of Maryland at College Park, 2002), 114. Other figures who attended include Isaac Albéniz, Albéric Magnard, Albert Roussel, Paul Poujaud, Vincent d'Indy, and Paul Dukas.

45 Benedictus often invited Séverac to his home, together with Ricardo Viñes, and composers Maurice Delage, Maurice Ravel, Florent Schmitt, Désiré-Emile Inghelbrecht, Emile Vuillermoz, Paul Ladmirault, and Manuel de Falla. Guests at the home of Louis de Serres included the writer Colette, as well as composers Gabriel Fauré, André Messager, Charles Bordes, and Vincent d'Indy.

46 Poems and prose were often read aloud at the home of the Princesse de Polignac and attendees included Léon-Paul Fargue and painter and musician Paul Sordes. For more information on the Princesse de Polignac, see Sylvia Kahan, *Music's Modern Muse: A Life*

Godebski and they continued to see each other at other such events.[47] These include gatherings at the home of composer René de Castéra as well as those at the home of composer Maurice Delage in 1903, where it is likely that Séverac heard for the first time Ravel perform *Pavane pour une infante défunte* and *Jeux d'eau*.[48] As Delage was a staunch pro-Debussyist, Debussy would often visit to perform his own works, including extracts from *Pelléas et Mélisande*. Other compositions were played, including those by Gabriel Fauré, Emmanuel Chabrier, as well as various Russian compositions, including symphonies by Borodin and various works by Balakirev.

Séverac and the Music of Richard Wagner

Séverac's perception of Wagner's music evolved dramatically between 1892 and 1914. As previously mentioned, Séverac's hearing a performance of Wagner's *Lohengrin* in 1892 inspired him to withdraw from law school and transfer to the Toulouse Conservatory. This enthusiasm for Wagner's music early in his career prompted him to indict the Toulouse public in print for not sponsoring many concerts containing Wagner's music.[49] Séverac again commented on Wagner's music in 1897 upon missing a performance of *Die Meistersinger von Nürnberg*:

> The big event of the week was Wagner's [*Die Meistersinger von Nürnberg*]. I couldn't go, but those that did attend were thrilled by the work and the performers ... Wagner's opera has been celebrated: it's a triumph for the great cause.[50]

Séverac's comments about Wagner's music contributing to the "great cause" would have also reflected the early attitudes of his composition teacher, d'Indy, who championed French works while simultaneously praising the music of Wagner. This is in contrast to the fact that d'Indy later accepted the presidency of the anti-German Ligue nationale pour la defense de la musique française in 1916, although his role here would have been an "honorary" one. This earlier pro-Wagner view held by Séverac therefore represented, for many, a modern view of the state of music in Paris at the time, but before the evolution towards an anti-German stance in the years leading up to World War I.

In 1898, Séverac again illustrated his interest in Wagner's music: "I don't know the work by Mendès on Wagner, but I intend to read it ... D'Indy rightly began a

---

of Winnaretta Singer, Princesse de Polignac (Rochester, NY: University of Rochester Press, 2003).

47 Cipa and Ida were brother and sister.

48 Aspry, "Déodat de Séverac," 237.

49 See Séverac, "Toulouse et l'évolution musicale contemporaine," *La renaissance latine* (August 15, 1902), 678–82.

50 Guillot, *Déodat de Séverac: la musique et les lettres*, 53 [Séverac letter to sister Marthe, 1897]. "Le grand événement de la semaine est des Maîtres chanteurs de Wagner. Je n'ai pu y aller, mais ceux qui y ont assiste ont été enthousiasmés de l'oeuvre et des artistes ... L'oeuvre de Wagner a été acclamée, enfin c'est un triomphe pour la grande cause."

remarkable seminar on the master of Bayreuth and I arrived at its climax."[51] This was followed with additional comments one year later, when Séverac attended a performance of Wagner's *Tristan und Isolde* at the Théâtre de la Monnaie in Brussels: "The performance of *Tristan* was for me an unforgettable and indescribable delight ... The man who was capable of writing this work is a giant before whom you must bow humbly and 'tip your hat.'"[52] Séverac went to hear *Das Rheingold* at a Lamoureux concert conducted by Camille Chevillard in 1900 and subsequently wrote an article on Wagner in a Toulouse publication, wherein he commented: "It would be easy to prove objectively the musical legitimacy of [*Der ring des Nibelungen*] to those who jealously want to ignore his genius."[53] As late as 1905, Séverac remarked: "I am hastily sending you this note so you have the time to tell your friends about *Tristan [und Isolde]*."[54]

Séverac's views began to evolve, however, upon his departure from Paris following his graduation from the Schola Cantorum. In a 1909 article for *Le temps*, for example, critic Pierre Lalo commented that in France, Wagner alone was capable of regenerating the music of young French musicians, which enlisted the response of several composers, including Albert Roussel, Florent Schmitt, Maurice Ravel, and Séverac.[55] Séverac replied in the form of a letter-response:

---

51 Ibid., 62. [Séverac letter to sister Jeanne, 1898.] Catulle Mendès (1841–1909) wrote on Wagner during the 1880s. "Je ne connais pas l'ouvrage de Mendès sur Wagner mais je me propose de le lire ... D'Indy justement à commencé une série d'études remarquables sur le maître de Bayreuth et en somme je suis arrivé ici au 'moment culminant' de son cours."

52 Ibid., 96. [Séverac letter to sister Jeannette.] "La représentation de *Tristan* a été pour moi une jouissance inoubliable et indéfinissable ... L'homme qui a été capable décrire cette oeuvre est un géant devant lequel il faut s'incliner humblement et 'enlever son chapeau.'"

Séverac was in Brussels together with Charles Bordes to hear pianist Maurice Bastin perform Séverac's *Sonate* at the Libre esthétique, a museum of modern art created in 1894 by pianist Octave Maus. An art exposition would take place there each spring, and Maus wanted to complement the exposition with accompanying conferences and concerts. These music events often included Wagner's music, as well as works by composers César Franck, Vincent d'Indy, Henri Duparc, Ernest Chausson, Charles Bordes, Pierre de Bréville, Gabriel Fauré, Emmanuel Chabrier, and Séverac. Bordes and Séverac both visited the Musée des beaux-arts while in Brussels, especially admiring the Flemish school of painting of the fifteenth and sixteenth centuries, as well as works by Claude Monet and symbolist Odilon Redon, with whom Séverac subsequently became close friends.

53 Déodat de Séverac, "Causerie musicale: A propos de *Tristan et Iseult* de Richard Wagner," *Le messager de Toulouse* (January 1, 1900). "Il serait aisé de prouver objectivement la légitimité musicale de l'auteur de la Tétralogie á ceux qui jalousement veulent encore ignorer son génie."

Camille Chevillard (1859–1923) was a conductor and composer who led the Lamoureux orchestra in the première of Debussy's *Nocturnes* in 1900 (Munich: Fink, 1982) and *La mer* (Paris: Durand, 1938) in 1905.

54 Guillot, *Déodat de Séverac: la musique et les lettres*, 239. [Séverac letter to Cipa Godebski, 1905.] "Je vous envoie ce mot à la hâte pour que vous avez le temps d'avertir quelque ami pour *Tristan [und Isolde]*."

55 Pierre Lalo, "La musique: concerts spirituels—proportion des oeuvres Wagnériennes et des autres," *Le temps* (April 13, 1909), 3.

You ask if I seek "a return to the Wagnerian influence." Why? In a country with masters like Fauré, d'Indy, Debussy, and Dukas, one may look at Germany and even Russia with head held high ... You also ask if I intend to "Wagnerize" my work. My intentions are quite simply to compose the music that comes to me ... but I strongly doubt that I will ever work in the German style! I was born far too close to the beautiful Mediterranean to be able to succeed at writing German music.[56]

Like the other contemporary French composers mentioned, Séverac's anti-Wagner attitudes evolved more fully during World War I, as evident in a letter to conductor Louis Hasselmans:[57]

The very great German masters mean nothing to me ... to my taste, the greatest Classical musicians are not "Made In Germany." Palestrina, Monteverdi, and Rameau are, in their expressive power, Mediterranean. German editors have profited from Romanticism, while we have long suffered from it. They have also profited from our scholarly squabbles in order to impose their domination and force us to ignore our own venerable masters.

They say ... "Wagner is very strong." But I detest Wagner. For as strong as he is, he has done great damage to contemporary theatrical music ... Wagner killed Opéra-Comique [and] ... he killed melody ... Wagner has made us such stupid snobs that the simple, charming and adorable music of composers like Méhul, Gounod, or even Gabriel Fauré, leads my friends to smile broadly ... Nothing is less artistic than Wagnerian music ... Germans cannot be artists ... And let us not forget that every single one of our Mediterranean olive groves, which carry in their branches more true poetry, more elegance and beauty, than all of their Black Forests.[58]

---

56 Déodat de Séverac, *Grand revue* (April 10, 1909), 564–5, in response to an article written by Pierre Lalo in *Le temps* (April, 3, 1909), 3. "Vous me demandez si je souhaite 'un retour de l'influence wagnérienne?' Pourquoi? Dans un pays des maîtres comme Fauré, d'Indy, Debussy, Dukas, on peut regarder l'Allemagne et même la Russie avec la tête haute ... Vous me demandez aussi: 's'il est dans mes intentions' de me wagnériser? Mes intentions sont tout simplement d'écrire la musique qui me viendra ... mais je doute fort que je travaille jamais dans le goût germanique! Je suis né beaucoup trop près de l'admirable Méditerranée pour pouvoir arriver à écrire de la musique allemande."

57 Louis Hasselmans (1878–1957) was a French conductor of Belgian extraction. Before turning to conducting, Hasselmans was a celebrated cellist, as principal of the Concerts Lamoureux and member of the Quatour Caplet. He was conductor of the Opéra-Comique from 1909 to 1911.

58 Déodat de Séverac, "Quelles conséquences aura la guerre pour l'art musical en France," *Le courrier de l'aude* (September 20, 1915). This was a partial reproduction of a letter from Séverac to orchestral conductor Louis Hasselmans. The article also appeared in *Soleil du midi* (November 8, 1915). "Les très grands maîtres nés en Allemagne n'ont pour moi rein ... à mon goût, les plus grands musiciens classiques ne sont pas 'Made in Germany.' Palestrina, Monteverdi, et Rameau sont des latins dans toute la force de l'expression. Les éditeurs d'Allemagne ont su profiter du romantisme qui nous a long-temps infestés, et de nos querelles d'école, pour nous imposer leur domination, et nous forcer à ignorer nos véritables maîtres.

"L'on dit ... 'Wagner est très fort;' mais je déteste Wagner pour si fort qu'il soit, car il a fait un mal immense à notre musique de théâtre contemporaine ... Wagner a tué l'opéra-comique ... il a tué la mélodie ... Wagner a fait de nous des snobs tellement stupides que la musique simple, charmante et adorable d'un Méhul, d'un Gounod et même d'un Gabriel Fauré fait

The chronological documentation of comments made by Séverac regarding Wagner's music indicates a growing evolution with regard to his anti-German stance in the years leading up to World War I, an evolution felt by many French composers at the time, including Debussy.[59]

Séverac and Claude Debussy

Some of Séverac's works composed between 1898 and 1907 contain Impressionist techniques, including seventh chords as tonic substitute, major seconds for colorist effect, and parallel fourths and fifths. Although Séverac's suggestive programmatic titles with corresponding poems also mirror stylistic characteristics of Claude Debussy and other Impressionist musicians, Séverac's pieces differ in their references to specific regional southern French and Catalan villages and festivals and are therefore considered regionalist.[60]

Some writers and critics spoke of Debussy, Ravel, and Séverac together as the three most prominent composers in France at the time, as illustrated by Henri Sauget commenting that Séverac, Debussy, and Ravel were considered to be a trio on the forefront of music of that period.[61] Camile Mauclair, in a 1906 article for *La revue musicale*, referred to Séverac as being the heir to Debussyism when he stated that "Séverac has been searching for, and after *Pelléas* [*et Mélisande*] has found, a new mode of expression."[62]

Séverac met Debussy in 1899 following a Société nationale event that included a première of two of Séverac's songs, "Prends mon âme" and "Les cors." Séverac recounted the event: "I met ... a man whom I did not know. He said to me: 'I like your music very much' ... It was Debussy!"[63] Séverac later came into contact with the composer on several occasions, including during performances of Séverac's *Sonate* for piano of 1899 and *Le chant de la terre* of 1900.[64] Séverac also met Debussy in 1902 at a Société nationale concert featuring Séverac's symphonic poem *Nymphes*

---

sourire beaucoup de mes camarades ... rien n'est moins artiste que la musique Wagnérienne ... Les Allemandes ne peuvent être des artistes ... et puis n'oublions pas qu'un seul de nos oliviers méditerranéens porte plus de poésie vraie, plus d'élégance et de beauté que toutes leurs forêts noires."

59 For more on Debussy and nationalist thought, see Jane Fulcher, *French Cultural Politics and Music* (Oxford: Oxford University Press, 1999).

60 These titles and references more similarly parallel the Andalusian compositions of Isaac Albéniz and Joaquin Turina. Séverac often included Andalusian augmented seconds and Phrygian scales in his compositions.

61 Henri Sauget, *Souvenir de Déodat*, 1983; reprinted by Graham Johnson, "Program notes to CD," *Songs by Déodat de Séverac*, performed by Graham Johnson, François Le Roux, and Patricia Rozario (Hyperion A66983, 1998), 2.

62 Camille Mauclair, "La musique," *La revue musicale* (November 15, 1906). "Séverac avoir cherché et trouvé, depuis *Pelléas* une expression nouvelle."

63 Louis Laloy, *La musique retrouvée, 1902–1927* (Paris: Plon, 1928), 134–5, reprinted by Aspry, "Déodat de Séverac," 103. "J'ai vu ... un monsieur que je ne connaissais pas, et qui m'a dit: j'aime beaucoup votre musique ... C'était Debussy!"

64 Laloy, *La musique retrouvée, 1902–1927*, 135.

et crépuscule, where Debussy "strongly congratulated" Séverac on the première.[65] French writer Colette also attested that the two composers were at a party at the home of Louis de Serres in which there was a "feverish atmosphere [around Debussy] of people wholly enamored of music. All my meetings with Claude Debussy took place in the sonorous warmth, the delicate fever of an exclusively musical atmosphere ... If Louis de Serres left the keyboard, Pierre de Bréville replaced him, or Charles Bordes, or Déodat de Séverac."[66]

In 1902, Séverac heard a performance of the vocal score to Debussy's *Pelléas et Mélisande*, which had a pronounced influence on his career:

> I am still working on the end of *Le retour* despite of having given myself the last lines. But I am hardly satisfied, for I sense that my music is bland and imprecise. Yes, there are moments where, despite encouragement from mentors and friends, one looks ahead with a certain apprehension ... In Art one thing alone is necessary: "searching" ... is it still possible to search after *Pelléas [et Mélisande]*? If one must simply reflect, it is sad and above all, worthless. Wasted time, for oneself and others.[67]

Séverac's Impressionist style in his opera *Le coeur du moulin* was greatly influenced by hearing *Pelléas*. In fact, in 1905, upon completion of his piano suite *En Languedoc*,

---

65 This is substantiated by Séverac's comments: "Yesterday, at rehearsal, a group of young musicians came up to me, strongly congratulating me (Debussy among others), and their opinion is more important to me than what those worthless critics put in the papers." ("Hier à la répétition, une foule de jeunes musiciens étaient venus, qui m'ont fortement congratule (Debussy entr'autres) et leur avis m'est plus cher que ceux des critiques généralement assez nuls des journaux au revues.") See Guillot, *Déodat de Séverac: la musique et les lettres*, 163. [Séverac letter to Séverac family, May 4, 1902.]

Debussy's high regard for Séverac's music is further corroborated by André Schaeffner, who stated: "Amongst his contemporaries, Debussy had the highest esteem for Séverac." ("Parmi les contemporains, Debussy estimait surtout Séverac.") Aspry, "Déodat de Séverac," 104.

66 Colette, *Oeuvres complètes* (Paris: Le Fleuron, se vend chez Flammarion, 1949), 301. Reprinted, edited, and translated by Edward Lockspeiser, *Debussy* (New York: McGraw-Hill, 1972), 138–42.

67 Henri Collet, *L'essor de la musique espagnole au Xxème siècle* (Eschig, 1929), 155–6. [Letter to René de Castéra, August, 1902] This was written upon hearing a vocal score of the opera with Cuban-born friend Joaquín Nin y Castellanos. "Le continue la fin du *Le retour* malgré m'ayant donne les derniers vers, mais je ne suis guère satisfait de ma musique que je sens incolore et impécise. Oui, il y a des moments où malgré les encouragements de maîtres et d'amis on regarde l'horizon avec une certaine apprehension ... Car en Art, une seule chose est nécessaire: trouver ... est-il possible de trouver encore après 'Pelléas'? Si l'on doit simplement refléter, c'est triste et surtout inutile. Temps perdu pour soi-même et pour les autres." Debussy asked Séverac if he could see his score to *Le retour:* "I am at this moment very busy with the recopying of *Le retour*, which I consider nearly finished ... Debussy, who asked me if he could hear it one of these days, was quite happy ... This truly means something to me." ("Je suis en ce moment très occupé par le recopiage intégral du *Le retour* que je considère à peu près comme terminé maintenant ... Debussy qui m'avait demandé de l'entendre ces jours-ci été fort content ... C'est bien quelque chose pour moi.") See Guillot, *Déodat de Séverac: la musique et les lettres*, 192. [Séverac letter to Alix, May, 1903.]

Séverac sent Debussy a copy of his score. Debussy later replied with a letter to Louis Laloy:

> If you're in touch with Séverac, tell him not to think me so stupid as to be ungrateful for what he sent me. He writes great music that feels good and one breathes with a full heart. Unfortunately, I've lost his address; how can I thank him?[68]

Debussy also referred Séverac to Albert Carré, director of the Opéra-Comique, after hearing Séverac play the score to *Le coeur du moulin* on the piano.[69] Even upon Séverac's permanent departure from Paris in 1907, Debussy and Séverac still corresponded, and Debussy remained familiar with new works composed by Séverac at the time. These included *Hélène de Sparte*—incidental music that Debussy heard performed in 1912 at the Théâtre du Châtelet in Paris. Debussy told Séverac: "This [overture to *Hélène de Sparte*] is exquisite, at once precise and Impressionist, deliciously orchestrated and rich with ideas."[70]

Séverac and Maurice Ravel

Séverac met Maurice Ravel in 1902 through Ricardo Viñes at a social gathering at the home of Cipa and Ida Godebski. As stated earlier, Ravel and Séverac were at several parties together, including that of painter Edouard Benedictus, a gathering given by René de Castéra, and a 1903 soirée given by Delage, where Séverac heard Ravel perform his *Pavane pour une infante défunte* and *Jeux d'eau*. Séverac and Ravel were also members of the Société nationale de musique until Ravel withdrew in 1909. Both were also associated with the Société musicale independante, formed

---

68 Laloy, *La musique retrouvée, 1902–1927*, 135. [Debussy letter to Louis Laloy, May, 1905.] "Si vous correspondez avec Séverac, dites-lui qu'il ne me croix peu assez stupide pour avoir été insensible à l'envoi qu'il m'a fait. Il fait de la musique qui sent bon et l'on y respire à plein coeur. J'ai malheueusement perdu son adresse: mais comment le remercier?"

69 Brody, "The Piano Works of Déodat de Séverac: A Stylistic Analysis", 38. This is coupled with the fact that Debussy volunteered to bring Séverac's score to Carré. Further corroboration is found in Séverac's following comments: "I would like (if possible) to show him [Carré] my score to *Le coeur du moulin* before his departure on the 12th. This is because Debussy has made arrangements to show it to Carré, but before showing it to him, I would love it if [d'Indy] would tell me if there is value [in the score]." ("Je veux (si possible) lui montrer ma partition du *Le coeur du moulin* avant son départ pour le XII. Ceci parce que Debussy m'avait engagé a l'exhiber à Carré, mais avant de faire cette exhibition, j'amerais assez que le Patron me dise si ça vaut le coup.") See Guillot, *Déodat de Séverac: la musique et les lettres*, 215. [Séverac letter to Auguste Sérieyx, June, 1904.]

In 1903, Séverac wrote to regionalist Jean Charles-Brun stating that he was a close friend of Debussy and would be happy to introduce Charles-Brun to the composer. See Pierre Guillot, "Claude Debussy and Déodat de Séverac," *Cahiers Debussy* (nouvelle série, no. 10, 1986), 3–16.

70 Canteloube, *Déodat de Séverac*, 31. [Debussy letter to Séverac after hearing *Hélène de Sparte* at the Théâtre du Châtelet, May, 1912.] "Ce numéro (l'ouverture) est tout à fait exquis, d'un dessin précis et impressionniste à la fois, savoureusement orchestré et riche d'idées."

by Ravel after his resignation from the Société nationale de musique; they also attended gatherings given by Le nouveaux jeune-France, where they performed their works. Séverac and Ravel also met at gatherings hosted by the Apaches.

Séverac's first written references to Ravel surface at the time Ravel was having difficulty getting his music accepted by judges of the Prix de Rome. Ravel did not win first prize during the five years in which he competed, these being 1900 to 1903, and 1905:

> Happily, I don't have to go before a jury of lambs and brutes who will once again declare Ravel's infamy and dismiss this exquisite artist ... Long live Ravel! Down with the lambs.[71]

Séverac's appreciation of Ravel's music is further illustrated by a similarity between certain works by both composers. Critic Pierre Lalo claimed that Ravel's "Une barque sur l'océan" and "La vallée des cloches" from the piano suite *Miroirs* demonstrated a resemblance to that of Séverac's earlier piano suite *En Languedoc*. In this 1906 article in *Le temps*, Lalo claimed that Ravel's work demonstrated in "a completely different manner, a very distant and transposed echo of the feeling which inspires *En Languedoc*, Séverac's most important work."[72] The author was partially referring to the fact that *Miroirs* and *En Languedoc* were five-movement suites for piano composed one year apart and both were introduced by pianist Ricardo Viñes. In addition, they both contain water imagery often musically symbolized by glissandos:

> One sees signs of an evolution ... in the five pieces for piano which were performed at the Société Nationale. Two of them, "Une barque sur l'océan" and "La vallée des cloches" ... have emotion ... This transformation seems not to follow from the influence of Debussy, but rather from that of a musician of the same generation as Ravel, and of whose profound and spontaneous sensitivity I told you last year ... Déodat de Séverac ... Maurice Ravel is without doubt, with Séverac, the best known of our young musicians, and the one whose talents are the most mature ... [Ravel] is ... different from his rival ... [Ravel] is all artifice and exterior ornaments while [Séverac] is all ingenuity and deep sentiment.[73]

---

71 Guillot, *Déodat de Séverac: la musique et les lettres*, 198. [Séverac letter to Michel-Dimitri Calvocoressi, 1903.] "Heureusement je n'aurai pas à passer devant un jury des yeux et de brutes qui a une fois de plus professé son 'infamie' en mettant au panier l'artiste délicieux qu'est l'ami Ravel ... Vive Ravel! À bas les veaux!"

The 1903 jury consisted of Théodore Dubois, Jules Massenet, Emile Paladilhe, Xavier Leroux, Paul Hillemacher, and Henry Roujon (Director of the School of Beaux-Arts and Secretary to the Academy of Beaux-Arts).

72 Lalo, *Le temps* (January 30, 1906), 3; reprinted and translated by Orenstein, *A Ravel Reader*, 78.

73 Lalo, *Le temps* (January 30, 1906), 3. "On trouve un signe d'une évolution ... dans les cinq pièces pour piano qui viennent d'être exécutées à la Société nationale. Deux d'entre elles, 'Une barque sur l'océan,' et 'La vallée des cloches,'... a une èmotion ... Cette transformation ne semble pas s'accomplir sous l'influence de Debussy, mais plutôt sous celle d'un musicien qui appartient à la même génération que Ravel, et dont je vous ait dit l'an dernier la sensibilité ... profonde et spontanée, Déodat de Séverac ... Maurice Ravel est sans doute, avec Séverac, le plus connu de nos jeunes musiciens, et celui dont le talent est le plus formé ... [Ravel] est

Lalo's preference for Séverac's music over that of Ravel upset the latter composer, and he disapproved of this comparison in an uncharacteristically cynical 1906 letter to Séverac:

> I ... wanted to excuse myself for plagiarizing you (as Lalo would say). But that's really not my fault. Besides, how could I have suspected that there would be such a close relationship between a boat on the ocean and a festive southern country house?!! I trust that you won't be too angry with me. Till next Saturday, an affectionate handshake.[74]

Although further correspondence between the two alludes to Séverac meeting with Ravel in 1908 and 1911, comments such as those of Lalo helped lead to Ravel's evolving disapproval of Séverac's music and career, which came to a head while Séverac was living in Catalonia.[75] Séverac, however, did not return this disapproval, as he heard for the first time Ravel's *Daphnis et Chloé* in 1912 and wrote: "I ... heard *Daphnis [et Chloé]* ... I have ... great joy and admiration for this work! It is suave!"[76] Despite the friendship between Ravel and Séverac, Ravel also felt that Séverac's career was declining at this time, in part, because of the perception that Séverac was professionally inactive after moving to the south of France.[77]

Séverac's Departure from Paris, 1907–1910

In 1907, upon graduating from the Schola Cantorum, Séverac left Paris permanently to live briefly in his childhood home in Saint-Félix-Caraman in the province of Languedoc.[78] It was at this time that he presented himself as municipal advisor to his arrondissement in Saint-Félix-Caraman, district of Revel, and was elected—a family precedent set by his father who had formerly held this position as well as that of mayor of Saint-Félix-Caraman.[79] Against all predictions, Séverac received,

---

... différent de son rival ... [Ravel] est tout en artifices et en ornaments extérieurs, tandis que [Séverac] est tout en sentiment ingénu et profond."

74 Ibid., 3; translated by Orenstein, *A Ravel Reader*, 77. [Ravel letter to Séverac, January 31, 1906.] In all fairness to Ravel, Lalo and Ravel disliked each other and Lalo consistently accused Ravel of imitating other composers.

75 Guillot, *Déodat de Séverac: la musique et les lettres*, 298. This letter states: "I saw Ravel yesterday evening." [Séverac letter to Cipa Godebski, 1908.] ("J'ai vu Ravel hier soir.") Ibid., 364. Another letter cites: "Yesterday evening, I dined at Ravel's house with the Cipas." [Séverac letter to sister Alix in 1911.] ("Hier soir j'ai diné chez Ravel avec les Cipa.")

76 Ibid., 381. [Séverac letter to Cipa Godebski, 1912.] "J'ai ... entendu Daphnis ... J'ai ... toute mon joie et toute mon admiration pour cette oeuvre! C'est suave!"

77 In order to illustrate that this was not the case, Séverac later composed *Pavane pour une taupe défunte*, in part, to be a satire on Ravel's piano work *Pavane pour une infante défunte*.

78 He also visited Barcelona that year together with southern French poet Victor Gastilleur in order to meet with Adrià Gual over discussions about Séverac's incidental music for *L'estudiant de Vich*.

79 Séverac, himself, had run unsuccessfully for this position in 1904, and ran again in 1912 and 1919. In 1919, he was appointed Secretary-Director of the Communal Assembly of the departmental archives of Haute-Garonne.

together with his associate, Auguste Get, a majority of votes.[80] During the electoral campaign, Séverac's slogan was, "I created the Lyre du vent d'autan," referring to a choral group Séverac founded in 1904 and placed under the direction of choral director Louis Amiel.[81]

Séverac's Early Years in Céret, 1910–14

By 1910, Séverac had settled in the town of Céret, a Catalan town in the Pyrenees mountains in the province of Roussillon.[82] This move was inspired by the desire to live close to French and Catalan friends in Céret's artistic community, including Manuel Hugué y Martinez, Pablo Picasso, Frank Haviland, Max Jacob, Juan Gris, Georges Braque, Moise Kisling, and André Derain. Yet it was also a decision prompted by the composer's fascination with the land and the music of its people.

Séverac served as organist at the church of St Pierre from the year of his arrival in Céret until his death 11 years later. In 1912, Séverac married Henriette Tardieu, an actress he knew as early as 1907. The birth of their daughter, Magali (named after Frédéric Mistral's "Cansoun de Magali" in *Mirèio*) placed more financial demands upon Séverac, who then took upon himself several commissions to compose popular music.[83] As late as 1919, Séverac wrote to his editor Alexis Rouart stating that he dreamed of leaving music to sell Spanish wines in Spain in order to earn a better living. Séverac commented on his dilemma: "I am ... obligated to do other work: arrangements of works by amateurs and orchestrations ... it is necessary to live ... In our time ... there are no longer any Mécènes or Médicis!!"[84] This emphasis on practical matters in the years leading up to World War I led many composers in Paris to show disdain for Séverac's evolving career, not only for the "popular" or light works that Séverac composed, but also for works performed en plein air, of which many composers in Paris demonstrated disapproval.[85] Additional criticism included comments that Séverac's characters within dramatic works had little psychological depth, and that his music was too personal, direct, and simple. Séverac attempted to

---

80 Séverac and his colleague, Auguste Get, received 2,025 votes, as compared to their "radical socialist" incumbent opponents who received a total of 2,001 votes. Séverac's partner Auguste Get was a member of a famous family of alcohol distillers. See Chapter 7 on piano music, specifically on composition *Pipperment-Get*. Regarding the opposition, François Raissac and his partner, Paul Ferrie, professor at the College of Revel, received 2,097 votes.
81 The group often performed at local festivals and political campaigns.
82 Séverac settled in Céret at the end of 1909 and beginning of 1910. After spending several months at the Hotel Armand, he rented a small house on Saint Ferréal Street where he began to compose *Héliogabale*. In 1911, the Catalan press announced Séverac's permanent move to Céret. See Canteloube, *Déodat de Séverac*, 24–5.
83 Séverac was struck by her beauty. They dated each other for five years before getting married in 1912, and their daughter Magali was conceived just before the occasion. Mistral later became Magali's godfather.
84 Canteloube, *Déodat de Séverac*, 40. [Reprint of Séverac letter to his editor, Alexis Rouart, 1911.] "Je suis ... obligé de faire d'autres travaux—arrangements d'oeuvres d'amateurs, orchestrations ... il faut vivre! ... De nos jours ... il n'y a plus de Mécène ni de Médicis!!"
85 See Chapter 10 for citations and greater detail.

remain indifferent, labeling his critics chichistes–those who complimented him in public but criticized him in private: "Let the heads of the chichistes say what they will. Let them mistake their desires for reality ... It is of no importance. We can let the chichistes wear each other down."[86] Séverac often turned to d'Indy for comfort at this time, as his former mentor continued to provide counsel. In a letter to Séverac, d'Indy spoke of Séverac's dilemma:

> Work slowly but surely. There are too many people in Paris—even among your friends——who complain about your "idleness" ... I much prefer the man who lets himself struggle with his work to all those little social climbers who feel they must trot out their stuff every few months ... and who produce insignificant nothings dressed up as ballets ... Work like you think, and don't let your "friends" tell you that "you have to do this or that" ... I will always tell you my sincere opinion, and if it does not coincide with your way of seeing things, then you needn't grant it any value.[87]

Séverac and World War I

Séverac sought to enlist as soon as war between France and Germany was declared, but being 42 years old, he was rejected for duty at the front. As a result, Séverac joined the medical corps and was posted in four towns in southern France between 1914 and 1919, including Carcassonne, Perpignan, Saint-Pons, and Prades. Much of this time was spent serving as a hospital attendant in Saint-Pons, near Céret. It was at this time that Séverac composed and performed marches and patriotic songs, including *Missia Victoiriae, Elégie héroique: aux morts pour la patrie* (paraphrase of *Pie Jesu*), *Marche militaire du 24th colonial*, a canticle on the poem "Ave Salutaris Fons Maria" (extract from *Cantata Perdriu*, by poet Josep Pons), several patriotic songs, and *Hosannah pour les héroes*. Séverac's work at this time, however, was interrupted by a severe kidney attack, and Séverac was then brought to a hospital within the town of Prades, where he remained for the rest of the war. His musical output decreased during these years.

On Armistice Day, all nearby villages came alive after what was considered by many to be four years of psychological numbness. Music was performed and Séverac obliged by performing on string bass with other musicians, as citizens marched in the streets. Séverac was reputed to have improvised a *Te Deum* on organ for townspeople

---

86 Aspry, "Déodat de Séverac," 536. "Laisse dire les chefs des 'chichistes'... laissons-les prendre leurs désirs pour des réalités ... Ça n'a aucune importance: Laissons les chichistes s'user mutuellement."

87 *Musée Déodat de Séverac*, reprinted by Aspry, "Déodat de Séverac," 585. [Autograph letter from d'Indy to Séverac, 1914.] "Travaillant lentement mais sûrement. Il y a tant de gens à Paris—même parmi vos amis—qui se lamentent sur votre état de 'farniente' ... Je préfère beaucoup le monsieur qui se laisse taxer d'une oeuvre, à tous nos petits arrivistes qui se croient tenus de pondre leur 'salon,' quatre fois par an ... et de mettre au monde une miniature tenue sous forme d'un ballet ... Travaillez comme vous pensez, et ne vous laissez dire par vos copains 'il faudrait faire ceci ou cela' ... Je vous dirai toujours sincèrement mon opinion, si elle ne cadrait pas avec votre nature ou votre manière de voir, il ne faudrait pas y attacher d'autre importance."

in the local church in Prades on the following day. He and his regiment subsequently demobilized in January, 1919, at which time Séverac returned to Céret.

Séverac and His Last Years, 1919–21

Séverac composed and finished several works in 1919 following the war, including his piano composition *Sous les lauriers-roses* and his violin work *Minyoneta: souvenirs de Céret*. Séverac was also invited to be part of the Rousillon delegation to visit the Palau de la Mùsica in Barcelona, in honor of Joseph Joffre, the field marshal of France during World War I. [88] Séverac played the organ before friends in the Orfeó Català at the Palau de la Mùsica while in Barcelona, improvising on *Lo cant del Vallespir* and *Lo cant dels Ocelles*.[89]

In the summer of 1920, Séverac contracted uremia, which did not prevent him from receiving the Medal of the Legion of Honor in September of that year. He attended a gathering upon invitation from the king of Belgium, together with composers Paul Dukas, Vincent d'Indy, Maurice Ravel, and Florent Schmitt. He also discussed his lifelong dream with Blanche Selva of building a conservatory in Barcelona, the Escola Mediterrània de Música, dedicated to training musicians in Mediterranean music; this dream, however, was not realized. His last public appearance took place in January of the following year, and Séverac died of uremia on March 24, 1921.

---

88 Joseph Jacques Césaire Joffre (1852–1931) was the maréchal de France, or Field Marshal during World War I. A field marshal in France was an officer ranking just below Commander-in-Chief.

89 The Orfeó Català was founded in 1891 by Anselm Clavé and directed by Lluis Millet, who emphasized the singing of music composed by ancient masters, as well as the chanson espagnol and chanson populaire occitane.

Chapter 3

Le Régionalisme

French regionalists criticized the Third Republic government for three primary reasons. First, Paris dominated in the making of administrative decisions for all provinces in France, and these regions often felt compelled to turn to the capital for advice and resources. Second, most regionalists thought that administrative divisions within France did not correspond either to economic or to sociological reality. Third, there was no intermediate unit with directly elected representatives to act as a buffer between the département and the state.[1]

Centralization within the French government had often been attributed to decrees instituted by revolutionaries following the French Revolution as well as by policies incorporated by Napoleon Bonaparte's administration—policies that divided France into 36,000 communes, of which the average population of each was a thousand people.

Independent civic life within the communes was negligible, since each commune had virtually no income with which to institute any autonomous activity. The amount of tax revenue that a commune could raise on its own was strictly controlled by the prefects, and approximately three-fourths of this income went to the state. Leftover funds often went towards public services, which were considered the financial responsibility of the communes, as was primary education, police services, road building, and repairs of public property. The more state legislation was introduced, the more the responsibility was placed on the communes. However, the power given to local communes was not proportionately increased. If a small village could not afford to build a school, it was dependent on the state for subsidies, and the state then made decisions regarding educational policy. If a village desired to raise and spend money, it had to obtain authorization from the state.

---

1 James B. Rowdybush, *The Hexagon and the Napoleonic State: A Study of Decentralization and Regional Reform in France* (PhD Dissertation, University of California, Berkeley, 1983), 224. France traditionally has been divided into provinces, or approximately 22 regions that define different geographical areas. From the time of Louis XVI to the French Revolution, the province was also used in administrative terminology to designate a particular territorial order; however, specific provinces were never defined with precision. Following the French Revolution, the département was established; this was a smaller unit within France that changed geographical boundaries from those of the province in order to help eliminate old loyalties that could undermine the unity of the Republic. Each département was headed by a préfet, a person who served as the main channel of communication between the citizens living within the département and the Paris government. Each département was then divided into one to nine arrondissements headed by sub-prefects. These were then split into approximately 100 to 150 communes. France is now divided into 96 départements, 384 arrondissements, and 36,414 communes.

Alexis de Tocqueville (1805–59) argued that this state centralization was begun not by French revolutionaries, but by the monarchy of the Ancien Régime. His contention in *Ancien régime et la révolution* (1856) was based on two assertions: first, that a myth was created by revolutionaries, who claimed that regionalism was the essence of the Ancien Regime and defended by counter-revolutionaries who had lost their regional power following the revolution; second, counter-revolutionaries claimed that the Ancien Régime had provided a golden age of provincial liberties violated by the French Revolution.[2]

Tocqueville proposed the cultivating of intermediary bodies between the individual and the state, since he believed they could safeguard individual liberty and democracy through self-government and citizen participation in local associations. However, in *De la démocratie en Amérique* (1835), he made a distinction between centralized government and centralized administration, contending that the state must retain the power to govern, but administrative functions must be left to local institutions. According to Tocqueville, a centralized administration often lacks support and therefore becomes vulnerable.[3]

The Industrial Revolution, which resulted in increased urban migration, helped exacerbate the intellectual conflict over the relative merits of centralization versus regionalism. According to censuses taken in 1896, 1901, and 1911, more than half of the French population living in Paris was born outside the metropolitan area. By 1911, there were five cities with a population of over 200,000 people.[4] White-collar positions formed the majority of new openings, including positions for cabinet ministers, magistrates, civil servants, and businessmen—thus helping to increase the middle-class population in urban areas and a significantly greater financial and industrial plutocracy. Blue-collar workers were also affected, however, as living standards and wages increased for industry employees.

Thus, industrial output in France tripled between 1870 and 1914, but the number of agricultural workers diminished. In 1870, approximately 52 percent of the active population was engaged in agriculture, and by 1910, the percentage had decreased to approximately 40 percent.[5] In his 1906 book *Le retour à la terre et la surproduction industrielle*, French Minister of Commerce Jules Méline lamented the steady decrease in farming that was continuing in rural France. Méline attributed this

---

2   See Robert Gildea, *The Past in French History* (New Haven, CT: Yale University Press, 1994), 166.

3   See Alexis de Tocqueville, *De la démocratie en Amérique* [1835] (Paris: Garnier-Flammarion, 1981), 9–10.

4   See Xavier de Planhol, *An Historical Geography of France*, translated by Janet Lloyd (Cambridge: Cambridge University Press, 1994), 401. The five towns were Paris, Lyon, Toulouse, Marseille, and Nice.

5   See Jules Méline, *Le retour à la terre et la surproduction industrielle* (Paris: Hachette et Cie., 1905). For further discourse on regionalism and agriculture, see René Bazin, *La terre qui meurt* (Paris: Calmann Lévy, 1899). René Bazin (1853–1932) was a member of l'Académie Française, and a professor of law at the Catholic University of Angers. He resigned in 1903 in order to devote himself to a literary career. His first published novel was *Stéphanette*, followed by *Une tache d'encre*. He was awarded the Chevalier of the Legion of Honor in 1900.

decrease to foreign competition, industrialization, a rural exodus, and the centralized power of the French government. Paradoxically, he then advocated that the state intervene for prevention of peasant migration to urban areas and the repatriation of city workers to rural territories "to protect us from troubles resulting from the too exclusive development of manufacture."[6] He stated that society "needs to strive to educate ... rural classes in a way that we instill in them a love for their labor. In this purpose, a different order of education is required, the chief end of which should be to bring out the beauties of nature and the advantages of life in the field. This is a task for our school teachers."[7] Méline's essay was characteristic of seemingly countless books and articles on decentralization in France throughout the second half of the nineteenth century. During the 1860s, over seventy books had been published on the topic.[8]

The term *régionalisme*, however, was unknown for most of the nineteenth century. The earliest extant example of its use is in an 1874 essay on Provençal culture by poet Léon Berluc-Perussis (1860–1902), a member of the Félibrige movement led by Provençal regionalist poet Frédéric Mistral, and dedicated to maintaining Provençal customs and language. Used in this cultural context, the word was later employed politically by writer-philosophers Maurice Barrès and Charles Maurras to counterbalance the perception of an excessively centralized bureaucracy in the French government.

Jean Charles-Brun

Ever since the French Revolution followed by Napoleon Bonaparte's decrees helped instigate the centralized state, many historians have characterized the history of political ideas as a debate between those who believed in the French Revolution and reactionaries. Regionalists have often been placed into the latter category, in part, because of anti-Dreyfusard attitudes held by many regionalists during the Dreyfus Affair towards the end of the nineteenth century. According to historian Julien Wright, however, the resultant "occultation" of régionalisme by various scholars becomes the product of oversimplifying the regionalist movement.[9]

Fin de siècle French regionalist Jean Charles-Brun (1870–1946) held views that represented a counter-argument to this purported oversimplification. Charles-Brun produced many books on decentralization at the beginning of the twentieth century, including *Le régionalisme* in 1911.[10] He formed groups such as the Fédéralist

---

6 Méline, *Le retour à la terre et la surproduction industrielle*, 121–3. Méline is citing a Belgian undertaking.

7 Ibid. The translation can be found in Méline, *The Return of the Land* (London: Chapman and Hall, Ltd., 1906).

8 These include F. Le Play, *La reforme sociale en France* (Paris: E. Dentu, 1866) and L.A. Prevost-Paradol, *La France nouvelle* (Paris: Michel Levy, 1868).

9 Julien Wright, *The Regionalist Movement in France, 1890-1914: Jean Charles-Brun and French Political Thought* (Oxford: Oxford University Press, 2003), 54.

10 Jean Charles-Brun, *Le régionalisme* (Paris: Bloud et Cie, 1911).

régionaliste français (FRF) in 1900 and the Action régionaliste in 1901, wherein both organizations promoted decentralization and regionalism in France.

Charles-Brun supported the ideals found in the 1789 Jacobin Declaration of the Rights of Man instigated following the French Revolution, thereby illustrating nuanced differences within regionalist associations. One reason why his contributions have often been neglected by posterity is that his portrayal contradicts the aforementioned paradigm that all regionalists are reactionaries. Charles-Brun's views were that of reconciliation rather than polarization, thereby downplaying the dichotomy between regionalists and the Third Republic government.

Charles-Brun believed that regionalism should be apolitical and inclusive and he tried to heal the religious, social, and political divisions that were at the heart of much regionalist rhetoric. He attempted to bridge a divide between regionalist literary ideas and contemporary economic and geographical theories, rather than declaring the more controversial political and social ideals held by figures such as Maurice Barrès and Charles Maurras.

Like Barrès and Maurras, Charles-Brun was originally a member of the Félibrige; in fact, Mistral saw Charles-Brun as a possible successor to Mistral's role as figurehead and leader of the movement. Charles-Brun, however, resigned from the organization over anti-Dreyfusard views held by many within the group, including Barrès and Maurras.

This information is significant, because Séverac dedicated his 1907 graduating thesis to Charles-Brun, which lends evidence to the fact that Séverac himself was not a polemicist who favored one type of regionalist organization over another and did not always hold the same ideas favored by many within the Félibrige organization.

Séverac and Politics: Charles Maurras and the Dreyfus Affair

It would nonetheless be an oversimplification to view Séverac as a naive musician who embraced regionalist philosophy solely for artistic reasons, as additional evidence tends to contradict this view. Séverac was not only a regionalist, but like his parents, a fervent Royalist as well as Legitimist, who possessed an interest in pays and patrie. Writer-philosophers Maurice Barrès and Charles Maurras also formed an allegiance to both regionalism and nationalism, while Séverac, although devoted to both, was most interested in his local region.[11]

Like other French aristocrats, Séverac's interest in Royalism centered around the desire to return the central power in France to the nobility, which had lost power following the French Revolution. Legitimists were among the most conservative of Royalists in that they opposed political compromises regarding the restoration of the monarchy established by the 1830 revolution, even when nobles gave up power

---

11 Portraits of the Duke of Bordeaux, future Count de Chambord, decorated the music salon room in Séverac's baronial birthplace home in Saint Félix-Caraman, while a portrait of Louis XVIII remained on the piano; Bertrand de Molleville, Séverac's great-grandfather, was a minister under Louis XVI.

by eventually leaving Paris and returning to their estates in their local pays. One resultant strategy among Legitimists, therefore, was to cultivate popular support in the provinces to which aristocrats had returned by asserting the distinctive identity of the provinces against the interference of the centralized state. This identity would be established sometimes through a separate language, or through popular culture, religious faith, an emphasis on a rural economy, or a nostalgic vision of a provincial past that glorified tradition and frowned upon change. Yet Séverac believed that maintaining these traditions did not require subjugating individuals in the name of these customs, as Séverac opposed all forms of oppression regardless of the origins of this persecution. This is evident in Séverac's comments about socialists in Paris: "The newspapers [publish about] ... the folly of certain (self-proclaimed) socialists ... [who] seem to ignore the lessons of history... [although] you know me enough to know that I have a horror of all inquisitions."[12]

This reference to inquisition centered around Séverac's interest in the Dreyfus Affair, an event in which Séverac, interestingly, took sides with Emile Zola (1840–1902), a famous French novelist who defended Dreyfus in public. This would have been in opposition to conservative thought in France, thereby illustrating Séverac's liberal political philosophy in this particular case, as he perceived Dreyfus to be an oppressed victim. Nonetheless, Séverac's views grew increasingly conservative as the impending war with Germany came nearer.

The Dreyfus Affair centered around Captain Alfred Dreyfus, a Jewish army staff captain who, in 1894, was wrongly convicted of handing military secrets to the Germans. One year later, some in French intelligence began to suspect another officer, Major Ferdinand Walsin-Esterházy. Many prophesied that if Esterházy were proven to be guilty, Dreyfus would be then cleared and therefore prejudiced and superficial inquiries leading to the initial accusation against Dreyfus made public. In 1897, Esterházy was publicly accused, but the verdict regarding Dreyfus was not reversed because of the opposition from the army, nationalists, and clerical workers. This crisis split the country into two factions. Some emphasized individualism and liberty by demanding the acquittal of Dreyfus—no matter what sacrifice to military and state prestige. One figure who maintained this philosophy was writer Emile Zola, whose open letter to the president of the Republic entitled "J'accuse" blamed generals and staff for knowingly convicting an innocent man. Those who were opposed to this stance often stressed order, obedience, and tradition, and thought that the prestige of the army and country would be in question if Dreyfus were acquitted. They further felt that one man was not worth the national loss. As Maurice Barrès stated, "There is only probability that Dreyfus is innocent, but it is absolutely certain that France is innocent."[13] The case was reopened in 1899 and Dreyfus was again pronounced guilty, though two out of five jurors voted for acquittal. Unspecified

---

12 Pierre Guillot, *Déodat de Séverac: la musique et les lettres* (Liège, Belgium: Pierre Mardaga, 2002), 191 [Séverac letter to his mother, 1903.] "Les journaux ... sottises que font certains (soi-disant) socialistes ... ils semblent ignorer les leçons de l'histoire ... vous me connaissez assez pour savoir que j'ai horreur de toutes les inquisitions."

13 Another constituency that held this philosophy consisted of anti-Semites. Maurice Barrès, *Scènes et doctrines du nationalisme* (Paris: Plon-Nourrit, 1925), 29; reprinted and

mitigating circumstances were cited in order to reduce the sentence to ten years. Dreyfus was eventually pardoned after spending time on Devil's Island.

Comments by Séverac relating to the Dreyfus Affair are scant yet revealing. In June of 1899, for example, President Emile Loubet had been struck with a stick by a demonstrator at a steeplechase in the town of Auteuil. Supporting Loubet was politically equated with backing Dreyfus, and therefore a riot ensued between Loubet supporters and the demonstrators who thought Loubet's policies erroneous. Forty-three people were arrested. Séverac responded to his sister's concern over a rumor that he had participated in the event:

> Who told you that I had been arrested at Longchamp? This is an enormous joke if only because I spent my Sunday with Bordes at the Schola Cantorum tranquilly ... I have nothing in common with [the demonstrators in] the struggles at Longchamp ... and I am perfectly unsullied.[14]

Further corroboration of Séverac's views regarding Dreyfus comes from Claire Vlach-Magnard, the grandchild of French composer Albéric Magnard. She attests that Magnard signed a *Manifeste des intellectuels* in 1898, in essence, a protest against the treatment of Dreyfus, and cites that Séverac also signed this manifesto.[15]

Regardless of Séverac's isolated example of French Republican sentiment, conservative philosophy becomes evident in his frequent visits to the home of writer-philosopher Charles Maurras (1868–1952) in Paris, whose ideas in "L'idée de décentralisation" Séverac found inspiring. In this essay, Maurras crystallized federalist concepts and those ideas surrounding decentralization that became important for nationalist factions in the last two decades of the nineteenth century.

Maurras's career began after regionalist philosopher-writer Maurice Barrès founded the Ligue de la patrie française in 1899, a group founded during the Dreyfus Affair in order to encourage nationalism and regionalism in France. Maurras worked with Barrès within this league and shared many of Barrès's ideas, but Maurras sought a firmer doctrinal foundation by wanting to restore the French monarchy. While Barrès urged discipline and tradition, Maurras sought to reinstate many of the classical ideals he felt existed before the French Revolution. Not finding this doctrine in Barrès's organization, a faction within the Ligue de la patrie française seceded and joined Maurras in founding the publication *L'action française*. The league subsequently became a militantly Royalist organization, and more than any other association before World War I, controlled the discourse of cultural politics in France. The league's publication was one of the few daily Royalist journals at the

---

translated by Michael Curtis, *Three Against the Republic* (Princeton, NJ: Princeton University Press, 1959), 149.

14 Guillot, *Déodat de Séverac: la musique et les lettres*, 85. [Séverac letter to sister, Jeanette, 1899.] "Qui vous a dit que j'avais été arrêté à Longchamp? C'est une énorme blague pour la raison bien simple que j'ai passé mon dimanche avec Bordes à la Schola tranquillement ... Il n'y a rien de commun avec les batailles de Longchamp ... et je suis parfaitement intact."

15 Claire Vlach-Magnard, *Correspondances de Albéric Magnard* (Paris: Société française de musicologie, 1997); Claire Vlach-Magnard states that there is evidence that Séverac was in the group who signed this manifesto.

time, with over ten thousand readers. Like the Ligue de la patrie française, *L'action française* focused its attention on political debate regarding French culture and continued to emphasize so-called authentic French traditions and values. Maurras took the philosophy one step further, however, when he specifically emphasized the importance of preserving the classical tradition in France in its pristine form. This included encouraging Royalism and becoming free of foreign cultural or racial elements, so as to exclude those perceived by some as not being inherently French.

Maurras made an important distinction between the post-revolutionary pays légal and the indigenous pays réel: the latter for Maurras comprised a national and regional culture, thus simultaneously endowing citizens with two patries, each commanding loyalty in different ways. While a citizen's roots were in a regional petit-pays, one nevertheless shared the common destiny and potential of the nation.

These two pays, however, eventually led to an inner tension within the league, that is, between advocates of authoritarian centralization, and the protectors of regional culture and rights. For Maurras, both ideologies were not only of equal significance, but were inherently inseparable, because political and cultural ideals arose originally from the same source. For Maurras, therefore, paying homage to both pays and patrie while promoting Classicism combined with tradition was synonymous with the restoration of the French monarchical state.

In truth, Maurras promoted a hierarchical society of medieval manor and town, wanting to substitute in place of the current administrative arrangement municipal councils and regional assemblies in which local aristocrats would be the controlling authorities. This restoration would, according to Maurras, succeed when local systems included stratification, privilege, hereditary power, and the inviolability of family property, the latter promoting a return to feudalism and the caste system. Interestingly, Maurras, who himself was not an aristocrat, and defended so-called provincial liberties, did not object when the Vichy government during World War II deprived local villages and municipal governments of many of their former powers, including the power to elect their own mayors. Maurras was eventually subjected to prison life for treason following World War II.

Séverac subscribed to the journal for the Action française, and his interest in the publication is evident in comments by publisher E.C. Ricart, who reminisced: "[Séverac and I] spoke of music, the Action française, of Moréas, Greeks, and Catalans that he loved."[16] In 1908, Séverac wrote a letter to Auguste Sérieyx, wherein he commented: "My cousin Edmond de Rigaud absolutely wants to meet you and tell you about a mission of which L'action française has put him in charge."[17]

Séverac adhered to Maurras's monarchist views, but unlike Maurras, who found pays and patrie inseparable, emphasized the idea of petit-pays for most of his life.

---

16 E.C. Ricart, *El gris i el cadmi* (Barcelona, Spain: Libreria Catalonia, 1926), translated into French by Martin Gobet, reprinted by Jean-Bernard Cahours d'Aspry, "Déodat de Séverac," (unpublished manuscript), 645. "Nous parlions de musique, de L'action française, de Moréas, des grecques, des catalans qu'il aimait."

17 Guillot, *Déodat de Séverac: la musique et les lettres*, 300. [Séverac letter to Auguste Sérieyx, 1908.] "Mon cousin Edmond de Rigaud voudrait absolument vous connaître et vous parler d'une mission dont L'action française l'a chargé."

Séverac's views began to evolve, however, with the advent of World War I. He became a visiting lecturer who preached nationalism at an Action française meeting in Paris during the war. Séverac's increasingly nationalist tendencies at this time are not only evident in his evolving distaste for Wagner's music, but also apparent in his adaptation of ideas promoted within the Ligue nationale pour la defense de la musique française. Séverac's nationalist beliefs thereby began to resemble those of Maurras more closely, as Séverac undertook to promote the idea that self-repatriation to the land of one's ancestors and petite-patrie was the only feasible way for the future of French national music.

The Ligue nationale pour la defense de la musique française was created in 1916, in part to forbid public performances of German music in France that was not in the public domain, and to simultaneously promote French music and musicians. Gustave Charpentier, Théodore Dubois, Vincent d'Indy, Charles Lecocq, Xavier Leroux, and Camille Saint-Saëns were all members of the organization. Saint-Saëns, who was enamored of German culture, espoused his version of the league's philosophy two years before the association was founded:[18]

> After the massacres of women and children, how can the French listen to Wagner? It is necessary to make this sacrifice of not reading or hearing the works of Wagner, because he thought Germany could use his work to conquer souls. Art is only a pretext; a universal Germany, that is the true goal."[19]

Saint-Saëns' brand of chauvinism over Wagner's music obfuscates the fact that Wagner's music was already in the public domain in the years leading up to World War I. Séverac did adopt Saint-Saëns' opinion during the war, however, as illustrated by Séverac's comments:

> If ... my name carried a bit more weight, I would put out a call to all French composers to organize a national show of strength in honor of Saint-Saëns in response to those who attack him for his anti-Germanism ... Because of pride, some wouldn't want to sacrifice their interests in their own musical schools in favor of purely national Art.[20]

---

18 For more information on Saint-Saëns and his views on Germany, see Camille Saint-Saëns, "Germanophile," *L'echo de Paris* (October 6, 1914), 1.

19 Ibid. "Apès les massacres de femmes et d'enfants, comment peut-il se trouver des Français pour entendre Wagner? Il fallait faire le sacrifice de ne plus entendre les oeuvres de Wagner parce qu'il considérait que son oeuvre était le moyen employé par l'Allemagne à la conquête des âmes. L'art n'était qu'un prétexte; la germanisation universelle, voilà le vrai but."

20 Pierre Guillot, *Déodat de Séverac: écrits sur la musique* (Liège, Belgium: Pierre Mardaga, 1993), 128. Despite the fact that Séverac gave a lecture for the league, he nonetheless did not join the organization. "Si ... mon nom ait un peu plus de poids, je ferais appel à tous les composit[eurs] français en vue d'organiser une manifestation nationale en l'honneur de St. Saëns pour répondre à ceux qui áttaquent bassement ce grand français à cause de son anti-germanisme ... Ceux qui, par orgueil, ne veulent pas sacrifier leurs intérêts d'école à l'Art purement national."

Séverac also admired and supported ideas promoted by philosopher, writer, and monarchist Léon Daudet (1867–1942), who co-founded the Action française together with Charles Maurras. Daudet was a polemicist who served as a deputy in the French government's Chamber of Deputies between 1919 and 1924.[21] Daudet's comments inspired Séverac to write him a letter, which Séverac later published.[22]

Maurice Barrès

French novelist and journalist Maurice Barrès (1862–1923) was a prominent regionalist writer on politics and culture. Originally from the region of Lorraine, he had moved to Paris in 1883 and produced the *Culte du moi* trilogy in 1888, a series of novels advocating a philosophy of individualism.[23] Barrès was elected to the French parliament in 1889 on an anti-republican platform stressing nationalism and an anti-capitalist desire for social reform. He also founded the newspaper *La cocarde*, in which he attempted to build a democratic socialist youth movement.[24] In 1898, he created the Ligue de la patrie française, a group organized in the heat of the Dreyfus Affair and dedicated to promoting both regionalism and nationalism in France.

Although Barrès believed in a national and regional culture, an inner conflict within the organization nonetheless grew between those who stressed nationalist authoritarian centralization and those who held more of an interest in promoting regional culture.

Barrès believed in administrative regionalism, as his régionalisme centered on the desire to free French provinces from the control of Parisian politicians and administrators who, Barrès believed, knew relatively little about the various regions they governed. He argued that a centralized government leads to absolutism and therefore a lack of freedom among its citizens, thus molding the minds of the

---

21 The Chamber of Deputies was the lower house of parliament during the Bourbon Restoration, July Monarchy, and Third Republic. It is equivalent to the American House of Representatives and members of these bodies are termed deputies, similar to American congresspersons or British members of parliament. The word Deputy refers to any member of a legislative body.

22 This letter was published in *Le feu* in 1917 with the title "Ne vous scandalisez plus!" Daudet once declared "The German temperament ... is ferocious, and the absence of tact is just a consequence of an absence of sensitivity. This ferocity is methodical, conceived coldly as an element of ethnic superiority, domination and conquest ... this civilization bleeds dry the French, the English, the Russians, and the Belgians ... without a thank you." ("Le tempérament allemand ... est un tempérament féroce chez qui le manque de tact n'est qu'une dépendance du manque de sensibilité. Cette férocité est méthodique, froidement conçue comme un élément de supériorité ethnique, de domination et de conquête ... La civilisation exige que le Français, l'Anglais, le Russe et le Belge ... le saigne sans merci sur le billot.") Statement made by Daudet, August 22, 1914, cited by Marcel Marnat, *Maurice Ravel* (Paris: Fayard, 1986), 44; recited by Guillot, *Déodat de Séverac: écrits sur la musique*, 128.

23 Maurice Barrès, *Le culte du moi* [1888] (Paris: Plon, 1966). *Le culte du moi* consists of three novels—*Sous l'oeil des Barbares*, *Un homme libre*, and *Le jardin de Bérénice*.

24 *La cocarde* (The Cockade) was a Paris newspaper published for six months from 1894 to 1895.

people to the various perceived necessities of the state. Barrès then called for new administrative and geographical boundaries, local democracies, and the devolution of centralized legislative and administrative authority.

Barrès essentially agreed with nineteenth-century French historian Hippolyte Taine (1828–93) that the state's domination of education decreased independent thinking among university faculty and administrators. In *Origines de la France contemporaine*, Taine had argued against centralized educational institutions. He indicted the Second Republic government in his anti-Jacobin account of the French Revolution and its aftermath.[25] Taine further asserted that these bureaucracies instituted centralized laws transforming the French school system into "national education factories" and that the government in Paris also dictated how children were to be educated, thereby consigning provincial schools to intellectual conformity and stagnation.[26]

For Barrès, an oligarchy of insiders imposed this uniformity on professors and students and therefore suppressed individuality. The intellectual uniformity arose from the teaching of "Kantian" philosophy that persuaded students to become "citizens of humanity at the expense of regional identity."[27] These theories thus highlighted humankind as an abstract universal entity and encouraged students to scorn local traditions, thereby deepening confusion among these pupils. In addition, Barrès observed that many provincial professors who taught these "Kantian" ideals were originally from Paris.

As a counter-measure, Barrès suggested that each region develop and maintain its own regional university, where pupils would learn through "examples from nature." He called for individuals to express their regional heritage in education, claiming that hymns and sacred songs on which a child ought to be nourished would encourage it in family life and regional activity.[28]

Barrès also argued that the study of humanities had engendered a distaste for manual work, hindering the French population from being able to handle agriculture, commerce, or industry. An emphasis on humanistic study lured prospective

---

25 See Hippolyte Taine, *Origines de la France contemporaine* [6 vols., 1876–93] (New York: H. Holt and Co., 1895); French edition (Paris: Hachette et Cie, 1899). For an English translation, see Hippolyte Taine, *Origins of Contemporary France*, translated by John Durand (New York: Peter Smith, 1931). "Post-Royalist governments" refer to governments following the French Revolution.

26 Increased centralization within French society also helped diminish regional differences among the provinces. Although the cause of this centralization is often justifiably ascribed to the French Revolution, Napoleon Bonaparte, and the Industrial Revolution, it was also inherent in the Ancien Régime. Agents of decentralization were often superseded by the king's absolute power. One such example was prompted by Duc de Richelieu, the chief minister of Louis XIII from 1624 until his death in 1642, who made the Conseil d'état one of the prominent agents of monarchical centralization by increasing its power. He eventually replaced many provincial governors with his loyal followers, therefore stifling opposition and eventually forbidding any intervention in administrative decisions and affairs of state. Richelieu was also a French cardinal and statesman.

27 Barrès, *Un homme libre* [1888] (Paris: Plon, 1966), xiv.

28 For more data on these views, see Curtis, *Three Against the Republic*, 167.

agriculturists away from the land from which they came, thus creating unemployed intellectuals and a generation of frustrated aesthetes. As a counter-measure, he suggested the establishment of vocational schools to promote employment for rural workers, emphasizing regional pride and practical skills among the working classes.

Barrès also claimed that centralization had encouraged students to uproot themselves and move to Paris. Indeed, he recalled that as a young student in Nancy, he himself had eagerly awaited the day when he would leave for Paris where "great men lived"—an indication that his viewpoint contained contradictions.[29] In his novel *Les déracinés* of 1897, Barrès depicts the moral and physical uprooting of seven young Lorrainers. The teacher of these seven in the provinces is Professor Bouteiller, who, through his devotion to Immanuel Kant, encourages the students to lose their sense of traditional morality. They are then uprooted and move to Paris with the desire to fulfill themselves to their utmost. Barrès therefore treats the teacher Bouteiller with disfavor, because Bouteiller implanted the concept of ambition and urban migration in his pupils.[30]

Barrès described this experience as alienating. The fates of the uprooted students differ: Racadot and Mouchefrin are of peasant origin and have little natural defense against what Barrès describes as intellectual anarchy. They become assassins. The character Racadot initially founds a journal that fails and squanders his inheritance. He tries to raise his social standing by severing family ties and rejecting his father's advice to seek a position in his local pays. Because Racadot gives up his home and traditional values, Barrès posits that he is bound to fail.

Renaudin becomes an unscrupulous political journalist and Suret-Lefort a successful Third Republic lawyer-politician. Sturel becomes an impassioned proponent of General Boulanger's ideas and Ruemerspacher develops into a historian who worships Hippolyte Taine.[31]

According to Barrès, these déracinés felt uprooted by the lack of traditional relationships in Paris and experienced isolation and disorientation by the precariousness of their social status. Barrès's call for a regional tranquillity, harmony, and simplicity that purportedly existed in rural areas reflects an alternative to these disastrous consequences. He described the benefits of remaining in one's indigenous region and feeling rooted, contrasting them with an uprooted urban life replete with philosophical skepticism, cynicism, flippancy, weakened morality, a lack of religious faith, and selfishness fueled by a capitalist market.[32] He further thought that migration to Paris could be discouraged by offering unique regional

---

29 Henri Mondor, "La jeunesse de Barrès: premières lectures de Barrès," *La revue de Paris* LXIII (January, 1956), 10.

30 Maurice Barrès, *Les déracinés*, 2 vols. (Paris: Bibliothèque-Charpentier, 1897).

31 General Georges Boulanger (1837–91) was minister of war in 1887, and his philosophies reflected those held by a conservative constituency in France following the defeat in the Franco-Prussian War. Boulanger and his supporters hoped to overthrow the Republic; however, this revolution never took place. Boulanger was later charged with state treason, and he therefore fled to Belgium where he committed suicide on the grave of his late mistress.

32 For more information on rootedness, see Simone Weil, *L'enracinement* (Paris: Gallimard, 1949).

opportunities for students at provincial institutions and by offering higher salaries to professors. Barrès's horticultural metaphor was criticized by his nemesis, the French writer André Gide (1869–1951) who, in *Incidences* (1924), reminded the public of the false metaphor, that in fact a plant can thrive when uprooted and transplanted.[33] Nonetheless, the word *déraciné* in Barrès's usage eventually became part of the French lexicon as its appearances increased.[34]

Barrès's central thesis regarding this uprootedness centered on a purported lack of attachment to what he referred to as a generational past, which could be found only in becoming absorbed in one's rural birthplace, since the dead survive in children as temporary custodians of ancestral tradition. "The soul which today lives in me is made of thousands of dead, and that sum, increased by the best of myself, will survive me when I am dead and forgotten."[35] In his philosophy of *la terre et les morts*, Barrès refers to the cult of an individual's psychic roots found in the earth and the dead. He defended "not the past, but what is eternal."[36]

However, for Barrès, ancestry and regional roots later became tied with race, which for him became a function of tradition and genetic heritage. In 1898, Barrès campaigned for election in Nancy and learned the difficulties of winning the election by not being anti-Semitic enough. His opponent accused him of "surface anti-Semitism" and this contributed to Barrès losing the election.

At the turn of the century, Barrès therefore made a philosophical leap from cultural to racial rootedness. At first, he believed that the former was a result of education and not blood, thereby assuming that Jews could be assimilated into French culture. Barrès repeatedly stated in his later writings that he believed there to be a direct link between physical and cultural qualities—a theory stated by contemporary racial theorists who believed that physical attributes, even physiognomy, were outward signs of inward grace and expressions of the folk soul. Barrès later made connections between political decentralization and xenophobia, arguing that once local self-government became a reality, Frenchmen would take steps to evict foreign workers from their regions. Barrès's leap from cultural to racial rootedness led self-proclaimed Fascist leaders of the mid 1930s (including Pierre Drieu La Rochelle and Robert Brasillach) to cite Barrès as their initial role model. Barrès's son Philippe Barrès, joined France's first fascist party Faiseau in 1925 and praised German Nazi ideology in 1933.

Despite Barrès's earnest pleas for regionalism, he was often charged with insincerity. Because Barrès spent his entire adult life in Paris, many doubted his honesty by believing that he was not interested in truth but in emotional comfort. As Barrès's biographer Pierre de Boisdeffre stated: "If Barrès had followed his own advice, he would never have left Lorraine, never settled in Paris, and never become the Barrès we know. Without Paris and the university, Louis Pasteur would have

---

33   André Gide, *Incidences* (Paris: Nouvelle revue française, 1924), 56.

34   Robert Soucy, *Fascism in France: The Case of Maurice Barrès* (Berkeley: University of California Press, 1972), 13.

35   Maurice Barrès, *Mes cahiers* XIII: 25 (Paris: Plon, 1929), reprinted by Curtis, *Three Against the Republic*, 113.

36   Ibid.

tended cows."[37] Another critic charged, "It is not Lorraine which has created Maurice Barrès; it is Maurice Barrès who has created Lorraine."[38]

In this regard, Barrès's secretary stated that between 1905 and 1914, Barrès demonstrated little interest in regionalist literature when books and pamphlets portraying customs, festivals, and folklore of Lorraine and other French provinces were mailed to him. He would say "It's all too tedious."[39] When Barrès returned periodically to his native Lorraine, he was reported to have made no effort to talk with the townspeople. Barrès's reply to such criticism was that "it doesn't matter where one lives or how one participates. Rootedness is an awareness of one's cultural heritage."[40]

Barrès's philosophy combined regionalism with nationalism in an effort to counteract a society perceived as increasingly decadent. Prior to Barrès's lifetime, French nationalism was often equated with humanitarianism and the ideals that prompted the French Revolution. Barrès, however, became more concerned with national self-interest coupled with an encroaching indifference to the fate of other nations. Barrès also developed an interest in economic and intellectual protectionism, a glorification of military power, and a belief that the individual becomes subordinate to the interests of the state; this latter conviction was eventually embodied in Barrès's views during the Dreyfus Affair and contradicted some of his earlier views found in *Culte de moi*. This curious conjoining of two seemingly antithetical paradigms became a way for Barrès to manipulate various constituencies within French society. Nationalists and regionalists shared the need to resist an outside power, and Barrès realized the necessity of appealing to these two groups: those who abhorred the excess administrative control that the Third Republic employed over the provinces, and French patriots asserting their Frenchness in order to countermand the encroachment of German culture and military power. For Barrès, music played a part in this marriage of regionalist and nationalist philosophy, and he encouraged families to sing hymns and sacred songs of the Catholic Church in an effort to invoke traditions that were antithetical to those articulated by the leftist Third Republic government. For Barrès, singing regional sacred and secular folk songs was another way to emphasize this local cultural heritage.

Séverac and Barrès

The regionalist writings of Maurice Barrès significantly influenced Séverac's 1907 thesis. Barrès's ideas shared by Séverac were also promulgated by the Ligue de la patrie française, the group organized by Barrès in the wake of the Dreyfus Affair

---

37 Pierre de Boisdeffre, *Métamorphose de la littérature: de Barrès à Malraux* (Paris: Alsatia, 1950), 46; reprinted and translated by Soucy, *Fascism in France: The Case of Maurice Barrès*, 98.

38 Soucy, *Fascism in France: The Case of Maurice Barrès*, 79.

39 Jérôme Tharaud, *Mes années chez Barrès* (Paris: Librairie Plon, 1928), 204–205; reprinted and translated by Soucy, *Fascism in France: The Case of Maurice Barrès*, 79–80.

40 Anthony Greaves, *Maurice Barrès*, translated by Greaves (Boston: G.K. Hall and Co., 1978), 18.

and dedicated to promoting regionalism and nationalism in France. Séverac's composition teacher Vincent d'Indy was a member of the organization, and appeared on the league's platform accompanying patriotic songs on the piano. During the Dreyfus Affair, d'Indy wrote to the organization that he had recruited Ernest Chausson and Pierre de Bréville. Jane Fulcher reminds us that by 1902 when the Schola Cantorum was in serious financial difficulties, d'Indy was writing letters of thanks to the Ligue de la patrie française, alluding to a financial association between the two organizations. She further argues that the Ligue de la patrie française helped support the institution in order to use the establishment as a vehicle to disseminate its doctrine.[41] There is no direct evidence that d'Indy was responsible for convincing Séverac to appropriate the theories of Barrès and the Ligue de la patrie française. Yet, given the potential financial link between the league and the Schola Cantorum, coupled with the close ten-year relationship between the professor and his student, it seems likely that young Séverac was aware of d'Indy's ideological leanings.

Séverac was more interested in regionalism than nationalism. He avoided discussions about racial rootedness and anti-Semitism as well as the glorification of military power, but when it came to regionalism, Séverac believed in Barrès's ideals. Barrès and Séverac shared disapproval of the centralized French government and the Paris Conservatoire, a similar philosophy regarding regionalism in education, and a common interest in régionalisme and its ties with nature, peasantry and ancestral roots. The regionalist Maurice Barrès called for new administrative and geographical boundaries, local democracy, and the devolution of centralized legislative and administrative authority. Séverac expanded these regionalist ideas to include the politicization of the fine arts, wherein the musical counterpart to the centralized bureaucracy of the French government was found in the bylaws of the Paris Conservatoire and in its relationship with provincial institutions. In Séverac's view, regional music schools were often corrupted when funded by the Paris Conservatoire, echoing Barrès's argument that provincial universities were highly compromised when sponsored by the state.

Séverac, in his 1907 thesis, consistently alluded to Barrès's déraciné philosophy and that of *la terre et les morts*:

> The young composer will therefore develop contrary to his instinct in the atmosphere of a cultural porridge; he will have to adapt himself to a soil that nature had not intended for

---

41 Jane Fulcher, *French Cultural Politics and Music* (Oxford: Oxford University Press, 1999), 16. Fulcher nonetheless overstates her case regarding the relationship between the Schola Cantorum and the Ligue de la patrie française. Steven Huebner notes that evidence of d'Indy's interaction with the Ligue de la patrie française was minimal. Huebner further contends that Fulcher's primary source for this information is Jean-Pierre Rioux, *Nationalisme et conservatisme: la ligue de la patrie française, 1899–1904* (Paris: Editions Beauchesne, 1977), in which Rioux makes points that are directly opposed to many of Fulcher's contentions. Rioux furthermore states that the league moved beyond the Dreyfus Affair and became committed to the Republic, as it avoided anti-Semitic discussion and became an arm of the French bourgeoisie. See Steven Huebner's review of Fulcher's book in *Music and Letters* (vol. 82, no. 2, 2001), 333–8. Also see Carlo Caballero's untitled review in the *Journal of the American Musicological Society* (vol. 55, no. 3, 2002), 563–78.

him. Gradually he will break the chain of old traditions that linked him to his ancestors and to his region.[42]

Séverac employed the term *déracinés* in several articles, including a 1911 essay for *Musica* where he stated: "We wondered why [these regionalists] who charmed us [with their music] would have no echo in the soul of our uprooted friends and exiles in Paris."[43] Séverac also used the word déraciné in his thesis, where he revealed his indebtedness to Barrès by his description of France's system of musical education:

> The young musician who will let himself be caught in ... the Prix de Rome ... is forbidden to show a personality that will not conform to the ideal of ... [the] uprooted ones ... Parisianism has done its work; they are ... uprooted ones of a higher class, but uprooted all the same. Since the Regional Conservatoires are only ... branches of the Conservatoire in Paris, [they] are given the responsibility to train their students in accordance with predetermined methodologies. [As a result, one] begins to *uproot* oneself (in accordance with the forceful expression of Maurice Barrès) when one is still a nursing baby.[44]

Séverac echoed Barrès's anti-centralization philosophy by chastising the Paris Conservatoire director Théodore Dubois and a number of conservatory composition professors for emphasizing a narrow range of musical genres and styles. He accused the administrator of applying pressure to music students who lived outside Paris to study at the conservatory, thus inhibiting student individuality and unique regional music traditions. Séverac severely criticized the centralized system that produced this phenomenon:

> Contemporary French music is engaged in a struggle ... with a formidable enemy, centralization ... Today's musicians ... however different they seem to be from one another in their methods of composition are all ... its benevolent victims. They compose music of Paris and for Paris; they stray progressively farther away from the native genius special to the diverse French provinces where they were born.
>
> Each region is endowed by nature with ... an essence, and a special flavor which it owes to the soil that supports it and to the sun which helps it to grow ... It has acquired

---

42 Séverac, "La centralisation et les petites chapelles musicales," *Le courrier musical*, 11e année, no. 3 (January 15, 1908), 40. "Le jeune compositeur se développera donc contre son instinct dans l'atmosphère d'un bouillon de culture; il devra s'adapter à un sol auquel la nature ne l'avait souvent pas destiné. Peu à peu il rompra la chaîne des vieilles traditions qui l'unissait à ses aieux et à sa région."

43 Séverac, "Chansons du Languedoc et du Roussillon," *Musica*, 10e année, no. 111 (December, 1911), 241. "Nous nous demandions pourquoi ce qui nous charmait n'aurait aucun écho dans l'âme de nos amis déracinés et éxilés à Paris."

44 Séverac, "La centralization et les petites chapelles musicales," 11e année, nos. 1, 3 (January 1, 15, 1908) collation, 4, 40. "Le jeune musicien qui se laissera prendre au ... Prix de Rome ... il lui est interdit de faire preuve d'une personnalité qui ne serait pas conformé à l'idéal de ce milieu ... de déracinés ... Le parisianisme a fait son oeuvre; ils sont ... des déracinés supérieurs, mais des déracinés tout de même ... Les Conservatoires régionalistes puisqu'ils sont ... de simples succursales du Conservatoire de Paris, chargés à ce titre de lui préparer des sujets suivant une recette déterminée, ont commencé à se *déracinér*, suivant la forte expression de M. Maurice Barrès, quand on est encore un nourrisson."

under diverse influences (climate, soil, culture) specific qualities. There is none of this in the majority of contemporary musical works ... This kind of uniformity ... is due to centralization.

The officials ... (opportunists) are placed under the high protection of the State, to which they owe in return at least external fidelity and a few works for national ceremonies.

Of what does the protection of the State consist? As soon as the student composer from a regional conservatory is able to realize fifths without mistakes, or without false relations a bass assigned by the director of the conservatory ... he can obtain a prize for harmony. The State immediately takes possession of his destiny. His township (sometimes sharing the cost with the state) gives him a modest sum, which enables him to live in Paris and to "mingle."

His first duty is to deposit ... at the door of the national Conservatoire all of his talents and his budding personality ... Here he is now in the hands of a master, himself controlled from above, who sets him on a diet of cantata ... "In order to succeed in being a genuine artist, one has to have the Prix de Rome." It is therefore indispensable to fashion the creative faculties of that kind of student so that he may achieve the particular ideal of the jury of the Institute ... Once winner of the glorious Prix de Rome, the young artist, if he is not a talent of the first rank, is condemned to continue. To win fame and acquire a fortune, he will also have to compose cantatas, or other pieces which will be used to inaugurate statues of "great citizens" and to magnify "triumphant Democracy."

About every two years, he will have an opera performed that will not be a great success with those of refined taste, but will satisfy the ... general public ... he will finally be able to assume his well deserved place in the Invalids of the Institute of France.[45]

---

45 Séverac's viewpoint expressed here concerned the Conservatoire before Fauré became director in 1905 and established reforms, even though Séverac published these ideas in 1907. Séverac, "La centralization et les petites chapelles musicales," 11e année, no. 1 (January 1, 1908), 1–3. "La Musique Française actuelle est aux prises ... avec un ennemi redoutable, la centralisation ... Les musiciens actuels sont ... pour si éloignés qu'ils soient en apparence les uns des autres par des procédés de composition, ils sont tous ... ses victimes bénévoles. Ils font de la musique de Paris et pour Paris; ils s'écartent ainsi progressivement et de plus en plus du génie propre aux diverses provinces françaises où ils sont nés.

Chaque région est dotée par une essence et une saveur spéciales qu'elles doivent au sol qui les soutient et au soleil qui les fait croître ... Ils ont acquis sous diverses influences (climat, terrain, culture) des qualités tellement spéciales ... Il n'en est pas ainsi dans la plupart des oeuvres musicales contemporaines ... Cette sorte d'uniformisation ... est due à la centralisation.

Les officiels ... (les opportunistes) sont placés sous la haute protection de l'Etat, auquel ils doivent en retour une fidélité au moins extérieure et quelques oeuvres pour les solennités nationales.

En quoi consiste la protection de l'Etat? Dès que l'élève compositeur d'un Conservatoire régional est capable de réaliser sans fautes des quintes et sans fausses relations une basse donnée par le directeur du conservatoire ... où il peut obtenir un prix d'harmonie. L'État s'empare aussitôt de sa destinée. Sa ville (quelquefois de moitié avec l'Etat) lui accorde un modeste secours qui lui permettra de vivre à Paris et de se "frotter."

Son premier devoir est de déposer ... à la porte du Conservatoire national tous ses dons et sa personnalité naissante ... Le voici maintenant entre les mains d'un maître dûment contrôlé en haut lieu, qui le met au régime de la cantate..."Pour arriver à être un véritable artiste il faut avoir le prix de Rome"; il est donc indispensable de façonner les facultés créatrices de l'étudiant de telle sorte qu'il réalise l'idéal spécial du jury de l'Institut ... Une fois grand

Séverac referred here to the negative impact of centralization within French art, which he believed was maintained by the French government and Paris Conservatoire. He further cited that prospective professional musicians were lured away from their native provinces in order to study at the Conservatoire, thereby suppressing regional identity. He identified a region's uniqueness through climate and soil, the former often spoken about in southern France in relationship to the sun, and the latter referring to ancestral land and the tradition of farming, again echoing concepts highlighted by Barrès.[46]

Séverac's allusion to a Faustian bargain between prospective students from the provinces and that of the Paris Conservatoire also applied to students admitted into the institution. Séverac accused composition students of being rewarded for narrowly composing in sanctioned styles and genres in order to advance to the final round of the Prix de Rome.

The Prix de Rome was conducted essentially in two stages. The preliminary round required the composition of a four-part fugue on a given subject and the setting of a short text for mixed chorus and orchestra. Out of 20 candidates, five or six were allowed to compete in the final round, in which they set an extended cantata text for solo voices and orchestra judged not solely by the composition faculty but also by members of the French Academy. Those jurors who were music professors often belonged to the most conservative of music circles and taught at the Paris Conservatoire. The winner was assured a modest stipend for four years, the first two of which were spent in Rome, the third in Germany or Austria, and the fourth in Rome or Paris.

Séverac's allegations are substantiated. Because of the importance of the prize, Conservatoire professors often emphasized choral music and cantata composition in their teaching. Jules Massenet stated that he focused on the cantata because he felt to do otherwise would have been impractical for the future of his students, among

---

Prix de Rome, le jeune artiste, s'il n'a pas en lui des dons à toute épreuve, est condamné à continuer. Pour atteindre aux honneurs et parvenir à la fortune, il devra encore composer des cantates, ou des choses dans ce genre, qui serviront à inaugurer les statues des "grands citoyens" et à magnifier la "Democratie triomphante."

Tous les deux ans environ, il fera jouer un opéra qui n'obtiendra pas à coup sûr les suffrages des amateurs raffinés, mais dont le ... gros public ... il pourra enfin prendre une place bien méritée aux Invalides de l'Institut de France."

46 Séverac also purported in his thesis that regionalists were either ignored in Paris, as provincials were considered vulgar by urbanites, or transformed into composing within a style lacking individuality. Séverac indicted proponents of centralization within music and claimed that they could be found in two separate and competing sects within the Société nationale de musique, the so-called "officiels, ou opportunistes," and "Les indépendants." He claimed that official composers were state-sponsored and were therefore controlled artists who composed works robbed of individuality and character and these works were primarily intended for national celebrations. So-called independent musicians did not live up to their title, according to Séverac, and themselves were of two warring factions, the "horizontalistes" (d'Indyistes) and the "verticalistes" (Debussyistes). He nonetheless provided a disclaimer that the figureheads were unwitting participants. Séverac's solution was to decentralize, as he believed that diversity was needed to create a truly national music.

whom were Alfred Bruneau, Gustave Charpentier, Charles Koechlin, and Florent Schmitt.[47] Professor Charles-Marie Widor initially warned against this narrow emphasis at the Conservatoire but adopted a more expedient attitude when assuming Théodore Dubois' composition chair in 1896. Composer Louis Vierne later remarked that Widor taught his organ students symphonic music and sonatas, insisting that they learn to analyze the forms of the work, but actively emphasized vocal genres in his composition class. "Occasionally he tried to make them write symphonic music, but most of his time was spent in the mill of the cantata and chorus, preparing for the trial examination. In the organ class, he seemed quite radical, but in composition, he had to make certain his students were competitive with rival classes."[48]

This accusation was corroborated by others, for Séverac was not the only source to criticize the Paris Conservatoire and the rigid compositional emphases dictated by the Prix de Rome. Music critic Pierre Lalo of *Le temps* described the biases that helped shape this situation and found the various directors of the Conservatoire partially responsible. He stated that Daniel Auber, director of the Conservatoire between 1842 and 1871, worked "for theater and [was] indifferent to other genres"; [49] that Ambroise Thomas, director between 1871 and 1896, was "one of France's most pathetic composers who, lacking true talent, tried to disguise his nothingness as a composer beneath a facade of administrative authority," and that Théodore Dubois, the director between 1896 and 1905, was an "administrative functionary who derived importance through his function as director alone, and not through his talent as a composer and musician."[50] These comments in the press and by Séverac allude to the fact that many felt the need for reform.

In 1892, a commission was established to recommend reforms for the Conservatoire, and some members, including d'Indy, argued for an emphasis on instrumental and non-operatic vocal genres. Lalo recounted Ambroise Thomas's indignant reaction to this philosophy: "But what musician of talent would want to lower himself by being a professor of symphonic music?"[51]

---

47 Jules Massenet, *My Recollections*, translated by H. Villiers Barnett (Freeport, NY: Books for Libraries Press, 1919, reprinted 1970), 117.

48 Louis Vierne, "Mémoires," *Diapason* 30, no. 2 (January, 1939), reprinted and translated by John Richard Near, "The Life and Work of Charles-Marie Widor" (DMA Dissertation, Boston University, 1985), 200.

49 Pierre Lalo (1866–1943), son of Edouard Lalo, was the music critic for *Le temps* from 1898 to 1914. He customarily spoke in favor of Wagner's music and championed Debussy's earlier music, but began criticizing Debussy's later works beginning with *La mer*.

50 Pierre Lalo, "La musique: les débuts du nouveau directeur—la direction de M. Fauré," *Le temps* (August 9, 1921), 3.

51 Lalo, "La musique: au Conservatoire—la grande commission de réformes de 1892," *Le temps* (August 8, 1901), 3. Also see Lalo, "La musique: le nouveau directeur du conservatoire," *Le temps* (June 20, 1905). "Quel musicien de talent voudrait se ravaler à être professeur de symphonie?" Changes in attitude began to take place once Fauré took over as director of the Paris Conservatoire in 1905. This view held by Thomas was formerly echoed by Théodore Dubois, who ironically started composing symphonies after leaving the Paris Conservatoire.

Vincent d'Indy, a member of the commission, drew up a proposal to reorganize the curriculum with a more rigorous study of instrumental music. The Conservatoire responded by eventually withdrawing funds that the reform commission needed, rendering it defunct. D'Indy eventually withdrew from the institution and helped establish the competing Schola Cantorum in 1897.[52]

***

Séverac's condemnation of centralization went beyond the Prix de Rome and the Paris Conservatoire. He called attention to schools and conservatories throughout France, including branches of the Paris Conservatoire, nationalized music schools, and municipal institutions. According to the composer, these schools were rewarded for their ties to the Paris Conservatoire. Séverac considered the local pedagogical biases of teaching in the same narrow range of genres and styles to be instituted through subventions, which required that these institutions conform to the program outlined by the Conseil supérieur des études du conservatoire national.

This belief was to a large degree valid, as out of 37 non-private regional music schools in France in 1907, approximately one-fourth were branches of the Conservatoire and roughly one-half were nationalized schools under the jurisdiction of the state government; only one-fourth of conservatories in France remained municipal schools (see Figure 3.1).[53] The nationalization of these schools transpired chiefly between the years 1884 and 1905 under the Third Republic. These nationalized institutions were originally municipal schools sponsored and subsidized by the state and placed under the control of the minister's delegates. Financial instability was the primary reason for requesting nationalization. Upon nationalization, however, schools were required to continue devoting at least the same yearly amount that the township or school had allotted in previous years from local income in order to pay for school expenses. The distribution of the budget needed to be approved by the minister, and the state then agreed to pay a percentage based on the institution's total allocated expenditures, which averaged between 20 and 30 percent of the total expenses. The amount would change from one year to the next, and the percentage, based on annual governmental policy revisions, could also be altered. Individual schools were then required to submit quarterly reports to the Minster, outlining their financial situation.

---

52 For more information on the history of the Paris Conservatoire, see Gail H. Woldu, "Gabriel Fauré as Director of the Conservatoire national de musique de déclamation, 1905–1920" (PhD Dissertation, Yale University, 1983); Woldu, "Gabriel Fauré, directeur du Conservatoire: les réformes de 1905," *Revue de musicologie*, 70/2 (1984), 199–28.

53 For more information, see Edmond Maurat, "L'enseignement de la musique en France et les conservatoires de province," *Encyclopédie de la musique et dictionnaire du Conservatoire*, vol. 2 (Paris: Librarie Delagrave, 1931), 3576–3616. Figure 3.1 consists of charts that I created based on gathering information about various municipal and national schools and the dates when they were established.

Figure 3.1 Status of Regional Conservatories in France (1907). Conservatory Branches, Nationalized Conservatories, and Municipal Schools

Nationalized Conservatories

Nationalized Conservatories of music were placed under the control of the Public Minister of Instruction of Fine Arts, under whom came the Deputy Secretary of State and Fine Arts, who in turn dictated rules to the Bureau of Theaters and Conservation of Palaces. There was also a consulting commission on music education, on which many well-known composers had served, including Alfred Bruneau and Paul Dukas—both of whom later became Inspector Generals of Music Education.

Town	Year Founded	Year Municipalized	Year Nationalized
Abbeville	1818	1821	1899
Aix-en-Provence	1849	1856	1884
Amiens	1891	------	1891
Bayonne	1876	1876	1884
Boulougne-sur-Mer	1830	------	1892
Cambrai	1821	------	1905
Chambéry	1865	------	1884
Douai	1806	1806	1884
Moulins	1887	1892	1893
Le Mans	1882	1882	1884
Saint-Omer	1884	------	1884
Sète	1882	1882	1884
Tarbes	1894	------	1921
Toulon	1900	1900	1905
Tours	1875	------	1886
Valenciennes	1835	1835	1884

Branches of Paris Conservatoire

Town	Year Founded	Year Municipalized	Year Converted To Branch
Lille	1803	1816	1826
Lyon	1872	1872	1874
Metz	1832	------	1841
Montpellier	1883	------	1890
Nancy	1881	------	1884
Nîmes	1863	1863	1903
Perpignan	1842	------	1892
Rennes	1865	1881	1884
Roubaix	1820	1820	1902
Toulouse	1820	1820	1826

Municipal Conservatories

Town	Year Founded	Year Municipalized
Angers	1890	1890
Arras	1830	1850
Avignon*	1828	1889
Besançon	1860	1860
Caen*	1835	1885
Marseille*	1822	1870
Oran	1907	1907
Saint Etienne*	1867	1891
Strasbourg	1855	1855
Tarbes	1894	1894
Tourcoing	1842	1882

* *Avignon*—founded 1828, closed 1829, opened 1835, closed 1836, opened 1845, closed 1848, opened 1853, closed 1870, opened and municipalized 1871, branch of Conservatory 1884, municipalized 1889.

* *Caen*—founded 1835, nationalized 1884, municipalized 1885.

* *Marseille*–founded 1822, municipalized 1830, branch of Conservatoire 1841, municipalized 1870.

* *Saint Etienne*—founded 1867, closed 1871, opened 1876, nationalized 1884, denationalized and municipalized, 1891.

The government required nationalized schools to comply with a program of studies drawn up by the Public Minister of Instruction of Fine Arts. Although the individual municipality prepared the curriculum, no modification of this program was allowed without the Minister's certification. The view of officials from the state government was that many nationalized schools had "outdated" syllabi that would require adjustments. This process had a leveling effect, since the inspections of exams, agendas, and competition requirements would inspire "effective programs of study and therefore a greater equivalence between schools and common objectives."[54] Séverac contended that these so-called "common objectives" resulted in homogenous compositional styles. He believed that superior institutions could grow and develop only when there existed a "separation of fine arts from the state," alluding to the separation of religion and state in 1905.[55] As a way of countering the claim that quality education came only through state centralization, Séverac asserted that these private music schools needed to have the strictest policy in admitting students.

---

54 Ibid, 3615.
55 Séverac, "La centralization et les petites chapelles musicales," 11e année, no. 5 (March 8, 1908), 142.

Séverac also criticized the practice of recruiting talented students away from the provinces into the Paris Conservatoire. Visiting inspectors would scout for talented pupils and submit their names to the Public Minister of Instruction of Fine Arts for attendance at the Paris Conservatoire. The Minister would often furnish travel grants, and since these inspected provincial conservatories were nationalized, the French government officially gave admission applicants from these institutions priority over those on a similar level from non-nationalized municipal or private schools.[56]

Séverac's alternative to the centralized music conservatory system was to build regional schools that based their pedagogy on what he referred to as folk music:

> The program of our regional school would be, of course, quite different from those one follows in today's schools or conservatories. The basis for it would be folk music, song, and dance. Instead of studying the principles of music in lamentable treatises elaborated by half-musicians, greedy and without taste, we would begin to spell out our notes to the texts of beautiful folk songs of the region, selected and graded according to their difficulty, in the form of *solfège*. At the same time, the pupil would learn the words of these poems, which are very often of an admirable lyricism and that would not be the least profitable part [of the student's experience] ... The usefulness of traditional folk song from the point of view of regional art is considerable ... Do you not believe that students taken from childhood and educated in the religion of folk song would be in a robust health and of a vigor rare today?[57]

Séverac's comments provide a polemical contrast between robust and vigorous students of regional folk art and "half-musicians" elaborating on corrupted national art music. From our standpoint, it is potentially problematic to reconcile these comments with Séverac's own practice, since although Séverac used folk elements in many of his compositions, these settings incorporated forms and genres found in

---

56 The Schola Cantorum also developed many outposts, but according to Bordes, each had its own autonomy. Nonetheless, these branches were required to conform to the philosophy of the Schola Cantorum in Paris. Local teachers were paid directly by the students and could teach on the Schola Cantorum premises for no charge, with the promise that they upheld the Schola Cantorum tradition and use "appropriate teaching material." See Charles Bordes, "Le Schola de Montpellier: société d'encouragement d'emulation à la musique," *AM Dossier* 1J53, cited by Andrea Musk, "Aspects of Regionalism in French Music during the Third Republic: the Schola Cantorum, d'Indy, Séverac and Canteloube," PhD Dissertation, Oxford University, 1999, 51.

57 Séverac, "La centralization et les petites chapelles musicales," 11e année, no. 5 (March 8, 1908), 143–4. "Le programme de notre école régionaliste serait, bien entendu, tout à fait différent de ceux que l'on suit dans les écoles ou conservatoires actuels. La base en serait la musique populaire, la chanson et la danse. Au lieu d'étudier les principes de la musique des traités lamentables élaborés par des musicastres cupides et sans goût, on commencerait à déchiffrer les notes sur les textes des belles chansons populaires de la région, choisies et graduées, suivant leur difficulté, sous forme de solfège. En même temps, l'élève apprendrait les paroles de ces poèmes qui sont si souvent d'un lyricisme admirable et cela ne serait pas la chose la moins profitable ... L'utilité de la chanson traditionnelle au point de vue de l'art régionaliste est considérable ... Croyez-vous que des élèves pris dès leur enfance et éduqués dans la religion de la chanson populaire n'auraient pas une santé robuste et une vigueur rares aujourd'hui?"

art music. Yet, Séverac's philosophy paralleled Barrès's emphasis on the "regional purity of folk culture" over the "corrupted" déracinés of corporate urban society.

Barrès and Séverac also privileged folk music when discussing peasants who lived in rural areas. Barrès wrote: "What I see in Lorraine, what I hear, is the peasant, the word of the peasant."[58] Séverac reminisced about rural peasants in his thesis:

> To travel through this country one will see this strange sight: common laborers or uncouth peasants capable of "discovering" some melodies of an absolutely personal character ... and at the same time discovering some poems, simple, it is true, but stamped with the most sparkling verve ... The first effect of the state's protection is, therefore, to remove from his country the young musician who has scarcely awakened to the life of Art, at an age at which one quickly forgets the old melodies sung by the shepherds in returning to the sheepfold.[59]

Séverac's regionalist solutions to administrative centralization within the fine arts included the building of regional music schools that emphasized the study of folk music. He also encouraged other composers to embrace the values Séverac believed to be held by the peasantry—ideas that paralleled Barrès's interest in regionalism with its associated values of family and tradition.

Frédéric Mistral

Another figure who championed supporting peasantry, régionalisme and rootedness was the Provençal regionalist poet Frédéric Joseph-Etienne Mistral (1830–1914), who received the Nobel prize in 1904. Mistral's published works include the highly acclaimed "Mirèio" (1859), an epic poem that praises pre-industrial communities and that became the subject for Charles Gounod's opera *Mireille* (1864).[60]

"Mirèio" is the story of a rich girl kept by her parents from a poor lover. She wanders across the country to the Church of the Three Marys but is overwhelmed by the effort and dies exhausted in the presence of her grieving parents and frenzied lover. Mistral weaves accounts of Provençal life, scenery, customs, and legends into

---

58 Curtis, *Three Against the Republic*, 229. The sentence is translated by Curtis.

59 Séverac, "La centralization et les petites chapelles musicales," 11e année, no. 1 (January 1, 1908); collation, 3, 6. "Parcourir ce pays et l'on verra cette chose inouie: de simples ouvriers ou de vulgaires paysans capables de 'trouver' des mélodies d'un caractère absolument personnel ... et 'trouvant' en même temps des poèmes simples il est vrai mais empreints de la verve la plus étincelante ... Le premier effet de la protection de l'État est donc d'éloigner de son pays le jeune musicien, qui s'éveille à peine à la vie de l'Art, à un âge où l'on oublie si vite les vieilles mélodies que chantent les pâtres en rentrant au bercail."

60 Frédéric Mistral, *Mirèio, pouèmo provençau* (Paris: H. Piazza, 1923). For a translation of Mistral's text, see Henri Mondor, *Nobel Prize Library: François Mauriac, Frédéric Mistral, and Theodor Mommsen,* translated by Annie Jackson (New York: Alexis Gregory, 1971), 125–225.

the poem, so that it becomes a rustic epic peopled by simple, unassuming characters. Most of Mistral's poems were concerned largely with local legend and tradition.[61]

Mistral's father was a wealthy farmer devoted to traditional customs and ancestral veneration, and his mother taught the young Mistral songs and religious traditions of their native Provence. Mistral grew to love the country songs and legends of his region, and often included images of shepherds and rural persons in his poetry. Mistral also possessed an interest in ancient Greece and Rome, in particular the works of Homer and Virgil.

Mistral later opened a museum in Arles dedicated to Provençal life and culture as a place to conserve, revive, and continue regional cultural life—part of his effort to reawaken an interest in regional folklore. In addition, Mistral became interested in the linguistic roots, orthography, and grammar of his native language, Provençal. He subsequently championed the development of a modern standard version of the language, rather than the downgraded patois to which he was accustomed as a child. Mistral later authored the two-volume Provençal dictionary and thesaurus *Lou trésor dóu Félibrige*.[62]

Mistral became convinced that the prohibition of the Provençal language in the centralized school system was the main reason for the migration of his compatriots to urban areas. As a result, Mistral's southern French philosophy also emphasized rootedness, political freedom, and economic and cultural regionalism. As the leader of the Félibrige movement, he helped to restore the Provençal language, customs, traditions, history, and poetry to southern France. This helped undermine the hegemony of the French academy, as many within the academy felt that the Félibrige promoted political separatism. The French government nonetheless applauded Mistral's regional poem "Mirèio," and the Félibrige reached its peak of influence at the beginning of the twentieth century.[63]

The members of the Félibrige never openly identified themselves with a political movement, and Mistral never claimed to be a separatist. Yet, he and the organization were hostile to the anti-clericalism and urbanism in the Third Republic government, and he often symbolically projected regionalism as a form of nationalism. Mistral once asserted that "the Félibrige can only be Girondin, federalist, religious, liberal, and respectful of traditions. Otherwise, it would have no reason to exist."[64] These religious values became evident in the organization's support of Catholic Provence over what Mistral perceived to be the Voltairean secular rationalism and progressive

---

61 Other poems include the collection *Li provençalo* (1852), a poem depicting sea, forests, and fishermen entitled "Calendau" (1867), "Lis isdo d'or" ("Islands of Gold") (1876), "Nerto" (1884), "La Rèino Jano" (1890), and an epic narrative consisting of vignettes about southern French regions entitled "Lou pouèmo dóu Rose" (1897).

62 See Frédéric Mistral, *Lou trésor dóu Félibrige ou Dictionnaire provençal-français*, 2 vols. (Aix-en-Provence: Veuve Remondet-Aubin, 1879–1887).

63 A group of seven poets who initially called themselves the Association of Provençal Poets founded the Félibrige in 1854. They set out to revive an interest in the customs and history of Provence. The word *félibres* (referring to a member of the Félibrige) comes from an old Provençal tale in which Jesus was found disputing others in the temple with "li sét félibre de la léi," which Mistral took to mean "the seven doctors of the law."

64 Gildea, *The Past in French History*, 208. The quote is translated by Gildea.

ideology of northern France. The Félibrige became one of the most important manifestations of régionalisme in late-nineteenth-century France.

Mistral also argued for regional pride in neighboring provinces, and he believed that this would help encourage an interest in southern France as a region. This view was based on his assertion that troubadours originated in Provence, but that they also flourished in the regions of Languedoc, Catalonia, and the Auvergne. This sentiment led to Mistral's pan-Latin concept, which considered the south of France a federation of provinces based on a linguistic union of Latin-based languages. This pan-Latin idea was furthered by various figures, including the journalist Louis Xavier de Ricard, Charles Beauquier, deputy of Doubs, and Antonin Perbosc, the Occitan poet from Languedoc who flourished in the wake of Mistral's success.[65] Mistral expressed his regionalist pan-Latin ideas in the following:

> Those who have not lived in the South, and above all in the midst of our rural populations, cannot understand the incompatibility, the insufficiency, the poverty of the language of the North as regards the customs, needs, and the organizations of those who live in southern France. Transplanting the French language to Provence is like clothing the bronzed, robust shoulders of a harvester in the cast-off of a Parisian dandy ... It would be so easy, so beautiful, and so true to have our children sing the great folk songs, specific to each province, not translated and deformed, but in the dialect of the region and of its forbears![66]

Séverac's interest in indigenous music paralleled his fascination with peasantry and nature, ideas largely inspired by the philosophies and poems of Frédéric Mistral. Mistral's regionalist outlook was intertwined with his reverence for nature, two elements that figure prominently in his poems, particularly those to which Séverac found a spiritual kinship. According to Joseph Canteloube, "[Séverac's] inspiration comes from country life and this obviously brings him close to [the philosophy of] Mistral."[67] The influence of Mistral's philosophies on those of Séverac is also evident in a quotation from the composer's thesis, where Séverac emulates Mistral's poetic southern French reverence for nature:

---

65 Mistral's *Ode aux catalans* (1859) helped establish a close alliance between the citizens of Provence and those of Roussillon, thus helping to inspire the Catalan Renaissance. Many from this province who helped promote the Catalan Renaissance in Rousillon accepted Mistral as an important spokesperson for the regionalist aesthetic, including Joseph Bonnafort and Joseph-Sebastien Pons.

66 Mistral, "Lettre de Frédéric Mistral," *Les chansons de France* (July 1, 1906), 4–5. "Ceux qui n'ont pas vécu dans le Midi, et surtout au milieu de nos populations rurales, ne peuvent se faire une idée de l'incompatibilité, de l'insuffisance, de la pauvreté de la langue du Nord vis-à-vis des moeurs, des besoins et de l'organisation des méridionaux. La langue française, transplantée en Provence, fait l'effet de la défroque d'un dandy parisien ... Il serait pourtant si facile, si joli et si honnête, de faire chanter à nos enfants la fleur des chansons populaires, particulières à chaque province, non pas traduites et déformées, mais dans le dialecte de la région et des aieux!"

67 Joseph Canteloube, *Déodat de Séverac* [1st Edition, Paris, 1929] (Beziers, France: Société de musicologie de Languedoc, 1984), 75. "Son inspiration a pour source la vie des champs et cela l'apparenté étroitement à Mistral."

> Poor sun-drenched Midi ... This corner of dreamland, where all chromaticism ... quivers ... and fades away under the pale iris silhouette of the Pyrenees. We should have ... the golden lyre of a Mistral to express the exquisite harmony of this vision.[68]

Séverac also spoke of his allegiance to Mistral and his philosophies in a letter to Joseph d'Arabaud in 1913:

> Naturally, we recognized ourselves in Mistral ... because of his original, meaningful, and deep work. If he had not been so much a part of us, we could have still honored him for his life and his work ... This great artist was one of those sons of the south of France, who, since "Mirèio," has renewed a full awareness of the virtues of the [land of the] sun.[69]

Séverac's interest in the Félibrige can be traced back to 1899, when southern French poet and friend Paul Rey (1873–1918) wrote Séverac a letter referring to the Félibrige: "Many members of the Félibrige school of Paris asked me to sing in different cities, their hometowns in the south of France."[70] Séverac later joined the Félibrige of Paris and attended several meetings at the Café Voltaire and Odéon.[71] Séverac established friendships with key figures within the organization.[72]

Séverac first met Mistral when the composer was a delegate to the Congrès des chants populaires, an event organized by Charles Bordes in Montpellier in 1905.[73] Bordes appointed Mistral as president of the event and Séverac and Amédée Gastouée

---

68 Séverac, "La Centralization et les petites chapelles musicales," 11e année, no. 1 (January 1, 1908), 5 "Pauvre Midi ensoleillé ... Ce coin de rêve où tout le chromatisme ... frissonne ... et s'éteint lointainement là-bas sous la silhouette d'iris pâle des Pyrénées. Il faudrait ... la lyre d'or d'un Mistral pour dire l'exquise harmonie de cette vision."

69 Aspry, "Déodat de Séverac," 558–9. "Tout naturellement, nous nous reconnaissions en Mistral ... par son oeuvre racée, significative, profonde, n'eut-il pas été si nôtre, que nous aurions pu l'honorer encore pour sa vie et pour son oeuvre ... Ce grand artiste était un de ces fils du midi qui, depuis Mirèio ont repris pleine conscience de la vertu du soleil."

70 Ibid., 80–81. [Paul Rey letter to Séverac, 1899.] "Plusieurs members de l'Ecole Félibréenne de Paris me demandée pour la chanter dans différentes villes, leurs cités natales du Midi."

71 Stéphane Giocanti, *Charles Maurras: félibre* (Paris, 1995), 73, cited by Andrea Musk, "Aspects of Regionalism in French Music during the Third Republic: the Schola Cantorum, d'Indy, Séverac and Canteloube," 128.

72 Ibid., 129.

73 The origin of the gathering began in 1905 when Bordes left Paris for Montpellier in order to improve his health. Bordes had also taken ambitious financial risks that failed with money that belonged to the Schola Cantorum—another reason for his departure. As Bordes cited: "It is about time that I left the Schola [Cantorum] if I do not want to destroy that which I created." Letter from Bordes to Guy Ropartz, December 6, 1900 (BN). ("Il n'est que temps que je m'éloigne de la Schola si je ne veux détruire ce que j'ai créé.").

Séverac spent three months in Montpellier with Bordes preparing for the event. Artistic participation included sopranos Emma Calvé and Marie de la Rouvière, harpsichordist Wanda Landowska (1877–1959), and members of the Quatuor vocal des chanteurs de Saint-Gervais. The group performed Rameau's ballet *La guirlande* and Paul Lacombe's *Rhapsodie du pays d'Oc*.

were asked to be secretaries of the secular and religious divisions respectively.[74] As a result, a friendship developed between Séverac and Mistral.[75] The combination of sacred and secular music at the event is apparent in the itinerary in Figure 3.2.

The 1906 congress was largely the result of work by Bordes, who helped champion the study of religious choral music as well as indigenous folk music from various provinces. The Congress, therefore, in combining religious music with that of folk art, reflected the philosophy of the Schola Cantorum. Amédée Gastouée, who was secretary of the religious division, included hymns, sacred Christmas music, and twelfth-century liturgical drama at the event.

Mistral's regionalist philosophy and interest in folk music helped inspire Séverac's evolving interest, which became especially evident at this event, when Séverac wrote an article honoring the gathering in a Montpellier publication:

> Up to the present day (excluding Grieg and the Russians), the only musicians who didn't blush in wooing this beautiful country air that is popular song ... were especially "contrapuntists" and ... in the tradition of Renaissance composers, like Vincent d'Indy and Felipe Pedrell, to name the most known. The traditional song [is] often the prototype of melody since it is self-sufficient. The congress that the Schola Cantorum is in the process of organizing in Montpellier comes therefore at a good time; it is likely to give the last and definitive impulse to the birth of a movement which I have already mentioned above. But it is necessary for all friends of the Languedocien tradition (félibréens, members of the Action Régionaliste) to support it with all their forces. It is necessary that all energies spread over and recognize one another and unite themselves in a common faith, and the noble cause of the popular song will triumph.[76]

---

74 Bordes himself had fervent views regarding régionalisme and led classes at the Schola Cantorum in folk music. Bordes articulated his views succinctly in "Le chant populaire," *Tribune de Saint-Gervais* (December, 1896), 184, reprinted and translated by Musk, "Aspects of Regionalism in French Music during the Third Republic: the Schola Cantorum, d'Indy, Séverac and Canteloube," 63.

75 Séverac spent time socially with Mistral during this period at singer Emma Calvé's home, the Château de Cabrières in Rouergue.

76 Déodat de Séverac, "Le renouveau de la chanson populaire," *L'action régionale de la Schola Cantorum*, reprinted in *Le mistral* (August 8, 1906); also included in Guillot, *Déodat de Séverac: écrits sur la musique*, 68. "Jusqu'à présent (si nous exceptions Grieg et les Russes), les seuls musiciens qui ne rougissaient pas de faire la cour à cette belle paysane qu'est la chanson populaire ... étaient surtout des "contrepuntistes" ... de la lignée des maîtres de la Renaissance, tels que Vincent d'Indy et Felipe Pedrell, pour ne nommer que les plus connus. La chanson de tradition étant souvent le prototype de la mélodie puisqu'elle se suffit à elle-même. Le congrès que la Schola est en train d'organiser à Montpellier vient donc bien à son heure; il est susceptible de donner la dernière et définitive impulsion au mouvement naissant dont je parlais plus haut. Mais il faut pour cela, que tous les amis de la tradition languedocienne (groupes félibréens, actions régionalistes) le soutiennent de toutes leurs forces. Il faut que les énergies encore éparsés se reconnaissent et s'unissent dans une foi commune et la noble cause de la chanson populaire triomphera."

Figure 3.2 Events during the 1906 *Congrès des chants populaires*

OPENING EVENT: Overture of the Sacred Music Session (Cathedral Saint-Pierre) with the concours of the Schola Chorale of Montpellier (Monsignor de Cabrières, presiding).

EVENING EVENT: Secular session, directed by Séverac and inaugurated by Mistral (honorary president) with performances by Wanda Landowska and Marie de la Rouvière.[77] This includes:

a) *La cansoun dis avi* performed by Rouvière (unpublished, gathered, and edited for the Congress by Charles Bordes)
b) Danses villageoises du XVIIe siècle (performed by Wanda Landowska)
c) *L'isle de Délos* (cantata for solo voice with orchestra, by Louis Clerambault)
d) *Chaconne d'Armide* (by Gluck).

DAY TWO, MORNING: Discussions begin—religious music session (directed by Amédée Gastoué, and includes examples of hymns and popular Christmas music).

DAY TWO, AFTERNOON: Secular music session, with focus on music of the troubadours (directed by Séverac).

DAY THREE: *Le drame liturgique des vierges sages et des vierges folles*, after a Latin manuscript from 1150, interpreted by the chanteurs de Saint-Gervais (presented by Amédée Gastoué). Discussions on the topic of "Music in Provence from the Seventeenth Century to the French Revolution."

DAY THREE, EVENING: Gala concert with Emma Calvé, Marie de la Rouvière, Marie Pironnay, and Wanda Landowska; orchestra under the direction of Charles Bordes.

DAY FOUR: Popular airs from Languedoc:

a) "La coeur d'amour" (extract from Felipe Pedrell's *Los Pyreneos*), directed by Paul Lacombe
b) "Le mas en fête" (from Séverac's *En Languedoc*), traditional dances (from Montpellier)
c) *Musiques galantes des XVIIè et XVIIIè siècle* (Wanda Landowska, harpsichordist)
d) *Plaisirs de la campagne* (pastoral cantata, by Campra), sung by Alie Villot, with Wanda Landowska participating

---

77 Marie de la Rouvière was a dramatic soprano from Provence. Séverac became enamored of her talent.

e) *La guirlande* (pastoral-ballet in one act by Jean-Philippe Rameau), Louis and Blanche Mante participating.

DAY FIVE: *Grand-messe grégorienne* (sung by two choirs at cathedral).[78]

In 1913, Séverac began composing an opera set to Mistral's "Poème du Rhône" ("Lou Rose"; 1892–96).[79] Mistral's work is comprised of texts taken from poems used in ancient Provençal songs. Originally based on the epic Greek poem "Argonautiques" by Apollonius from Rhodes, "Poème du Rhône" is the story of a Rhône river ferrywoman and a quest for gold. The work also provided the model for Virgil's fourth book of the *Aeneid*.

Séverac chose Gabriel Boissy as the librettist for the opera, and in a letter from Mistral to Boissy, the poet spoke of Séverac's work-in progress:

> My dear Boissy, I am happy to see you take up again the project of Paul Mariéton on the subject of the "Poème du Rhône," put into musical drama by Déodat de Séverac. I gladly authorize you to write the libretto, only on the condition that the composer commits to finishing it and having the work performed in the theater within a time specified—and not too long, because of my age, one cannot wait too long for the [work's] completion. I have plenty of confidence in you as a musician, as you are, like no other, nourished with our Félibrige ideas.[80]

Séverac traveled to Aix-en-Provence in 1913 in order to meet with the poet and discuss the setting of the "Poème du Rhône" to music. Gabriel Boissy described the apparent friendship between Séverac and Mistral at their meeting:

> Déodat was very close to [Mistral]. He had tears in his eyes upon seeing his [venerated master]. The atmosphere [of the festival] was busy with crowds and the [sound of] fifes and tambourines.[81]

This would be the last time that the two would meet, as the poet died the following year. Mistral's death, together with the outbreak of the World War I, discouraged Séverac from finishing the project.[82]

---

78 Aspry, "Déodat de Séverac", 265–7.

79 Frédéric Mistral, "Lou pouèmo dóu Rose" ("Le poème du Rhône en XII chants"), Provençal text and French translation by Frédéric Mistral (Paris: A. Lemerre, 1897).

80 Aspry, "Déodat de Séverac", 558. "Mon cher Boissy, je suis heureux de vous voir reprendre, le projet de notre Paul Mariéton, au sujet du Poème du Rhône, mis en drame musical par Déodat de Séverac et volontiers je vous autorise à écrire le livret, seulement à condition que le compositeur s'engage à terminer et à mettre son oeuvre au théâtre dans un temps donné—et pas trop long, à cause de mon âge on ne peut plus traiter pour trop longue échéance. J'ai pleine confiance en vous comme un musicien, vous êtes autant que personne, nourri de nos idées félibréennes."

81 Ibid, 559–60. "Déodat était près du vieux maître. Il avait les larmes aux yeux de voir de quelle vénération celui-ci était l'objet. L'atmosphère était bourdonnante de la foule et des aubades des fifres et des tambourins."

82 In 1918, the Ligue d'oc was founded—a regionalist league in the spirit of the Félibrige. Camille Soula named Séverac co-president with the poet Antonin Perbosc. It was

Séverac's regionalist philosophy and interest in folk music, as influenced by Mistral, subsequently had an influence on other composers, including Joseph Canteloube, who, in turn, incorporated folk elements into his own compositions. The two musicians met in Paris in 1904 when studying composition with Vincent d'Indy. They often took walks together and met at cafes while discussing their shared philosophy of régionalisme, as evident in a later 1917 letter from Séverac to Canteloube: "I remember with happiness the bygone days in the old neighborhood with our long chats and common dreams of régionalisme."[83] The Auvergne composer also recalled another conversation with Séverac regarding regionalism and folk music:

> As I confessed to Déodat de Séverac, I had little interest in the various musical factions of the time, he said to me, "Do as I do, my old friend! Sing of your own country, your land." I did exactly that and began to collect the traditional songs of the Auvergne and of Quercy. Struck by their charm, their poetry, their grandeur and their beauty; feeling or guessing all that they had absorbed through the ages, I devoted myself wholly to this task of collection and extended my coverage to the whole of France. It was not so much the folklorist aspect that attracted me, but rather the musical beauty of the majority of these songs. That is why I swore to myself to make them known and by bringing out their full worth in their setting, by surrounding them with as much of their natural poetry as possible, rather than a vulgar rhetorical accompaniment.[84]

Although Séverac claimed that "the usefulness of traditional folk song from the point of view of regional art is considerable," he rarely used actual French folk melodies in

---

thought that both carried with them the future of the Félibrige cultural Renaissance. However, the league did not survive and Séverac died in 1921. The league was replaced by the Chorale Déodat de Séverac, dedicated to promoting southern French art.

83 Françoise Raginel Cougniaud, *Joseph Canteloube* (Béziers, France: Société de musicologie de Languedoc, 1988), 28.. "Je me souviens avec bonheur de nos anciens jours du vieux quartier, de nos longues causeries et de nos rêves communs de régionalisme."

84 Canteloube, "Comment juger le divorce opposant la musique moderne et le public," *Pour ou contre la musique moderne* (Paris: Flammarion, 1957). "Comme je lui [Séverac] avouais le peu d'intérêt que m'inspiraient les clans musicaux, il me dit—'Faites comme moi, mon vieux! Chantez votre pays, votre terre!' Je le fis et commençai à recueillir les chants traditionnels de l'Auvergne et du Quercy. Pris par leur charme, leur poésie, leur grandeur et leur beauté, sentant ou devinant tout ce dont ils s'étaient imprégnés au cours des âges, je me livrais tout entier à cette collecte que j'étendis à toute la France. Ce n'est pas ici le Folklore qui m'attirait, mais la beauté musicale de la plupart des chants. C'est pourquoi je me jurai à moi-même d'en répandre la connaissance, en les mettant en valeur dans leur cadre, en les entourant de toute la poésie naturelle possible, et non pas d'une vulgaire rhétorique d'accompagnement."

In a 1907 article for *Le courrier musical*, critic François Sternay revealed similarities between Canteloube's *Dans la montagne* (suite for violin and piano) and Séverac's piano suite *En Languedoc*, stating that "the melodic line [in both pieces] is very pure, and the love of nature is very well expressed." ("La ligne mélodique est très pure, et l'amour de la nature est très puissamment exprimeé.") See *Le courrier musical* (Paris, March, 1907), cited by Françoise Raginel Cougniaud, *Joseph Canteloube* (Béziers, France: Société de musicologie de Languedoc, 1988), 33.

his earlier compositions, but instead used characteristics inherent in the folk-music style. In an article for *Eaux-vives*, Canteloube commented on the fact that Séverac possessed a natural melodic gift—one that eliminated a need for appropriating actual folk melodies.[85]

Vincent d'Indy and Régionalisme

Regionalist attitudes were also promoted by Vincent d'Indy, who often embellished these concepts with religious overtones, and much of this philosophy was incorporated into the Schola Cantorum curriculum. The Schola Cantorum was subsequently criticized by proponents of the Paris Conservatoire for instigating these so-called Catholic philosophies into the curriculum, thereby defying new national laws regarding the separation of church and state. D'Indy was himself chastised for receiving funds from the Catholic Church, beginning in 1898, in the form of donations from the Institut Catholique de Paris. Critic and Paris Conservatoire student Emile Vuillermoz describes his view regarding this relationship between the Schola Cantorum and the church:

> Let us not forget that [the Schola Cantorum] was active at the moment of the law governing religious congregations and the separation of the church and the state [after 1905]! ... My opinion is that the "d'Indystes" were simply an unauthorized congregation ... and hid their true identity behind a musical front.[86]

Practicing Catholicism within public life was considered by many to be one form of conservatism within contemporary France, an approach often coupled with nationalist pro-military attitudes in part stimulated by the Dreyfus Affair; these ideas were often combined with feelings of nostalgia for the Ancien Régime which activated pro-monarchy sentiments.[87] D'Indy and Séverac held these views as an important part of their regionalist philosophies.

D'Indy's regional interests were reflected in his instigating the teaching of folk music at the Schola Cantorum, which was subsequently adopted by two primary regional factions in Paris: Breton regionalists, including Joseph-Guy Ropartz, Paul

---

85 Canteloube, *Eaux-vives* (February, 1953), 19.

86 See Emile Vuillermoz, "La Schola et le Conservatoire," *Le mercure de France* (September 16, 1909), 234–43.

It is true that the L'action française was not officially Catholic and Charles Maurras was agnostic, but the organization did support the restoration of Roman Catholicism as the state religion after the 1905 law on separation of church and state. Maurras thought Catholicism a major entity in social cohesion and stability. A vast majority of members of L'Action française were practicing members of the Catholic faith, including a significant number of clergymen. Because Maurras often maintained a utilitarian view of religion, some Catholics regarded the organization with distrust. Pope Pius XI condemned L'action française in 1926.

87 Vincent d'Indy, "A Propos du Prix de Rome: le régionalisme musical," *La revue musicale* (June, 1902), 246, reprinted and translated by Musk, "Aspects of Regionalism in French Music during the Third Republic: the Schola Cantorum, d'Indy, Séverac and Canteloube," 47.

Le Flem, Paul Ladmirault, and Charles de Sivry, and southern regionalists, among whom were Vincent d'Indy, René de Castéra, Joseph Canteloube, Raoul Laparra, Blanche Selva, Charles Bordes, Ricardo Viñes, Manuel de Falla, Isaac Albéniz, and Séverac. D'Indy's regionalist attitudes found their genesis in his ancestral home in the Ardèche. He discussed his affinity for this area:

> Each province is able to become a fatherland of art in the same way as the fatherland; each province ... must be a more fertile source than the big city where everything is centralized and seemingly catalogued by the lowest denominator.[88]

D'Indy's passion for ancestral lands is also evident in a letter written in his youth: "It was there in our beloved mountains, that for the first time I experienced the beautiful and glimpsed the ideal."[89] Like Bordes and Séverac, many of d'Indy's compositions reflect this rural heritage, such as *Poème des montagnes* (1881), *Symphonie sur un chant montagnard français* (1886), *Fantaisie sur des thèmes populaires français* (1888), and *Jour d'été à la montagne* (1905)—the latter evoking a nostalgic view of country life in the Cévennes region through indigenous folk elements.

D'Indy's ideas also centered around the perceived destructive forces of the urban music hall and cabaret, apparent in d'Indy's writings about Beethoven:

> [Life] is [for me] no longer the domain of the city dweller on a pleasant day out, but that of the peasant who also celebrated holidays by drinking, dancing, and singing. Song and dances take on a more hearty and characteristic appearance under the open sky than in the lukewarm suburban cabarets.[90]

This view of so-called lukewarm cabarets set against the purity of outdoors is reminiscent of Séverac's ennoblement of the peasants over their city-dwelling compatriots, evident in his 1907 thesis as well as letters written during his later years in Catalonia.[91]

---

88 Jean de la Laurencie, "Quelques souvenirs Vivarais," *Revue du Vivarais*, vol. 39 (March–April, 1932), reprinted and translated by Musk, "Aspects of Regionalism in French Music during the Third Republic: the Schola Cantorum, d'Indy, Séverac and Canteloube", 109.

89 Vincent d'Indy, *Beethoven* (Paris, 1911), 68, reprinted and translated by Musk, "Aspects of Regionalism in French Music during the Third Republic: the Schola Cantorum, d'Indy, Séverac and Canteloube," 100.

90 Séverac's predilection for outdoor venues will be discussed more thoroughly in Chapter 10.

91 For d'Indy, regionalism was also intertwined with nationalism, and he believed in cultivating this regionalism for the purpose of stimulating national renewal. As d'Indy remarked, "all artists concerned with the creation of national unity should be attached emotionally, mentally, and where possible, physically to his own petite patrie." See d'Indy, *Beethoven*, 67, reprinted and translated by Musk, "Aspects of Regionalism in French Music during the Third Republic: the Schola Cantorum, d'Indy, Séverac and Canteloube," 99.

Séverac's studies with d'Indy, not including composition, consisted of three classes: the first analyzing symphony and opera, the second examining folk music and sonata, and the third studying counterpoint. D'Indy's most provocative writing on regionalist ideas in symphonic music is found in "L'expression," from Vincent d'Indy, *Cours de composition*

D'Indy also commented on his ideas in his preface to *Chansons populaires du Vivarais*

> I have had to banish from this collection the texts adapted to vaudeville—bastardized representations of the genre—as well as a number of modern compositions that lacked poetic or musical interest, because the folk song is only granted its licensee thanks to the impersonal efforts ... of the principal worker.[92]

Andrea Musk notes that d'Indy clearly indicated in *Chansons populaires du Vivarais* his desire to exclude so-called vaudeville songs because they supposedly lacked tradition. For d'Indy, folk songs were allegedly rooted in the Gregorian chant tradition, corroborated by the fact that both contain a monodic texture, rhythmic freedom, and modality.[93] She also comments on d'Indy's interest in Beethoven as progenitor of régionalisme, as found in d'Indy's book on Beethoven. Musk further reminds us that d'Indy viewed Beethoven's *Symphony no. 6 in F, op. 68* ("Pastoral") not as a realist depiction of sounds from the countryside, but as the spirit of the countryside rendered through Beethoven's soul and intellect. D'Indy further commented that the impetus was not nature in general, but a distinct locality that became part of Beethoven's life.[94]

Musk claims that d'Indy's regionalism is best exemplified in *Jour d'été à la montagne* (1905), a symphonic triptych based on a summer day in the Cévennes mountains of his youth. As in many of Séverac's compositions, d'Indy's work combines nature and religion. Rather then nature per se, however, d'Indy enjoined a specific locality together with Catholicism. Folk music within the composition was collected by d'Indy, and a hymn melody in the third movement was adapted from a cantilena for the Feast of the Assumption that d'Indy heard at a church in the mountains.[95] According to d'Indy, it is an identical transcription, save for the rhythm,

---

musicale, vol. 1 (Paris: Durand, 1903). For more information on d'Indy, see Stéphane Giocanti, "Vincent d'Indy et le régionalisme musical," *La France latine*, vol. 113 (1991); Auguste Sérieyx, *Vincent d'Indy* (Paris: Albert Messein, 1914); Andrew Thomson, *Vincent d'Indy and His World* (Oxford: Clarendon Press, 1996); Vincent d'Indy, *La Schola Cantorum, son histoire depuis sa fondation jusqu'en 1925* (Paris, Bloud et Gay, 1927), and Manuela Schwartz, ed. *Vincent d'Indy et son temps* (Sprimont, Belgium: Mardaga Press, 2006). This latter work edited by Schwartz includes a chapter on French folk songs for a cappella chorus: see Bernadette Lespinard, "Vincent d'Indy et la naissance d'un genre nouveau: les chansons populaires françaises arrangées pour choeur mixte a capella," in *Vincent d'Indy et son temps*, edited by Manuela Schwartz, 283–300.

92 Vincent d'Indy, *Chansons populaires du Vivarais* (Paris: A. Durand, 1900), 2; translated by Musk, "Aspects of Regionalism in French Music during the Third Republic: the Schola Cantorum, d'Indy, Séverac and Canteloube," 65.

93 Musk, "Aspects of Regionalism in French Music during the Third Republic: the Schola Cantorum, d'Indy, Séverac and Canteloube," 65.

94 Ibid., 104.

95 For more information, see Joseph Canteloube's *D'Indy* (Paris: Laurens, 1951), as well as Stefan Keym, "De la 'Divine Bonté' à l' 'Antéchrist?' *Jour d'été à la montagne* de Vincent d'Indy compare à *Eine Alpensinfonie* de Richard Strauss," and Stéphane Giocanti,

of a Gregorian chant belonging to the Office of First Vespers of the Feast of the Assumption.[96]

Musk further points out that there is a direct analogy between this work and visual triptychs dating to the early Christian era, when painters formed three panels symbolizing the Trinity in which they would narrate a single story or devotional prayer for the purpose of personal meditation.[97] The central panel would be the focus of devotion and the outer panels would fold towards each other in order to provide continuity. D'Indy's analogy to the triptych would therefore be found in the three movements of *Jour d'été à la montagne*: "Aurore: un lever de soleil sans nuages," "Jour: après-midi sous les pins," and "Soir: retour au gîte avec des dernières éclaircies sur les cimes des pins, puis ... la nuit," describing different parts of the day in the countryside.

"Aurore" opens with nocturnal creatures making sounds as dawn breaks. Light emerges gradually and the climax in the music occurs with the emergence of the sun. "Jour" is primarily a reverie combined with country dances, a thunderstorm, and return to calm surroundings. "Soir" evokes the return of peasants and a call to prayer in the form of a hymn. Melancholy gradually appears as the sun disappears and night ensues.[98]

According to d'Indy, this is a narrated story, but there also appears a sense of timelessness, so that this idyllic landscape becomes a retreat from the outside world. These ideas parallel Séverac's reverence for nature scenes coupled with religious faith.[99]

"Vincent d'Indy est-il un compositeur religieux?," both in *Vincent d'Indy et son temps*, edited by Manuela Schwartz, 195–210, 255–62.

96 D'Indy, *Cours de composition musicale*, in collaboration with Auguste Sérieyx, vol. 2, bk. 2 (Paris: Durand et Cie, 1909), 329; reprinted by Musk, "Aspects of Regionalism in French Music during the Third Republic: the Schola Cantorum, d'Indy, Séverac and Canteloube," 116.

97 Ibid., 110.

98 D'Indy letter to Marcel Labey (Les Faugs, August 17, 1905), Paris, BN, la 90, reprinted and translated by Musk, "Aspects of Regionalism in French Music during the Third Republic: the Schola Cantorum, d'Indy, Séverac and Canteloube," 110. For more information on *Jour d'été à la montagne*, see Stéphane Giocanti, "Vincent d'Indy est-il un compositeur religieux?," in *Vincent d'Indy et son temps*, edited by Manuela Schwartz, 255–62.

99 Another programmatic work by d'Indy with titles similar to those found in Séverac's piano music is *Tableaux de voyage*, op. 33 (13 pieces for piano). The composition had its première in 1891 and d'Indy later orchestrated 6 out of 13 of these movements (*Tableaux de voyage*, op. 36, suite d'orchestre). What is significant is that this work contains many characteristics and programmatic themes and titles found in Séverac's piano music, including meter in groupings of 5 (5/8 in "Preamble"), also found in Séverac's works, including "Le jour de la foire, au mas," from *En Languedoc*; traveling while experiencing the wonders of nature ("En marche"), similarly discovered in Séverac's *Cerdaña*; resting during a journey ("Halte au soir"), also experienced in Séverac's "Halte à la fontaine" section of "A cheval, dans la prairie," from *En Languedoc*; enjoying a village festival after traveling ("Fête de village"), also witnessed in Séverac's "Les fêtes," from *Cerdaña*; and bells ringing warning of a storm ("Le glas"), the latter found in Séverac's *Le glas* section of "La grêle," from *Le chant de la terre*.

The Angelus

This call to prayer in d'Indy's music coupled with idyllic landscapes and a sense of timelessness is also captured in much of Séverac's music. Bucolic landscapes were subsequently evoked by Séverac in his songs and piano suites, the latter consisting primarily of *Le chant de la terre*, *En Languedoc*, and *Cerdaña*. In *Le chant de la terre*, for example, Séverac does not describe a day in the mountains, but a seasonal year for a farmer and his family, beginning with the planting of seeds and concluding with a wedding following a crop harvest. Although there is no evidence that Séverac appropriated the concepts found in d'Indy's work, it would be extremely unlikely that Séverac was not aware of d'Indy's regionalist leanings in *Jour d'été à la montagne*.[100]

More significantly for Séverac, however, were extra-musical influences, including the paintings of Jean-François Millet (1814–75) and the Barbizon school. Millet, the son of a peasant farmer from Normandy, grew up with Catholic Puritan parents with stern religious sentiments. Millet's childhood included learning Virgil's *Georgics* and the psalms from the Bible. As a result, Millet associated Christianity with nature and pastoral poetry, thereby later depicting Catholic prayer in outdoor rural settings.[101]

Although Flemish painters of the sixteenth century had previously depicted laboring peasants often as peripheral or comic characters, Millet was the first artist to endow rural life with a dignity and monumentality that transcended realism, recreating the peasant as an almost heroic figure. Millet characterized these figures as valiant in their arduous labor, and characterized within what appears to be a timeless existence.[102]

Millet's paintings were often criticized as possessing socialist traits, or appearing as socialistic manifestos to appeal to the mob. According to many critics, this attitude thereby raised peasantry to an almost equal status to that of the elite, in the same way that certain critics of Séverac's en plein air theatrical works claimed that outdoor venues allowed various classes to mingle, inadvertently promoting greater equality among these classes.[103] These ideas would seemingly contradict Séverac's Royalist

---

100 *Le chant de la terre* predates *Jour d'été à la montagne* and *En Languedoc* was composed the same year in which d'Indy's work was completed. *Cerdaña* was written several years after d'Indy's composition was published.

101 For more information on Millet and the Barbizon school, see John Mollett, *The Painters of Barbizon* (London: Sampson Low, Marston, 1890), and Jean Bouret, *The Barbizon School and 19th-Century French Landscape Painting* (London: Thames and Hudson, 1973). For more sociological study of the Barbizon school, see Timothy James Clark, *The Absolute Bourgeois: Artists and Politics in France, 1848–1851* (London: Thames and Hudson, 1973). For a study of the ramifications of Millet's *L'angélus*, see Salvador Dali, *Le mythe tragique de l'angélus de Millet* (Paris: Société nouvelle des éditions Jean-Jacques Pauvert, 1963, 1978).

102 See Chapter 10 for a more detailed discussion on Séverac's philosophy regarding en plein air works.

103 These rural agricultural themes are found in Millet's *The Sower* (1850), *Haymaker* (1850), *Harvesters* (1853), *Sheep-shearers* (1853), *Peasant Grafting a Tree* (1855), and most significantly for Séverac, *The Gleaners* (1857) and *The Angélus* (1859). He employed these

stance, but is reconciled in the myth of an aristocrat's benign love for peasants and their labor, or as a patriarchal provincial figure overseeing his petit-pays.[104]

Interestingly, many of Millet's critics failed to comment on his deep religious convictions found in paintings depicting peasants praying in the fields, as in his painting *L'angélus*. An angelus is a Roman Catholic devotional prayer recited at 6 a.m., noon, and 6 p.m. every day of the year, except during Paschal Tide, when the Regina Coeli is recited instead.[105] The angelus was designed to commemorate the Annunciation, that is, the angel Gabriel's announcement of the Incarnation (Luke 1:26–38). A festival takes place on March 25 in celebration of the event, and a bell is rung as a call to farmers working outdoors, as well as to others in the village, to recite the prayer. This prayer would have been spoken in medieval Latin ("Angélus Domini," or "Angel of the Lord").[106]

Séverac depicted the angelus with bell tones in parallel fourths and fifths within various compositions, coupled with performance indications within the score as well as suggestive movement titles indicating the overall programmatic intent of the composition. The angelus was also depicted by other composers, painters, and writers of the time. Francis Jammes (1868–1938), for example, wrote *De l'angélus de l'aube à l'angélus du soir* (1900), completed the same year in which Séverac finished his piano suite *Le chant de la terre*. Séverac read this work and paid homage to Jammes in his 1907 thesis. Although other French composers alluded to the angelus, no composer depicted the tradition as much as Séverac.[107]

---

two latter titles in certain scores as descriptive references, including his piano suites *Cerdaña* and *Le chant de la terre*. Gleaners are those who gather grain left behind by reapers.

104 Paschal Tide represents 50 days from Easter Sunday to the Pentecost, or the first Vespers of Low Sunday to the first Vespers of Trinity Sunday.

105 The prayer often included a triple repetition of the Hail Mary, to which, in later times, three introductory versicles with concluding versicle and prayer would have been added, the latter belonging to the Antiphon of Our Lady, "Alma Redemptoris." The prayer was originally intended to be chanted on one's knees, but Pope Leo XIII modified this in 1884 by allowing a standing posture, as seen in Millet's painting *L'angélus*.

106 Other composers include Debussy in his song "Les angélus." The angelus was employed by Séverac in many works, including six songs, "L'éveil de Pâques" (1899), "Chanson de Blaisine" (1900), "Le ciel est, par-dessus le toit" (1901), "A l'aube dans la montagne" (1903), "Temps de neige" (1905), and "Chanson pour le petit cheval" (1910–13). Piano works that specifically indicate angelus bells in the score include measure 40 of "Les semailles," from the piano suite *Le chant de la terre*; *En Languedoc*, where Séverac cites *Angélus du soir* in measure 191 of "Vers le mas en fête"; and *Au loin sonne l'angélus de l'aube*, in measure 126 of "Le jour de la foire, au mas." Séverac also included the angelus several times in his opera *Le coeur du moulin*.

107 Other types of prayer are specified in Séverac's piano suites, as in *Les rogations* and *Le glas*, in measures 188 and 204 in "La grêle," from *Le chant de la terre*. Nuptial bells are included in measure 73 of "Les moissons," from the same suite, and Séverac calls for *Cloches au loin*, in measure 13 of "Epilogue: le jour des noces," also from *Le chant de la terre*. In "Coin de cimetière, au printemps," from *En Languedoc*, "Le chant doucement marqué, comme des cloches lointaines" is indicated within the *Dies Irae* section. Millet's "The Gleaners" is also echoed by Séverac in his piano suite *Cerdaña*, where he employs the term "Gleaners" in the score.

Illustration 3.1   Jean-François Millet, *L'angélus*. Permission courtesy of Réunion des Musées Nationaux/Art Resource, NY

Regionalism and the Concept of Returning Home

One of the recurring regionalist themes in Séverac's music is the idea of returning home. Perhaps Séverac and other regionalists who lived in Paris felt guilty for leaving their native pays, and this guilt was coupled with nostalgic feelings of longing for their pastoral province. Returning home became an idée fixe within their lives. Séverac, unlike many other regionalists, did move back to the south of France, albeit in an adopted homeland in the Catalan province of Roussillon.

The story in Séverac's opera *Le coeur du moulin*, for example, concerns Jacques, who is returning to his native village after years of finding fame and fortune elsewhere. In this story, Jacques returns only to find Marie, the love of his life, married. This story echoes many ancient tales, including Tennyson's *Enoch Arden*, where Enoch, the sailor, becomes shipwrecked and stranded on an island, only to eventually return home many years later where he discovers his wife remarried to someone else.

Séverac stressed this concept of returning home in his piano suites *En Languedoc* and *Cerdaña*. In *Cerdaña*, programmatic titles and accompanying description describe mules as the mode of travel in which to return home. Séverac's incidental music to

Les Antibels is composed for a tragedy within a rustic setting, where Jan returns to his native village after military service in order to help his mother. Séverac's *Didon et Enée* centers around Dido waiting for Aeneas to return home from the war. The story found in Séverac's *Le retour* is of Steno, who, after selling the house and land of his ancestors in order to live in a distant city, returns to his pays to wed Simone, who has waited for his return.

Yet the concept of home meant many other things for Séverac, including feelings of nostalgia for nature experienced in Séverac's boyhood, the Christian use of home as metaphor for heaven, nostalgia for his aristocratic ancestral home together with images of countryside peasants, and the idea of traditions he learned during his childhood. Perhaps for Séverac, as well as for other regionalists, home also symbolized childhood feelings of security, comfort, familiarity, and simplicity. Mistral's Félibrige emphasized these ideals, as did works by Barrès, Maurras, and d'Indy.

PART II
Compositions from the Paris Years, 1896–1909

Chapter 4

Severac, Christianity, and Organ Music

Regionalists favored the Catholic Church as an institution for political as well as religious reasons, so their alliance was often a marriage of convenience. Barrès stressed the teaching of sacred songs and hymns in schools, despite the fact that he possessed little religious conviction for much of his life. He argued that traditional religious institutions aided regionalists through their emphasis on family. Barrès also wanted these institutions to fight new decrees instituted by the centralized Third Republic government, including the dissolution of monasteries in 1903, the separation of church and state in 1905, and the creation of a newly nationalized secular educational system. Regionalist poet Frédéric Mistral also supported sacred institutions, as illustrated in his claim that the Félibrige was inherently religious.[1]

Not only was religion and its relationship with politics adamantly discussed in Paris during this time, but religion and music also became a hotly debated topic. Many figures at the Paris Conservatoire, for example, indicted the Schola Cantorum as being more interested in religion than music, including Paris Conservatoire composition pupil Emile Vuillermoz, who complained that "the Schola (modern meditative school) taught philosophy, morality, and spiritualism instead of composition."[2] Novelist Romain Rolland also described what he perceived as the religious role of the Schola Cantorum in his popular novel *Jean Christophe*:

> The members of the [Schola] had taken a name reminiscent of a clerical institution which had flourished thirteen or fourteen centuries ago ... Christophe ... saw that it was a Catholic cult ... [These people] attributed every defect in art and every vice of humanity [to] the Renaissance, the Reformation, present-day Judaism, which [they] lumped together in one category.[3]

This debate also led to a battle between various fin de siècle French composers over what were the roots of French music. In 1899, the Minister of Public Instruction assembled various musicians together in order to form a historical canon as a way of presenting a unified history of French music. Alfred Bruneau, a professed follower of the Third Republic and leading Dreyfusard, suggested that the lineage began with the secular compositions of Adam de la Halle (1237–88) and continued with those

---

1 See Chapter 3 on Mistral.
2 See Emile Vuillermoz, "La Schola et le Conservatoire," *Mercure de France* (September 16, 1909), 234–43. Emile Vuillermoz (1878–1960) studied composition with Fauré and then turned to music criticism.
3 Romain Rolland, *Jean Christophe* (Paris: P. Ollendorf, 1905), reprinted in *Jean Christophe*, translated by Gilbert Cannan (New York: Henry Holt and Co., 1911), p. 55.

of Clément Janequin (1485–1560). Janequin composed Parisian chansons, a type of song embodying an elegant simplicity and rational spirit.

D'Indy objected to this lineage by criticizing Bruneau for being anti-clerical and for possessing a bias against sacred music, and thereby suggested that Gallic music had its roots in Gregorian chant, medieval organum, and the sacred music of Palestrina and Monteverdi. Vincent d'Indy himself was a devoted Catholic who believed that music existed in order to elevate the spirit of humanity. This theory was inspired by his interest in medieval philosophy, wherein the relationship between master and pupil was to have been bound together by religious faith.[4] A battle over cultural identity therefore ensued between regionalists from the Schola Cantorum who supported d'Indy's beliefs, and Third Republic defenders of Bruneau's index, most of whom were studying or teaching at the Paris Conservatoire.[5]

Séverac found fault with those on both sides of the religious battle, as his Catholic beliefs did not often extend into political conflicts. This is illustrated in a personal letter to his family:

> I despise injustice regardless of its origins ... For some, it is Christianity that produced the Inquisition ... The [Christian] ideas are beautiful. It's too bad that there are those who in the name of these ideas act like rogues. Truth endures despite them ... God continues His work. Nature embodies his life and the sun sings above the clouds ... fortunately, God understands the causes, and because of this he excuses and pardons that which we censor without any hesitation *in his name*. We who are certain of the boundless kindness of Jesus; if, in spite of this, we are led to weep, the cause is in our own weakness. This weakness makes Jesus love us ever more, because he senses our inability to sail alone on the waves.[6]

The origins of Séverac's seemingly tolerant Christian philosophy becomes apparent in his poetry to accompany *Loin des villes*, an early title to what later became his

---

4 Séverac himself referred to d'Indy as "a monk of the Middle Ages" in his 1907 thesis.

5 See Jane Fulcher, *French Cultural Politics and Music* (Oxford: Oxford University Press, 1999) and Brian Jack Hart, "The Symphony in Theory and Practice in France, 1900-1914" (PhD Dissertation, Indiana University, 1994). Bruneau was the leading Dreyfusard among composers, and was interested in establishing the French tradition as one of solely secular works.

6 Pierre Guillot, *Déodat de Séverac: la musique et les lettres* (Liège, Belgium: Pierre Mardaga, 2002), 136, 191, and Blanche Selva, *Déodat de Séverac* (Paris: Librairie Delagrave, 1930), 36. [Conflation of two letters, Séverac letter to Mme Gilbert de Séverac, 1903, and Séverac letter to sister Alix, 1901.] Italics belong to Séverac. "Je hais l'injustice d'où qu'elle vienne ... Pour certains autres c'étaient le Christianisme qui produisait l'Inquisition ... Les idées sont belles. Tant pis pour les hommes qui au nom de ces idées se conduisent en chenapans. La Vérité subsistera malgré eux ... le Bon Dieu continue à faire son métier. La Nature reprend sa vie et le Soleil chante au dessus des nuages ... heureusement Dieu connaît les causes, et pour cela il excuse et pardonne ce que nous condamnons *en son nom* sans plus d'hésitation. Nous qui sommes certains de l'infinie bonté de Jésus. Et si nous pleurons malgré cela, la cause en est a notre faiblesse; cette faiblesse qui fait que Jésus nous aime davantage encore, car il sent notre incapacité de 'voguer seuls sur les flots.'"

piano suite *En Languedoc*. The poetry reads: "My father was good and believed in God, but in a God so tender and lenient that a theologian would have cursed him had he known him."[7] Additional comments from a letter to his mother provide further indications regarding Séverac's Christian philosophy: "Love, pity, the spirit of forgiveness; these are the greatest virtues and the dearest to God."[8]

Séverac had maintained an interest in religious music ever since childhood, but his enthusiasm for sacred music was ignited further when he traveled to Solesmes with Charles Bordes and became inspired by hearing plainchant. As Séverac stated upon his return: "Never had drama or symphony provoked so much emotion and joy in me! Gregorian chant melodies represent the *pinnacle* of Art."[9] It is also apparent that Séverac's interest in sacred compositions from the Renaissance and Middle Ages greatly increased during the ten years of study at the Schola Cantorum, as discernible in his extended use of church modes and chant in his own compositions. This was largely the result of his choral conducting experience under the tutelage of Charles Bordes, who stimulated Séverac's interest in Renaissance composers and modal composition. As early as 1897, Bordes invited Séverac to conduct the Schola Cantorum chorus in a performance of several Renaissance works.[10] As a result of this event and other gatherings championed by Bordes, Séverac began to increasingly emphasize chant modes within his sacred compositions.[11]

---

7   Guillot, *Déodat de Séverac: écrits sur la musique* (Liège, Belgium: Pierre Mardaga, 1993), 64. "Mon père était bon et croyait en Dieu mais en un Dieu si tendre et si clément que les théologiens l'auraient maudit s'ils l'avaient su."

8   Selva, *Déodat de Séverac*, 37. [Séverac letter to mother, 1903.] "L'amour, la pitié, l'esprit de pardon sont les plus grandes vertus et les plus chères à Dieu."

9   Ibid., 47. [Séverac letter to family, 1897.] "Jamais drame ni symphonie ne m'ont procuré autant d'émotion et de joie! La mélodie grégorienne est le *summum* de l'art."

10   Ibid., 32.

11   *Ave Verum* was one such work, a motet composed in 1898 for soprano and tenor, with organ. The work was published the following year. There are four other manuscript versions of this work without dates at Séverac's baronial birthplace of Saint-Félix de Lauragais. Séverac described the process of composing the work, which contains conjunct and modal melodic lines: "I hope that the motet for two voices does not seem too difficult. In terms of form, it is a sort of chorale. It is therefore necessary ... that there be enough nuance in the execution, so that the opposing melodic lines imitate each other. A little rallentando and decrescendo [is necessary] at the end of each phrase." Guillot, *Déodat de Séverac: la musique et les lettres*, 46. [Séverac letter to sister Jeanne, 1897]. "J'espère que le motet à deux voix ne semblera pas trop difficile. Comme forme c'est une espèce de choral. Il faut donc assez ... de nuances dans l'exécution pour faire des oppositions entre les dessins que s'imitent. Un petit ralenti et un decrescendo régulier à chaque fin de phrase."

Ave Maria was another sacred work that Séverac submitted to Bordes and d'Indy for advice, and he subsequently reported that both approved of the work: "Bordes found my *Ave Maria* very interesting. D'Indy just sang my praises to the class and took the original in order to study it more closely." Ibid., 60. [Séverac letter to sister Jeannette, 1898.] ("Bordes avait trouvé mon Ave Maria très intéressant. D'Indy m'a complimente tout à l'heure à la classe et a emporté l'original pour l'étudier de plus près.") A third work was Séverac's motet *Homo quidam* for three equal voices, tenors, baritones, and basses, with organ. D'Indy, among others, heard the première of this work. Selva, *Déodat de Séverac*, 82.

Organ Music

Séverac's background as an organist dates to his childhood. His first learning experiences as an organist came from studying harmonium with his father, which continued until Séverac began tutelage with organist Louis Amile.

These lessons took place in the local church in Saint-Félix-Caraman, built in 1303 and therefore one of the most ancient in southern France. The organ on which Séverac practiced was an eighteenth-century Rabiny refurbished in 1872 and contained three keyboard manuals.[12] Séverac thereafter studied organ at the Dominican Collège de Sorèze in Toulouse between 1886 and 1891, where he attended middle school, at which time he also accompanied singers on the organ in the college chapel. Séverac finally moved to Paris in 1896 where he began lessons with Guilmant at the Schola Cantorum.

One mission of the Schola Cantorum was to enrich the organ repertoire, which would be improved by employing melodic ideals found in medieval vocal incantation, an idea first printed in *La tribune de Saint-Gervais* in 1895, when the first edition announced the many principles of the new society.[13] Employing melodies reminiscent of chant was, in part, inspired by monk, scholar, and plainchant editor Joseph Pothier (1835–1923), who, together with other Benedictine monks from Solesmes, published *Mélodies grégoriennes d'après la tradition* of 1880. In this treatise, Pothier defined his principles surrounding the restoration, notation, and performance of plainchant melodies based on fourteenth-century neumatic manuscript sources.[14] These concepts, initially proposed by Abbé Canon Augustin Gontier (1802–81) in *Méthode raisonnée de plainchant: le plein-chant considéré dans son rythme, sa tonalité et ses modes*, were later emphasized by Pothier's assistant, Dom André Mocquereau (1849–1930) in *Paléographie musicale*:[15]

> [Our goal] is to raise Gregorian chant from the abject state into which it has fallen, to pursue the work of its restoration until complete justice is done, and it has recovered its full ancient beauty which renders it so proper from divine worship.[16]

---

12 Joseph Rabiny (1732–1813) was the nephew of Karl Joseph Riepp (1710–75), a French organ builder of German birth. Rabiny subsequently took over his uncle's workshop.

13 See Vincent d'Indy, *La tribune de Saint-Gervais: bulletin mensuel de la Schola*, vol. 1 (Paris: Schola Cantorum, 1895). The publication ran in 26 volumes between 1895 and 1929.

14 Joseph Pothier, *Mélodies grégoriennes d'après la tradition* (Tournai, France: Société Saint Jean l'Evangéliste Desclée et Cie, 1880).

15 Augustin Gontier, *Méthode raisonnée de plain-chant: le plain-chant considéré dans son rythme, sa tonalité et ses modes* (Paris, 1859); reprinted in *Metodo ragionato di canto piano: il canto piano nel suo ritmo, nella sua tonalità, nei suoi modi* (Rome: Torre d'Orfeo, 1993).

16 André Mocquereau, *Paléographie musicale*, 1st series, x (Tournai, France: Société Saint Jean l'Evangéliste Desclée et Cie, 1922). Twenty-one volumes were published from 1889 to 1914 and from 1921 to 1954. Mocquereau was a Benedictine monk and French scholar of plainchant, who worked for 13 years as Pothier's assistant. He succeeded Pothier as choirmaster in 1889.

This so-called abject state found in previous performance practice heavily emphasized each tone, which arose from editions that contained arbitrary rhythmic subdivisions through the employment of measure bar lines within the score. Pothier's new restorations contained no bar lines in order to promote suppleness of phrasing during performances. Since original chant notation had no fixed or absolute note values, the music was therefore to be sung in a "natural and non-metrical" style, determined by two factors: the tonic accent of the Latin text, and the natural divisions of the text placed into words and phrases. Units were therefore organized according to Latin word accentuation, or "oratorical rhythm," which achieved a sense of musical and syntactical coherence.[17] The result was a transformation from comparatively inauthentic settings of liturgical melodies to more textually and rhythmically accurate plainsong. Pothier subsequently published Gregorian chant in *Liber gradualis* of 1883, and the scholarly journal *Revue grégorienne* was founded in 1911 as a result of his work. Although Pothier's *Liber gradualis* aroused opposition from proponents of a previous edition entitled *Graduale romanum* of 1871,[18] Pope Leo XIIII nonetheless began to encourage the work of Pothier and later appointed a commission to edit and publish Pothier's interpretations, which were subsequently declared official and obligatory.

These innovations were vital for the Schola Cantorum, as Pothier often performed and taught workshops at the institution during Séverac's tenure, a relationship established by Charles Bordes in 1895. Séverac attended many of these events:

> We had a lecture on "The Role of Gregorian and Palestrina Chants in Art," given by the famous Dom Pothier ... He told us the role that we must play as future artists, composers, and organists, in the future union of, or better, in the restoration of links between true art and religion ... Abbé Larrieu attended the conference.[19]

In 1900, Pothier participated in the Assises de musique religieuse et classique de la Schola (Conference of Religious and Classical Music at the Schola), under the artistic leadership of Guilmant.[20] Guilmant was as influential as Bordes in promoting the musical and religious aesthetics espoused by Pothier, and Guilmant's organ music was often inspired by Pothier's philosophies. As one of the most accomplished improvisers of sacred organ repertoire, Guilmant's liturgical output was often based on plainchant and Pothier's concepts surrounding the rhythmic interpretation of this

---

17 Richard Sherr, "Plainchant," *The New Grove Dictionary of Music and Musicians*, vol. 19, online edition (Oxford: Oxford University Press, 2006), 857.

18 Friedrich Pustet, *Graduale romanum* (Regensburg: Société St.-Jean l'Evangelist et Desclée et Cie, 1871).

19 Guillot, *Déodat de Séverac: la musique et les lettres*, 55–6. [Séverac letter to father, Gilbert de Séverac, 1897.] "Nous avons eu une conférence sur 'Le rôle du chant grégorien et palestrinien dans l'Art' faite par le fameux Dom Pothier ... Il nous a dit le rôle que nous devions jouer nous futurs artistes, compositeurs, organistes, dans l'union future, ou mieux, dans la restauration des liens de l'art vrai avec la religion ... Abbé Larrieu avait assisté à la conference."

20 Guilmant became professor of organ at the Paris Conservatoire in 1896 to replace Charles-Marie Widor, while also remaining as professor at the Schola Cantorum, which he co-founded.

chant.[21] As a spokesperson, Guilmant espoused his views on incorporating plainchant into liturgical organ music in *La tribune de Saint-Gervais*:[22]

> In our services, the grand-orgue is called upon generally to make itself heard in alternation with the choir: at mass, at the Kyrie, Gloria, Sanctus and Agnus Dei; at vespers, after the psalms; at the hymn, at the Magnificat. A certain number of organists have the habit ... of playing small pieces [in alternation] which have nothing in common with that which the choir chants, and that seems to me bad from a musical point of view because the melody ought to follow [the chant] in its rhythm and tonality ... It is necessary that, in the pieces which alternate, the organist play the Gregorian melody, or at least some versets which are based on these themes. I think that there are some very interesting things to write in the polyphonic style with the ancient tonalities [modes], and on these chants which are so beautiful. The German organists have composed some pieces based on the melody of chorales, forming a literature for the organ which is particularly rich; why should we not do the same with our Catholic melodies?[23]

This philosophy had an impact on many of Guilmant's pupils. In addition, Guilmant had a reputation as an excellent teacher and patient mentor, a fact corroborated by Séverac. He observed that Guilmant often interacted with students as a bon vivant, especially evident when Guilmant took his students out to cafes until late in the evening.[24]

Guilmant often gave lessons on a harmonium during his early tenure, as the Schola Cantorum did not yet possess an organ.[25] Records nonetheless indicate that Séverac began study with Guilmant in 1898 on an organ, most likely at La Trinité, where Guilmant was employed as resident organist. Séverac proceeded to play on various instruments in Paris, including the three-manual Cavaillé-Coll symphonic organ at Sainte-Clotilde, where Guilmant and other organists heard Séverac play.[26]

---

21 These works include *L'organiste liturgique*, op. 65 (which contain versets; Boca Raton, FL: Masters Music Publications, 2001), *Lamentation*, op. 45, no. 1 (New York: G. Shirmer, 1876), as well as music set to liturgical prayers and offertories, and *Impression grégorienne*, op. 90 (*Pièces nouvelles pour orgue*, Paris: A. Durand, 1904), the latter not literally quoting plainchant.

22 The Schola Cantorum subsequently began a series of publications of Vespers organ music similar to those in Guilmant's collection *Les vêpres du commun des saints*.

23 Alexandre Guilmant, "Du rôle de l'orgue dans les offices liturgiques," *La tribune de Saint-Gervais* 1 (September 1895), 11–12. Reprinted and translated by Edward Zimmerman and Lawrence Archbold, "Why Should We Not Do the Same with Our Catholic Melodies?: Guilmant's *L'organiste liturgique*, op. 65," in Lawrence Archbold and William J. Peterson, eds, *French Organ Music From the Revolution to Franck and Widor* (Rochester, NY: University of Rochester Press, 1995), 203.

24 Vincent d'Indy, *La Schola Cantorum, son histoire depuis sa fondation jusqu'en 1925* (Paris: Bloud et Gay, 1927), 33. D'Indy is citing comments by Louis Vierne.

25 Jean-Bernard Cahours d'Aspry, "Déodat de Séverac" (unpublished manuscript), 67.

26 César Franck (1822–90) played organ at Sainte-Clotilde from 1858 to 1890, but it was not yet a fashionable place upon his arrival. He later drew his students to Sunday masses at the church, including his pupil d'Indy, who heard Franck improvise. This led many others to attend the church, thereby leading to its fame as a venue in which to hear excellent organ improvisation. Although Franck's ability to improvise became legendary, comparisons on a

Guilmant's emphasis on ideals found in plainchant found its way into his organ teaching, which subsequently had an influence on Séverac's compositional approach. Guilmant required, for example, that Séverac improvise on plainchant melodies wherein phrases were to be rendered with the same suppleness and lyricism suggested by Pothier's editions, while including melodic embellishments and passing tones. These elements were first incorporated into Séverac's earliest surviving organ work, *Suite en mi* (1897–9), which Guilmant performed for Séverac at the professor's home.[27] Other characteristics in this work influenced by Guilmant include conjunct melodies, stark harmonies, modality, homogeneous texture, and limited registration.

Suite en Mi

Suite en mi, although dedicated to Guilmant, was correspondingly influenced by d'Indy.[28] Séverac submitted *Suite en mi* to d'Indy before publication, corroborated by Séverac's comments on d'Indy's reaction:

> D'Indy returned to me my organ suite that I gave to him before submitting it to the printers ... I will transcribe for you a note written by [d'Indy] at the end of my score; "This is quite good." In any case, this gives me great pleasure ... Human weakness hopes that when one has seriously worked on a piece, it will be recognized as "good" by competent people ... Tomorrow, the printers begin printing it.[29]

Bordes published the completed first movement to Séverac's *Suite en mi* in *Répertoire moderne de musique vocale et d'orgue de la Schola Cantorum* as part of a project undertaken from 1897 to 1899, in which 500 works by various composers were published. Bordes was initially inspired to undertake such a venture to counter the claim by professors at the Paris Conservatoire that he occupied himself only with

---

purely technical level with his contemporaries, Camille Saint-Saëns at the Madeleine, and Widor and Guilmant at Saint-Sulpice and La Trinité, has led to comments about Franck's less accomplished technique.

27 Many of Séverac's organ compositions were unpublished manuscripts that remain lost. These include 20 versets for harmonium (date unknown), *Sub Tuum* of 1889 (two motets for voice and organ), *Elévation* of 1890, and *Prélude in C* of 1892. Works composed while at the Schola Cantorum include *Intermède* (date unknown), *Canon par diminution* (date unknown), *Prélude de quatuor* of 1898, and *Marche religieuse* for organ, written in 1899. Late unpublished works that combine organ with other instruments include a set of variations for organ, oboe, violin, and cello based on the Catalan hymn *L'oracio de l'hort*, entitled *El divino de l'hort* (1916).

28 Séverac, *L'oeuvre pour orgue: suite en mi* (Longchamp: Editions Europart-Music, 1994).

29 Guillot, *Déodat de Séverac: écrits sur la musique*, 123. [Séverac letter to family, January 16, 1901.] "D'Indy m'a rendu ma Suite d'orgue que je lui avais confiée avant de la remettre au graveur ... Je vous transcris textuellement la note mise par le maître à la fin de ma partition. 'C'est tout à fait bien.' Cela me fait grand plaisir ... Le faiblesse humaine veut que, lorsqu'on a sérieusement travaillé à un ouvrage, il soit reconnu 'bon' par les gens compétents ... Demain le graveur commencera à faire les planches."

Gregorian chant and the music of Palestrina. Two months later, the movement was reprinted in the musical supplement to *La tribune de Saint-Gervais*, also facilitated by Bordes.[30] Séverac then had the entire suite published in 1901.

This work was given its première by Georges Ibos at a Société nationale de musique concert one year after its inception. Ibos replaced Paris Conservatoire pupil Juliette Toutain, who was prevented from performing the work by Théodore Dubois, then the director of the conservatory.[31] Although Dubois was a colleague of Franck at Sainte-Clotilde, the Paris Conservatoire was in direct competition with the Schola Cantorum, as the Schola Cantorum opposed most policies adapted by Dubois' institution. The success of the Schola Cantorum and its directors was often commented upon in newspapers and journals, further upsetting Dubois, and exacerbated by Séverac's 1896 defection from the Paris Conservatoire to the Schola Cantorum.

Suite en mi is in four movements: "Prélude," "Choral et Variations," "Fantaisie pastorale," and "Fugue," and Séverac combines two primary styles here—those emphasized on responsive and delicate actions found in the classical organs similar to the Rabiny in Saint-Félix de Lauragais, including the aforementioned suppleness and lyricism, and those rendered on symphonic organs capable of producing the sumptuousness and force typical of organ symphonies by Charles-Marie Widor and Louis Vierne.[32]

Characteristics in the suite that are prominent in d'Indy's music include cyclicism, chromaticism, and liturgical idées fixes, or "theme generators." The work is ensconced in counterpoint while containing both rhythmic and melodic repetition, fragmentation, and thematic allusion.

The opening "Prélude," for example, contains an initial chromatic appoggiatura in the form of an ascending minor second motive of E sharp to F sharp within the key of E minor, which thereby helps create tonal instability.[33]

---

30 See d'Indy, *La tribune de Saint-Gervais* (August, 1899).

31 Juliette Toutain was a pupil of Fauré.

32 See Daniel Paquette, CD program notes, *Déodat de Séverac: l'oeuvre pour orgue*, translated by David Nussenbaum; Erato Records, performed by Pierre Guillot (Erato, STU71224, 1985).

33 Ibid.

Example 4.1   Measures 1–5 of "Prélude," from *Suite en mi*

This motive occurs throughout the suite. In "Prélude," for example, the initial appoggiatura is repeated mostly in eighth note rhythms in virtually every measure, therefore becoming a major melodic as well as rhythmic element within the work. The opening to the second movement "Choral et Variations" contains the same ascending motive, this time as a major second in a somewhat slower rhythm of quarter notes.

Séverac's cyclic approach also becomes apparent when the same recurring motive is found in the fourth-movement fugue, now with a diatonic descending pattern of C to B, which is then employed as the incipit of the fugue subject. The subject is repeated in various forms throughout the fugue, including the incipit as passing tones, thereby illustrating Guilmant's pedagogical ideals.[34]

---

34 Séverac's formal strictness in the fugue is found in the use of an exposition, strettos, and augmented themes, albeit without countersubject.

Example 4.2   Measures 1–5 of "Fugue," from *Suite en mi*

Like other French organists involved in régionalisme, Séverac fused liturgical attributes found in chant together with regional elements. What makes this suite unusual, however, is Séverac's desire to personalize rural ideals by making allusions to specific localities. Séverac's "Fantaisie pastorale," from *Suite en mi*, for example, although containing a motive reminiscent of plainchant, also alludes to rustic origins in upbeat accents and long drones and pedal points suggesting the cornemusa, the bagpipe found in the southern French provinces, primarily Roussillon.[35] The cornemusa played a prominent part in local holidays and dances by accompanying Catalan sardanas, and was used in these cobla ensembles from the twelfth to the second half of the nineteenth centuries; in fact, the cornemusa was initially combined with the drum and fluviol, or one-handed flute, to form what was once the indispensable base of the cobla ensemble.

---

[35] Regionalist organ compositions were not uncommon and include such works as Camille Saint-Saëns' *Rhapsodie sur des cantiques Bretons* (New York: G. Schirmer, 1876).

Example 4.3   Measures 42–52 of "Fantaisie pastorale," from *Suite en mi*

The cobla ensemble also included shawm-like double reed instruments, or tiples and tenors. Séverac heard these instruments growing up near the Pyrenees mountains of southern France. His childhood included studying oboe as a result of this inspiration, as its timbre continued to remind him of its rustic origins. These pastoral roots are suggested in *Suite en mi* with the employment of the oboe stop in the opening to the third movement "Fantaisie pastorale."[36] The title of the movement further alludes to the en plein air aesthetic surrounding these two Catalan instruments.

Although Séverac often included cyclic elements in his early works, by 1902 he began to modify his use of the cyclic process, turning to the suite as a model for an increasingly rhapsodic, modified cyclic construction. With this technique, the composer found a balance between recurring elements as a method of unification and a way of narrating program music. Séverac often foreshadowed upcoming motives and reminisced over past programmatic themes, while always creating these recurring relationships. In this way, Séverac fused this program music together with incipient regional characteristics.

Petite Suite Scholastique

Regionalist elements combined with a liturgical style is found in Séverac's second organ suite *Petite suite scholastique, sur un thème de carillon languedocien* of 1912, or "Five Pieces for Organ or Harmonium."[37] The work, written 11 years after *Suite en mi* and published one year later, is in five movements: "Prélude" (Entrance),

---

36 Like most French organ composers in fin de siècle France, Séverac requested the precise timbre by stating organ registration.

37 *Orgelmusik der französischen romantik: petite suite scholastique* (Sankt Augustin, Germany: J. Butz, 1991), originally published, 1913.

"Méditation: pièce chromatique" (Offertory), "Prière-Choral" (Chorale Prayer), "Cantilène mélancolique" (Communion), and "Fanfare fuguée" (Exit).

Although composed during Séverac's tenure in Catalonia, this work does not incorporate allusions to sardana rhythms or cobla instrumentation. In fact, Séverac envisioned the work to have a liturgical function in the form of a five-part mass, which resembles the style of his early period. Nonetheless, it is based on a regional carillon theme from the French province of Languedoc which pervades all five movements.

Example 4.4   *Carillon languedocien* theme

This cyclic theme is incorporated in a quasi-fugal manner within the first movement "Prélude," where imitative polyphony in eighth notes is based on a subject, but not repeated intact, as would versions of a subject within the exposition of a fugue. This incipit of the carillon theme is employed in "Prélude" within a thick chromatic texture, united by long appoggiaturas and intensified by augmentation.[38] The antecedent of the theme is continually reiterated within the key of F minor.

Example 4.5   Measures 1–3 of "Prélude," from *Petite suite scholastique*

In the second movement "Méditation," the first four intervals of the carillon theme are repeated throughout. These pitches occur in the key of B flat major, but within highly chromatic passages coupled with a slower harmonic rhythm. As in the first movement, the theme occurs within stepwise motion, but differs in that it contains interchangeable major–minor modal interplay. This is in contrast to the first movement, which possesses all minor intervals within the opening theme.[39]

---

38   "Prélude" is dedicated to Abbé Bonnet, archpriest in the Catalan town of Céret, where Séverac, Picasso, and other artists were living. "Prière-Choral" is dedicated to Abbé Adoui, Vicar of Saint-Félix-Caraman. "Méditation," dedicated to Abbé Jean de Bonnefoy, priest in the town of Nailloux, recalls various organ works of Louis Vierne in title as well as aesthetic. Vierne also composed organ works based on carillon themes, including *Carillon de Westminister* ("Pièces de fantaisie en quatre suites").

39   Cadences in both are approached by upper and lower neighbors.

The theme returns in a more literal fashion within the third movement "Prière-Choral," albeit transposed to B flat minor, and in the fourth movement "Cantilène mélancolique," it returns to the original key but now metrically transformed into 9/8.

Within the final movement "Fanfare fuguée," the theme is harmonically and rhythmically augmented into a jaunty 12/8 meter within F major, thereby highlighting Séverac's overall predilection for major–minor modal interchanges by commencing the suite in a minor key while concluding in the parallel major.

***

Despite the fact that Séverac's surviving organ music remains scant, his organ style is nonetheless incorporated into many other genres. In *Versets pour les vêpres d'un confesseur non pontife, d'après les thèmes liturgiques*, a work based on a tradition established by Guilmant building on Gregorian chant themes, the "Fidelis servus et prudens" section contains long trumpet tones in the upper voice combined with modality.[40] The treatment of this section is similar to that found in Séverac's tragédie-lyrique *Héliogabale*, when Gregorian chant text is heard during the baptism scene of Claudius in Act II, Scene 4.

The carillon theme in "Cantilène mélancholique" from *Petite suite scholastique* is comparable to passages within the 'Angélus du soir' section of "Vers le mas en fête," from Séverac's piano suite *En Languedoc*.[41] This comparison is not only made because the piano work contain an almost elegiac sweetness reminiscent of sections found in *Petite suite scholastique*, but also because the melodic major second interplay in the carillon theme within the organ work echoes angelus bells, which Séverac imitates in many of his piano works.

Example 4.6a   From Measure 3 to "Cantilène mélancolique," from *Petite suite scholastique*

---

40   Paquette, CD program notes, *Déodat de Séverac: l'oeuvre pour orgue*, 2–3. The work includes "Domine quinque talenta," "Euge serve bone," "Fidelis servus et prudens," "Beatus III servus," and "Serve bone fidelis."

41   This interplay is also evident in other compositions, including Séverac's opera *Le coeur du moulin*, wherein the same two intervals are highlighted, as Séverac indicates l'angélus within the score.

Example 4.6b   Measures 192–195 of "Vers le mas en fête," from *En Languedoc*

Additional organ-like passages similar to those found in both organ suites discussed here are located in "Sur l'étang, le soir" ("On the Pond, Evening"), from Séverac's piano suite *En Languedoc*. These include a succession of chords moving in parallel motion sustained by an active bass. Three clefs common in organ works are notated to accommodate this structure.

Example 4.7a   Measures 49–53 of "Prélude," from *Suite en mi*

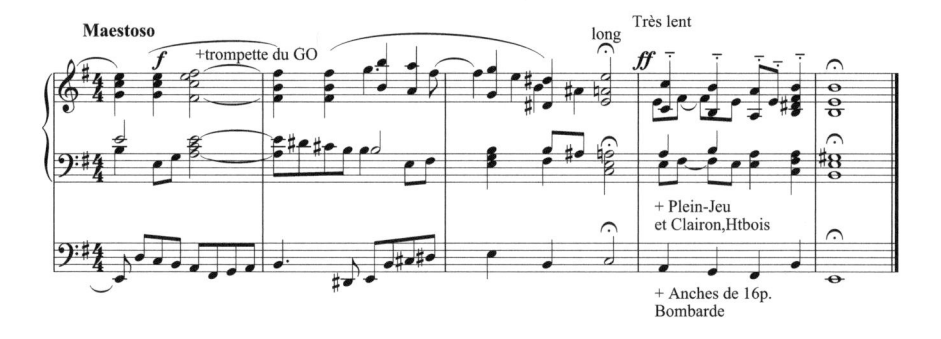

Example 4.7b   Measures 101–109 from "Sur l'étang, le soir," from *En Languedoc*

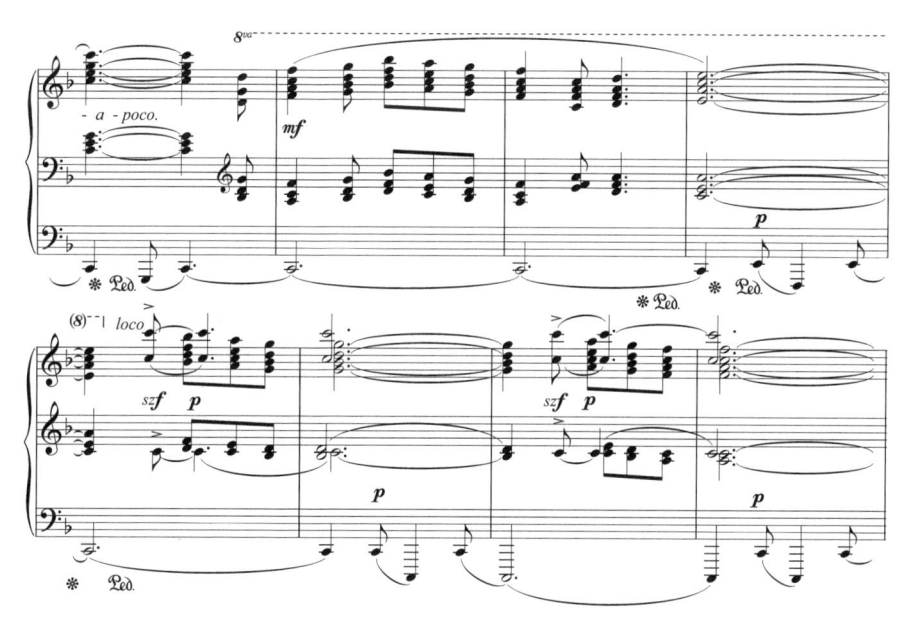

Another genre where organ-like elements can be found is in the piano part to one of Séverac's mélodies, "Les cors" ("The Horns" 1898), set to a text by southern French poet Paul Rey. The piano writing in this song contains upper register figurations suggestive of organ technique. This is combined with a baroque-like organ cadenza at the conclusion of the song.[42]

---

42 Other types of prayer are specified in Séverac's piano suites, as in the sections entitled 'Les rogations' and 'Le glas,' in "La grêle," from *Le chant de la terre*. Nuptial bells are included in "Les moissons," from the same suite, and Séverac calls for 'Cloches au loin', in "Epilogue: le jour des noces," also from *Le chant de la terre*. In "Coin de cimetière, au printemps," from *En Languedoc*, 'Le chant doucement marqué, comme des cloches lointaines' is indicated within the 'Dies Irae' section.

See Graham Johnson, "Program notes to CD," *Songs by Déodat de Séverac*, performed by Graham Johnson, François Le Roux, and Patricia Rozario (Hyperion A66983, 1998), 20. Johnson notes that this is the only song influenced by the "brooding" style of Albéric Magnard. Magnard taught Séverac during d'Indy's leave of absence.

Debussy's song "Le son du cor" (from *Trois mélodies*, 1901) contains open fifth intervals on the piano together with an obscured rhythm in 9/8 meter, while the vocal line is in 3/4.

As stated, Séverac's organ works reflected an interest in medieval and Renaissance sacred music as well as southern French folk idioms. These characteristics were emphasized within the Schola Cantorum curriculum by d'Indy, Guilmant, and Bordes, who collectively employed these genres and elements into their own compositions. Séverac's exposure to and subsequent interest in Gregorian chant and provincial identity led to his incorporating these elements into his two published organ suites, *Suite en mi* and *Petite suite scholastique*. Yet Séverac's organ music is unusual in that he pays homage to regionalism in personal and specific ways, so that certain localities within France are suggested.[43]

Eighth notes are therefore set against eighth note triplets. Séverac's song predates Debussy's work by three years.

43 Though Séverac helped wounded soldiers during World War I and was himself later confined to a medical center due to kidney failure, he nonetheless found opportunities to play and improvise on organs within hospital chapels, thereby retaining his relationship with the instrument.

Chapter 5

Songs

Séverac composed 51 songs for solo voice and piano. These consist of three collections with three pieces in each set, two songs originally written for the theater, 13 individual compositions that remain unpublished, as well as 29 separately published works. Séverac also harmonized three groups of indigenous French melodies that he gathered from written sources, some of which were originally collected from the oral tradition during the early part of the nineteenth century. Séverac then applied modified restatements of pre-existing melodies while also adding instrumental refrains.

Most of Séverac's works are mélodies and some are written as chansons. As Pierre Bernac cites in *The Interpretation of French Song*: "There is, in French, a very sharp difference between *mélodie* and *chanson*. *Mélodie*, which is the French equivalent of *lied*, denotes serious song, concert song, whereas *chanson* refers to a folk song, a popular song or night-club songs. If some composers of mélodies occasionally use the word *chanson* in the title of their songs, it is to suggest that they are intentionally in a very simple style, or in folk song style: i.e., Poulenc: *Chansons villageoises*. It may also be because the word *chanson* has been used in the title of the poem: Duparc: *Chanson triste*."[1]

The majority of Séverac's songs are either through-composed or in modified-strophic form, and the few that are strophic are either children's songs or folk-like pieces. There is much registral and textural change within most of his mélodies, and Séverac incorporated a moderate degree of modulation. Ostinatos are often prevalent, as are varied rhythms, harmonies, and textures. The song "Aubade" contains the greatest amount of measures, 110 within an allegretto tempo, and the least amount is found in "Temps de neige," with a total of 38 measures without tempo indication; the average song composed by Séverac contains approximately 45 measures, with tempos ranging from lent to allegretto.

Séverac often chose symbolist poems as the basis for his mélodies, including works by Charles Baudelaire, Paul Verlaine, and Belgian symbolist Maurice Maeterlinck, whose play *Pelléas et Melisande* was set by Debussy in the opera of the same name.[2] Séverac also chose various regionalist poets from southern France, including Paul Rey, Prosper Estieu, and Marguerite Navarre. Historical poets include the eighteenth-century regionalist Goudouli and medieval poet Charles d'Orléans. Séverac also set music to works by Edgar Allan Poe, Emile Verhaeren, François Coppée, Henri Gauthiers-Villars, and Louise Espinasse-Mongenet. Séverac himself wrote the words to two of his mélodies.

---

1   Pierre Bernac, *The Interpretation of French Song* (New York: Norton, 1978), xiii–xiv.
2   Although Baudelaire was not, strictly speaking, a symbolist poet, his work *Correspondances* was one of the first poems to suggest the idea of symbolism in nineteenth-century French poetry.

Séverac's songs span his entire career. His unpublished songs date from his youth and published works span a 20-year period from 1896 to three years before his death. Stylistically the songs are diverse and reflect a varying level of sophistication. The songs are influenced by characteristics employed by various composers, including diatonic and triadic harmonies found in certain songs of Hector Berlioz, the harmonic ambiguity of Richard Wagner and Modest Mussorgsky, declamatory phrases found in Claude Debussy's *Pelléas et Melisande*, Impressionist characteristics, which include acciaccaturas, unresolved dominant seventh and parallel ninth chords, added sixth and seventh intervals employed as colorist devices, whole-tone scales, and onomatopoeia in the form of church bells. Some of Séverac's songs employ historical forms, allusions, and references, such as an eighteenth-century period pastiche imitating the harpsichord, a medieval rondeau, and modality combined with an absence of bar lines alluding to Gregorian chant. Many of the aforementioned characteristics are related to chronological stages within Séverac's lifetime. Earlier songs reflect characteristics emphasized at the Schola Cantorum followed by songs that contain Impressionist elements. Other elements are employed irrespective of these developments, such as historical allusions. Yet Séverac's uniqueness is apparent in regionalist works which include texts by southern French poets that often describe nature, as well as songs that contain characteristics found in Catalan and Andalusian music.[3]

Schola Cantorum Influence

One of Séverac's earliest published songs is "Ritournelle" ("Ritornello," 1896), set to words by François Coppée (1842–1908) and which includes elements found in the early French Romantic style of Hector Berlioz, particularly in "Villanelle" from *Les nuits d'été*.[4] Both songs contain staccato chords and repeated note accompaniment, all with elements common in the mid-classical period, such as conjunct and highly tonal melodies combined with simple triadic harmonies; these characteristics are then embedded within an early Romantic period decorum.[5] The title "Ritournelle" refers to a modified musical but not poetic restatement of the primary stanza, as well as the employment of an instrumental refrain.

---

3 Songs containing Catalan and Andalusian elements are presented in this chapter rather than in Part III of this book because of the small number of examples employed. There are not enough songs within these two styles to warrant separating these songs and placing them into a different chapter.

4 Séverac's songs composed before 1897 contain simple accompaniments. His earliest songs performed in Paris date from 1897 and include the rondellus "Prends mon âme" ("Take my Soul," 1898), composed to a text by Paul Rey and performed at the Société nationale de musique in 1899. Others include "Les Huns" (1898), set to Paul Rey's text and containing modality also found in many other works influenced by Schola Cantorum values, including "Les hiboux."

5 Graham Johnson notes that this song's piquant qualities are also found in Bizet's *L'arlésienne*, Suite no. 1 (1872), and its impish characteristics are found in Edouard Lalo's songs. See Graham Johnson, "Program notes to CD," *Songs by Déodat de Séverac*, performed by Graham Johnson, François Le Roux, and Patricia Rozario (Hyperion A66983, 1998), 11.

Although Séverac did later collect folk songs and harmonize them within this classical period aesthetic, the sprightly but elegant style is rare in Séverac's songs.

Example 5.1a   Measures 1–6 of Berlioz' "Villanelle"

Example 5.1b   Measures 1–5 of Séverac's "Ritournelle"

Another of Séverac's earlier songs is "Les hiboux" ("Owls," 1898), in which the owl is depicted with grace notes sounded to open fourth intervals. This work, set to a text by Charles Baudelaire, is slow and haunting, illustrating the stationary and mysterious character of the owl. The accompaniment possesses a mournful quality that foreshadows similar passages in Séverac's opera *Le coeur du moulin* (1909).[6] In this mélodie, Séverac employs unresolved dominant seventh chords, which briefly alternate with added sixth and seventh intervals as colorist devices, a technique later used with greater abandon during his Impressionist phase.

---

6   This mournful quality is found in many of Modest Mussorgsky's songs.

Séverac's first compositional stage was influenced by characteristics promoted within the Schola Cantorum.[7] The piano accompaniment in "Les cors" ("The Horns"), for example, set to a text by Paul Rey, suggests organ improvisation, since the lower register bass coupled with upper register figurations imply organ technique. There is also a baroque-like cadenza at the end of the work alluding to the organ. This occurrence follows references to eighteenth-century hunting horns.[8]

Another work containing characteristics championed at the Schola Cantorum is "Renouveau" ("Spring" 1898), dedicated to Charles Bordes. Historical self-consciousness is reflected by the opening theme in the piano, which is written in the Dorian mode while the song is set to a text by medieval poet Charles d'Orléans (1394–1465). The song contains octosyllabic lines and the text is a rondel, denoting a type of Latin text structurally similar to that found in the medieval rondeau, dating from the eleventh century and a forerunner of the French rondeau. The conjunct melody sounded by the piano in this song not only alludes to medieval music, but the vocal line also emphasizes triplets employed during the Middle Ages to symbolize the trinity. Séverac's chosen meters oscillate between 3/4, 6/8, 9/8, and 12/8 nineteen times.

Rather than placing an emphasis on spring, the text highlights a winter that has passed, and the slow-moving Dorian mode in the melody helps maintain the stark aesthetic found in the text: "The season has laid its mantle by, of wind and cold and rain."[9] This particular text by d'Orléans was later set by Debussy after Séverac composed this song, and Saint-Saëns subsequently used the poem two decades later.[10]

---

[7] Much of the harmony in this work is similar to various songs by Chausson, Duparc, and Franck.

[8] Séverac most likely employed this device as a reference to eighteenth-century organ music.

[9] Déodat de Séverac, *Trois mélodies et quatre pages pianistiques inédites* (Paris: Presses de l'Université de Paris-Sorbonne, 2002), 13. "Le temps a laissié son manteau de vent, de froidure et de pluye."

[10] Séverac's "Renouveau" was composed in 1904 and Saint-Saëns' version was written in 1921.

Example 5.2 Measures 1–7 of "Renouveau"

Another song paying homage to Schola Cantorum values is "Soleils couchants," or "Paysages tristes" ("Setting Suns," or "Sad Landscapes"), composed in 1898 and dedicated to d'Indy. The song alludes to Gregorian chant in the lack of bar lines and the use of repeated notes, modal structure, and lack of instructions for dynamics. The music is set to a text by Paul Verlaine (1844–96) containing lines of five syllables each. The music speaks of the barrenness and melancholy of twilight by flirting with the Dorian and Aeolian modes, as B natural and B flat are used interchangeably.[11] Parallel fifth intervals in the bass also provide an aura of archaism.[12]

---

11 Igor Stravinsky and Edgar Varèse later set this text to music.
12 This sense of archaism is often found in many of Debussy's songs.

Example 5.3 Beginning of "Paysages tristes" ("Soleils couchants")

Impressionist Works

The first song to abandon Schola Cantorum influences and embrace Impressionism is the regionalist song "L'éveil de Pâques" ("Easter Awakening," 1899), set to a text by the celebrated Belgian poet Emile Verhaeren (1855–1916).[13] This is one of Séverac's earliest works to highlight onomatopoeia in the form of Easter church bells.[14] Impressionist techniques include the whole-tone scale played by the piano within the second stanza and a slower harmonic rhythm and tempo within the third verse. The latter section also demonstrates Séverac's appreciation for Christian faith clothed within his regionalist aesthetic: "Figures of Christ pass by, offering charity; and I am good and clean and upright by my will, although old sins always freeze my soul."[15] The song concludes following a brief interlude in the piano, which then returns to the original tempo and rhythm for the final stanza. Major second intervals are employed here as a final allusion to bells.

Another Impressionist song with references to bells is "Le ciel est, par-dessus le toit" ("The Sky is Above the Roof," 1901). The text, written by Paul Verlaine, was employed by Gabriel Fauré in "Prison" and by Reynaldo Hahn in "D'une prison," and describes Verlaine shooting Arthur Rimbaud following a disagreement, for which Verlaine was subsequently imprisoned.[16] The work had its première at the Société nationale de musique in 1901 and was reviewed favorably by critic Pierre Lalo, who stated: "This young musician has a natural expression of gold which is nothing to look down upon, and which lets us have hope for the future."[17]

The song evokes a soft melancholy accompanied by fluid bell-like sonorities reflecting the text: "The bell you see in the sky gently rings."[18] There are often

---

13 Séverac had the première of his *Sonate* for piano (1900) in Brussels and Vincent d'Indy had many of his works, including his opera *Fervaal*, performed in Belgium, so there was a direct connection between Schola Cantorum composers and premières in Belgium. Séverac also used texts by other Belgian poets (including Maeterlinck's "L'infidèle"). See Michel Stockhem, "Vincent d'Indy en Belgique: réseaux et influences," in *Vincent d'Indy et son temps*, edited by Manuela Schwartz (Sprimont, Belgium: Mardaga Press, 2006), 87–98.

14 Johnson, "Program notes to CD," *Songs by Déodat de Séverac*, 27. "L'éveil de Pâques." "Les vieilles mains d'argent des coutumes locales, et carillons et bruit de fête à pleins bourdons."

This multi-layered quasi-bell étude begins by outlining a parallel octave pentatonic scale within the low registers of the piano, in some ways echoing Mussorgsky's "The Hut on Fowl's Legs," from *Pictures at an Exhibition*.

15 Ibid. "Des Christs passent dans l'air et font leur charité; et je suis bon et net et droit par volonté, bien que le vieux péché gèle toujours mon âme."

16 Joseph Canteloube states that Séverac composed this song when he was still a student at the Toulouse Conservatory, despite contrary evidence to it being composed in 1901. See Joseph Canteloube, *Déodat de Séverac* [1st Edition, Paris, 1929] (Béziers, France: Société de musicologie de Languedoc, 1984), 43.

17 Jean-Bernard Cahours d'Aspry, "Déodat de Séverac" (unpublished manuscript), 127. "Ce jeune musicien a un don d'expression naturelle qui n'est point à dédaigner et qui laisse concevoir des espérances pour l'avenir."

18 Séverac, *Douze mélodies* (Paris: Rouart, Lerolle et Cie., 1924), 2. "La cloche, dans le ciel qu'on voit, Doucement tinte."

simultaneous conflicting harmonies and this is often combined with a seemingly arbitrary alteration of directional tones within structurally important chords.[19] Séverac also employed flatted seventh chords and added sixth tones. Acciaccaturas within the piano writing allude to birds, while a whole-tone scale accompanies the text: "A bird you see on the tree plaintively sings."[20]

Séverac's "Un rêve" ("A Dream," 1901) illustrates the influence of Debussy's *Pelléas et Mélisande*, primarily in the use of undulating bass rhythms suggesting the twilight world of half-shades and speech rhythms in place of discernible melody.[21] The song's dotted rhythm is employed as a unifying device. Text painting is also apparent as E major descends to E flat on the word "dream" when the text reads: "That holy dream, that holy dream, while the whole world grumbled."[22] Séverac's text is taken from a poem by Edgar Allan Poe (1809–49) and translated by symbolist poet Stéphane Mallarmé (1842–98). The work is dedicated to Séverac's friend and colleague, symbolist painter Odilon Redon (1840–1916), who in 1902 suggested to Séverac that he set Poe's poem to music.[23]

Another song is "Temps de neige" of 1903 ("Snowfall"), set to the text of Henri Gauthiers-Villars.[24] Carillon sounds are heard in open fourth intervals preceded by acciaccaturas, but there is no section in the text referring to bell sounds. Instead, a silent whitened landscape is suggested by pandiatonic piano writing.[25]

One of Séverac's most poignant melodies is found in "Chanson de la nuit durable" of 1910 ("Song of Endless Night"), composed upon moving to the Catalan province of Roussillon. The song contains a broad arch-like structure combined with harmonic sensuality and a nocturnal ambiance.[26] The text, written by Louise Espinasse-Mongenet, is haunting in its imagery and Séverac matches this richness with constantly shifting harmonies. The song is about an enduring relationship, as a man asks a woman whom he loves to wander with him underneath the stars and

---

19 Elaine Brody, "The Piano Works of Déodat de Séverac: A Stylistic Analysis" (PhD Dissertation, New York University, 1964), 343.

20 Séverac, *Douze mélodies*, 2–3. "Un oiseau, sur l'arbre qu'on voit, chante sa plainte." The general poetic mood of this song is reminiscent of Debussy's "En sourdine" and "Clair de lune," from his song cycle *Fêtes galantes*, also set to texts by Verlaine. The work also resembles Charles Bordes' "Sur un vieil air," and the shimmering perpetual motion in the piano is also indicative of Albert Roussel's "Le jardin mouillé."

21 The orchestral-like pianism in "Un rêve" also echoes Debussy's "La flûte de Pan" and "Le tombeau des naïades," from Debussy's song cycle *Chanson de bilitis* (1901; Paris: Jobert, 1971).

22 Ibid., 11. "Ce rêve béni, ce rêve béni, pendant que le monde entier grondait."

23 The work had its première at the Libre esthétique in Brussels in 1905.

24 The work is in a modified ternary form.

25 This pandiatonicism resembles Debussy's "The Snow is Dancing," from his piano suite *Children's Corner*. Debussy's work had its première three years after Séverac composed this song.

26 These characteristics are reminiscent of songs by other composers who employ Impressionist techniques, including Debussy in "Le balcon." [1888; Paris: A. Durand, 1904]. In Debussy's song, the first line of each verse is repeated at the end of the verse. Elements from Chausson's "Cantique à l'épouse" (1896) are also apparent in the nocturnal ambience within Séverac's song.

find comfort in him. He then compares this form of happiness to mortals who die in oblivion but without strife, where they will not awaken or be ruled by space and time—but the only thing that will survive is their love surviving through the ages. A close relationship between music and text is apparent when Séverac sustains a chord with the words: "I wish the hours were dead for us, no more time!"[27] When the word "time" appears, a faster moving rhythm begins in the form of a gentle ostinato, which continues for six measures.[28] This song is Séverac's last to incorporate Impressionist characteristics, but here he combines these elements with modality.[29] These elements are apparent in the opening flourish on a pentatonic scale, similar to the opening of "En tartane," from his piano suite *Cerdaña*. The ensuing A major chord with added seconds and sixths again reflects the Impressionist style. This is followed by Impressionist harmonic ambiguity when the song becomes stagnant harmonically. Séverac juxtaposed repeated major second grace notes here together with an ambiguous B–F tritone dyad.

Regionalist Works

Séverac's régionalisme within his mélodies is reflected in his fondness for texts which describe specific outdoor scenes and is what helps make his songs personal and relatively unique. Some regionalist works include characteristics borrowed from his progenitors as well as contemporaries, while others are less derivative. One song containing Impressionist techniques intertwined with régionalisme is "A l'aube dans la montagne" of 1903 ("At Dawn in the Mountains"). Séverac evokes far-away sounds of dawn angelus bells as the composition alludes to folk-like music from the Pyrenees mountains. This is combined with a symbolist text written by Séverac, as well as Impressionist harmonies, thereby causing Séverac to be nicknamed the "Mistral of Sonorities."[30] Séverac spoke of the song:

> While the Angelus bells sleep, the atmosphere is calm, almost still. It evokes a sort of vague murmur, shivers which pass through nature as it awakens. Little by little, dawn comes. The melody is inflamed like the heavens while the accompanying tones multiply and vibrate more and more. By small successive touches, of increasingly vivaciousness, modulations follow a vocal line that ascends higher and higher, thus translating daybreak ... that awakens. Then the Angelus bells awaken.[31]

---

27 Ibid., 28. "Je veux que les heures devant nous soient mortes!"
28 Ibid. "Il n'y aura plus de temps."
29 This modality suggests Franck's influence.
30 Johnson, "Program notes to CD," *Songs by Déodat de Séverac*, 33.
31 Jean-Bernard Cahours d'Aspry, *Déodat de Séverac: musicien du soleil méditerranéen* (Belgium: Séguier, 2002), 87–8. "Tandis que l'angélus sommeille encore dans les clochers, précise le compositeur, l'atmosphère est calme, presque immobile. Elle évoque dans une sorte de murmure en peu vague les frissons qui passent dans la nature qui s'éveille. Peu a peu l'aube se lève. La mélodie s'enflamme comme le ciel tandis que les timbres de l'accompagnement se multiplient et vibrent de plus en plus. Par petites touches successives, de vivacité croissante, les modulations se succèdent sur une ligne vocale de plus en plus haute, traduisant l'aurore ... qui s'éveille. Alors l'Angélus s'éveille dans les clochers."

Impressionist techniques are part of this relationship between music and words. The song begins with a G minor chord with an added sixth, which then proceeds to the Impressionist device of unresolved parallel ninth chords. A whole-tone scale is sounded in the middle section as the text reads: "Wood thrushes chirr in the brush, towards the laughing echoes."[32] Bell-like sonorities are heard in the middle register of the piano as F against E flat and added upper register grace notes enhance carillon sounds.

The music in "A l'aube dans la montagne" closely reflects the text. Examples transpire throughout the song, as when the text reads "poplars in their pride stretch their branches," while the melody leaps up a major seventh, or in the lyrics "the crimson heights above," as the melody ascends a perfect fifth.[33] The song is in G minor but finally resolves in a culminating climax on a G major chord with an added sixth, thereby raising the key from minor to major and therefore symbolizing the rising sun in the poem.

This song also reflects the influence of speech rhythms and French prosody found in Debussy's *Pelléas et Mélisande*. In fact, Séverac heard Debussy perform sections of the opera just before composing the work. Syllabic text settings with conjunct melodies create the quasi-recitative style, as the song builds in tension over a long period, again reminiscent of Debussy's work.[34] The text speaks of dawn and the sounds of nature, and the music and setting here is reminiscent of Act IV, Scene 4 of *Pelléas et Mélisande*.[35]

---

[32] Séverac, 16. "Les grives stridulent, dans les taillis, vers les échos rieurs."

[33] Ibid., 14-15 "autour des peupliers qui fusent à l'infini;" "des sommets en sanglantés."

[34] Graham Johnson notes that this song also resembles André Caplet's "Fôret" in this regard. See Johnson, "Program notes to CD," *Songs by Déodat de Séverac*, 33.

[35] Johnson draws parallels between the last section of the song ("Lors, une rumeur de joie s'élève des hameaux et des villes") and the climax of *Pelléas et Mélisande*, where Pelléas is about to die and sings "toutes les étoiles tombent." He also compares the sextuplet piano accompaniment in the song's final page to Debussy's piano work *L'isle joyeuse*.

Example 5.4a   Measures 32–34 of Séverac's "A l'aube dans la montagne"

Example 5.4b   6 Measures at Rehearsal 35 of Act IV, Scene 4 of Debussy's *Pelléas et Mélisande* (piano-vocal score)

[Musical notation with vocal line text:]
C'est le der_nier soir... le der_nier soir... Il faut que tout fi_nis_ se... J'ai jou_ comme un en_fant au_ tour d' une cho_ se que je ne soup con nais pas.___ J'ai jou é en reve, au tour des piè_ ges de la des_ti_ né ___ e...

The regionalist song "Le chevrier" ("The Goat Herd;" 1897–98) is Séverac's earliest song heralding the southern countryside. The text, written in Provence by southern French poet Paul Rey, speaks of a nomadic goat herder's loneliness and lack of love in the mountains of southern France. The opening piano line reflects this by depicting a flute played by the goat herder, a reference Séverac used in many other works, including the opening to his piano suite *Cerdaña*. The melodic line in this song suggests folk music through cadential upper neighbor half-step figures as well as lower neighbor whole-step interplay, which culminate in a suspension with D flat sounded together with an F minor chord, eventually resolving to the pitch C in the final measure.[36] The use of this dramatic device in "Le chevrier" distinguishes this

---

[36] The music touches upon several other influences, including the songs of Henri Duparc. In Duparc's song "Au pays où se fait la guerre," for example, oscillating tremolos simulate orchestral swells employed by Wagner in his orchestral writing; Johnson, "Program notes to CD,"

song from others by Séverac in its inherently Wagnerian style. Additional Wagnerian influence includes a through-composed structure with stanzas that are broken up with ever-changing melodic contours.

Finally, another regionalist work is "Chanson de Blaisine" of 1900 ("Blaisine's Song"), which was originally composed as incidental music for a one-act drama by Maurice Magre entitled *L'ouvrier qui pleure*.[37] Séverac instructed that the song was to be sung in the wings off-stage. The music suggests folk music from Languedoc in its melodic shape and piano line. Additionally, as in "Le Chevrier," the piano writing imitates the southern French Pyrenees flute. "Chanson de Blaisine" also makes references to Spain and mule drivers with two allusions to mule bells, similarly found in Séverac's piano suite *Cerdaña* composed a decade later.

Late Works

Séverac employed at least three different styles while living in Catalonia during the last decade of his life. One approach was to use a contained Romanticism found in his "Ma poupée chérie" of 1914 ("My Dearest Dolly"), composed for and dedicated to his daughter Magali.[38] The simplicity of this "Berceuse-chanson pour une petite (ou grande) fille" is reminiscent of Séverac's set of piano pieces depicting childhood found in *En vacances*, composed the same year as "Ma poupée chérie."[39]

Séverac's late regionalist works reflecting Catalan and Andalusian elements are found in *Trois pièces en langue d'oc* ("Three Pieces on Languedoc Poems," 1910), which consist of "Chanson pour le petit cheval" ("Song for the Little Horse"), "Aubade," and "Chant pour Noël" ("Christmas song").[40]

"Chanson pour le petit cheval" is set to a text by Languedoc poet Prosper Estieu and contains Spanish elements, including triplet rhythms leading to Phrygian cadences characteristic of much Andalusian popular music.[41] The canter of a pony on a parched southern French landscape is imitated by the piano. There are also allusions to bells in the inner voices with a more ominous death knell that reflects the text: "Let us turn around and escape this death knell! My love! My love! My

---

Songs by Déodat de Séverac, 12–13. For more information on Wagner's influence on French song, see Ralph Scott Grover, "The Influence of Franck, Wagner, and Debussy on Representative Works of Ernest Chausson" (PhD Dissertation, University of North Carolina at Chapel Hill, 1966).

37 The manuscript to the play *L'ouvrier qui pleure* remains at the Toulouse town library.

38 Various composers created works depicting children, including Debussy, Ravel, and Russian composer Modest Mussorgsky. Mussorgsky's song cycle *The Nursery*, for example, was within this vein, despite Mussorgsky's more harmonically complex language.

39 Rocking rhythms here also suggest Schumann's piano work *Kinderszenen*, op. 15.

40 *Trois pièces en langue d'oc* is sometimes cited in the Catalan language as *Flors d'occitania*, "Chanson pour le petit cheval" as "Canson pel cabalet," and "Chant pour Noël" as "Cant per Nadal."

41 These elements are reminiscent of Ravel's "Alborada del gracioso," from his piano work *Miroirs* (1904–5).

love is dead!"[42] "Aubade" was composed to a text by poet Marguerite Navarre, who was one of Séverac's literary friends from Languedoc. Like "A l'aube dans la montagne," the song evokes dawn. The work, however, is an eighteenth-century evocation and therefore period pastiche. The piano part suggests a harpsichord or spinet, corroborated by Séverac's instructions: "cherchez une sonorité d'épinette."

"Chant de Noël" is set in a folk-like 6/8 meter to a text by Languedoc poet Goudouli and translated by Paul Gravollet. It is in the style of canticles from Languedoc published in *Recueil de cantiques spirituels provençaux et français* (1759).[43]

Harmonized Folk Songs

This section is not intended to be a detailed analysis of Séverac's harmonizations, but rather a brief discussion of these arrangements, thus providing a glimpse into the types of folk songs in which Séverac was interested, and the manner in which he treated these songs in his arrangements.

Séverac became involved in a project in 1906 at the Schola Cantorum designed to collect French songs from written and oral sources and have them published. Arrangements of these songs were included and arrangers were placed under the auspices of the Schola Cantorum with Louis Bourgault-Ducoudray as head of the committee. On the committee were Louis Laloy, Alexis Rouart, Julien Tiersot, Gabriel Fauré, Vincent d'Indy, Frédéric Mistral, and Séverac.[44] The society created a journal published three times yearly entitled *Chansons de France* and provided Séverac with the opportunity to edit publications containing folk music.[45]

---

42 Séverac, *Douze mélodies*, 36. "Retournons-nous, pour fuir ce glas! Ma mie! ma mie! ma mie est morte."

43 A. Caen, *Recueil de cantiques spirituels provençaux et français* (original publication, 1759, 2nd ed. P. Chalopin, Imprimeur-Librarie, c.1800).

Another work by Séverac composed at this time is *Canço dels invadits* ("No Passereu"), set to a text by Apeles Mestres. Other songs include "Les Hussards de la Garde," "Dans les prisons de Nantes," (two versions), and "Jean des Grignottes."

44 Despite the fact that the Schola Cantorum officially gave priority to indigenous French folk music, there were some figures from the Paris Conservatoire who also studied indigenous music, including Louis Bourgault-Ducoudray (1840–1910), Professor of Music History at the Paris Conservatoire from 1878–1908, and Maurice Emmanuel (1862–1938), who replaced Bourgault-Ducoudray in 1909.

45 According to Andrea Musk, Séverac began to theorize that southern French folk song was influenced by that of Algeria, and that a study of Algerian songs would help musicians better comprehend the development of folk song in France. He even proposed a trip to Algeria, but was denied the funds. Minutes of correspondence between the Ministère de l'instruction publique et des beaux-arts detail Séverac's contention, corroborated by Bordes and Bourgault-Ducoudray. See *Minute de lettre: ministère de l'instruction publique et des beaux-arts*, January 27, 1911; Private Collection, restated in Andrea Musk, "Aspects of Regionalism in French Music during the Third Republic: the Schola Cantorum, d'Indy, Séverac and Canteloube" (PhD Dissertation, Oxford University, 1999), 136.

The publication lasted until 1913 and issued arrangements by various composers, including Vincent d'Indy's *Chansons du Vivarais*, Jean Poueigh's songs from the Gascogne and Haut Languedoc regions, René de Castéra's harmonizations of the Landes region, Paul Ladmirault's collection of songs from Brittany, Julien Tiersot's *La Bresse*, and Joseph Canteloube's songs from the Auvergne and Quercy regions. Séverac himself harmonized three groups of indigenous French songs— *Les vieilles chansons de France* (1905), *Chansons du XVIII siècle* (1905, 1907) and *Chansons populaires harmonisées* (1906).[46] Séverac harmonized these songs to pre-existing melodies that he gathered from various written sources, some of which were collected from oral sources by others during the early part of the nineteenth century. Séverac then applied modified restatements of pre-existing melodies while also adding instrumental refrains for voice and piano.

Many of Séverac's arrangements were for the popular singer Yvette Guilbert (1865–1944), whose role at the Salle d'Harnicourt and other salon venues was to perform folk song recitals supported by changes of costume, all with an array of facial expressions and gestures not encouraged in the more traditional concert halls where art song was performed. Guilbert's characters included murderers, drug addicts, as well as comedy parts and pastoral figures, the latter sometimes arising in the form of shepherds and shepherdesses. Her songs often contained conversations where she delineated characters with different voices. Her performances were designed to disturb as well as amuse, and she was therefore admired by such composers as Giuseppe Verdi and Charles Gounod. Some of Séverac's folk song harmonizations were first performed by Guilbert in 1904.

Guilbert also participated in male roles, including drinking songs such as "Pour le jour des rois" ("For Twelfth Night"), found in Book I to Séverac's collection *Chansons du XVII et XVIII siècle*. She sang about love rivalry in "Offrande" ("Offering") as well as vowel sounds alluding to risqué behavior in "Ba be bi bo bu!," both collected by Séverac and harmonized in this collection. Guilbert also delivered courtship dialogue in "Le cotillon couleur de rose" ("The Pink Shirt"), which made allusions to Marie Antoinette, also included in Séverac's publication. "Ne dérangez pas le monde" ("Don't Interfere with Folk"), from Book I of this work, was an eighteenth-century song referring to risqué courtship and seduction. The piano depicts audacious pinches and underhanded squeezes and became an effective

---

46 Séverac, *Chansons du XVIIIème siècle* (Paris: Rouart, Lerolle et Cie, 1906); *Les vieilles chansons de France* (Paris: Rouart, Lerolle et Cie, 1906). In both Books I and II, Séverac harmonized songs from various regions within France that he gathered from written sources, some of which were collected from oral sources by others during the early part of the nineteenth century. Séverac then applied refrains. Pieces in Book I include "Ba be bi bo bu!," "R'muons le cotillon," "Zon, zon, zon!," "Le vieil époux," "Pour le jour des rois," "Le berger indiscret," "V'là c'que c'est qu'd'aller au bois," "Prière du matin," "Ne dérangez pas le monde," and "Offrande." Book II includes "Vaudeville des batelières de St. Cloud," "Musette," "Le beau Daphnis," "L'amour en cage," "Le vin de Catherine," "Nicodème," "L'homme n'est jamais content," "La fileuse," and "Cécilia." *Les vieilles chansons de France* includes "La peureuse," "La ronde," "L'Auvergnat," "Le manchon," "Ma mère, il me tuera," "La semaine de la mariée," "Les gens qui sont jeunes," "Le roi a fait battre tambour," "Les belles manières," and "Le boudoir d'aspasie."

performance piece for Guilbert. "Musette," from Book II of Séverac's *Chansons du XVII et XVIII siècle*, reflects the early twentieth-century craze for the hurdy-gurdy employed during Marie Antoinette's era when the drone was an important element in music. "Le roi a fait battre tambour" ("The King Ordered the Drum to be Beaten"), from *Les vieilles chansons de France*, alludes to a bygone aristocratic era; in this song, a conversation between a king and one of his subjects leads to a tragic and fatal relationship. Séverac's piano sonorities during the "Rataplan" chorus suggest the rattling of a Basque drum, and the treble line here complements the ominous rumblings in the bass.[47]

***

As suggested, harmonizations of folk songs differ in style from Séverac's mélodies, the latter including characteristics inherent in early nineteenth-century Romanticism, late nineteenth-century extended tonality, and Impressionist characteristics, including declamatory phrases found in Debussy's *Pelléas et Mélisande*. Yet Séverac's songs are unique in that many are composed through the lens of southern French régionalisme, with en plein air references to flutes played by goat herders in the southern French mountains and onomatopoeia in the form of church bells calling farmers to outdoor prayer. In this manner, Séverac suggested specific regional localities, which reflected his regionalist aesthetic.

---

47 Other works, such as "Philis" (1907), were not part of the above collections. "Philis" is a rondeau chanté, which contains the superscription: "d'après un manuscrit du XVIIIe siècle."

Chapter 6

Opera: *Le Coeur du Moulin* (The Heart of the Mill) (1909)
Pièce Lyrique en Deux Actes, Poème de Maurice Magre

In 1903, Séverac composed a regionalist theater work in one act entitled *Le retour*, set to a libretto by poet-novelist Maurice Magre (1877–1941).[1] He then expanded the composition into two acts and orchestrated it under the title *Le coeur du moulin*, or *Chat-huant*.[2] Séverac offered the work to d'Indy upon his mentor's request, and although d'Indy's response was that of cautious counselor, he nonetheless encouraged Séverac to submit the composition to the Concours musical de la ville de Paris. Séverac commented on the process:

> Mine would be a scandalous presence at the Schola [Cantorum] ... these competitions are silly ... Dear d'Indy is in the process of defending me and ... happily, Messager ... is well-disposed toward *Le coeur du moulin* ... I played *Le coeur du moulin* for some friends before dropping it off ... and they were entirely enchanted.[3]

Séverac's insecurity regarding the merit of *Le coeur du moulin* led him to consider his opera to be a "scandalous presence" at the Schola Cantorum. This reference to conductor André Messager is significant, because Messager was a juror who subsequently helped admit Séverac to the final round.[4] Séverac did not receive first

---

1 Magre was known in literary circles and founded the journals *Les essais d'art jeune* and *L'effort*.

2 Séverac, *Le coeur du moulin: pièce lyrique en deux actes*, piano-vocal score (Paris: Edition Mutuelle), 1909. An orchestral-vocal version is owned by Editions Salabert and is available for rent.

3 Pierre Guillot, *Déodat de Séverac: la musique et les lettres* (Liège, Belgium: Pierre Mardaga, 2002), 203, 208. [Conflation of three letters: Séverac letter to Mme de Castéra, December 15, 1903, Séverac letter to his mother, December 20, 1903, and Séverac letter to Mme Paul de Bonnefoy, January 16, 1904.] "Je serais un objet de scandale à la Schola [Cantorum] ... c'est idiot ces concours." "Le bon d'Indy est en train de me défendre et ... heureusement que Messager ... est très bien dispose." "Les camarades auxquels j'ai joué *Le coeur du moulin* avant de le déposer ... ont été complètement enchantés."

4 Séverac was elated at this: "This is enormous for me, not because of the prize ... but because ... this is a way of having my work heard. Without this I would normally have had to wait for two to three years for that!" Guillot, *Déodat de Séverac: la musique et les lettres*, 208. [Séverac letter to sister Alix, January 20, 1904.] ("C'est énorme pour moi, non pas à cause du

prize, however; in their report, the jury explained that *Le coeur du moulin* was a "symbolic, sinewy, and bold work," but was dismissed because of its perceived "confined proportions."[5] This would have been a reference to the introspective nature of Séverac's music and Magre's poetry, which was in direct opposition to more dramatic and politically charged operas. Debussy nonetheless offered to present the work to Albert Carré, director of the Opéra-Comique, so that Carré might consider performing the composition.[6] This led to a hearing in 1906:

> Séverac played the two acts which were to be read by Carré [this year]. Very good musical things, somewhat in the form of Debussy, but not in harmony. A wonderful artist, Selva accompanied marvelously.[7]

---

prix ... mais parce que ... ils auront ainsi une audition de mon oeuvre, chose qu'il me faudrait attendre deux ou trois ans sans cela!")

André Messager was a composer of light operas and conductor at the Opéra-Comique. The 1903 jury consisted of Théodore Dubois, Jules Massenet, Emile Paladilhe, Xavier Leroux, Paul Hillemacher, and Henry Roujon (Director of the School of Beaux-Arts and Secretary to the Academy of Beaux-Arts). Vincent d'Indy had to excuse himself as a result of a meeting in Poland.

5   Samuel Rousseau, *Rapport sur le concours musica., 1900–1903* (Paris: De la ville de Paris, Chaix, 1904); also see Guillot, *Déodat de Séverac: la musique et les lettres*, 208.

6   Albert Carré finally agreed to a 1909 première following various changes Séverac made to the opera between 1905 and 1908. Carré was nonetheless indifferent to the project. This fact is corroborated by Paul Dukas' ironic counsel to Séverac: "Carré does not seem excited to perform your work, it seems to me. Translate your work therefore to the title *El horn del molino*, and he will conduct it quickly. He conducts Puccini three times a week." ("Carré ne se presse guère de vous jouer, ce me semble? Faites donc traduire votre ouvrage sous le titre *El cor del molino*, il passera comme une lettre à l'Italie place Favart et l'on joue Puccini trois fois la semaine.") [1909 letter from Paul Dukas to Séverac.] See Vladimir Jankélévitch, *La présence lontaine: Albéniz, Séverac, Mompou* (Paris: Editions du Seuil, 1983), 101, 137.

Carré gave the title role of Jacques at the première to singer Jean Perier and the role of Marie to Carré's wife. Apparently, Jean Perier was so effective in his role that Madame Carré feared being overshadowed, and therefore asked her husband to discharge the singer. "The Dances of the Treilleses" in the second act also appeared to be highly effective in rehearsals, and Madame Carré, again fearing that these picturesque dances took attention away from her personal success, asked her husband to suppress them under the pretext that the stage was too small and the ballet would therefore overwhelm the decor; Carré therefore had the ballet removed. Séverac vehemently argued with Carré about this decision, claiming that the ballet music contained the exposition of a principal theme that dealt with the action. Withdrawing the section would therefore make much of the opera incomprehensible, to which Carré replied: "I don't give a damn about your music!" D'Indy later performed Séverac's ballet music in a concert at the Société nationale de musique. See Guillot, *Déodat de Séverac: la musique et les lettres*, 330, and Jean-Bernard Cahours d'Aspry, "Déodat de Séverac" (unpublished manuscript), 345. "Votre musique, je m'en fous!"

7   This was mentioned by Séverac's friend Mme de Saint Marceaux in her journal, dated January 26, 1906, the same day that she heard *Le coeur du moulin*, reprinted in Guillot, *Déodat de Séverac: la musique et les lettres*, 256. "Séverac fait exécuter les deux actes qui vont être lus à Carré. De très bonnes choses musicales, un peu dans la forme Debussy mais pas dans l'harmonie. Un bel artiste, Selva accompagne merveilleusement."

Opera: Le Coeur du Moulin *(The Heart of the Mill) (1909)*

The story of *Le coeur du moulin* takes place at the end of the eighteenth century on the outskirts of Séverac's birthplace village of Saint-Félix-Caraman. On stage is to be an old well surrounded by Mediterranean olive, fig, cypress, and sunshade pine trees. There is a path leading to the village, and there are rows of grapevine continuing far into the distance, eventually leading into a group of small hills. In the far distant horizon is the silhouette of the Pyrenees mountains.

The action begins on a September afternoon during the wine harvest. After a short symphonic prelude, one hears the song of wine growers in the hills. Women and children come out of the village carrying their snacks, including Marie and her friend, Louisons, who enter with baskets underneath their arms.

Jacques, a child of his pays, who left his home town to find his fortune elsewhere, subsequently returns to his native land. He is heard singing from far away as a result of his elation at seeing his homeland again. He recalls with emotion the familiar landscape of his childhood, as voices of nature call him to ancient memories. Yet he is also anxious to reunite with Marie, the love of his life whom he left behind. They then see each other in the distance, and the opera becomes more dramatic as they meet and profess their love for each other. Marie then confesses that she is married, but admits to him that she has always loved him and still desires to be with him. The workers in this wine-growing region then enter. Marie's husband, Pierre, sings his love for Marie and Jacques' mother subsequently arrives, at which time the workers leave to allow mother and son their reunion. This encounter occurs, but not before Marie agrees to a meeting with Jacques that evening.

Act II opens with a traditional holiday among the wine-growers of Languedoc. They dance the "Danse des treilles" and at the end of the dance, a miller tries to reason with Marie to forget Jacques. Marie leaves and Jacques then enters, and the miller thereupon counsels Jacques to leave his native pays. Jacques' mother arrives and becomes dismayed after learning of her son's intentions. Indecisive and tortured, Jacques seeks advice from his mother and she replies in tears that it is Jacques' duty to make his own way far away from his native pays. Memories of his childhood reappear, and after saying farewell, Jacques leaves his home village. Marie, after learning of Jacques' departure, explodes into sobs while voices of the village and land around her sing.[8]

Despite derivative qualities, *Le coeur du moulin* is nonetheless unique in various ways. There are countless tonal passages, including folk-like strophic songs that imply southern French régionalisme. Magre's text suggests characters that are often naïve and provincial, and many of these moments are tonal or pentatonic, further enhancing this naïveté. The outcome of this work is also significant in that Jacques' departure is no more violent than Aaron Copland's mid-century *The Tender Land*, where home is also evoked as a primary concept. This is what Carré found objectionable and atypical of most contemporary opera, as even the characters in Debussy's *Pelléas and Mélisande* encountered death.

Séverac emphasized the concept of returning home in *Le coeur du moulin* as metaphor, embodied through several symbols, including Catholic angelus bells

---

8   The story is not a new one and is somewhat reminiscent of Tennyson's *Enoch Arden* (Enoch Arden *and Other Poems*, Boston: Houghton Mifflin, 1895).

calling toiling farmers to prayer. Rural peasants are therefore reminded of a celestial home, church, and tradition, all characteristic of fin de siècle régionalisme. The first reference occurs in Act I, Scene 2, when Jacques is on the outskirts of the village returning to his native home. He hears angelus bells in the distance and sings about this in perfect fourths and fifths, while the orchestra accompanies in diminished arpeggios. When Jacques and Marie first meet in the third scene of the same act, they sing on the whole-tone scale while referring to angleus bells they hear within the town. They therefore associate the rediscovering of each other to feelings embodied by home. Before parting, they again mention the angelus while singing with the orchestra in unresolved ninth chords, thereby creating a sense of uneasiness in leaving. Towards the end of the final act, bells recur while "voices of nature" sing their advice to Jacques regarding his decision to stay or leave his native pays. Whole-tone scales again sound, while Jacques sings within a major–minor modal interchange, the latter alluding to his sense of conflict in making an agonizing but necessary decision.

The music and concept surrounding the work was indisputably influenced by Debussy's *Pelléas et Mélisande*, of which Séverac heard the composer perform from a piano-vocal score in 1902, the same year in which Séverac began composing his opera. Séverac also heard a performance of the opera at the première later that same year.[9] Both works share a similar poetic conception and are comparatively introverted dramas without grandiloquence. The two compositions contain supple and free declamation, therefore reinforcing the rhythmic and dynamic inflections of the French language. Both contain quasi-recitative and parlando styles, leitmotives, a balance between verbal and musical rhythm, and non-functional harmony in the form of modality, altered chords, and unresolved parallel seventh, ninth, and eleventh chords; both also avoid traditional tonal cadences.

The similarity between the two operas was not lost on critics, composers, and other audience members, as attested to by critic Gaston Dubreuilh in a review of the 1909 première of Séverac's work:

> In spite of the rupture with the Wagnerian method, the constant use of the leitmotive assures the musical unity of the work, but it is a sort of recitative specific to the French language as theorized by Jean-Jacques Rousseau: "the best recitative is where one sings the least." [According to Rousseau], recitatives must consist of small intervals, so as not to raise or lower the voice much. [In Séverac's work, there are] a few sustained sounds, never any bursts, and still less screaming, nothing that might resemble song, little inequality in the length or value of the notes, nor in their degrees; and yet, the music of *Le coeur du moulin*, as in *Pelléas [et Mélisande]*, is never monotonous. This is due to its harmonious and symphonic richness.[10]

---

9   See Chapter 9 for more detail about Séverac attending the première of *Pelléas et Mélisande* (1902).

10   Gaston Dubreuilh, *Les nouvelles* (December 9, 1909), reprinted in Aspry, "Déodat de Séverac," 371. "Malgre la rupture avec la méthode Wagnérienne, l'emploi constant du leitmotive assure l'unité musicale de l'ouvrage; mais c'est un type de recitatif propre à la langue française comme Jean Jacques Rousseau avait theorisé. 'Le meilleur recitatif est celui ou l'on chante le moins,' disait-il. Il doit rouler entre de forts petits intervalles, n'élever ni

Dubreuilh, although aware of Wagner's influence on French music, alluded here to a new style that utilized French declamation more effectively, as initially defined by *Pelléas et Mélisande* and subsequently adapted by Séverac.

Other critics focused on the negative consequences of emulating Debussy. Gabrielle Cavellier wrote that Séverac used "antiquated formulas influenced by Debussyism," and other writers criticized Séverac as being a musician with much talent, but one that didn't know how to become liberated from the influence of Debussyism.[11]

Louis Laloy, however, defended Séverac's work in this regard by stating that "It is clear ... that originality is not even conceivable, that every work has its precedents, if not its models, that an artist only finds his way when he follows the lead of those to whom his taste is similar."[12] Gabriel Fauré concurred:

> Does the score of *Le coeur du moulin* resemble other works? Without a doubt. But what artist, at the beginning of his career, does not undergo the influence of one or several of his predecessors? Doesn't Mozart shine throughout Beethoven's first works? And doesn't one hear echoes of Weber's *Euryanthe* while listening to *Lohengrin*? Nothing is invented in music, and you could even claim that the personality, the originality, the novelty, resides far less in what is expressed than in how it is expressed.[13]

Other comments mostly centered around the perceived weakness of Maurice Magre's libretto, and Séverac himself was aware of the libretto's shortcomings. His criticisms spoke of its highly verbal character, much of which was not perceived as being pertinent to the action; yet Séverac felt that these sections created ambiance during picturesque moments, thereby reflecting the poetry of the countryside. Critic Louis Laloy commented on the libretto and its relationship to the music:

> The language is too abstract ... Such dramas of Maeterlinck were only accessible to a large following after the harmony of the notes had prolonged the vibration of the words. Séverac is eminently capable of such a mission, but he will never address it with this

---

abaisser beaucoup la voix. Peu de sons soutenus; jamais d'éclats, encore moins de cris, rien qui ressemble au chant, peu d'intégalité dans la dures, ou valeur des notes, ainsi que dans leurs degrés. Et pourtant, la musique du *Le coeur du moulin*, comme celle de *Pelléas [et Mélisande]*, n'est jamais monotone. Cela tient à sa richesse harmonieuse et symphonique."

11 Gabrielle Cavellier, *Coulisses* (January 1, 1910), reprinted in: Aspry, "Déodat de Séverac", 383–4. "... des formules surannées aux influences debussystes."

12 Aspry, "Déodat de Séverac", 386. "Il est clair ... qu'une originalité absolue n'est pas même concevable que toute oeuvre a ses précédents, sinon ses modèles, qu'un artiste ne trouve sa voie qu'en prenant pour guide ceux à qui son goût l'apparente."

13 Gabriel Fauré, "Les théâtres," *Le figaro* (December 9, 1909), 4–5; reprinted in Aspry, "Déodat de Séverac", 385. "La partition du *Le coeur du moulin* ne ressent-elle d'influences manifestes? Incontestablement, mais quel est l'artiste qui, au début de sa carrière—quant ce n'est pas durant toute sa carrière—n'a pas subi l'influence de l'un ou de plusieurs de ses devanciers? Est-ce qu'à travers les premières oeuvres de Beethoven ne transparait pas Mozart? Et n'entend-on point, en écoutant *Lohengrin*, des echos d'*Euryanthe*? D'ailleurs, on n'invente rien en musique, et l'on pourrait affirmer même que la personnalité, l'orginalité, la nouveauté, resident bien moins dans ce que l'on exprime que dans la manière dont on l'exprime."

libretto ... By misfortune, Magre missed exactly what gives life to the slightest inventions of this poet, so sure of his candor: its sensitivity ... Magre wants to be a poet and merely a poet. He doesn't have the knack for psychology; nature alone inspires him. The human heart does not interest him, but the "heart of the mill."[14]

Séverac's opera is permeated with leitmotives and they are often intended to evoke emotional reminiscences, as attested to by Séverac in the introduction to his score:

> The musical themes in *Le coeur du moulin* do not only play the abstract role of leitmotives, as in most modern works, but they are, for the heroes of the drama, and particularly for Jacques, true characters that speak.[15]

There are essentially seven primary leitmotives that represent principal themes. These include duty, treason, good-heartedness, love, wisdom, friendship, and nature, as well as secondary motives.[16] Characters in the opera are often themselves symbols of these seven themes in the same way that Golaud's main motif in Debussy's *Pelléas et Mélisande* is more about anxiety than Golaud.[17] Steven Huebner notes that in *Pelléas et Mélisande*, Golaud's primary motif appears in several places where the connection to the character appears to be tangential.[18]

Jacques' mother plays an integral role in the opera as she represents sympathy, home, roots, instinct, and the law of nature; however, she also speaks for wisdom and especially duty, which is sometimes in direct opposition to the laws of nature and home. Towards the end of the work, for example, voices of nature tell Jacques

---

14 Louis Laloy, "La Musique," *La grande revue* (December 25, 1909), 818, reprinted in Aspry, "Déodat de Séverac", 367. "Le langue est trop abstraite ... Tel drame de Maeterlinck n'est devenu accessible à un nombreux public qu'après que l'harmonie des notes eut prolongé la vibration des mots. Séverac est éminemment apte à une telle mission, et il ne s'adressera jamais, pour lui fournir des livrets ... Par malheur, il lui manque justement ce qui donne la vie aux moindres inventions de ce poète si sur de sa candeur; la sensibilité ... Magre se veut poète, et purement poète. Il n'a cure de psychologie; la nature seule l'inspire; ce n'est pas le coeur humain qui l'interesse: c'est le coeur du moulin."

Another claim by various critics, including composer Alfred Bruneau, was that Séverac's regional roots in this work was apparent in that it had a very southern French temperament. Vladimir Jankélévitch agreed: "In spite of the work's similarity in some ways to Debussy, the atmosphere in *Le coeur du moulin* is different, the internal lighting and sense of light is different. The light of Debussy is oceanic; that of Séverac, southern France!" Jankélévitch's remarks from *La presence lointaine: Albéniz, Séverac, Mompou* are reprinted in Aspry, "Déodat de Séverac", 386. "Malgré sa proximité de Debussy, l'atmosphère du *Le coeur du moulin* est différente, l'éclairage interne est different, le sens de la lumière dans les tissus est différents. La lumière de Debussy est océanique, celle de Séverac est méridionale."

15 Pierre Guillot, "Claude Debussy et Déodat de Séverac," *Cahiers Debussy*, no. 10 (1986), 11. "Les thèmes musicaux du *Le coeur du moulin* ne jouent pas seulement un rôle abstrait de leitmotive, comme dans la plupart des oeuvres modernes, mais ils sont, pour les héros du drame, et particulièrement pour Jacques, de véritables personnages qui parlent."

16 Guillot, "Claude Debussy et Déodat de Séverac," 15.

17 Steven Huebner, *French Opera at the* fin de siècle (Oxford: Oxford University Press, 1999), 474.

18 Ibid.

to remain in the village, which is contrary to his mother's advice, as she counsels Jacques on the virtues of wisdom and duty—advice that persuades Jacques to leave the village. In this opera, therefore, the duty motive becomes synonymous with that of Jacques' mother. Since responsibility to one's duty is painful for Jacques, as it is in conflict with his desires and needs, the duty motive is often in the form of a tritone. This is first heard in Act I, Scene 7, where Jacques and his mother reunite for the first time:

Example 6.1   Measure 3 of Act I, Scene 7 to *Le coeur du moulin* (piano-vocal score)

In Act II, Scene 4, Jacques pleads with his mother to sympathize with his desire not to leave the village in order to be with Marie. He sings to his mother within perfect fourth and fifth intervals; however, in Scene 5, Jacques plaintively asks his mother what he should do in the face of this dilemma, wherein the tritone is again outlined, this time in an ascending motive of B flat to E. The tritone prophesies her response calling for an allegiance to duty.

Example 6.2   Excerpt from Act II, Scene 5 to *Le coeur du moulin* (piano-vocal score)

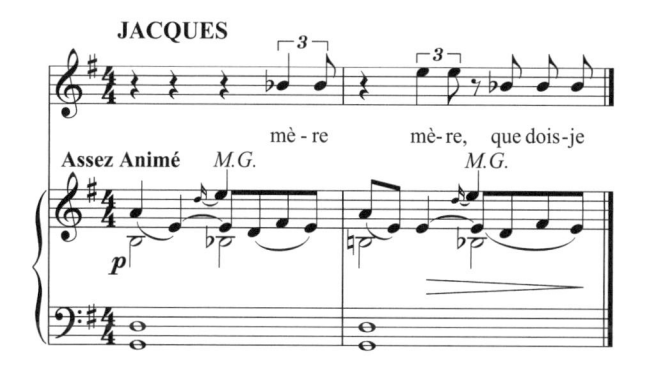

Duty is not only an enemy to the laws of nature and home, but is also resistant to betrayal. Deception seems imminent, as Jacques is prepared to meet Marie alone later that day, thus signifying Marie's disloyalty to her husband Pierre. This betrayal is indicated in the form of a treason motive first heard in the opening scene of the opera, where Marie is speaking to her friend Louison about her dream. In this reverie, Marie betrays her husband, as a tritone is outlined with orchestral tremolos.

Example 6.3   Excerpt from Act I, Scene 1 to *Le coeur du moulin* (piano-vocal score)

When Jacques and Marie meet for the first time in the opera, Marie cries out that she is in the process of betrayal. Instead of opening with sixteenth notes, as in her dream, fear and confusion during this meeting is rhythmically depicted in quarter note triplet rhythms accompanied by a tritone. These cries of betrayal are echoed several times here, the last sounded by Marie in a polytonal structure of D flat together with A flat.

Marie's intention to deceive Pierre is in direct contrast to Pierre's motive, which is equated with good-heartedness and joy, first heard early in the opera. Pierre's ecstatic manner is heard when singing on a pentatonic scale, thereby alluding to an almost naïve sense of innocence and abandon.

Jacques has his own song, commonly known as "Chanson de Jacques," because Séverac also set it to piano accompaniment to be performed as a separate work. It is labeled by Séverac as a "folk-like song," or "chanson dans le style populaire ancien," in which Jacques experiences joy at rediscovering his homeland. Much of the dotted rhythm in the melody here sounds within the pentatonic scale based on E, rising a semitone every stanza. This occurs first on F, subsequently on F sharp, and finally to G, all which suggest Jacques' increasing hope upon seeing his birthplace. The technique resembles Act I, Scene 1 to *Pelléas et Mélisande*, where Debussy's passage ascends a semitone followed by a whole tone, a technique that d'Indy likened to early baroque period stile rappresentativo.[19] In Séverac's case, however, this occurs at the beginning of each new verse within a strophic and tonal passage. This melody to this song therefore becomes one of the primary themes of the drama, as it contains reprises that intervene during picturesque scenes.[20]

In addition to an owl which represents wisdom, there are also four voices that constitute the "Heart of the Mill" and are found in dream personalities from childhood. These come to Jacques towards the end of the opera, and include a fairy that inspires dancing and symbolizes similar ideals to that of the angelus, a beggar, a "Christmas voice," and a wheat fairy. These voices often come in the form of a double choir, no doubt influenced by polyphonic Renaissance works that Séverac conducted under the guidance of Charles Bordes. The choir often sounds offstage, particularly when Jacques is about to recount memories of his village and native land. The fairy first emerges after Jacques' initial reference to the angelus, as a distinct folk-like dance rhythm sounds in the orchestra. This recurs once more in Act II, Scene 6, when various voices of nature speak to Jacques regarding his dilemma and decision as to whether he should leave. A similar folk-like dance rhythm ensues.[21]

***

As stated, Séverac's leitmotives play an important role and additional characters are also given specific phrases or harmonies. The use of these leitmotives, phrases, and harmonies suggest Debussy's influence, as found in *Pelléas et Mélisande*. Yet although *Le coeur du moulin* shares many characteristics found in Debussy's work, *Le coeur du moulin* is unique in several ways, including the use of folk-like song. Many musicians found this style effective. *Le coeur du moulin* was appreciated by those who thought *Pelléas et Mélisande* revolutionary and who believed Séverac to be continuing within that tradition. As composer Charles Koechlin remarked:

> [*Le coeur du moulin*] will probably be little understood by what one calls the "general public," with their dense spirits and vulgar, superficial minds. They are only pleased by violent and sudden turns of events, hate true music and have little patience for the

---

19 Vincent d'Indy, "Pelléas et Mélisande," *L'occident* (June, 1902), cited in Huebner, *French Opera at the* Fin de Siècle, 471.

20 Joseph Canteloube, *Déodat de Séverac* [1st Edition, Paris, 1929] (Beziers, France: Société de musicologie de Languedoc, 1984), 61.

21 The "Christmas voice," symbolizing nostalgia and church is heard towards the end of the opera immediately before the dance. The voice sounds in the bass within a minor key. The wheat fairy, representing food and life, as well as fields reminiscent of home, sounds in a folk-like dance in triple meter within the key of B minor. The beggar sings in 9/8 meter within the key of G with added sixths, providing an Impressionist-like aesthetic.

expressiveness of deep-seated sentiments: that is, everything beautiful in a lyric drama. This beauty exists in *Le coeur du moulin*.[22]

---

22 Charles Koechlin, "Chronique musicale: *L'or du Rhin*," *Gazette des beaux-arts*, 51e année, vol. 2, no. 63 (December, 1909), 492–4; reprinted in Aspry, "Déodat de Séverac," 366. "Elle sera peu comprise sans doute de ce qu'on appelle si justement le 'gros' public, réunion d'esprits épais, vulgaires et superficiels, ne se plaisant qu'aux coups de théâtre violents, détestant la vraie musique, qualifiant de longueurs tout ce qui est expression développée d'un sentiment profond: tout ce qui, précisément, est la grande beauté d'un drame lyrique. Cette beauté existe dans *Le coeur du moulin*."

Chapter 7

Piano Music

Séverac's style in his piano music varies more than in any of his other genres. Many of his works are regionalist in their programmatic references in the score and titles to the various movements. His *Sonate* of 1899 illustrates Sonata-Allegro form, and *Le chant de la terre* (1900) incorporates régionalisme together with modality in a style characteristic of ideals emphasized at the Schola Cantorum, as well as major–minor modal shifts coupled with lean lines and a texture characteristic of French Romanticism. Onomatopoeia is employed in *Le chant de la terre* in the form of sounds and sights from a southern French farm, which is alluded to by Séverac's programmatic descriptions. Specific locales are represented, including Andalusian references in the form of flamenco cante jondo and guitar.

En Languedoc (1904) accommodates Impressionist elements, yet the formal plan is derived from extra-musical regionalist associations and the harmonic integration of the separate movements. Séverac employed rapid arpeggios, a series of unresolved dominant seventh chords, whole-tone scales, chromatic side-stepping, parallel block chords, and unprepared modulations. *Cerdaña* (1908–11) contains Andalusian and Catalan regionalist characteristics, and separate movements exist wherein thematic, rhythmic, and harmonic resemblances contribute to the element of unification. Both *En Languedoc* and *Cerdaña* originated as separate pieces that Séverac composed at different periods and decided afterwards to assemble in suites.

En vacances I (1911) reflects the piano writing of Robert Schumann, and works such as *En vacances II* (1911), *Baigneuses au soleil* (1908), and *Sous les lauriers-roses* (1919) illustrate characteristics found in the piano music of Emmanuel Chabrier. Séverac's piano music is nonetheless unique in various ways. In most of Séverac's piano music, for example, harmony and harmonic color becomes the controlling element rather than melody. This chapter will therefore consider these piano compositions individually, with the exception of *Cerdaña* and *Sous les lauriers-roses*, which will be analyzed in Chapter 10 when works influenced by Catalan and Andalusian music will be discussed.

Sonate (1899)

I. Adagio-Allegro
II. Elégie
III. Allegro-Scherzando
IV. Allegro-Finale

Séverac developed his earlier cyclic style while studying composition with Vincent d'Indy at the Schola Cantorum. Although d'Indy fervently adhered to cyclic form in his own compositions, he may have taken a different approach with those of Séverac. Canteloube recalled Séverac's story:

> When Séverac showed him [d'Indy] his four-movement piano *Sonate*—it [maintained a] total adherence to the sacred principle of cyclic form which met with criticism. D'Indy penciled in "I don't see the necessity of bringing all of the themes back like this."[1]

The composition to which Canteloube referred is the *Sonate* for piano in B flat minor.[2] The four movements are "Adagio-Allegro," in Sonata-Allegro form, "Elégie," composed in homage to Séverac's late father and sister and in ternary form (ABA), "Allegro-Scherzando," and an "Allegro-Finale," which contains the cyclic recapitulation of previous themes from the other three movements. The work was premièred in 1901 at the Libre esthétique in Brussels by the dedicatee, 17-year-old pianist Maurice Bastin.[3] Séverac described its reception in a letter to his mother several weeks later:[4]

> I had my sonata performed in the concert hall. Bastin was perfect ... My sonata received more applause than I had expected, given the cold reputation of Brussels audiences. Monsieur Kufferath, the editor of *Guide musical* (a very famous journal) came to congratulate d'Indy and asked him to introduce me. And now, I have been invited to have my works heard each year at the Libre esthétique ... something I accepted with enthusiasm.[5]

---

1 Andrew Thomson, *Vincent d'Indy and His World* (Oxford: Clarendon Press, 1996), 32. This passage is translated by the author.

2 Séverac, *Sonate pour piano* (Paris: Edition de Pierre Guillot, 1991). There is only one manuscript of *Sonate* kept in Séverac's baronial birthplace home in Saint-Félix de Lauragais. There is a recording of *Sonate*: see Isabelle Legoux Laboureau, 1984 (Disc Revolum REV 051 RVM 360).

3 Maurice Bastin (1884–1983) was born in Belgium and subsequently studied at the Schola Cantorum where he became friends with Séverac. He was appointed conductor at the Théâtre de la Monnaie in Brussels in 1919.

4 The work was performed two additional times following the Brussels première. The first was at a school concert in Paris and a second in northern France during a concert tour. The score was lost following this event. In 1980, University of Maryland DMA student Margaret Otwell rediscovered the score at Séverac's house in Saint-Félix de Lauragais. See Margaret Otwell, "The Piano Works of Déodat de Séverac: A Complete Recording" (DMA Dissertation, University of Maryland at College Park, 1981), 31.

5 Pierre Guillot, *Déodat de Séverac: la musique et les lettres* (Liège, Belgium: Pierre Mardaga, 2002), 139. [Séverac letter to family, March 25, 1901.] " J'ai fait répéter ma Sonate dans la salle de concert. Bastin a été parfait ... Ma *Sonate* a été accueillie par des applaudissements que je ne prévoyais pas, étant donné la réputation de froideur des bruxellois. Monsieur Kufferath, le directeur du *Guide musical* (revue très célèbre) est venu féliciter d'Indy et a demandé à me connaître. Et maintenant, on m'a invité à faire entendre chaque année mes oeuvres à Libre esthétique ... chose que j'ai acceptée avec enthousiasme."

Despite d'Indy's protest regarding what he considered to be the work's excessively cyclic elements, Séverac nonetheless retained much cyclic structure when revising the work, as he employed related thematic material in all of the movements.[6] Although Beethoven's music served as a primary model for Séverac's *Sonate*, it is nonetheless d'Indy's views regarding Beethoven through Franck's lineage that often reveals itself in Séverac's work. Sonata-Allegro form within the first movement is one example of this, where Séverac adhered to an adagio introduction followed by three primary themes within the exposition, a development which includes modulatory passages on these three ideas, followed by the recapitulation which brings back all three themes; the movement concludes with a coda. This structure is broken down in Figure 7.1.

Cyclicism can be observed in the opening theme of the first movement, which is quoted and transposed in the opening to the second movement "Elégie," as evident in the following:[7]

Example 7.1a   Measures 1–2, *Sonate*, first movement

---

6   Maurice Kufferath was also a professor of counterpoint at the Conservatoire du Bruxelles. For more information, see Michel Stockhem, "Vincent d'Indy en Belgique: réseaux et influences," *Vincent d'Indy et son temps*, in Manuela Schwartz, editor (Sprimont, Belgium: Mardaga Press, 2006). 92–5.

7   D'Indy himself often incorporated cyclicism in his works, including *Symphonie sur un chant montagnard français*, op. 25. Cyclicism was a primary principle of composition for d'Indy and is discussed in his treatise. See Vincent d'Indy, "Le sonate cyclique," *Cours de composition musicale*, in collaboration with Auguste Sérieyx, vol. 1 (Paris: Durand et Cie, 1903).

Example 7.1b   Measures 1–2, *Sonate*, second movement

Figure 7.1   Sonata-Allegro Form in *Sonate*, 1st Movement

Measures	Form	Key
1–8	Introduction: Adagio	B flat minor
9–46	Exposition, Theme I	B flat minor
47–56	Exposition, Transition	modulation
57–93	Exposition, Theme II	D flat major
	(Dolce, meno allegro quasi canzona)	
94–111	Exposition, Closing theme	D flat minor
112–224	Development	F minor-modulation
225–227	Recapitulation of *Adagio*	modulation
228–277	Recapitulation of Theme I	B flat minor
278–293	Recapitulation of Theme II	B flat major
294–302	Recapitulation of Closing Theme	B flat major
303–387	Coda	B flat minor

All of the movements contain the initial theme stated at the beginning of the sonata, and the final movement recalls all of the previous themes contained in the work. It is the final measures of this last movement to which d'Indy referred as being excessively cyclic. For example, it is interesting to compare the similar chord structure and descending octave line found in the last measures of the fourth movement to that in the first movement. This is most pronounced in measures 256 and 305, as shown below:

Example 7.2a   Measure 256, *Sonate*, fourth movement, descending octave line

Example 7.2b   Measure 305, *Sonate*, first movement, descending octave line

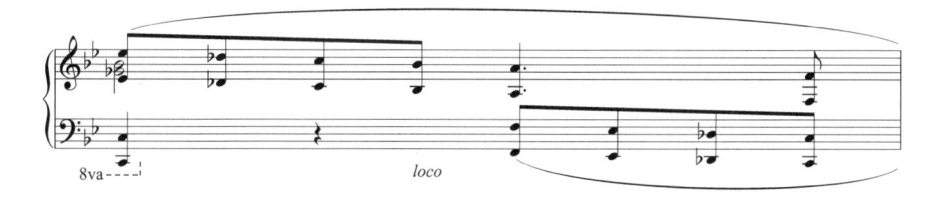

A similar rhythmic pattern and half- and whole-step lower neighbor interval motion found in the first movement occurs towards the end of the final movement, as illustrated here:

Example 7.3a   Measures 349–352, *Sonate*, first movement, rhythmic pattern and major 2nd interval motion

Example 7.3b   Measures 265–266, *Sonate*, fourth movement

There is also a similar chord structure, melodic line, and use of parallelism in both the third and fourth movements, as demonstrated below:

Example 7.4a   Measures 60–73, *Sonate*, third movement, Melody and Parallelism

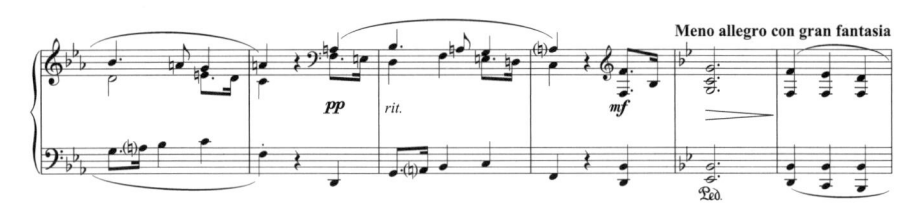

Example 7.4b   Measures 106–110, *Sonate*, fourth movement

***Le Chant de la Terre, Poème Géorgique pour Piano* (1899-1900)**
(The Song of the Earth: Poem of Agriculture and Rural Life for Piano)

I. Prologue
II. Le labour (The Plowing of the Field)
III. Les semailles (The Planting of the Seeds)
IV. Intermezzo: conte à la veillée (The Story of the Old One)
V. La grêle (The Hailstorm)
VI. Les moissons (The Harvest)
VII. Epilogue: le jour des noces (The Wedding Day)

In 1898, Séverac wrote letters to his family describing his persistent feelings of nostalgia for the countryside in his native region. This paralleled the composing of his first piano suite *Le chant de la terre* (The Song of the Earth), composed between 1899 and 1900, which reflected his interest in multi-movement programmatic works. Within these movements, Séverac emphasized regionalism by paying homage to the farmers of southern France, by referring to seasonal planting, a hailstorm, a harvest, and a wedding ceremony.[8]

Séverac's use of the term *géorgique* illustrates his interest in classical literature by alluding to Roman poet Virgil's *Géorgiques*, written in four books circa 36–29 BC, which celebrated agriculture and rural life. The word *géorgique* itself refers to cultivating land and tilling soil, apparent in Virgil's work:

> And boy–discoverer of the curved plow
> And bearing a young cypress root, uptorn
> Sylvan, and Gods all and Goddesses,
> Who make the fields your care, both ye who nurse
> The tender unsown increase,
> And from heaven
> Shed on man's sowing the riches of your rain
> What makes the cornfield smile beneath what star
> Maecenas, it is meet to turn the sod
> Or marry elm with vine; how tend the steer;
> What pains for cattle—keeping or what proof
> Of patient real serves for thrifty bees
> Such are my themes.[9]

---

[8] Séverac encloses his own poetry for each movement in a manner that resembles Virgil's work. The use of the Dorian mode and occasional absence of bar lines highlights the regional quality of this work and occasionally resembles Gregorian chant.

[9] Virgil, *Georgiques*, 29 BC Excerpts from *Georgic I*, translated by John Dryden and J.B. Greenough, www. classics.mit.edu.

Séverac's suite was also influenced by the contemporary French poet Francis Jammes, who wrote his own Christian version of *Géorgiques*. Post-Impressionist painter Paul Cézanne also created a work entitled *Géorgiques*, which would have been known to Séverac, as the composer referred to Cézanne in his 1907 thesis.

The Intermezzo in *Le chant de la terre* serves as a dividing point between the preceding three movements and the three movements that follow; Séverac also composed programmatic verses for each movement of the suite. There was a first edition in prose format, but the second version containing free verse, influenced in part by poet Emile Verhaeren, was the one adopted for the première and is the one discussed in this chapter.[10]

The first complete performance of *Le chant de la terre* took place at the Libre esthétique in Brussels in 1902, a concert performed by pianist Jean de Chastain. The event was also associated with an exposition of living painters, as well as an Henri de Toulouse-Lautrec (1864–1901) retrospective.[11]

Although Séverac included cyclic elements in his *Sonate*, by 1900, he began to modify his use of the process. At this time, he turned to the suite as a model for increasingly rhapsodic, modified cyclic constructions. He also used regional elements in these programmatic compositions. With this approach, he found a balance between recurring thematic elements as a unifying device and program music narration. Séverac often foreshadowed upcoming motives and reminisced over earlier programmatic themes by incorporating certain rhythmic, melodic, or harmonic elements taken from these primary motives. These components were often inserted in their complete form, therefore being non-developmental.

This work emerges conceptually as a one-movement piece, despite formal delineation between so-called movements. The different sections are characterized by intermittent departures from the fundamental mood as expressed in the opening theme. There is also a recurrence of rhythmic, melodic, and harmonic elements in all of the movements. There are constant metric changes with hemiola effects coupled with stratified textures. Additional characteristics include conjunct melodies, modality, consistent employment of the flatted supertonic, Phrygian scales, descending minor tetrachords, plainsong melody, omission of barlines to avoid accents and promote irregular meter, ostinato patterns, as well as dance rhythms accompanied by imitations of folk instruments.

Musical characteristics found in the work illustrate the influence of d'Indy's *Poème des montagnes* (1881), another piano suite alluding to nature through modality. There is also a consistent use of onomatopoeia in the work's reference to church bells in the form of parallel fourths and fifths, included in L'angélus section of "Les semailles," the 'Les rogations' and 'Le glas' segments in "La grêle," and 'L'aimée' section in the final movement, when wedding bells are represented by parallel sixths.

In addition to the work's modality, cyclicism, and onomatopoeia, Séverac also included distinct melodies, another characteristic emphasized within the Schola

---

10 Elaine Brody, "The Piano Works of Déodat de Séverac: A Stylistic Analysis" (PhD Dissertation, New York University, 1964), 95. *Le chant de la terre* was dedicated to Belgian critic and pianist Octave Maus (1856–1919), published initially by Edition Mutuelle (1903), and subsequently by Rouart Lerolle (plates now property of Editions Salabert). Emile Verhaeren (1855–1916) was a Belgian poet, art critic, and author of short stories and theater works.

11 Séverac met Schola Cantorum pianist Blanche Selva for the first time at this event. She performed the suite in the Paris première at a Société nationale concert one year later.

Cantorum. There is also an avoidance of explicit cadential resolutions as seemingly arbitrary altered chords are included, as are tendency tones, which are often replaced with non-directional modal constructions. Frequent ostinatos are constructed as pedal points on tones other than the root, and textural stratification, or multiple levels of activity, also occur.

The flatted supertonic and notable absence of leading tones in the composition both create an inherently modal effect by avoiding functional harmonic cadences. Whole-tone scales occur infrequently and appear primarily in the final epilogue "Le jour des noces." The tonal scheme of most of the suite moves in thirds, sometimes with enharmonics, which progresses as follows: D minor, F sharp, B flat, and D minor. Seventh chords abound in the work, mostly on the subdominant, dominant, and submediant. Chromaticism exists in transitional scale figures, especially within the bass. Grace notes often occur as structural features of the melody rather than as embellishments.

Most of the separate movements are in ternary or modified ternary form. The opening "Prologue" contains two statements of the primary theme, one in free rhythm and the second in measured time. Elaine Brody states that these seven movements are part of a bogen structure, or ABCDCBA.[12] Brody, however, also notes that all seven movements together constitute a semi-sonata form, with the exposition of themes and first thematic group occurring in "Le labour," and a second thematic group with new melodic material ensuing in "Les semailles." The angelus in "Les semailles" then represents the closing theme of the exposition, and also contains a codetta with a second closing group.[13] The development would then be contained in the "Intermezzo" and "La grêle," which includes new melodic material, but with frequent chromaticism and much modulation. These key changes take place without previous preparation or are coupled with unconventional pivot chords, which imply previous preparation. The recapitulation then appears in "Les moissons," in which the primary theme from the exposition is recalled; "Le jour des noces" is therefore considered by Brody to be the coda.

Regional folk-like music is included in *Le chant de la terre*, where conjunct melodies and the absence of leading tones are apparent in the opening to the second movement "Les semailles." The melody contains the six-note scale F sharp–G sharp–A sharp–B–C sharp–D sharp–F sharp, derived from the major scale, but omits the leading tone of E sharp. In addition, the range is limited to the interval of a fifth in measures 1–6, as in B, C sharp, D sharp, F sharp. The example also includes a conjunct modal construction commonly found in French folk songs. Yet, one cannot ignore the Lydian modal implications as well as whole-tone interaction, as B in the right hand part is counteracted by the B sharp in the left hand portion, therefore giving the passage a certain modal ambiguity.

---

12 Brody, "The Piano Works of Déodat de Séverac: A Stylistic Analysis", 104. A bogen structure is an arch form. Séverac transcribed *Le chant de la terre* for small orchestra in 1912, which up until recently was lost. It was lately rediscovered in England and acquired by a citizen of Luxembourg, who subsequently had the work performed.

13 Ibid., 97.

Example 7.5   Conjunct Modal Construction, Measures 1–7 of *Le chant de la terre* for piano, second movement ("Les semailles")

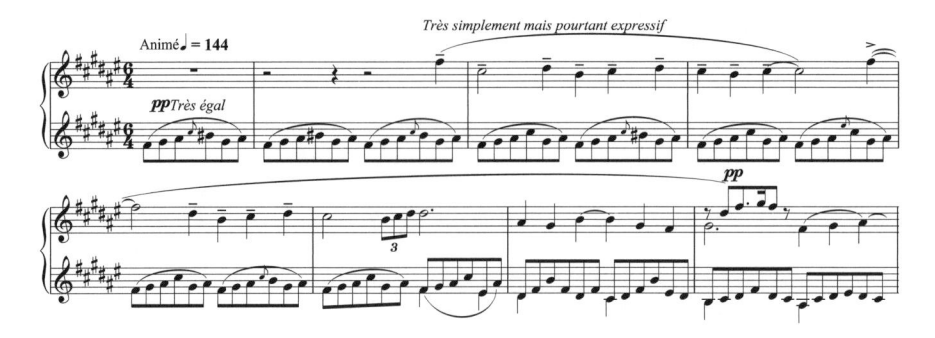

Another example of conjunct melody occurs in the opening to the "Intermezzo" ("Conte à la veillée"). A 5/4 meter appears, alluding to irregular meter found in some French folk music, a technique also employed by d'Indy. The naïveté of the melody in the "Intermezzo" is gradually contradicted by increasing chromaticism in the harmonization, as evident below:

Example 7.6   Measures 1–8 of the "Intermezzo" section of *Le chant de la terre*

As previously mentioned, most movements in *Le chant de la terre* share onomatopoeia in the form of church bells, as well as modality, cyclicism, distinct melodies, avoidance of explicit cadences, non-directional folk-like modal constructions, ostinatos, textural stratification, absence of leading tones, and ternary or modified ternary form. Differences between movements nonetheless occur and should be mentioned briefly in the following breakdown, in which each movement is coupled with accompanying poetry written by Séverac.

Prologue

Séverac created a regional and rural atmosphere in "Prologue" with the use of the flatted supertonic and notable absence of leading tones, which helped avoid functional harmonic cadences and created an inherently modal effect, thereby imitating folk music as well as Gregorian chant. One motive forms the thematic material for all but one movement and is frequently and directly quoted. The chant-like melody initially occurs in the "Prologue" within the Dorian mode. It is referred to by Séverac as 'Le chant,' or 'L'âme de la terre' (The Song, or The Soul of the Earth), and is the primary means of unification within the suite.

Example 7.7   Opening Prologue to *Le chant de la terre*

In this excerpt, it is likely that Séverac omitted bar lines as a way of avoiding accents and regular meter in order to reflect Dom Pothier's 1880 edition of Gregorian chant entitled *Mélodies grégoriennes d'après la tradition*, thus providing a reverent and almost spiritual character to farming life. Pothier purposely omitted bar lines in order to allow for a more supple flow within melodic phrases, a practice with which Séverac was familiar, as Pothier gave lectures at the Schola Cantorum when Séverac was a student. Nonetheless, the modal ambiance in this section also echoes folk chants de labour (or plowing songs), sung by toiling peasants in the Languedoc region, that were subsequently collected by Joseph Canteloube from written and oral sources and placed into his collection *Anthologie des chants populaires français*.[14] In fact, the second movement to this suite is labeled "Le labour" and its modality resembles chants de labour within Canteloube's anthology. The theme in the "Prologue" is also transposed and quoted in all the other movements, with the exception of the "Intermezzo." Example 7.8 illustrates this:

---

14   Joseph Canteloube, *Anthologie des chants populaires français groupés par provinces*, 4 vols. (Paris: Durand, 1951), 95.

Example 7.8   "Les moissons," Measures 1–8, *Le chant de la terre*

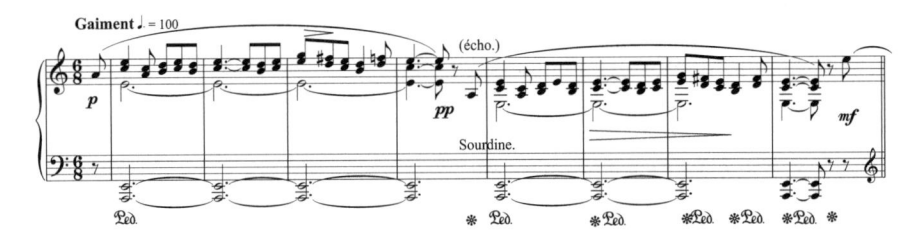

Le Labour (The Plowing of the Field)

> The length of the field kneaded from limestone and shale
> His torso arched, his arms clutching the plowshare
> The cowherd persists
> Guiding the mindlessly willful cattle
> Against the rocks' steely stubbornness
> And the bloody furrow; in visions of lilies,
> The chimerical visions evaporate.
> He dreams of joyful tomorrows,
> Golden morns, stormy nights;
> Cursed passersby, savage pillagers,
> But he continues
> Musing on the evening's opal hue,
> Wondering if his beloved longs for him in the forest's edge.[15]

"Le labour" furnishes a chorale transformation of the theme, thus suggesting an almost sacred quality of the land. Séverac's regionalism here foreshadows "Coin de cimetière, au printemps," from his piano suite *En Languedoc*, which similarly

---

15 Pierre Guillot, *Déodat de Séverac: écrits sur la musique.* (Liège, Belgium: Pierre Mardaga, 1993), 41–2.

"Le labour"

> Le long du champ pétri de calcaire et de marne
> torse ployé en arc et bras rivé au soc
> le bouvier s'acharne
> tendant l'effort des boeufs au vouloir identique
> contre l'entétement d'acier du roc
> et du sillon sanglant, liliales
> s'évaporent les visions chimériques
> il songe aux lendemains de joie
> aux matins d'or, aux nuits d'orage
> passants maudits, pilleurs sauvages
> mais il va ferme et droit
> en songeant le soir, sur fond d'opale
> l'Aimée l'espère au seuil des bois.

instructs that a certain movement sound as if coming from a distance, and pedals should therefore be blurred. Much of the writing is in the low bass register depicting the heaviness of the peasant's labor. This reflects the text, which does not suggest a romanticized view of farming, but instead emphasizes its difficulties. The second theme is the 'bien-aimée' melody. The movement also contains tritones, whole-tone scales, chromatic side-stepping, parallel block chords, and a series of unresolved dominant seventh chords.

Les Semailles (The Planting of the Seeds)

>By the furrows of the tamed field
>the sower goes, silent ...
>And then returns, without worries
>His arm offered to mysterious tomorrows
>His golden gesture,
>—scattered sparks—from dawn until evening
>Throws the seed of his hopes
>To sleeping Fate
>But the dark, Distant bell-tower
>Lights up with an *Angélus*
>And the lucid souls of the elected
>A light toward trails and paths
>Or watch over the crosses,
>The sower stops
>and, bending his head
>listens in prayer ... then stands up
>And turns back
>toward the open Destiny where his dreams lie.[16]

The angelus in "Les semailles" is depicted by parallel fourth and fifth intervals and heard in a mixolydian mode, while the accompanying figure suggests a Lydian mode.

---

16 Ibid., 42.

"Les semailles"

>Par les sillons du champ dompté
>le semeur va, silencieux ...
>et puis revient, à pas comptés
>le bras tendu vers les mystérieux
>Son geste d'or,
>—étincelles éparpillées—de l'aube au soir
>jette le grain de son espoir
>au Destin qui dort
>Mais le clocher sombre et lointain
>S'illumine d'un *Angelus*
>Et des ogives, en vol oblique,
>les âmes claires des élus
>s'envolent vers les sentiers et les chemins

The 'B' section continues a bass ostinato from the 'A' section within the Phrygian mode, and the recapitulation of the 'A' section is compressed by eliminating six measures; a codetta concludes the movement. This movement represents Séverac's early flirtations with Impressionism, as it is labeled 'tranquille, très doux et lointain,' and the performer is told to 'enlevez la sourdine.'

Intermezzo: Conte à la Veillée (Story of the Old One)

>Close to the hearth,
>Upon a beechwood stool
>the grandmother spins endlessly
>She sits there, surrounded by her agedness,
>For how long, no one knows,
>Binding and releasing
>The web of her wisdom.
>Night arrives, daughters and sons
>surround her, venerate her.
>Then, with a slow voice.
>Drawing in her sons
>With her knowledge
>She begins an ancient legend
>And all listen, saying nothing
>In their piety, happy to see,
>Curious to learn.[17]

"Intermezzo" is the story of a grandmother spending an evening surrounded by her family before a hearth during sunset, as she recalls history and legends. The

---

>où veillent les croix
>Le semeur s'arrête
>et, courbant la tête
>écoute et prie puis se relève
>et s'en revient
>vers le destin béant où git son rêve.
>17 Ibid.

"Intermezzo"

>Auprés de l'âtre,
>sur un escabeau de hêtre
>l'aieule file indiscontinûment
>Elle est lá, auréolée de sa viellesse
>on ignore depuis quelle ére
>liant et déliant
>les écheveaux de sa sagesse
>La nuit venue, les filles et les fils
>l'entourent, la venérent
>alors elle, d'une voix lente,
>tout en nouant les fils

movement contains two unrelated subsections within the 'B' section, which alternate two meters in the form of 5/4 (2/4 + 3/4, and 3/4 + 2/4) and 4/4. This provides an elusiveness to what is otherwise a highly non-elusive tonal movement. Much of this movement contains the primary theme of the suite, unbarred with lowered seventh degrees and tritone intervals. The 'A' section returns with full chords.

La Grêle (The Hailstorm)

> Like shocks of broken trees,
> Descending to the deep valleys
> In the distance; the organ far off rumbles,
> An old hobo of years past
> Who circles around the world
> And reappears, the same days
> The same places, burning towns,
> Pillaging fields in heavy clamors.
> Death awakens and dreams, to the sky,
> Behind the livid mist
> Pale after drinking the harvester's blood
> And misery's frosty flowers:
> A small, perfidious tomb.
> One deaf and savage clamor
> Of despair and self-revolt
> Climbs the farmhouses and villages
> But soon, in spite of the clashes
> Of the fraying hurricane
> Women go to the heart of the woods
> Strewing the soil with blood-stained flowers
> And tears of compassion;
> The bells ring into their eyes.[18]

Onomatopoeia in the form of church bells also occur within this suite, but unlike most bell tones suggested in various Impressionist works, including those by Debussy

---

> de son savoir,
> commence une antique légende
> et tous écoutent, sans rien dire,
> en leur piété, heureux de voir,
> curieux d'apprendre."

18 Ibid., 43.

"La grêle"

> Comme des chocs d'arbres cassés
> dévalant aux vallées profondes,
> au loin, là-bas, l'ouragan gronde
> vieux chemineau des ans passés
> qui marche en cercle autour du monde
> et reparait aux mêmes jours,
> aux mêmes lieux, brûlant les bourgs,

and Ravel, the bell tone combinations in Séverac's work are explicit references to oncoming storms or call those within the area to specific forms of daily prayer. Séverac accomplishes this by placing local terms into the score while providing programmatic references in the various movement titles. In the fourth movement, "La grêle," or "The Hailstorm," for example, a storm is heard in the outer segments, initially occurring in a long 'A' section within the mixolydian mode. This unfolds gradually over 88 measures and then retreats, as the inner 'B' section is indicated with the term 'Les rogations', referring to a solemn prayer or supplication chanted during the three days preceding Ascension day. This is reflected in a conjunct chant-like melody moving in parallel octaves while quick modal changes occur: B sharp, F sharp minor, C sharp Phrygian, C sharp Aeolian, E major, A Mixolydian, and F sharp Dorian. E flat dominant seventh chords then resolve to D minor. Thirteen measures later, the term 'Le glas', or "freezing to the bone," is indicated, a regional idiom alluding to a certain type of hailstorm that permeated the region near the Pyrenees mountains, warning of which was given to local citizens by church bell tones. These sounds are evoked through a diatonic melody supported by parallel fourth interval motion and major second and seventh intervals. The second half of the 'B' section again refers to 'Le glas', eventually leading to the return of the 'A' section. The keys and modes are frequently established with the aid of secondary dominant chords. Ostinato figures also occur in "La grêle," including a perfect fifth on D and an augmented fifth on A flat.

Les Moissons (The Harvest)

> This is the gold that falls
> Beneath the clear crescent
> The gold that bends
> Beneath the blond zephyr
> Gossiping children,
> Along the hedgerows,
> Harvest sheaves of joy
> While the girls pass by the woods,

> pillant les champs en fracas lourds.
> La mort s'éveille et songe, au ciel
> derriére la brume livide
> à boire le sang des récoltes;
> et la misére en fleurs de gel
> tombe serrée, tombe perfide
> une clameur sourde et sauvage
> de désespoir qui se révolte
> monte des mas et des villages
> mais bientôt, malgré les fracas
> de l'ouragan qui s'effiloche
> les femmes vont au fond des bois
> jonchant le sol de fleurs sanglantes
> et des larmes compatissantes
> perlent soudain aux yeux des cloches.

with laughs and flowers,
toward their loves
This is the gold that bends
Beneath the clear crescent
Of the Reaper-King![19]

"Les moissons" depicts the harvest and is the only movement after the "Prologue" to open with 'Le chant'. In this work, the movement recalls two themes, the initial theme provided in the prologue, as well as the 'bien-aimée' melody from "Le labour." After the harvest, the melody notated in the score by Séverac as 'l'aimée,' appears as a faint resemblance to that marked by Séverac as 'd'aimée,' in "Le labour." Wedding bells in the form of parallel fourths then announce the Epilogue, entitled "Le jour des noces." There is no clear return to the 'A' section, but instead a coda, which contains the original chant in an inner voice. More folk instrument imitations with disjunct melodies oscillate away from and back to the modal center of the movement.

Le Jour des Noces (The Wedding Day)

    Under the lime blossoms; in the whirlwind of sun
    Couples frolic
    The old eviscerate barrels
    Bagpipes and blowtorches whine above
    The passing Wind, which caresses and flees
    The Earth, a tepid and nacre vapor,
    Rises and dissipates, teasing and tender
    Through its dance,
    Under the barrels the old ramble on
    Through the dark, distant bell-tower's prophetic notes

---

19   Ibid., 43–4.

"Les moissons"

    Voici l'or qui choit
    sous le croissant clair,
    voici l'or qui ploie
    sous le zéphir blond
    Les enfants jaseurs
    le long des sillons,
    glanent les gerbes de leur Joie
    et les belles vont par les bois,
    avec des rires et des fleurs,
    vers leurs amours
    voici l'or qui ploie
    sous le zéphir blond
    voici l'or qui choit
    sous le croissant clair
    du Moissonneur-Roi!

The holy joy of Love
Spring about on the plain.[20]

The final 67 measures of the last movement, "Le jour des noces," contains twelve metric changes and end with a hemiola effect that employs 6/16 as compound duple meter. Timbre is also suggested, as the depiction of wedding bells is combined with sound representations of a shawm, a reference by Séverac to Catalan instruments. Another folk-like citation, in what is Séverac's earliest reference to Andalusian music and the influence of Albéniz, appears in the opening plucked guitar figuration consisting of alternating arpeggiated fourths and fifths. This leads to the return of the 'A' section, which is followed by the original 'Le chant' theme. Guitar figurations return, and these are succeeded by a coda, which consists of fragments from 'Le chant', coupled with wedding bells suggested by parallel fourths.

En Languedoc (In Languedoc), Suite pour Piano (1903–4)
Originally entitled *Loin des villes* (Far From Cities)

I. Vers le mas en fête (To the Farmhouse During a Holiday)
II. Sur l'étang, le soir (On the Pond, Evening)
III. A cheval dans le prairie (On Horseback, on the Prairie)
IV. Coin de cimetière, au printemps (In the Corner of the Cemetery, In Spring)
V. Le jour de la foire, au mas (The Day of the Fair, At the Farmhouse)

> My father was good and loved the fields
> those restful fields where love wilted
> when the shepherds sing with the wind
> that shivers in the gray trees
> those evening fields veiled in dreams of blue
> My father was good and believed in God
> But in so tender and lenient a God
> That a theologian would have cursed him

---

20 Ibid., 44.

"Le jour des noces"

> Sous les tilleuls; en tourbillon de soleil
> les couples s'ébattent
> Les vieux éventrent les tonneaux
> Cornemuses et chalumeaux nasillent au dessus
> de Vent qui passe, caresse et fuit
> De la Terre, une vapeur tiede et nacrée
> s'éleve qui se perd, frôleuse et câline
> á travers les danses
> Sous les tonneaux les vieux radotent
> Lors du clocher sombre et lointain en prophetiques notes
> la sainte joie d'Aimer
> s'élance par la plaine.

Had he known him. When I was small
He often took me on his knees
and said quietly, "Love love
And loathe hate. Love the day
And the night when you dream." I listened to him
Because of his gentle gaze
And he showed me the golden countryside
And the golden mane of the setting sun
Sometimes he led us with mother
And my little sisters: Jeanne, Lili,
And Marthe, whom God took from us
—Oh! God who makes us cry!—he led us
on the hillside, along white roads
Why did he say: "This is beautiful!"
These woods and the wind that laughs in the branches,
and these golden mists that hang up above!
Why did he say: "This is beautiful!"
I don't know, but it was nevertheless beautiful.
And it was good to love these things
And these plain-clothed people that lived there,
On these fields reaped and sown
With golden rain, the life of Men.
Since you also know of the soft confessions
Along the long roads, that the bended trees
And calm waters make to poets,
You, who would wander, far, far from the towns
On the hillsides veiled in dreams of blue
Listen! A good wind has risen tonight
Come, drink in the evening, at twilight
The aged trees sing for us ... listen!
Oh you who would wander, far from the towns,
Come with me, my country sings ... listen!
Since you would wander far from the towns
On the hillsides veiled in dreams of blue
(Séverac's poetry to accompany *Loin des villes*[21])

---

21 Ibid., 64–5.

Mon père était bon et aimait les champs
les champs paisibles où l'amour tressaille
quand les bergers chantent avec le vent
qui frémit en des arbres de grisaille,
les champs du soir voilés de rêve bleu.
Mon père etait bon et croyait en Dieu
mais en un Dieu si tendre et si clément
que les théologiens l'auraient maudit
s'ils l'avaient su. Lorsque j'étais petit
souvent il me prenait sur ses genoux
puis il disait tout bas: 'Aime l'amour
et déteste la haine. Aime le jour
et la nuit quand on rêve.' Je l'écoutais

Loin des villes was an early title to what later became Séverac's regional programmatic piano suite *En Languedoc*. Séverac subsequently thought the former title not specific enough and replaced it with one explicitly alluding to his native province.[22] *Loin des villes* contained four of the five movements later incorporated into *En Languedoc*, omitting Séverac's earliest Impressionist piano work, "Coin de cimetière, au printemps."

En Languedoc reflects Séverac's love of nature and idealization of routines and daily lives of villagers. "Sur l'étang, le soir" and "Le jour de la foire, au mas" were composed in 1903 and first performed in Brussels by Ricardo Viñes that same year. "Coin de cimetière, au printemps" and "A cheval, dans la prairie" were incorporated into the suite a year later and similarly had their première in Brussels. "Vers le mas en fête" was completed in 1905. The first complete performance of all five movements under its final title took place on March 25, 1905 at the Schola Cantorum, with Ricardo Viñes performing in what was the first concert of works composed exclusively by Séverac. The suite was performed by Blanche Selva at the Société nationale one year later. *En Languedoc* was subsequently published by Edition Mutuelle, the company

---

Parce qu'il avait un regard très doux
et qu'il me montrait la campagne d'or
et les cheveux d'or des soleils couchants.
Parfois il nous menait avec maman
et les petites soeurs: Jeanne, Lili
et cette Marthe que Dieu nous a prise
—Oh! Dieu qui fais pleurer!—il nous menait
sur les côteaux, le long des routes blanches.
Pourquoi disait-il: 'Que cela est beau!
Ces bois et le vent qui rit dans les branches.
et ces brumes d'or qui planent là-haut!
Pourquoi disait-il: 'Que cela est beau!'
Je ne sais pas mais c'était beau quand même
et c'était bon d'aimer ces choses-là
et ces gens mal-vêtus qui vivaient là
sur ces champs qu'on déchire et où l'on sème
avec de l'or en pluie, la vie des Hommes
Puisque tu sais aussi les doux aveux
que font aux poètes, le long des routes
les arbres penchés et les eaux tranquilles,
toi qui voudrais errer, bien loin des villes
sur les coteaux voilés de rêve bleu
écoute, un bon vent ce soir s'est levé
viennent boire le soir, au crépuscule,
les vieux arbres chantent pour nous ... écoute!
o toi qui voudrais errer, loin des villes,
avec moi, viens, mon pays chante ... écoute!
puisque to voudrais errer loin des villes
sur des coteaux voilés de rêve bleu

22 See Guillot, *Déodat de Séverac: la musique et les lettres*, 221. [Séverac letter to Ricardo Viñes, November, 1904.]

established by Séverac's close friend and colleague René de Castéra, who published many works by Schola Cantorum students and disciples.[23]

Critic Pierre Lalo favorably reviewed *En Languedoc* in *Le temps*, commenting: "[Séverac's music] springs from nature, it is filled with the fragrance of the land, and there one breathes a perfume of the sun." The sun here is a veiled reference to southern French music, as other writers of the period often used the word when describing music by Séverac and other southern French musicians, including Joseph Canteloube.[24] Séverac's suite was also inspired by the works and philosophies of Mistral. The essence of Mistral's poetry on which this suite was based depicts daily lives of villagers and the excitement of the country fair. It also contemplates the beauty of southern France and the monotony of labor undertaken by agrarian inhabitants.

"Vers le mas en fête" ("To the Farmhouse During a Holiday") is dedicated to Ricardo Viñes and depicts a journey to a Mas, or farm during festival season. The composer quotes a dedication taken from the first chapter of Mistral's poem *Mireio*: "We sing only for you, oh shepherds and folk of the farm."[25] The movement contains three sections, the first labeled 'Par le chemin du torrent,' the second 'Halte à la fontaine,' and the third 'Le mas en fête.' The programmatic regionalist references suggest a young man returning to his home in the country after a long absence. Each section, therefore, describes the traveler at various stages in the journey home. 'Par le chemin du torrent' portrays the traveler hurrying home while passing a rushing mountain stream, and in the 'Halte à la fontaine' section, the traveler stops en route to rest at a spring, while 'Le mas en fête' describes the traveler's arrival at the farm in the midst of a festive celebration. The coda in this movement contains the ringing of the 'Angélus du soir,' evoking a post-festival calm at the farm during sunset.[26]

The second movement, "Sur l'étang, le soir" ("On the Pond, Evening"), dedicated to Gustave Bret, depicts nature in the Languedoc province with the following introductory quote by Séverac: "This night, oh beloved, we will go and dream on the lake, in the old rowboat."[27] Canteloube claims that the movement was inspired by Séverac watching fireworks with a friend over the Saint-Ferréal pond near Narbonne. Some scholars note a similarity between organ-like passages within this movement and those in Debussy's "La cathédrale engloutie."[28]

---

23 Rouart Lerolle took over the plates for publication in 1919.

24 Pierre Lalo, "La musique: concerts—à la Schola Cantorum, les oeuvres de Déodat de Séverac, un musicien nouveau," *Le temps* (July 7, 1905), 3. "Elle sort de la nature, elle est pleine de l'odeur du terroir, on respire le parfum du sol."

25 Frédéric Mistral, *Mirèio, pouèmo provençau* (Paris: H. Piazza, 1923), Chapter 1. "Cantan que per vautre, o Pastre e gènt di Mas."

26 Séverac, *Déodat de Séverac: Piano Album* (Paris: Editions Salabert, 1991), 83.

27 Brody, "The Piano Works of Déodat de Séverac: A Stylistic Analysis," 147. "Cette nuit, ô bien-aimée, nous irons rêver sur le lac, dans la vieille barque." Gustave Bret was a well-known organist and composer.

28 Canteloube's comment about Narbonne can be found in Canteloube, *Déodat de Séverac* [1st Edition, Paris, 1929] (Béziers, France: Société de musicologie de Languedoc, 1984), 50. Similarities between a passage in Séverac's "Sur l'étang, le soir" and Debussy's "La cathédrale engloutie" can be located in Pierre Guillot, "Claude Debussy and Déodat de

"A cheval, dans la prairie" (On Horseback, on the Prairie), dedicated to "Monsieur A. d'Avezac de Castéra," contains three sections, 'Départ,' 'Halte à la fontaine,' and 'Retour.' Canteloube claims that Séverac was inspired to compose the work after witnessing the activities of a chicken near his home village of Saint-Félix-Caraman. 'Départ' nonetheless evokes a galloping horse, 'Halte à la fontaine' recalls the memory of a previous episode, and the galloping horse resumes his paces in 'Retour'.

"Coin de cimetière, au printemps" was composed the same year that Séverac left his native village of Saint-Félix de Lauragais for Paris. His father and sister had died earlier that year, and the work's title refers to the local village cemetery, as distant bells are indicated by the performance instructions 'Le chant doucement marqué; comme des cloches lointaines.'[29] Although the piece contains major second and minor seventh intervals characteristic of music by Debussy, the title and impetus for the work is regional, and paralleled the aesthetic found in Barrès's philosophy of *la terre et les morts*. Both Barrès's philosophy and Séverac's composition refer to death, ancestry, and the reverence for one's local pays. The movement is dedicated to Viñes.

The final movement, "Le jour de la foire, au mas" ("The Day of the Fair at the Farmhouse"), is dedicated to Henri Estienne, and incorporates the introductory quote: "Tomorrow, arise before the dawn and we will follow the long, twinkling herds."[30] The movement begins and ends with the fluviol, or flute of a goat herder, and alludes to action at the farm on the day of the fair. The traveler is gathering animals to sell, while swarming crowds appear joyous. Following a short episode, the performance indications 'Au loin sonne l'angélus de l'aube' cues a transposed version of the angelus of the first movement. The additional directions 'Comme un bruissement de sonnailles' and 'Comme un chant de coq' provide animation subtitles to noises suggesting chickens and roosters.[31] Séverac's earliest significant use of pentatonicism occurs within this movement.

In *En Languedoc*, Séverac modified his use of cyclic elements, thereby demonstrating his stylistic evolution. Rather than employing earlier cyclic techniques that often emphasized recurring melodies within a work, as in *Le chant de la terre*, cyclic elements in *En Languedoc* come in the form of rhythmic motives and interval relationships. For example, in the first movement, "Vers le mas en fête," the section described as 'Halte à la fontaine' contains in the right-hand figuration the major-second and perfect-fourth interval C–D–G, as evident below:

Séverac," *Cahiers Debussy* (nouvelle série, no. 10, 1986), 12–15. Debussy composed the two preludes after Séverac composed *En Languedoc*. According to Alfred Cortot, "Sur l'etang, le soir" was influenced by Chabrier's "Sous-Bois" and "Paysages." This is somewhat evident in the interplay of parallel fourth and fifth intervals in both works by Chabrier and Séverac's work, as well as major second intervals employed as coloristic devices, chromaticism, and a prominent use of triadic tonal harmony. See Jean-Bernard Cahours d'Aspry, "Déodat de Séverac" (unpublished manuscript), 204.

29 Séverac, *Déodat de Séverac: Piano Album*, 108.

30 Brody, "The Piano Works of Déodat de Séverac: A Stylistic Analysis," 147. "Demain, lève-toi avant l'aube; nous suivrons les longs troupeaux tintinnabulants."

31 Ibid., 113, 118–19.

Example 7.9   Interval structure in 'Halte à la fontaine' section, Measures 94–95, *En Languedoc*, first movement ("Vers le mas en fête")

These intervals are emphasized throughout the work. In measure 185, the seconds and fourths return in a higher register, whereby upper stems show inversion techniques based on the notes C–D–G.

Example 7.10   Interval structure, Measures 183–190, *En Languedoc*, first movement, "Vers le mas en fête"

In the opening to the second movement ("Sur l'etang, le soir"), the two intervals are again highlighted, this time in the form of F–B flat, B flat–C, and G–C:

Example 7.11   Interval structure, Measures 3–5, *En Languedoc*, second movement ("Sur l'étang, le soir")

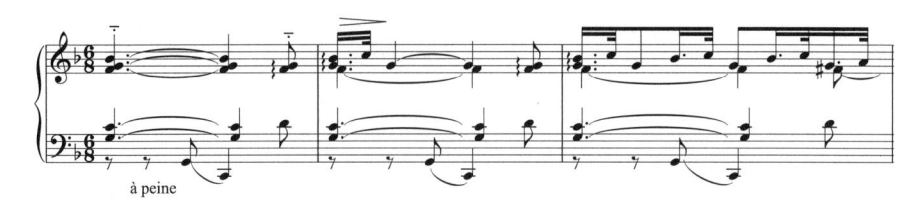

In the 'Halte à la fontaine' section of the third movement, " A cheval dans la prairie," the seconds and fourths are sounded at length:

Example 7.12   Interval structure, Measures 108–111 of *En Languedoc*, third movement ("A cheval dans la prairie")

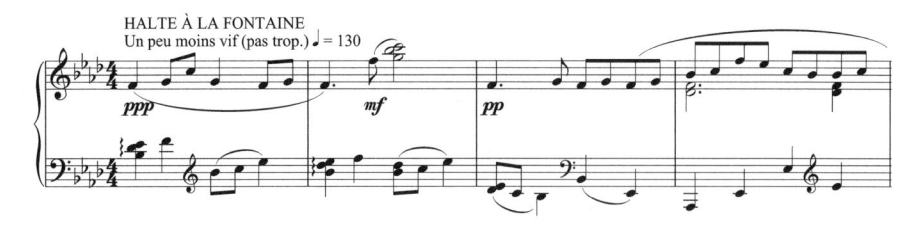

Towards the end of the movement, the intervals are entered as minor seconds in rhythmic augmentation. The diminishing of major seconds into minor second intervals is coupled with accompanying perfect fourth intervals.[32]

Example 7.13   Interval structure within augmentation in *En Languedoc*, third movement ("A cheval dans la prairie")

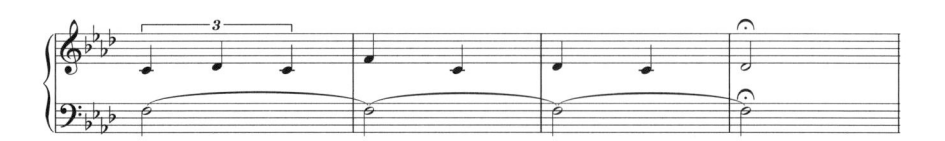

The sections entitled 'Angélus de soir', as well as the 'Halte à la fontaine' theme in the first and third movements, suggest the use of program music to enhance the cyclical structure. In the first and third movements, a specific melody or motive

---

32   These sections emphasizing quartal harmonies are often the result of added-note chords.

returns at the end. The size of these recapitulations vary in length, from two to four measures to verbatim repetitions, at times extended by a codetta. Unlike the cyclic melody in *Le chant de la terre*, however, cyclic melodies in *En Languedoc* do not carry the responsibility for unifying the entire group of pieces. Pedal points, rhythmic patterns, and moods are the recurring elements that bind each piece into a unit, rather than traditional melodic and harmonic structure. New motives often emerge in subordinate positions and ultimately assume increased importance. This often thins out textures, which allows rhythmic or melodic motives to eventually take precedence over surrounding material.

Other techniques employed by Séverac include wide pitch ranges in the bass and treble, stratified textures, trills, ostinatos, comparatively soft dynamics, pedal points similar to those employed by Debussy in many of his piano works, as well as multiple levels of sonority, parallelism, clustered dissonance, pentatonicism, modality, glissandi, and rapid arpeggios.[33] While glissandi and rapid arpeggios employed by Debussy often had atmospheric intentions, most employed by Séverac in *En Languedoc* served to expand the upbeat at points of articulation in order to suggest more emphasis on the following bar:[34]

Example 7.14 Rapid Arpeggios in Measures 128–129 in "Vers le mas en fête," from *En Languedoc*

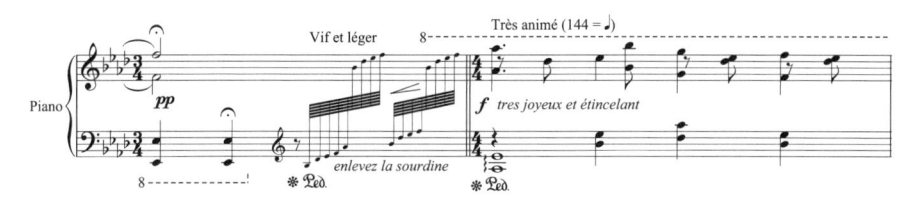

Although meter shifts and asymmetrical phrasing are common in this suite, rhythm often maintains less significance, except in "A cheval, dans la prairie," in which the rhythm helps suggest the beating of horse hooves.

Most of Séverac's melodies in *En Languedoc* are not exclusively part of a triadic structure, but are often modal with flatted leading tones and flatted supertonics. Altered dominant seventh chords are prominent, as are tonic chords with added sixths, thus creating a rich harmonic palette.

---

33 These characteristrics are also found in Debussy's *Préludes* and *Etudes* for piano, which were interestingly composed after *En Languedoc*. Nonetheless, Lisztian configurations in Ravel's *Jeux d'eau* (1901) can be found in *En Languedoc*.

34 Ibid., 154. Compositions by Chabrier, Albéniz, and Bordes also influenced *En Languedoc* through Séverac's use of dance rhythms, imitation of instruments, and sounds from native festivities. This was especially characteristic of Albéniz's music, which often glorified the sights and sounds in various sections of Spain. These include Albéniz's *Fête-Dieu à Seville* and "Triana," from *Iberia* (1905–9; New York: Dover, 1987).

Miscellaneous Works

Séverac composed various individual piano pieces as well as groupings of pieces into larger works. The following is not intended to be an exhaustive study of individual works, but to be a list of other piano pieces that merit attention.

Le Soldat de Plomb: Histoire "Vrai" en Trois Récits, 4 hands (1904)
(The Lead Soldier)

Le soldat de plomb was published by Edition Mutuelle as part of a Schola Cantorum project to gather works depicting childhood.[35] Maurice Denis illustrated the publication with color designs on Japanese paper, and subjects of these illustrations included Séverac, d'Indy, and pianists Blanche Selva and René de Castéra. The composition had its première at the Société nationale de musique in 1905, followed by a performance at the Libre esthétique.

The three movements are "Sérénade interrompue," "Quat' jours de boîte," and "Défile nuptial," and suggest the story of a soldier and his paramour. In "Sérénade interrompue," a toy solider serenades a doll, in "Quat' jours de boîte," the distraught toy soldier is uncertain about his chances of marrying the doll, but obtains permission to marry her by the end of the movement, and in "Défile nuptial," the two marry. This work contains ostinatos, added sixth chords, major second intervals as colorist devices, and pedal points to help convey the story. The work is of intermediate difficulty intended to be played by adults.

Stances à Madame de Pompadour (1907)
(Stanzas to Madame de Pompadour)

Madame de Pompadour (1721–64) was the mistress of Louis XV (1710–74). *Stances à Madame de Pompadour* is therefore a neo-baroque work inspired by the harpsichord and originally intended to be part of a suite entitled *Le parc aux cerfs*. Its first known publication occurred in a supplement of *Musica* in 1909.[36] The work is a poem for piano in modified strophic form, with the melody repeated several times with ornamental modifications. The 'B' section includes a series of unresolved dominant seventh chords, and the outer sections contain rapid harmonic rhythm. There are also echo effects in the style of the French baroque keyboard composers.

---

35 This also included Bizet's *Jeux d'enfants* for piano, 4 hands (1872).

36 Blanche Selva claimed that this suite was originally published in *La Schola paroissiale*, but this edition has not been found. The manuscript to *Le parc aux cerfs* has been lost.

Pippermint-Get: Valse Brillante pour le Concert (1907)
(Peppermint Candy: Brilliant Concert Waltz)

Pippermint-Get was part of a trend among French composers to create waltzes influenced by cafe music.[37] It is a parody of dance hall music based on *La valse lente*, an extremely popular tune in fin de siècle Paris. The title *Pippermint-Get* came from the name of a liquor produced locally by Auguste Get, whom Séverac met in 1907 when they ran for political office together following Séverac's graduation from the Schola Cantorum.[38]

Baigneuses au Soleil: Souvenir de Banyuls-Sur-Mer (1908)
(Sunbathing: Memory of Banyuls-Sur-Mer)

Baigneuses au soleil is an étude pittoresque in ternary form dedicated to pianist Alfred Cortot and was composed during the summer following Séverac's graduation from the Schola Cantorum in 1907. The première took place in 1909 at the Libre esthétique in Brussels, with Blanche Selva performing, and in Paris at the Société nationale de musique that same year. The work evokes the seashore in Impressionist ways, including the use of wide ranges on the keyboard, echo effects, crystalline textures, glissandos, voices on multiple levels, pedal points, ornamentation, asymmetrical phrasing, soft dynamics within the high treble range, and frequent metric changes, the latter often used to avoid composing over bar lines. The melody nonetheless becomes the controlling element, in contrast to Séverac's other piano works, where harmony and harmonic color are often more prominent. The melodic theme consists of a dotted-note rhythmic pattern that appears twice, first in the developmental 'B' section of the work, and subsequently in a skeletal version towards the end of the composition.

En Vacances: Au Château et dans le Parc, Petites Pièces Romantiques de Moyenne Difficulté pour Piano (1911)
(On Holiday: In the Chateau and in the Park, Small Romantic Pieces of Moderate Difficulty for Piano)

I. Invocation à Schumann (Invocation to Schumann)
II. Les caresses de grand'maman (Grandmother's Caresses)
III. Les petites voisines en visite (Young Neighbors Come to Visit)
IV. Toto déguisé en Suisse d'église (Toto Disguised in a Swiss Church)
V. Mimi se déguise en marquise (Mimi Dressed up as a Marquise)
VI. Ronde dans le parc (Dance in the Park)
VII. Où l'on entend une vieille boîte à musique (Upon Hearing an Old Music Box)
VIII. Valse romantique (Romantic Waltz)

---

37 Three versions were published by Rouart in 1907, one for piano and two for orchestra.

38 The liquor was produced in Rêves, a Languedoc market town near Séverac's home village of Saint-Félix-Caraman; Otwell, "The Piano Works of Déodat de Séverac: A Complete Recording," 87.

En vacances is in a style typical of particular compositions composed by Séverac between 1911 and 1914, in which he employed a tempered Romantic period aesthetic. The style of each movement as well as programmatic titles illustrate the influence of Schumann's *Kinderszenen*, further corroborated by the title to Séverac's opening movement, "Invocation à Schumann," which paraphrases Schumann's opening movement "Von Fremden der Ländern und Menschen."[39] These elements are also found in Séverac's song, "Ma poupée chérie" (1914), written for his infant daughter, which also depicts childhood.

En vacances is technically accessible for young pianists, evident in Séverac's avoidance of extreme ranges, closely blocked chords, extended pedal points, and fortissimo passages. Instead, Séverac incorporated repeated single notes in the form of pedal points, ostinatos, multiple levels of texture, highly tonal harmonies, occasional modality, flatted seventh intervals instead of leading tones, Phrygian and plagal cadences, and asymmetrical and overlapping phrases. Major–minor modal shifts often occur when Séverac incorporates major thirds within minor key melodies. Flat keys are preferred, as is typical in most of Séverac's piano works, but here the pieces remain within simple keys: C–F–D–A–B flat–E flat. Each of the eight movements is a miniature in ternary form and the structure remains the only means of unification within each movement.[40] 'B' themes are often derived from 'A' section material, which are usually themselves divided into two sections.

---

39 Similar works composed at the time include Schumann's *Album für die Jugend*, op. 68, Fauré's piano suite for four hands, *Dolly*, op. 56 (1894–7), Debussy's *Children's Corner* for piano (1908), and Ravel's ballet *Ma mère l'oye* (1911). "Invocation à Schumann" is dedicated "pour l'ami L. Froment," "Les caresses de grand'maman" is dedicated to Séverac's niece Césette de Bonnefoy, "Les petites voisines en visite," "pour Cricri Synnestwedt," "Toto déguisé en Suisse d'église" to René de Castéra's son, Gaston, "Mimi se déguise en marquise" to Maria Godebska (who was one of the individuals to whom Ravel dedicated *Ma mère l'oye*), the daughter of Cipa Godebska, "Ronde dans le parc" to Max Carrère, the son of a journalist for *La dépêche*, "Où l'on entend une vieille boîte à musique" to a young cousin of Séverac, Mimi de Rigaud, and "Valse romantique" to another young cousin, Marie de Saint-Cyr.

40 There are a few additional piano works that have recently been published, which includes *Scènes des champs* ("Pastorale: Scenes from the Country") of 1897, a work in binary form that alternates between G minor and E flat major within cut time interchanging with sextuple meter. The autograph manuscript was left unfinished at measure 48, and was recently completed and published by Isabelle Giordanetto. *Impromptu dans le caractère romantique* ("Impromptu in the Romantic Style") of 1898 is a finished work in rondo form. *Valse métèque* ("Waltz of the Immigrants") of 1898 is a slow waltz in F major, but the end of the autograph score is illegible and was recently completed by Isabelle Giordanetto. *Danse du "tonneau" et du "bidon"* ("Dance of the Cask and the Kettle") of 1907 is a work that Séverac adapted from his lyrical farce *Le roi Pinard*. See Déodat de Séverac, *Trois mélodies et quatre pages pianistiques inédites* (Paris: Presses de l'Université de Paris-Sorbonne, 2002). "Scènes des champs, no. 1 (Edition Giordanetto); "Pastorale" (Edition Shiono); "Valse métèque" (Edition Giordanetto); "Danse du 'tonneau' et du 'bidon'" (Edition Aline Fauré).

En Vacances II: Petites Pièces Romantiques de Moyenne Difficulté pour Piano (1911)
(On Holiday II: Small Romantic Pieces of Medium Difficulty for Piano)

I. La fontaine de Chopin (The Fountain of Chopin)
II. La vasque aux colombes (The Fountain Basin with Doves)
III. Les deux mousquetaires (The Two Musketeers)

In 1921, Rouart Lerolle issued a posthumous group of pieces collected from several of Séverac's works left in manuscript form. Séverac had completed "La fontaine de Chopin" and "Les deux mousquetaires" in 1911, while Blanche Selva finished the second half of "La vasque aux colombes" following Séverac's death; she was aided by Séverac's own sketches.

"La fontaine de Chopin" is representative of a trend during Séverac's time of writing in the style of another composer. The work is homophonic and chromatic, and contains fewer motives when compared to Séverac's other piano works. In "Les deux mousquetaires: canon sans danger dans le style pompier," two musketeers chasing one another are depicted through polyphonic passages, illustrating Séverac's return to the counterpoint characteristic of his music during his early years at the Schola Cantorum. It is one of the few linear piano works composed by Séverac when compared to his preference for multiple textures over pedal points in other works. "La vasque aux colombes" is written in an early eighteenth-century baroque style, with transparent textures, four-bar phrases, rapid harmonic rhythm, walking bass, and the employment of motive as a primary method of unification. This ternary work contains a juxtaposition of unrelated tonalities.

***

As previously mentioned, Séverac's piano music includes a wide range of characteristics and temperaments.[41] This includes major–minor modal shifts coupled with linear lines in *Le chant de la terre*, Impressionist elements in *En Languedoc*, and Romanticism in the style of Robert Schumann's *Kinderszenen* in *En vacances*. These works are nonetheless unique in that harmonic color becomes the controlling element rather than melody—characteristics in direct contrast to those found in Séverac's piano works based on Catalan music, which will be discussed in Chapter 10.

---

41 *Sérénade au clair de lune* (Serenade to the Moonlight, 1898) was composed as a piano piece and Séverac later orchestrated it for chamber ensemble in 1913. It is built on a theme that goes through a series of modulations. Different instrumental solos are heard in the chamber music version. The work was published in 1913 by Editions Lointier in Nice and the chamber music version has been recently recorded for orchestra. See "Déodat de Séverac: inédits oeuvres pour orchestre," performed by Robert Benzi and L'orchestre de la Suisse Romande" (Espace2 RSR6197, 2006).

Chapter 8

Unpublished, Unfinished, Lost, and Recently Published Works

One of the challenges with regard to Séverac's output centers around the number of compositions that were either unfinished, unpublished, or lost. Some works have been discovered in recent years and published, thanks, in part, to the initial attention that Elaine Brody gave to Séverac's piano music in her 1964 dissertation.[1] More needs to be accomplished in uncovering additional manuscripts, however, which will then provide us with a fuller view of Séverac as a composer.

Séverac's unpublished works date as far back as his youth. His earlier works written in 1898 during his first year at the Schola Cantorum include *Promenade en mer également* for piano, as well as *Preludio* and *Air de ballet*. Séverac composed piano works before this time by fluently improvising on organ or piano, but his mother and friends would often chastise him for neglecting to notate many of these compositions.[2] Letters written by Alfred Cortot to Blanche Selva following Séverac's death cite that some of his best music went with him to the grave, and that Séverac seemed unconcerned about preserving many of these works.[3] When Céret poet Pierre Camo solicited Séverac to compose a one-act opera with a sardana based on Catalan popular melodies, Séverac subsequently assured Camo that the work was already in his head and all that remained was to transcribe it to paper. Séverac's Catalan colleague Gustave Violet also described Séverac's reticence to notate compositions:

> How unfortunate that the [Te Deum] was not notated ... [Séverac] created it without putting it [to paper]. He had a superb memory ... It is in this way that he played to me often a magnificent piece on the *Cloître d'Elne* of which one hasn't found a trace among his papers.[4]

It is possible that Séverac's reluctance to preserve his compositions by notating them was due to his fear of producing what he thought society would consider mediocre works, as hints regarding his insecurity are reflected in various comments, including

---

1   See Chapter 1.
2   Elaine Brody, "The Piano Works of Déodat de Séverac: A Stylistic Analysis" (PhD Dissertation, New York University, 1964), 28.
3   Letter written April 13, 1962; see Alfred Cortot, *La musique française de piano*, II, (1930–48; Paris: Presses Universitaires de France; nouv. éd., 1981), 201–23. Marc Lafargue also maintained this fact in Marc Lafargue, "Souvenirs mêlés," *Les Marges*, later reprinted in Lafargue, *Le coq catalan* (March 24 and 31, 1923).
4   Gustave Violet, "Hommage à Séverac" (Paris, 1952).

one in 1919, when he stated "I am not sure of myself ... I don't have an idea as to the value of my work ... Certain moments it appears to me [to be worthy]. Other times I doubt ... If I have not succeeded, it is because I am unable to express what I feel."[5] Some of this doubt is unfounded, however, as many of Séverac's colleagues have described the fact that he improvised superb works.[6]

Additional comments by Séverac refer to his discomfort with his music upon hearing a new generation of works composed within a more economical style that began to evolve during Séverac's years in Catalonia: "I see music more and more today as an art that must be condensed ... In all my work, there is useless padding, and developments that are too long."[7] These so-called condensed works between 1910 and 1921 would have included music by Stravinsky.

Another reason why Séverac did not finish many of his compositions is because of his need to earn a living, which took time away from finishing many pieces. Séverac's only child was born during this time, and she demanded attention as well as income. This need to survive financially is corroborated in a letter by Séverac, who wrote to his editor in Marseille: "If I do not send you more music, it is because I am ... obliged to create other works—arrangements of amateur works and orchestrations, which provide me with money that I need."[8]

Despite these issues, it is nonetheless important to discuss certain unpublished and unfinished works because it will not only provide an incentive to locate these manuscripts, but also aid in further understanding Séverac's stylistic evolution. The purpose of this chapter, therefore, is not to analyze every known incomplete work by Séverac, but to discuss more significant works that are either lost, or not published, or incomplete. So-called significant works are determined in terms of quality alluded to by colleagues and by analyzing incomplete or recently discovered manuscripts.

---

5   Brody, "The Piano Works of Déodat de Séverac: A Stylistic Analysis", 312. This feeling of insecurity was common among many composers of the time, especially composers dedicated to Franck's music. Paul Dukas felt unsure about many of his works and refused to release virtually any composition after 1912, and eventually destroyed them.

6   Jean-Bernard Cahours d'Aspry, "Déodat de Séverac" (unpublished manuscript), 318, and Brody, translated by author, "The Piano Works of Déodat de Séverac: A Stylistic Analysis," 312.

7   Pierre Guillot, *Déodat de Séverac: la musique et les lettres* (Liège, Belgium: Pierre Mardaga, 2002), 76. [Séverac in a letter to René de Castéra, June 6, 1918.] "Je vois aujourd'hui et de plus en plus la musique comme un art que doit être condensé ... Dans toutes mes oeuvres, il y a des développements trop longs, du délayage inutile."

8   Joseph Canteloube, *Déodat de Séverac* [1st Edition, Paris, 1929] (Béziers, France: Société de musicologie de Languedoc, 1984), 40. [Séverac letter to editor in Marseille, 1911.] "Si je ne vous envoie pas davantage de musique, c'est que je suis ... obligé de faire d'autres travaux—arrangements d'oeuvres d'amateurs, orchestrations, qui me rapportent de l'argent dont j'ai besoin."

Orchestral Music

Nymphes au Crepuscule (1901–1902) [Incomplete]
(Nymphs at Dawn)

One work in the Impressionist style is *Nymphes au crépuscule*, a choral-orchestral work composed between 1901 and 1902 and dedicated to pianist Alfred Cortot.[9] Séverac evoked images and impressions of nature near the Pyrenees mountains, thereby including the subtitle *Tableau musical*.[10] There are several sections indicated, including *L'emeraude des vagues au crépuscule, Le lys des nymphes,* and *Le saphir et l'or qui les auréolant*. Séverac indicated different themes in this work to represent various characters, primarily a faun, nymphs, and a forest voice.

The composition evokes a lake in the middle of a forest in autumn twilight. An owl shrieks as autumn leaves fall and a young faun is heard at the edge of the lake playing a lute that accompanies a poem of love. Voices of invisible nymphs respond from afar. The faun repeats its song, but this time, only a sorrowful groaning is heard in reply as a sorcerer appears. The faun then tries to pull itself away from the sorcerer, and the voice of the forest subsequently proclaims the misfortune of love as the owl shrieks from afar. The faun subsequently hears silence in the forest and becomes calmer as nymphs come closer and envelop it, and laughter and joy then evolve throughout the night.

Séverac initially received advice from d'Indy regarding the work, as attested by a letter wherein Séverac summarized the work:

> I tried ... to evoke images and impressions of nature ... Have I succeeded? I do not know. In any case, I have submitted it to d'Indy and will tell you his criticisms ... I like best those creatures from dreams that conform to nature and are not tainted by civilization.[11]

Séverac's complex harmonies are used to evoke dreams and nature, as Séverac suggests in a letter to his family after hearing from d'Indy concerning the work:

> [D'Indy] found my last symphonic poem Nymphes au crépuscule good, despite some chords "which are not stirred up by verse" ... D'Indy is nevertheless not very shocked by my unexpected harmonies.[12]

---

9   The first text is in manuscript form, though incomplete. The second was printed in the program at the première. There are two additional versions of this work, one for piano and the other for piano, four hands.

10   The work was initially entitled *Nymphes* in the original manuscript and subsequently *Nymphes au crépuscule* in the program accompanying the première.

11   Guillot, *Déodat de Séverac: la musique et les lettres*, 153, 159. [Letter to sister Alix, February, 1902; Séverac letter to family, March, 1902.] "J'ai essayé ... d'évoquer des images, des impressions de nature ... Ai-je réussi? Je ne sais. En tous cas je l'ai remis à d'Indy et je vous dirai ses critiques ... J'aime mieux des personnages de rêve conformes à la nature non frélatée par les civilisations."

12   Ibid., 154. [Séverac letter to family, March, 1902.] "Il a trouvé très bien mon dernier poème symphonique *Nymphes au crépuscule* malgré quelques accords 'qui ne sont pas piqués des vers' ... D'Indy n'est pourtant pas tres effarouché de ces harmonies imprévues."

These unexpected harmonies no doubt refer to those found in Séverac's Impressionist style, which includes whole tone scales and dominant ninth chords. Not only did d'Indy encourage Séverac with regards to this new style, but there are pages in Séverac's manuscript containing d'Indy's orchestration suggestions supporting this approach.[13] This further corroborates the fact that although d'Indy spoke of "harmony" as being a false science, he was nonetheless a supportive and flexible pedagogue.[14] In fact, d'Indy conducted the première of the work at a Société nationale de musique concert in 1902. Séverac wrote in anticipation of the event:

> Happily for me, d'Indy ... has helped me considerably [with my compositions]. The orchestra ... will play it ... Tuesday evening. It is true that this orchestra is good enough, as it consists of members of the Concert Colonne and Concert Lamoureux; but my score is very delicate. There is a host of tiny details that need to be drawn out, but not exaggerated. However, I believe I have succeeded in giving the impression that I wanted.[15]

The work was well received; Debussy attended the première and "strongly congratulated" Séverac after the performance.[16] Furthermore, there is much evidence, thematically, as well as musically, that *Nymphes au crépuscule* is one of Séverac's earliest works to have been influenced by Debussy, especially by *Prélude à "L'après-midi d'un faune"* and *Nocturnes*. The faun is employed in the title to Debussy's *Prélude à "L'après-midi d'un faune"* as well as in the program to Séverac's *Nymphes au crépuscule*. Both also share specific characteristics, including whole-tone scales, glissandos, unresolved parallel ninth and dominant ninth chords, polyrhythms, soft dynamic ranges, solos, non-homogenized sound, *lontano* or far-away sounds, delicate percussion, harps, and a faun theme depicted by a flute. Pierre Guillot compares the two works:[17]

Example 8.1a   Measures 13–15 (Faun Theme) from *Nymphes au crépuscule*

---

13 D'Indy suggested that Séverac combine harps with celeste.

14 See Chapter 2. It must also be observed that d'Indy himself used Impressionist harmonies in *Jour d'été à la montagne*, op. 61, and *Symphonie sur un chant montagnard 'cevenole,'* op. 25.

15 Guillot, *Déodat de Séverac: la musique et les lettres*, 163. [Séverac letter to family, 1902.] "Heureusement pour moi d'Indy ... m'aide considérablement. L'orchestre ... jouera ... mardi-soir. Il est vraie que cet orchestre est assez bon, étant composé par moitié de membres du Concert Colonne et du Concert Lamoureux; mais ma partition est très délicate; il y a une foule de petits détails qu'il faut faire ressortir sans les exagerer; cependant je crois avoir réussi à donner l'impression voulue par moi."

16 Aspry, "Déodat de Séverac" (unpublished manuscript), 154.

17 See Pierre Guillot, "Claude Debussy and Déodat de Séverac," *Cahiers Debussy* (nouvelle série, no. 10, 1986), 9, 15.

Example 8.1b Measures 1–3 (Faun Theme) from Claude Debussy's *Prélude à "L'après-midi d'un faune"*

Séverac scored the work for piccolo, two flutes, two oboes, one English horn, two clarinets, one bass clarinet, three bassoons, four French horns, three trumpets, three trombones, one tuba, two harps, one celeste, and percussion, including triangle and cymbals. Also included are violins I and II, violas, and divided cellos and basses, reflecting a division prominent in many of Debussy's compositions.[18] In fact, with the exception of brass used in *Nymphes au crépuscule*, the orchestration in the work is similar to that of Debussy's *Prélude à "L'après-midi d'un faune"* and *Nocturnes*, as both composers emphasized woodwinds and French horn. Séverac's employment of sopranos and altos in the wings also resembles Debussy's "Sirènes," from *Nocturnes*.[19] Because of Séverac's friendship with Debussy coupled with a keen interest in his music, it would be unlikely that Séverac would be unaware of Debussy's work during this time.[20] Séverac's score was completed in 1902, but there were several measures lacking that rendered the autograph manuscript incomplete. The work has nonetheless recently been completed in two separate versions, one by French musicologist and organist Pierre Guillot, and another by conductor Roberto Benzi, Director of l'Orchestre de la Suisse Romande.[21]

Poèmes des Saisons: Tableaux Symphoniques (1900) [Lost]
(Poems of the Seasons)

One of Séverac's earliest compositions to remain lost consists of two out of four intended symphonic movements to be collectively entitled *Poèmes des saisons*, an orchestral work reflecting the four seasons. Individual movement titles suggest the beginnings of Séverac's Impressionist style: "L'automne: impression automnale" and "Chant d'ombre en la nuit d'hiver." Although there is no documentation to imply that Séverac composed the two remaining movements evoking spring and summer, there is evidence that he intended to compose these two pieces: "D'Indy has accepted ['L'automne: impression automnale' and 'Chant d'ombre en la nuit

---

18 These include Debussy's *Jeux* for orchestra of 1913.

19 The rhythm in *Nymphes au crépuscule* evolves into a military-like march, reminiscent of Debussy's "Fêtes," from *Nocturnes* for orchestra.

20 Debussy composed *Nocturnes* between 1897 and 1899, and two of the movements in Debussy's *Nocturnes*, "Nuages" and "Fêtes," had their première at the Lamoureux in December, 1899. The first complete performance of *Nocturnes* took place in October of 1901. It is possible that Séverac could have heard the performance of some or all of the movements to *Nocturnes* before completing *Nymphes au crépuscule*.

21 The work has been recently recorded. See "Déodat de Séverac: inédits oeuvres pour orchestre," performed by Robert Benzi and L'orchestre de la Suisse Romande "(Espace2 RSR6197, 2006).

d'hiver,'], despite their new form and has strongly encouraged me to continue [composing 'Au printemps' and 'En été'], which I will do."[22] Séverac began the two movements evoking autumn and winter in 1899 and finished them the following year:

> I finished two of my Poèmes des saisons. Let's hope that d'Indy finds them to his liking, but I do not know if the form will appear to him too insignificant, because I tried a new system ... It is dangerous [to do so] ... but it costs me nothing to try.[23]

Séverac's so-called new system also suggests this newly adopted Impressionist style. There is little evidence as to what happened to Séverac's manuscripts for these works.

Didon et Enée (1901) [Lost]
(Dido and Aeneas)

Séverac enjoyed classical literature, particularly Virgil, and this is reflected in *Didon et Enée*, a symphonic poem based on *The Aneid*. Séverac began the quadripartite composition in 1899 and the première took place at the Schola Cantorum two years later. Séverac's first inclination was to compose the work for orchestra, but due to time constraints, scored it only for piano, four hands. He eventually orchestrated it for a London competition; the work, however, was not accepted, due to the fact that symphonic poems were not allowed into the competition. Séverac described the situation with the competition jury:

> It appeared ... on the competition program ... that symphonic poems were not admitted [into the competition] and that the academy would establish a special competition in two years time [for this genre]. Maus added that, as this work made a great impression on the jury, he had no doubt, said it would be a success at this next competition devoted ... to symphonic poems.[24]

There is no documentation as to whether Séverac submitted this work two years later to the proposed competition jury. Therefore, the orchestral version was never performed and Séverac later claimed to have lost the score.[25]

---

22 Guillot, *Déodat de Séverac: la musique et les lettres*, 90. [Séverac letter to sister Alix.] "D'Indy les a acceptés malgré leur forme nouvelle et m'a fort encouragé à continuer les autres, ce que je vais faire."

23 Aspry, "Déodat de Séverac" (unpublished manuscript), 109. [Séverac letter to sister Jeanne, June, 1900.] "J'ai terminée deux de mes *Poèmes des saisons*. Espérons que d'Indy les trouvera à son goût mais je ne sais si la forme ne lui paraîtra pas trop menue, car j'ai essayé une formule nouvelle ... C'est dangereux ... mais rien ne me coûte d'essayer."

24 Guillot, *Déodat de Séverac: la musique et les lettres*, 159. [Séverac letter to family, 1902.] "Il paraît ... sur le programme du coucours ... que le poème symphonique n'était pas admis et que l'académie en ferait un concours spécial dans deux ans. Maus a ajouté qu'étant donné 'la grande impression produite par *Enée* sur le jury, il ne doutant pas du succès pour le prochain concours' reservé ... au dit poème symphonique."

25 Aspry, "Déodat de Séverac" (unpublished manuscript), 129, 242–3.

Musique de Scène

Le Mirage, Deux Mélodies pour Soprano et Orchestre sur des Vers de Léon Damart (1903) [Unpublished]
(The Mirage)

Séverac composed much incidental music during the last decade of his life. *Le mirage*, however, was performed as early as 1904 when Séverac was still a student at the Schola Cantorum.[26] This symbolist drama in verse by Léon Damart stipulates that all moral sickness is inspired by the imagination. The story includes fairies within a nocturnal Black Forest where lives an old German alchemist by the name of Jacobus Nicht. Nicht has the reputation of being an incomparably dressed magician who helps all sick people who implore him for his services. He administers water accompanied with words that speak to the heart of patients, thereby curing their tormented souls. Two youthful clients, Elias Floch and Margareth, doubt his talents, as they doubt most things in life, including the power of love. They nonetheless visit him for help and he induces Elias to think that Margareth is Shakespeare's Juliet and therefore impels him to find love.

Séverac's Impressionist music for this work consists of two songs and a finale appearing in three parts of the drama. The first song, "Claudicants cahir, caha," (Légèrement animé) was written for flute, oboe, clarinet, bassoon, string quartet, and soprano, the latter singing the role of Dolcio. The second song, "Le ciel s'entrouvre," (Lent, comme un choral) takes place in the middle of a mystical love scene and the music of the finale occurs on the last words of the play: "Will I awaken from this ephemeral dream?," reflecting Damart's symbolist aesthetic also embraced by Debussy.[27]

The work contains much modality and chromaticism. Séverac conducted the première at the Théâtre du Casino de Royen from the manuscript. The composition was never published, but there are two autograph scores of the work, the orchestral-vocal score at the Bibliothèque nationale that Séverac used, and a piano-vocal score at Séverac's baronial birthplace home in Saint-Félix de Lauragais. There is also a handwritten copy completed recently by a professional copyist and available for viewing at Séverac's birthplace home.

Mugueto (1911) [Lost]

Mugueto of 1911 is incidental music to a lyrical and dramatic work in three acts based on a Languedoc novel by Marguerite Navarre. It was commissioned for a Félibrige holiday organized in Rabastens in honor of Auger Gailhard, a sixteenth-century Languedoc poet. He was one of the last troubadours, enjoying the favor of King Charles IX and King Henri IV.

---

26 The performance of this work took place at the Théâtre Foncillon à Royer.
27 Jean-Bernard Cahours d'Aspry, *Déodat de Séverac* (Biarritz: Atlantica, 2001), 127. "Vais-je me réveiller de ce rêve ephémère?"

Mugueto is set in the Gascogne region of France during harvest time. Spirit fairies preside over sunrise and disappear as harvesters emerge, who then sing "Chanson du blé." Mugueto enters as the group leaves, and she is then alone with François, who avows his love for her. After he leaves, Mugueto, who has never loved, asks the birds and flowers for help in knowing this emotion. She then meets a stranger by the name of Marcellir and the two discuss their past. Marcellir is poor and without family and Mugueto pities him and therefore tells him that he can work for her father. Mugueto then falls in love with Marcellir.

Act II opens with a village holiday and Mugueto and Marcellir are in love, but Mugueto sees Marcellir and a woman named Jacquette together and asks them for an explanation, whereupon Marcellir confesses his interest in Jacquette. Meanwhile, young peasants arrive singing a song about the Languedoc region of France in "Chanson d'amour", which is treated in canon form.

Act III opens with sorcerers incanting at sunrise. Mugueto begins to realize that egoist love is not sacrificial love and decides that she must die, because to her, life has become intolerable. Peasants sing a melancholy and tearful berceuse of death, composed in the style of an ancient folk melody.[28]

Le Retour (date unknown) [Lost]
(The Return)

Additional lost works by Séverac include *Le retour*, a work for theater in one act by Maurice Magre, the librettist for *Le coeur du moulin*. The story centers around Steno, who, after selling the house and land of his fathers in order to live in nearby cities, returns to his pays to wed Simone, who has waited for his return. She refused to wed a rich farmer in order to be faithful to Steno. Symbolism abounds in this work, which is reinforced through the absence of personalities as characters represent archetypes, including a farmer, wine harvester, bird, and ox.

Victoire de Samothrace (date unknown) [Lost]
(Victory of Samothrace)

Victoire de Samothrace is a tragic play by Abel Gance (1889–1981) which contains seven pieces of music that Séverac composed for the play: "Les ailes qui dormant," "L'éveil des ailes," "Les ailes blanches," "Les ailes d'or," "Les ailes rouges," "Les ailes bleues," and "Les ailes éteincelles." The historical story is based on the victory in 307 BC of the ruler Ptolemy and his Syrian daughter, Helle, daughter of Antigone.

---

28 Aspry, "Déodat de Séverac" (unpublished manuscript), 493.

Piano Music

Le Tombeau de Gaugin (1906) [Lost]
(The Tomb of Gaugin)

Séverac loved the art of Paul Gaugin and kept an original painting by the artist on his piano. Evidence of the existence of a piano work entitled *Le tombeau de Gaugin*, or *La mort de Gaugin*, is corroborated by Ricardo Viñes, who wrote in his journal: "Séverac played his *Le chant de la terre*, part of *En Languedoc*, and the debut of *La mort de Gaugin*, which is marvelous."[29] Cipa Godebski arranged to have the work performed at the Salon d'automne in 1906 in a room consecrated to Gaugin, who had died three years earlier. There is no evidence, however, of the work having ever been performed at this event. Canteloube discovered the manuscript upon Séverac's death in 1921, but the notation is illegible.

Cantata

Mediterranéenne (1904) [Lost]
(The Mediterranean)

Mediterranéenne was one of Séverac's earliest works to pay homage to the south of France, Spain, and Italy. He wanted the composition to characterize Mediterranean culture, an interest which also inspired Séverac to plan on building a conservatory in Barcelona. The school was to be called the Escola Mediterrània de Música and dedicated to training Mediterranean musicians with indigenous music; these plans, however, did not materialize.[30]

Mediterranéenne was written as a cantata for orchestra and singer with a text by southern French poet François-Paul Alibert (1873–1953). Canteloube stated that he heard Séverac play a piano transcription of all five movements in 1906, and that it was "an admirable work with color and a grandiose expression that created a profound impression."[31]

---

29 Suzy Lévy, *Journal inédit de Ricardo Viñes: Odilon Redon et le milieu occultiste, 1897–1915* (Paris, 1987), 71.

30 Séverac often visited a friend in Puigcerdà, the poet, critic, and journalist José Maria Junoy, who, together with Séverac, had contemplated the opening of a Mediterranean conservatory in Barcelona. Junoy researched artists who adhered to his ideals, and in Séverac found someone whose ideas corresponded to his own; Aspry, "Déodat de Séverac" (unpublished manuscript), 326.

31 Canteloube, *Déodat de Séverac*, 22. "Une oeuvre admirable de couleur et d'une expression grandiose."

Work for the Theater

La Fille de la Terre (1913) [Lost]
(The Girl of the Land)

La fille de la terre is a tragédie populaire by Emile Sicard, which had its première under the direction of Joseph Lignon at the Théâtre de plein air de Coursan before 8,000 spectators. This work depicts heroic and legendary deeds within rustic life. People do not receive traditional names in this piece, but are given generic titles symbolic of their ideal function. Séverac composed three symphonic preludes for the work, with each prelude symbolizing a different part of the day—dawn, late afternoon, and evening. There is a fugue evoking dawn, a melancholic song describing late afternoon, and a nocturne within a waltz rhythm for evening, the latter including local bells combined with lyrical poetry. Séverac also composed several principal themes, including a motive suggesting serenity, another based on dance rhythms, a third labeled "largo quasi religioso," and a fourth termed "Theme of the Land," which is sung by a soprano.

Les Antibels (1907–19) [Lost]
(The Antibels)

Les Antibels is an opera based on a tragedy within a rustic setting written by Emile Pouvillon (1840–1906) and first performed in 1899 without music.[32] The story centers around Jan, who returns to his native village from military service in order to help his mother. Séverac began composing the work in 1907 and worked on the music for much of his life, but most of the composition was never notated, except for certain themes. Canteloube mentioned that the work had been composed in its entirety within Séverac's head and many of Séverac's friends heard the five acts that Séverac committed to memory in a performance with Séverac at the piano.[33]

Le Roi Pinard (formerly, La Princesse d'Okifari) (1907–19) [Lost orchestral manuscript]
(King Pinard: King of the Vineyard)

Le roi Pinard ("Pinard I, roi du clos") is an operetta, or opéra bouffe, in three acts and four scenes on a libretto by Séverac. The work was completed in 1919 and dedicated to French soldiers who fought in World War I. Séverac subsequently attempted to have the work performed by an opera company in southern France, but the institution categorically refused to perform a contemporary composition; the piece therefore never received a première.

The action takes place during the sixteenth century on the imaginary island of Hokifari, which enjoys an ideal climate where marvelous fruits, flowers, and wines are produced. Characters in the story include the reigning King Pinard I, his

---

32 The performance took place at L'Odéon theater.
33 Ibid.

daughter Neurozita, the Minister of the Interior, Prince Bleutet, and the courtesan Mademoiselle Chiffan.[34]

Although the orchestral-vocal score is lost, there does exist an autograph manuscript of the work for voice and piano. Séverac's grandson Gilbert Blacque-Belair asked composer Yvon Bourrel to finish orchestrating the work based on fragments, and as a result, Bourrel completed a suite in 1991 in six movements that is faithful to the original piano-vocal score. The suite is scored for two flutes, one piccolo, two oboes, one English horn, one bassoon, two French horns, one trumpet, and strings. Included in *Suite d'après le roi Pinard* is "Prélude," "Madrigal," "Complainte," "Valse," "Rondeau," and "Finale." The prelude is melodramatic and the madrigal contains dance music from the operetta, which was to be sung by a mezzo-soprano choir. This dance music was transcribed in the suite for two flutes and includes a melancholy vocal habanera with an English horn solo. Also included in the opera is a waltz parody, ballet music, and a rondeau.

***

As stated, there are many reasons as to why many of Séverac's works have been lost, unfinished, or unpublished. Séverac's need to earn a living through orchestrating works by other composers took time away from finishing his own compositions. His carefree nature of not writing down various works that he improvised at the piano was another issue, as was his insecurity as to the value of his compositions. Musicians have nonetheless been completing unfinished works by Séverac while other complete compositions have recently been published. There is nonetheless still much work to do in uncovering many of Séverac's lost manuscripts.

---

34 Aspry, "Déodat de Séverac" (unpublished manuscript), 648–50.

PART III
Catalan Music, 1910–1921

Chapter 9
Catalan Regionalism: Politics and Music

Catalonian Political and Cultural History

Before analyzing Catalan folk and popular elements employed in Séverac's later works, it is helpful to review briefly the historical and cultural background of Catalonia, as well as Catalan music instruments and dances. We can then examine more fully the contents in Séverac's Catalan-based works as well as the Catalan regionalism that inspired the composer's interest in the region's indigenous culture.

Catalonia is comprised of the northeastern tip of the Iberian peninsula between the Pyrenees mountains, the Mediterranean sea, and the Ebro basin. It was an autonomous country during the early part of the first millennium AD until Charlemagne annexed the territory to the Franks at the end of the eighth century.[1] Almost 200 years later, the territory recovered its independence from the Franks and became a sovereign nation, and this independence lasted until the beginning of the sixteenth century. In 1516, the territory was integrated into the Spanish empire under the Hapsburg dynasty.[2]

In 1640, the Catalans rebelled against Philip IV, a conflict not quelled until 1659. It was at this time that Spain seized control of the southern region of Catalonia while the region north of the Pyrenees, later referred to as the French province of Roussillon, was annexed by France and quickly became economically and culturally integrated into the country, thus splitting the region.[3] Another Catalan outbreak in order to gain political autonomy took place in 1705. Catalonia surrendered in 1714, at which time Philip V abolished all Catalan political institutions and imposed Castilian laws, with the territory thereby losing its independence. Napoleon subsequently attempted unsuccessfully to

---

1   The indigenous language is spoken in a much larger area that includes the Catalan regions annexed to France in 1659.

2   In the twelfth century, Languedoc and Catalonia became united under a common sovereign. It was at this time that the first literary texts in Catalan appeared. The poetry of the Provençal troubadours became popular at the Barcelona court and by the thirteenth century, Provençal had replaced Latin as the official language of culture and court. Catalan eventually became the language of literature and philosophy, and this trend reached its zenith during the fifteenth century.

The difference between the Provençal and Catalan languages are largely politically rather than linguistically motivated. There are nonetheless some differences: regarding morphology, verb conjugations in both languages are slightly different. Catalan had a distinctive past tense formation known as periphrastic preterite formed from a variant of the verb "to go," plus the infinitive of the verb, which does not exist in Provençal. There are some minor phonological differences; in written form, Provençal and Catalan are relatively compatible.

3   Although Spain took control of southern Catalonia, the Catalan constitutional system was still preserved. Catalan patriotism largely transpired in Spanish Catalonia.

annex Spanish Catalonia, and this experience helped make Catalans aware that their territory was juxtaposed between two centralist regimes with assimilationist intentions.

It was early in the nineteenth century that many Catalan writers and artists realized the futility of political struggle. Instead, they accorded a greater power to music and literature to help achieve cultural independence. As a result, literary works of this Catalan Renaissance reflected Catalan regionalism and independence. The Catalan Renaixença coincided with the Romantic movement and took place between 1820 and 1890, ending with the subsequent popularity of modernisme in Catalan literature.[4] A poet who contributed to the Catalan Renaissance was Joaquim Rubió y Ors (1839–89, pseudonym Lo Gayter del Llobregat) who, in a prologue to his set of poems *Poesias catalanas* (1843), reinforced the growing perception that "Catalonia can still aspire to independence, not political independence, but certainly literary independence."[5]

Catalan poets created works in their indigenous language. The poet Bonaventura Carles Aribau became the first important creator of Romantic poetry in the Catalan language. He helped inspire the Renaixença through a description of his feelings of nostalgia towards his country and language in *La pàtria* (1833).[6] Other poets, such as Jacint Verdaguer (1845–1902) and Joan Maragall (1860–1911) followed suit.[7] Further regional patriotism was prompted by the recreation of medieval literary contests, or

---

4 Modernisme (1888–1911) is not to be confused with modernism. It represented the Catalan equivalent to other fin de siècle movements. The central city for this style was Barcelona and proponents of Modernisme opposed the religiousness and tradition inherent in the Renaixença. The Renaixença in French Catalonia began and ended approximately 25 years later than that of Spanish Catalonia.

5 Albert Balcells, *Catalan Nationalism*, translated by Jacqueline Hall (New York: St. Martin's Press, 1996), 26. Translation of Lo Gayter del Llobregat, *Poesias catalanas* vol. 1 (Barcelona: Edició Poliglota—Estampa de Jaume Jepus y Roviralta, 1888). Ors was an accomplished scholar of poetry in the nineteenth century. His works represent an attempt to re-establish the tradition of Catalan verse. His first poems were published in the *Diario de Barcelona* between 1839 and 1840. Ors created works under the pseudonym of Lo Gaiter del Llobregat and created works that reflected the new spiritual independence of the Catalan people.

6 Bonaventura Carles Aribau was the editor of the journal *El europeo* between 1823 and 1824. This publication was a significant landmark as the first important Catalan publication in the nineteenth century. *La pàtria* was a poem with nostalgic leanings towards Catalonia and the Catalan language—a poem that helped usher in the Catalan Renaixença.

7 Joan Maragall joined the staff of *Diario de Barcelona* as a private secretary—a post he held until 1903. As a journalist, Maragall wrote on political and social questions, but he also reviewed many theater productions of modernist playwrights. Maragall considered modernisme (or décadentisme) in poetry as simply the Romantic movement emerging after an interlude of naturalism. His poems include "Poésies" (1895), "Visions i cants" (1900), "Les disperses" (1903), "Enllà" (1906), and "Sequències" (1911). He was encouraged by the Catalan composer Felipe Pedrell, who set early sections of the poem "Visions, el comte arnau" to music. Jacint Verdaguer (1845–1902) won first prize at the Jocs Florals of 1877 through his epic poem in ten cantos *Atlàntida*, which was used by Manuel de Falla in his unfinished oratorio completed by Ernesto Halfter. Verdaguer's second epic poem, "Canigó" (1885), depicts the legendary origins of Catalonia through a direct confrontation between pagan and Christian themes. "Canigó" is a folk tale of a young Christian knight enchanted by mountain spirits in the Pyrénées. The poem is set against the background of the Moorish

Jocs Florals ("floral games"). The Jocs Florals was first organized in the fourteenth century and winners were awarded jewels in the form of flowers.[8] The celebration was eventually discontinued in the seventeenth century and not reinstated until the nineteenth century. The first of these occasions during the nineteenth century took place in Barcelona, and this 1859 event also helped give the Catalan Renaissance an institutional identity.

Several journals were published in the Catalan language in the 1870s, including *La campana de Gràcia* and *L'esquella de lá Torratxa*. In 1879, Valentí Almirall helped popularize political Catalanism and Catalan self-government through the creation of the first Catalan-language newspaper *El diari Català*. Catalan theater also flourished, including Serafí Soler's important work *Pitarra*. Catalan patriotism was also displayed socially through church societies, choral organizations, walking clubs, nationalist associations, and sardana dancing groups.[9]

Catalan Folk Music and Dance: The Sardana and Cobla

It has been suggested that the sardana dance had its roots in the secular round dances of ancient Greece (500–300 BC) and is believed to have been brought to Catalonia during the twelfth century.[10] One possible precursor to sardana music is the ronde ("ball redon" or "ball rodó")—a Catalan ballad that often accompanied round dances.

---

invasion of Roussillon, and the final defeat of pagan spirits is symbolized by the founding of the Benedictine monastery of Sant Marti del Canigó.

8 Arthur Terry, *Catalan Literature* (London: Ernest Benn Limited, 1972), 94.
9 These events were emphasized more in Spanish Catalonia then French Catalonia.
10 Gilbert Chase, *The Music of Spain* (New York: Dover Publication, Inc., 1941), 253. Much information regarding these dances during antiquity is known through iconographical references and historical documents, including writings by Greek geographer Strabo (66 BC– AD 29), who spoke of Iberian men and women dancing while holding hands. However, both sexes mostly danced apart from each other, and it was not until the Renaissance that men and women began to dance together. The word *sardana* is the feminine form of the Catalan adjective sarda, or in ancient times, sart or sarta, from the Latin word sardus, sardi, sardesc, or sardesca. However, ancient people often gave it the name cerdana, cerretes, or ceretani—which had its origins in the Catalan cerda or cerdana, derived from the adjective ceretanus or ceritanus. The name sarda or cerda is derived from the word cerdan—a person who lives in Cerdana. In fourteenth-century Perpignan (a town in French Catalonia), families often have last names such as Sarda, Serda, Cerda, Sardana, Serdana, Cerdana, and Serdanet. The following is a list of published references to the sardana together with the specific word chosen: cerdanes (1595), cerdana (1585, 1625, 1800s), cerdana, propre danse de Cerdagne (1611), sardanas (1573, 1655), serdana (1602), sardena (1616), sardanes (1619), sardanilla (1647), and sardana (1200s, 1605, 1700s). For more information on the sardana, see Josep Maria Mas i Solench, *Diccionari breu de la sardana* (Santa Culom a de Farners—J.M. Mas i Solench, 1981), Josep Maria Mas i Solench, *La sardana, dansa nacional de catalunya* (Barcelona: Generalitat de Catalunya, 1993), Aureli Capmany, *La sardana a catalunya* (Barcelona: Montaneri i Simón, 1948), Rubin Jenkins, *The Sardana Dancers* (London: J. Cape, 1964), Henry Pépratx-Saisset, *La sardane, la danse des catalans; son symbole, sa magie, ses énigmes* (Perpignan, France: Labau, 1956), and Max Havart, "Coblas, sardanes, danses, musiques catalanes," *Revista terra nostra* nos. 98–9 (1999).

Illustration 9.1 *Sardana Dancers in Saint-Félix de Lauragais*. Permission courtesy of the Bibliothèque Festival Déodat de Séverac, Toulouse, France

This fact is apparent in twelfth-century ceramic paintings found in sculpted monuments and therefore lends evidence that the ronde was danced in Catalonia as early as this time.[11] The sardana is also said to be related to the contrapàs llarch, a genre in which music, words, and dance were incorporated into a popular liturgical representation of a Christian Passion drama.[12] In addition, some scholars have theorized that the origins of the sardana can be traced to plainchant, which later evolved into goigs, hymns with couplets followed by a refrain usually dedicated to the Virgin Mary, a saint, or other religious subjects.[13] The oldest known reference to the sardana is in a Castilian poem by the Spanish poet Antonio Lo Frasso, who described the sardana as a dance popular in the Barcelona region:

> So they can jump and dance
> Eating chickens, hens and rabbits
> Shepherds, nymphs, go hand-in-hand
> Dancing a thousand sardanas on the plain.[14]

In 1573, there appeared a mandate from the bishop of Gerone, who suppressed what he considered "abuses habitually carried on in the cathedral and other churches in the diocese," referring to the dancing of the sardana inside the church.[15] Twenty-two years later, a letter from the bishop of Vich forbade the dancing of sardanas inside the church, allowing them instead to be danced in front of cathedrals and therefore not to distract church members.[16] During the same era, the dance was cited by the Castilian playwright Lope de Vega (1562–1635) in his work *El maestro de danzar* (1585):

---

11 Pépratx-Saisset, *La sardane, la danse des catalans; son symbole, sa magie, ses énigmes*, 67. It has also been suggested that the ronde influenced the sardana in its use of triple-meter patterns.

12 The contrapàs dance is also believed to be of Greek origin and initially danced by any number of people forming a circle with connected hands. The contrapàs is comprised of four types—the contrapàs llarch (long), the curt, the sarda, and the persigola. The sarda was also prominent in French Catalonia during the second half of the nineteenth century. According to Albert Mattes, the tradition was not only important in the mountain regions, but also played by fisherman at seaport villages. See Albert Mattes, *L'indépendant des Pyrénées-Orientales* (May 24, August 11, December 12, 1926).

13 There is often a mixture of religious and secular elements in many of these works that are often associated with dance. The combining of religious ceremonies with sacred dance does exist, although the juxtaposition is unusual. A variety of goigs are preserved in the fourteenth-century *Llibre vermell*.

14 F. Pujol, "Sardana, cançoner popular de catalanya," vol. 1 (*Diccionari de la danza*), 446. The poem was written c.1550–65. "Para bien saltar, bailar, bien mascardo Comiendo, pollos, gallinas y conejos pastores, nimphas van mano a mano bailando mil cerdanâs por el llano."

15 For documentation, see Pépratx-Saisset, *La sardane, la danse des catalans; son symbole, sa magie, ses énigmes*, 47. "Abus habituellement commis dans la cathédrale et autres églises du diocese."

16 Ibid.

> Feliciana—What were you dancing?
> Aldomaro—The sardana.
> Feliciana—It is good for women.
> Aldomaro—For a chosen mask
> and now for this hidden one
> it is full of remedies.[17]

One of the earliest detailed accounts of the sardana is found in a 1611 dictionary published in Madrid by Sebastian Covarrubias entitled *El tesoro de la lengua española*. A Catalan verse describes the Barcelona holiday of Carnestoltes with a remark about the sardana:

> Many of those who dance
> Without getting tired
> Do the sardana
> And others dancing the simple lo ball pla
> All of them hand-in-hand.[18]

This reference to the sardana as inherently benign is belied by a 1619 file regarding a sorcery claim in Terrassa, where there appeared a reference to "nothing less than the devil in person in red clothes—playing a very raucous flute on an ode of sardanes, which made witches dance."[19]

The social role of sardana dance events was mentioned in a 1647 Castilian poem composed for a Barcelona holiday in honor of the birth of the daughter of a certain viceroy:

> There the gallant
> Had the sun so close
> That, under the sound of the sardanilla
> Put the cart on the other side.[20]

A Jesuit priest from Béziers by the name of Father Vanière witnessed the dance in the early eighteenth century, where he alluded to a metaphysical dualism with regard to the nature of the dance by employing the word "fury," but proclaiming the experience beautiful:

---

17 Lope de Vega, *El maestro de danzar* (Act II, Scene 17), 1585. "Feliciana—Que danzabas? Aldomaro—La cerdana. Feliciana—Para mugeres es buena. Aldomaro—Para mascara escogida y esta de agora fingida esta de remedios llena."

18 Sebastian Covarrubias, *El tesoro de la lengua española* (Madrid). "Molts dels que danser sense que es cansen fan la Sardana i *lo ball pla* tots mà per mà."

19 Pépratx-Saisset, *La sardane, la danse des catalans; son symbole, sa magie, ses énigmes*, 48. "Riens moins que le diable en personne, tout de rouge vêtu—jouait d'une flûte qui faisait le son très rauque et sur un mode de sardanes pour faire danser deux bruixes."

20 Pépratx-Saisset, *La sardane, la danse des catalans; son symbole, sa magie, ses énigmes*, 47. "Alli et galan pretendiente tuvo el sol tan de su mano que al son de la sardanilla hizo dan voelta al carro."

The hands united ... in the middle of the square, while out of the windows people looked at them moving their feet and hands according to the rhythm and the song, their bodies were bent, making furious movements ... They were running toward one another sometimes turning and facing each other with a sudden move, often to the [accompaniment of] the lyre ... The people applauded this beautiful spectacle.[21]

Although sardanas were for social events, women were originally the only ones allowed to participate, eventually leading to groups consisting solely of men, as observed in 1823 when "Henry" (b.1778), a historian and conservator in the Perpignan Library, described his reaction to the sardana:

> The sardana, at least the contrapas was danced by men only in Perpignan on the Place de la loge. It is a fact that there is a solemn and even religious character within the contrapas and sardana to which the most ancient texts bear witness.[22]

The first sardanas to be later notated were composed by Joan Llandric in 1840, but it was only when Josep "Pep" Ventura (1817–75) created richer sounding compositions that the composed sardana became widely popular among musicians. Ventura's works contained well-crafted melodies and harmonies not constrained by strict rhythms. As a result, he became regarded as the father of the modern sardana.

Ventura's decision to invigorate the genre began when he fell in love with the daughter of a popular musician in Figueras, who wanted his daughter to marry a musician. Ventura was not a musician at the time but worked diligently until he soon was able to become a member of a local cobla, a group of musicians who play sardana music. He then traveled to villages collecting popular dance melodies from sardanas, with which he then expanded the form and created what is now referred to as the sardana llarga. Ventura composed 500 of these works, and they later became the canonical repertoire that influenced other Catalan musicians.[23] One such composer was Enric Morera (1865–1942), who set his sardanas to Catalan poems and subsequently made arrangements of his original compositions for choral groups.[24]

---

21 Ibid., 55. Castilians in Barcelona during the eighteenth century thought the sardana subversive and attempted to halt the proliferation of the dance and other forms of Catalan culture by prohibiting the teaching and speaking of Catalan in schools. "Les mains unies ... au milieu de la place, cependant que des fenêtres profondes, le peuple les regarde, agitant leurs pieds et leurs mains selon la cadence et le chant ou, le corps ployé, se livrant à des mouvements endiablés ... Elles courant l'un vers l'autre, tantôt se tourant le dos, tantôt se faisant face par une volte soudaine. Souvent, au signal de la lyre ... Le peuple applaudit ce beau spectacle."

22 Ibid., 56. "La sardane, était du moins le contrapas dansé par des hommes seulement à Perpignan, sur la place de la Loge. C'est un fait que le caractère solennel et même religieux du contrapas et de la sardine—dont témoignent les plus anciens textes."

23 Ventura's most favored sardana compositions were often inspired by popular song, including *Per tu pioro*, *Toc d'oracio*, *Arri moreu*, *Ai quines noies*, *Or son les oguetes*, *Totes voten hereu*, *El cant dels avcells*, and *El pardal*.

24 Morera's best known sardanas are *L'emporda* and *La santa espina*. Morera once commented: "The sardana is a dance, a hymn, a song; it is Catalonia." See Chase, *The Music*

Sardana Music

Certain scholars have argued that the sardana is not, strictly speaking, a folk dance, since both music and choreography have been largely composed by known individuals during the nineteenth century.[25] However, the genre is strongly rooted in Catalan rural folk rhythms and is thus generally considered by other scholars to be of a folk aesthetic. In favor of the second interpretation, the sardana has become the symbol for Catalan national unity and identity.[26] Its widespread presence among various social classes and both genders underscores the populist nature of this elegant and solemn communal circle dance. Legend has it that the dance was originally intended for women only, and that men began gradually to create and dance their own contrapàs, and then forbade women to participate. Eventually, both sexes danced together.

When dancing a sardana, participants hold hands in a circle and dance simple steps, while new dancers enter at will. The steps first move twice to the right, then to the left, and to the right again. The toe is pointed before each set of steps are taken. For this reason, the music is considered repetitive and hypnotic until a sudden change of tempo and pitch occurs. Usually in duple meter, sardana compositions closely resemble Provençal folk music, since they often contain duple subdivisions which alternate with intervening triple subdivisions. The melodic line helps determine the rhythm, characteristically comprised of metrical combinations:

---

of Spain, 255. ("La sardane est une danse, un hymne, un chant; c'est le Catalogne"). Other composers of sardana-influenced music include Anselm Clavé (1824–74), Juli Garreta (1875–1925), who composed 60 sardanas, Vincens Bou (1886–1962), Joan Carreras (1823–1900), and Josep Serra (1874–1939), whose first sardana was *El primer piu*. Franco prohibited the performances of sardanas in Spanish Catalonia during the early twentieth century in an attempt to thwart separatist sentiments. Lluis Millet (1867–1941) was Pedrell's pupil and co-founder of the Orfeó Català.

25 These scholars include Max Havart and Gilbert Chase. See Havart's publication cited earlier as well as Chase, *The Music of Spain*, 236–7.

26 See Chase, *The Music of Spain*, 237.

Example 9.1 Metrical Variants within Sardana Structure[27]

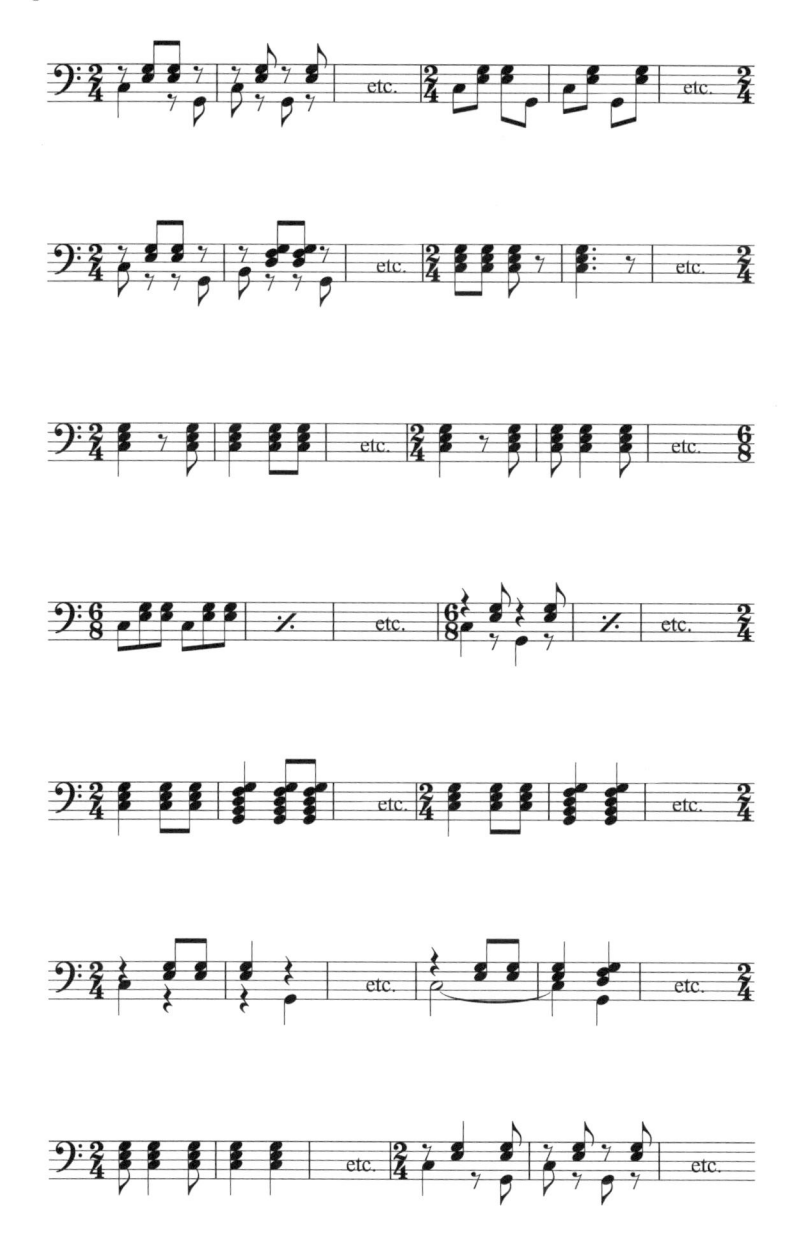

Each sardana is divided into two sections–the motif curt (short), generally of a sad character and approximately 20 to 50 measures in length, and the motif llarg (long), typically of a happier quality and 40 to 100 measures in length. A typical sardana might be approximately 35 measures of curts repeated three times,

---

27 Havart, "Coblas, sardanes, danses, musiques catalanes," 77–8.

followed by 81 measures of llargs stated six times for a total of 626 measures, or about 11 minutes of music.

Curt sections are often melancholy and played in the minor keys of A, D, G, C, B, or C sharp, while llarg sections are in quadruple meter and usually more festive, typically in the relative major. Although llarg sections are often lively, they begin quietly for approximately 8 to 12 measures and then become increasingly animated.[28] Then, a march-like moment announces an impending energetic finale.[29]

The Cobla Ensemble

The cobla ensemble consists of ten musicians playing eleven instruments, including two tenors, two tiples, one fluviol-tambori, two horns, two trumpets, one trombone, and one string bass.

The tiple (or prima) is a four-holed double reed instrument primarily used in the cobla for fast solo passages. It is sounded in the key of F, and is therefore heard a perfect fourth higher than written. It has a range of two octaves and a fifth. The tiple evolved from the shawm, of which four different types were in Western orchestras up to the seventeenth century—that of the soprano, tenor, alto, and bass. The instrument virtually disappeared from orchestras during the eighteenth century, with the exception of the bass shawm in ensembles in Brittany under the name of *bombarde*, and the soprano and tenor which survived in Spanish and French Catalonia. They were then labeled tiples and tenors.

The tenor is a double-reed wind instrument that dates from 1840 and has a less "sweet" sound than that of the tiple.[30] The instrument is in the key of B flat and is heard a whole step lower than written. Its lower register sounds solemn, its medium notes often evoke sweet and calm moods, and both registers are frequently employed during the quieter opening section of the sardana. The high register sounds passionate, sometimes violent, and is usually reserved for the more energetic llarg section finale. The tenor plays the primary melody and is often accompanied by horns and bass.

Brass instruments and the string bass are prominent in the modern cobla, including trumpets in the key of B flat that sound a whole step lower than written. They are often played together with horns and bass, and sound below that of the tiple and tenor. The string bass uses essentially three pitches; that is, the tonic, sub-dominant, and dominant tones. Trombones rarely play as soloists.

---

28 Twice as many dance steps are taken in the llarg section. Arms are raised to shoulder level during this section, and four steps (rather than two) are taken in both directions. The steps are similar to that of the old contrapàs.

29 In summary, the form of the sardana is as follows: first—calm mode (curt), then animated mode with triple rhythm, then dancing jumps accompanied by strong accents in the music, and finally dancers hopping. As a result of this complexity, dancing the sardana becomes more mental than physical in that one has to keep track of the number of measures in each section of music.

30 The tenor is often played together with horns and bass. In 1855, metal keys were added and the register was modified. The sonority was amplified as the size of the instrument was enlarged.

The fluviol is a small piccolo-like wooden flute that is included in the cobla. The instrument was traditionally played with the left hand alone while the right hand played a drum with drumstick. The wooden fluviol sounds similar to the piccolo and contains a two-octave range. It is in the key of F and sounds a perfect eleventh higher than written. Trills are effective on this instrument, and fluviols often evoke a pastoral or rustic character. The instrument is also used for solos or combined with horns, bass, trombones, and trumpets. Simple rhythms are continually emphasized.

Sardanas begin with an improvised fluviol solo introduction of ten measures. This opening prepares the musicians in the cobla as well as the dancers, who need to synchronize the first movement with the downbeat in the music. The fluviol introduction is never pre-composed and sounds similar to the one reproduced here:

Example 9.2 Typical Fluviol Introductory Solo[31]

When written into score format, the instruments in the cobla are as follows:

Figure 9.1 Sardana Structure and Score Format for Cobla

Sardana structure:

>ritournelle (not danced, ten measures)
>curt, curt
>llarg, llarg
>curt, curt
>llarg, llarg
>ritournelle (two measures not danced)
>llarg
>ritournelle
>llarg

Score format for contemporary cobla:

>1 fluviol with drum
>2 tiples (primas)
>2 tenors
>2 trumpets

---

31 Havart, "Coblas, sardanes, danses, musiques catalanes," 79.

1 trombone
2 flugelhorns
1 string bass[32]

The first sardanas (sardanes curts) were accompanied by the bagpipe (cornemusa), used in the cobla from the twelfth century to the 1860s. The cornemusa was initially combined with the tambourine and fluviol to form what was once the indispensable base of the cobla.[33] Then, when the cornemusa disappeared from the ensemble during the 1860s, two tenors and one saxophone took its place. Thus, the cobla was enlarged to include six musicians.

Two cornets were also added at the end of the nineteenth century, as were a trombone, two horns, and a string bass. This combination became the standard instrumentation, with the tiple, tenor, and fluviol representing the most important instruments within the ensemble.

This expansion of the cobla was regretted by many, including Etienne Arago, who recorded the change towards the end of the nineteenth century:

The cornemuse has also been dethroned
The ophicleide is its usurper
And from this jump on the vigorous hand
While raising in the air its female dancer
Where the dancer proudly triumphed
O my friends, speak, what have you done?[34]

Albert Manyach-Mattes spoke of the dilemma Pep Ventura faced when he helped change the instrumentation of the cobla ensemble:

Without wanting to question the talent or merit of Ventura as a renovator of the sardana, we must express here some reservation on the subject of this transformation of the cobla. It is without doubt that the cobla became the fashion of the day in the 1840s and many times since lost a lot of its character by the abandonment of the bagpipe, and by the introduction of other string and wind instruments. On the other hand, too radical modifications cannot take place without serious consequences on popular Catalan dances and airs. The contrapas, one of great rhythmic diversity, was altered because of the changes in instrumentation ... [It was] played in the past by two or three musicians knowing by heart the sung version and playing it with great accuracy; the difficulty began when it became necessary to write [the music] down—and to write it down for a group of eight to ten musicians, playing without a conductor and guided only by the consistency of the rhythm. We think that it would be of great interest to research and study the various ancient contrapas and sardana

---

32 The sardanas played by coblas are often in the key of C, G and F and their relative minor keys.

33 This two-person ensemble is often referred to as a *demi-cobla*.

34 Albert Mattes, *L'indépendant de Pyrénées-Orientales* (January 14, 1924): "La cornemuse est aussi détrônée l'ophicléide est son usurpateur et de ce saut sur la main vigoureuse, En élevant dans les airs sa danseuse où le danseur fièrement triomphait, O mes amis, parlez, qu'avez-vous fait?"

melodies closely and to play them again with the help of ancient instruments for which they were created.[35]

The evolution of the cobla during the nineteenth century helped create a need for new sardanas, which were subsequently composed by Pep Ventura, Anselm Clavé, and other Catalan composers. In his classical works, Séverac then emphasized the rhythmic structure when quoting or evoking these newly composed sardanas. This rhythmic adaptation was combined with innovative formal structures and harmonic modulation.

Catalonia and Art Music

The interest in Catalan art music was primarily inspired by Felipe Pedrell (1841–1922), who helped define Catalan regionalism in music by creating works that were historical, and by emphasizing indigenous elements in compositions that are independent of historical themes.[36]

Pedrell did editorial work in Barcelona up to 1894, and taught in Madrid between 1894 and 1904, returning to Barcelona in 1904. Pedrell often wrote for the journal *Revista musical catalaña* (1904–36), an important publication in the manifestation of the Catalan Renaissance. The journal was developed by L'Orfeó Català creator Lluis Millet (1867–1941). Pedrell also began editing the *Hispania schola musica sacra* in 1888, a journal that emphasized Renaissance composers from the fifteenth

---

35 Ibid. For more information on the subject, also see: Pujol, "Sardana, cançoner popular de catalanya," 393. "Sans vouloir nullement mettre en cause le talent ni le mérite de Pep Ventura comme rénovateur de la sardane, nous devons exprimer ici quelques réserves au sujet de cette transformation de la cobla. Il n'est pas douteux que la cobla, ainsi mise au goût du jour dès 1840 et plusieurs fois depuis n'ait perdu beaucoup de son caractère, tant par l'abandon de l'instrument de base qu'était la cornemuse que par l'introduction d'autres instruments à cordes ou à vent. D'autre part, des modifications trop radicales n'ont pu demeurer sans conséquences graves sur les airs et les danses populaires catalanes. C'est ainsi que la musique du contrapas, d'une extraordinaire diversité rythmique, se modifia dans les versions instrumentales que l'on voulut adapter aux nouveaux instruments ... Joué autrefois par deux ou trois musiciens sachant par coeur la version chantée et la jouant avec le maximum d'exactitude, la difficulté commença quand il fallut l'écrire, et l'écrire pour un ensemble de huit à dix musiciens, jouant sans chef d'orchestre, guidés seulement par la permanence du rythme.

Nous pensons qu'il serait d'un extréme intérét de rechercher et d'étudier de près les anciennes mélodies des divers contrapas et sardanes curtes et de les jouer à nouveau à l'aide des anciens instruments pour lesquels elles étaient faites."

36 Manuel de Falla wrote about Pedrell in the following: "Pedrell was a master in the highest form of the word; by his word and by his example, he has ... opened to musicians of Spain a road leading to the creation of a noble and deeply national art, a path that one believed to be already closed, and was without hope in the beginning of the last century." Manuel de Falla, "Felipe Pedrell," *La revue musicale*, 4e année, no. 4 (February 1, 1923), 1–11. ("Pedrell fut un maître dans la plus haute acceptation du mot: par sa parole et par son exemple, il a montré et ouvert aux musiciens d'Espagne un chemin sûr conduisant à la création d'un art noble et profondément national, un chemin que l'on croyait déjà fermé, sans espoir, au début du siècle dernier").

to seventeenth centuries. Other important Catalan journals include *La illustración musical española y americana* (1888–96) and *La música religiosa en España* (1896–9).

Pedrell's opera trilogy, *Los pirineos* (The Pyrenees, 1890–91), contains a Catalan text and subject that centers on the successful struggle by Catalonians during the thirteenth century to free themselves from the domination of the Papacy. Pedrell's other Catalan works include his cantata, *La glosa* (1905), *Lo cant de la montanya* (symphonic scenes; 1877), and his lyric drama, *El comte arnau* (The Three Sowers, 1904), a work that highlights an indigenous medieval legend and uses a Catalonian round woven into the texture.

Pedrell contributed scholarly articles to various other publications, including the Schola Cantorum's *La tribune de Saint-Gervais*. In an essay in the journal *Illustración musical hispano-americana*, Pedrell not only praised the mission of the Schola Cantorum, but also alluded to an anti-secularist outlook similar to that of Barrès:

> The Schola Cantorum lends incalculable services to religious art and delivers rough blows to the routine that kills all noble aspirations, as much in France as in Spain, countries which up to the present day did not originally have a respect for classical religious works and their glorious composers.[37]

Pedrell also created compositions based on folk song. In his manifesto *Por nuestra música* (1891), Pedrell articulated a nationalist and regionalist philosophy of composition, and he argued that a culture must build its own musical style by incorporating national and folk song into art music.[38] He further added that it was not necessary for a nationalist indigenous work to contain the history or culture of their nation. It was important only to include motifs and rhythms characteristic of that culture's indigenous music. Although Pedrell's ideas regarding regionalism and nationalism in music were largely Spanish, these concepts resonated with Catalan musicians and with French colleagues in Paris. In this way, Pedrell found common ground with Vincent d'Indy, and Pedrell's philosophies were therefore similar to those incorporated into the curriculum at the Schola Cantorum:

---

37 Felipe Pedrell, *Illustración musical hispano-americana* (October 30, 1894), 153–4. "La Schola Cantorum prestará servicios incalculables al arte religioso y asestará rudos gulpes a esa tutina que mata toda nobie aspiración lo musmo en Francia que en España, países que hasta ahora no han respondido como debian a respetar a poner en predicación las obras clasico religiosas de sus gloriosos maestros. Francia y la Schola Cantorum sin embargo se ha adelantado a España y será vergonzoso que los extranjeros salven de la ruina lo qaue mosotros no hernos pod du salvar."

38 Felipe Pedrell, *Por nuestra música* [1891] (Bellaterra, Spain: Publicacions de la Universitat Autònoma de Barcelona, 1991). There were many composers and ensembles that responded to Pedrell's manifesto, including the Orfeó Català, a choral organization created in 1891 by Lluis Millet and Amadeo Vives (1871–1932) and dedicated to reviving Catalan popular song. This Barcelona-based ensemble was committed to accomplishing in Spain what Charles Bordes had done in Paris with the Chanteurs de Saint-Gervais. The two organizations were similar in their revival of popular song and ancient polyphonic music. The choir often sang at the Palau de la Mùsica catalana in Barcelona.

The character of a truly national music is found not only in popular song and in the instinct of primitive periods, but also in the genius and the masterpieces of art; thus an opinion common to Vincent d'Indy who in teaching, demonstrated the parallel evolution of music with poetry, painting, and architecture.[39]

Pedrell's emphasis on regionalism, popular song, religious choral music, and medieval chant also closely resembled the official philosophy at the Schola Cantorum. Pedrell was a musicologist and editor who pursued the intellectual study of music, including polyphonic music from the twelfth century—an endeavor also prominent at the Schola Cantorum.

Pedrell's admiration for the accomplishments of d'Indy and other Schola Cantorum administrators led him to encourage various Catalan musicians to study at the institution. This included Pedrell's nephew, who subsequently attended the school. A relationship between Catalan artists and French musicians at the Schola Cantorum ensued, which was stimulated by correspondence between Pedrell and Charles Bordes.[40] An 1894 letter from Bordes to Pedrell foreshadowed upcoming exchanges between Pedrell and the Schola Cantorum:

> I should like to thank you for having met us in Barcelona and for allowing us to make contact with an artist like yourself. I am only a simple popularizer. Could I ever create for the old ... French what you have created for the old ... Spanish. I read with great interest your small brochure for serving national Spanish music, and this gave me the greatest desire to know your works, especially your *Pyrénées*. I absolutely share in your view and your national dream and I hope that your voice can be heard ... Maybe we could do something. Perhaps you will agree to conduct a concert of [music from] the young Spanish school in Paris this winter? If yes, then perhaps I can get you an orchestra—absolutely free of charge, of course.[41]

---

39 Pedrell, *Pour notre musique* (Barcelona, Spain: J.B. Pujol, 1893), 23. "Le caractère d'une musique vraiment nationale se trouve non seulement dans la chanson populaire et dans l'instinct des époques primitives, mais encore dans le génie et les chefs-d'oeuvre de l'art; pensée qui rejoint celle de Vincent d'Indy qui dans son enseignement démontrait l'évolution parallèle de la musique avec la poésie, la peinture et l'architecture."

40 In 1889, the Minister of Education commissioned Bordes to assemble a collection of early Basque music, which was published in 1897. Bordes later composed works based on Basque themes, including the *Suite basque* for flute and string quartet (1888) and the *Rhapsodie basque* for piano and orchestra (1890).

41 Letter from Charles Bordes to Felipe Pedrell, Saint-Jean-de-Luz, August 31, 1894, E. Bd. M 964. Cited in Montserrat Bergadà Armengol, "Les pianistes catalans à Paris entre 1875 et 1925." (PhD Dissertation: Université Rabelais de Tours, 1997), 182. "Je vous félicite d'avoir pu nous rencontrer à Barcelone et de nous permettre d'entrer en relation avec un artiste comme vous. Je ne suis qu'un simple vulgarisateur de tout ce que vous voulez. Pourrais-je jamais faire pour les vieux ... français ce que vous faites pour les vieux ... espagnols. J'ai lu avec grand intérêt votre petite brochure pour servir la musique nationale espagnole et cela m'a donné le plus vif désir de connaître vos oeuvres surtout vos *Pyrénées*. Je partage absolument votre façon de voir et votre rêve national et je souhaite que votre voix soit entendue ... Peut-être pourrions-nous quelque chose. Consentiriez-vous à diriger un concert de la jeune école espagnole à Paris cet hiver? Si oui peut-être suis-je à même de vous procurer un orchestre absolument gracieusement bien entendu."

Bordes traveled to Barcelona soon after he wrote this letter, as well as subsequent visits from other musicians from the Schola Cantorum seven years later. In 1899, Pedrell was invited to Avignon as a Mediterranean representative in order to establish a relationship between southern French and Catalan musicians; Pedrell performed concerts containing Catalan music during this time. The following year, the French première of Pedrell's *Pyrénées* took place at the Schola Cantorum. Catalan musicians reciprocated in 1902, when the Orfeó Català invited Charles Bordes to Spain in order to give two concerts with his choral organization. Bordes and Pedrell subsequently organized the Assises de la Schola, a Catalan event that corresponded to the French Fête de la musique religieuse.[42] The eventual collaboration between French students of the Schola Cantorum and Catalan musicians becomes evident in the *Revista musical catalana*, a bulletin established by the Orfeó Català in 1904:[43]

> The Schola Cantorum is where protégés were living together fraternally under the same roof. [It was] housing students coming from different regions of Spain, despite their differences [that were] due to the various languages that they spoke. The Andalusian Turina, the Catalan Civil, Gilbert Sangra, the Basque Guridi, Usandizaga, everybody knows that the Schola [contains] the ethnic diversity of the Iberian peninsula.[44]

The references to Catalan and Spanish musicians illustrates that music by Catalan and Spanish composers was becoming increasingly popular in Paris at the turn of the nineteenth century. In a survey taken by Montserrat Bergadà Armengol based on 28 Spanish and Catalan piano compositions edited in Paris between 1875 and 1900, 65 percent were considered by her to be salon pieces (waltzes, gavottes, marches, reveries, serenades, and meditations), and 35 percent were thought to be works of Spanish or Catalan character.[45] Between 1900 and 1925, however, 61 percent of the works surveyed were considered Spanish or Catalan. Figures 9.2 and 9.3 contain lists of Catalan and Spanish musicians studying or teaching at the Schola Cantorum and Paris Conservatoire from 1904 to 1925.[46]

---

42 Alexandre Guilmant performed organ recitals in Barcelona at L'exposition universelle of 1888. His correspondence with Pedrell began in 1896, when he graciously declined an invitation to Bilbao.

43 The Orfeó Català was a choral group created in 1891 dedicated to promoting Catalan composers and music. The *Revista musical catalana* served the Orfeó Català in much the same way that the *Tablettes de la Schola* served the Schola Cantorum.

44 F.A. Desde Paris, "Des de Paris; El cant popular religiós," *Revista musical catalana*, vol. 10, no. 120 (December, 1913), 344–7. "La Schola Cantorum que ha vist conviute fraternalment arracetats sua son sostre hospitalari estudiants vinguts de diferents regions d'Espanya, tots molt amies I no obstant ben dissemblants els un dels altres tant pel caracter com per la llengua que pariaven l'andalus Turina els catalans civil, Gilbert Sangrà, els Basques Guridi Usandizaga. Tothom sap a la Schola la diversitat etnica que enclou la peninsula iberica."

45 Principal composers included are Matias Miquel, Santiago Riera, and Esteban Marti. The most popular forms consisted of Spanish dances, including the jota, Spanish tango, and the habanera.

46 Armengol, "Les pianistes catalans à Paris entre 1875 et 1925," 151–2. This includes works by Francisco Contés, Esteban Marti, Santiago Riera, Isaac Albéniz, Frederico Mompou, Joaquín Cassadó, and Gaspar Cassadó.

Séverac subsequently became a beneficiary of this phenomenon, as he met many Catalan artists in Paris and also heard concerts containing Catalan music, which significantly affected his later compositional style. Séverac became friends with Isaac Albéniz (1860–1909), pianists Ricardo Viñes (1876–1943) and Joaquín Nin (1879–1949), painter Pablo Picasso (1881–1973), and sculptor Manuel Martinez-Hugué (Manolo; 1872–1945). In addition, Séverac had the opportunity to hear several concerts in Paris containing Catalan music. Before analyzing Séverac's Catalan-based compositions, it is therefore important to observe the initial source of inspiration for these later works, so we can more fully understand the evolution of Séverac's compositional style.

Figure 9.2   Catalan and Spanish Musicians at the Schola Cantorum between 1894 and 1925

1. Isaac Albéniz (1860–1909). Studied composition at the Schola Cantorum with Vincent d'Indy, 1894–8. Professor from 1898 to 1901.

2. Luis Bonaterra (1890–1952). Studied composition and piano with Moritz Mozkowski at the Schola Cantorum, 1910–20. Member of the *Trio hispania*.

3. Francisco Civil (b.1895, death date unknown). Studied composition with Vincent d'Indy, and also studied organ and piano accompaniment at the Schola Cantorum, 1904–17.

4. José Civil (dates unknown). Studied composition with Vincent d'Indy at the Schola Cantorum, 1904–21.

5. Fladio Costa (dates unkown). Studied composition with Vincent d'Indy at the Schola Cantorum, c.1905. Member of the Trio pichot costa (1913).

6. Juan Gibert Camins (1890–1966). Studied composition with Vincent d'Indy at the Schola Cantorum, 1910–28.

7. Vincente Maria de Gibert (1879–1939). Studied Gregorian chant, counterpoint, organ, and composition with Vincent d'Indy at the Schola Cantorum, 1904–7. Obtained his diploma in 1906. Also a pupil of Luis Millet and Felipe Pedrell. He composed Catalan chanson populaires for mixed choir in the spirit of the Schola Cantorum and Orfeó Català and wrote religious melodies for voice and piano, chamber works, and symphonies.

8. Augustin Grau (1893–1964). Studied piano and composition at the Schola Cantorum, c.1908–10.

9. Joaquín Nin (1879–1949). Although Nin was born in Havana, he moved to Barcelona when he was one year old and stayed there until 1900, at which time he moved to Paris to study at the Schola Cantorum. He studied piano with Mozkowski, and also harmony, counterpoint, and composition at the

Schola Cantorum with Vincent d'Indy, 1902–8, 1911. Professor from 1913 to 1939. He harmonized Catalan folk songs and had them published.

10. Carlos Pedrell (1878–1941). Nephew of Felipe Pedrell; studied composition under Vincent d'Indy and Pierre de Bréville at the Schola Cantorum.

11. Domingo Sangra (dates unknown). Studied violin, chamber music, harmony, and composition with Vincent d'Indy at the Schola Cantorum, c.1905–10.

12. Blanche Selva (1884–1942). Professor at Schola Cantorum, 1901–22.

13. Joaquín Turina (1882–1949). Not Catalan, but Spanish; born Seville, died Madrid. Studied composition with Vincent d'Indy at the Schola Cantorum, 1905–14, and studied piano with Moritz Moszkowski.[47]

Figure 9.3   Catalan and Spanish Musicians at the Paris Conservatoire between 1894 and 1925

1. Mario Calado (1862–1926). At Conservatoire, 1879–90.

2. Pau Casals (1876–1973). In Paris, 1898, Conservatoire dates unknown.

3. Francisco Cortes (b.1873). At Conservatoire, c.1893.

4. Manuel de Falla (1876–1946). In Paris, 1907–14.

5. Enrique Granados (1867–1916). At Conservatoire, 1887–89, 1905, 1909, 1911, 1914.

6. Joaquín Malats (1872–1912). At Conservatoire, 1890–96, 1903–4, 1907.

7. Esteban Marti (1871–1925). At Conservatoire, dates unkown.

8. Martias Miquel (1863–1907). At Conservatoire, 1883–1907.

9. Federico Mompou (1893–1987). At Conservatoire, 1911–13, 1921–41; received letter of recommendation from Granados.

10. Juan Bautista Pellicer (1862–1930). At Conservatoire.

11. Juan Pujol (1835–98). At Conservatoire, 1850–70, 1882.

12. Alejandro Ribó (1878–1957). At Conservatoire, c.1896.

---

47 Ibid., 35–6. In 1898, the year of the creation of the Schola Cantorum school, Catalan pianists at the Conservatoire began to decrease. The Schola Cantorum was established in 1894, the school was formed in 1898, and the school expanded in 1900. Catalans in Paris reached a statistical peak from 1886 to 1890.

13. Santiago Riera (1867–1959). Professor at Conservatoire, 1886–1959.

14. Mercedes Rigalt (b.1876). Professor at Conservatoire, 1891–9.

15. José-María Suandizaga (1887–1915). In Paris, 1901–6, Conservatoire dates unknown.

16. Florencio Torrent (b.1854, death date unkown). Dates at Conservatoire not known.

17. Joaquín Turina (1881–1949). Not Catalan. Born in Seville and took composition lessons from d'Indy at the Schola Cantorum in Paris, 1906–13. Studied piano with Moritz Moszkowski.

18. Ricardo Viñes (1875–1943). At Conservatoire, 1889–94.

Isaac Albéniz

One of the most important Catalan musicians to have an impact on Séverac's compositional direction was Isaac Albéniz (1860–1909), who taught at the Schola Cantorum between 1898 and 1901.[48] As a result of Albéniz's compositions and influence, Séverac also composed works containing Andalusian motives, including the use of Phrygian scales and triplet cadential figures. In addition, regional Andalusian titles in Albéniz's works often portray local festivals in the same way that Séverac depicts Catalan celebrations in his music. Séverac's approach therefore not only included imitations of the fluviol and sardana, but also programmatic references to specific villages and festivals in Catalonia.

Albéniz was initially a student at the Schola Cantorum and studied composition with Vincent d'Indy. During this time, d'Indy helped Albéniz to reorchestrate his orchestral suite *Catalonia* (1899) and conducted the work at its 1899 Société nationale première. D'Indy also helped Albéniz reorchestrate his opera *Pepita Jimenez* (1896–7).[49] In 1898, Albéniz then became Professor of Piano and Séverac became his assistant. There is little information about what Séverac learned in Albéniz's piano classes; however, Albéniz was reported to have been a lenient teacher who highlighted rhythm and sonority more than technique.[50]

Albéniz socialized with his students, and after piano classes, the professor would often invite his pupils to a Montparnasse patisserie in order to have conversations

---

48 Vincent d'Indy began corresponding with Albéniz in 1895, when Albéniz invited d'Indy to Barcelona in order to conduct a series of five concerts. D'Indy returned in 1898 for a second visit and made subsequent visits in 1909, 1914, and 1917. Séverac met Albéniz in 1898. Letter from Vincent d'Indy to Isaac Albéniz, April 1, 1895, E. Bd. M 986. Cited in Armegnol, "Les pianistes catalans à Paris entre 1875 et 1925," 181–4.

49 This work had its première in 1896 in Barcelona.

50 Jacqueline Kalfa, "Isaac Albéniz à Paris: une patrie retrouvée 1893–1909," *Revue internationale de musique française* vol. 9, no. 9 (June, 1988), 26.

over Spanish wine and champagne.[51] Although there is no evidence that Séverac attended these social events, it would be highly unlikely for him not to be present at some of them. It is known that Albéniz and Séverac attended many of the same social gatherings, including those at the home of Blanche Selva.[52] Canteloube commented that "we got together often on Sundays with Séverac at Blanche Selva's house ... One often met Albéniz there."[53]

Albéniz initially met Séverac when he was appointed assistant to the Catalan composer at the Schola Cantorum in 1898, and it is likely that he first heard Albéniz's music when the piano work *La vega* of 1889 was performed in Paris that same year.[54] This work contains Andalusian flamenco rhythms and ostinato guitar patterns, and these elements had an influence on Séverac's compositional style.[55]

Another Andalusian work by Albéniz that had an influence on Séverac's music was *Iberia* (1906–9), which contain Phrygian scales, triplet cadential figures, flamenco rhythms, and ostinato guitar patterns. These characteristics are present in Séverac's piano works, including *Cerdaña* (1908–11) and *Sous les lauriers-roses* of 1919. In addition, *Iberia* (Book I) had its Paris première in 1906, and we know that Séverac was familiar with this composition through comments made by the Belgian lawyer, writer, and art critic Octave Maus (1856–1919), who recalled hearing the work with Séverac present at Blanche Selva's home:[56]

> Ah! These Sundays at Selva's [home]. D'Indy listened to ... Baigneuses au soleil by Séverac, and remained stunned at the outpouring of water and the miracles of light that came from [Séverac's composition] ... which was outlined by the interpreter. Séverac

---

51 Gabriel Laplane, *Albéniz: 1860–1909* (Geneva: Editions du milieu du monde, 1956), 57.

52 Blanche Selva (1884–1942) was a Catalan pianist who taught at the Schola Cantorum. Séverac studied with Selva and they later became friends.

53 Jean-Bernard Cahours d'Aspry, "Déodat de Séverac" (unpublished manuscript), 230. "Le dimanche nous nous retrouvions souvent, avec Séverac, chez Blanche Selva ... On rencontrait là généralement Albéniz."

54 The work was delivered in a concert given by pianist Vianna da Motta on January 21, 1899.

55 A collaborative effort took place among pupils and professors at the Schola Cantorum—a collection of assorted children's piano pieces which included a movement by Albéniz entitled "Joyeuse rencontre" ("A Joyful Encounter"), taken from a two-movement work, *Yvonne en visite! Deux pièces pour piano* (Boca Raton, Florida: Masters Music, 1993). The title of this movement was alluded to by Séverac 12 years later in *Cerdaña*, wherein the movement "Les fêtes" was dedicated to Laura Albéniz (the composer's daughter) and a specific section within the movement is titled 'Charmante rencontre.' This lends even greater credence to the assertion that Séverac's access to Albéniz's compositions had a profound effect on his later compositional style. Pianist Ricardo Viñes performed Albéniz's *Granada* in 1900 and *Seguidillas* in 1901 at the Sociéte nationale. Pianist Blanche Selva performed many of Albéniz's compositions beginning in 1905 and these events were often reviewed by the Parisian press.

56 For more information on Octave Maus, see Michel Stockhem, "Vincent d'Indy en Belgique: réseaux et influences," in *Vincent d'Indy et son temps*, edited by Manuela Schwartz (Sprimont, Belgium: Mardaga Press, 2006), 87–100.

felt the same rapture upon hearing the twelve pieces of Iberia ... Seven or eight people to whom I was introduced and who were present were d'Indy, Roussel, Séverac, and René and Carlos de Castéra ... I had heard Albéniz play an unforgettable performance of the third book of Iberia and Roussel and Séverac promised to come hear their works at Le Havre.[57]

Séverac thought highly of *Iberia*, as evident from his remark that "one cannot hear a piece in *Iberia* without ... being taken with a nostalgia for this beautiful land."[58]

Albéniz left Paris in 1901 as a result of failing health, and Séverac and Albéniz subsequently corresponded by letter.[59] These letters illustrate that although Séverac's relationship with Albéniz was initially that of respectful pupil to professor, by 1905, the two musicians had become close friends. In 1903, Séverac signed a letter to Albéniz "your devoted and great admirer, Séverac." By 1905, he had switched to more familiar terms, signing a note to Albéniz with "Dear and ideal friend, Séverac."[60]

Séverac later visited Albéniz in Nice two years before the Catalan composer's death in 1909. Selva recalls Séverac's story:

Albéniz then lived near Nice, at the Château Saint-Laurent, a spacious place in which one found a huge music room with an organ ... It was Albéniz himself who opened the door. As he asked his visitor what he wanted, Déodat attempted to transform his voice, and responded "I am a poor musician without money or a place to stay who asks for hospitality" ... At this moment, Albéniz recognized him ... During his stay ... Albéniz played the organ where he improvised, and Déodat at the piano reproduced his theme that he developed in turn. When Séverac's improvisation was especially effective, Albéniz enthusiastically let go of his organ to embrace him at the piano ... Albéniz embraced him ... tears flowing from his eyes.[61]

---

57 Madeleine Octave Maus, *Trente années de lutte pour l'art, 1894–1914* (Brussels: Librairie l'oiseau bleu, 1926), 28. "Ah! Ces dimanches de Selva. D'Indy écoutait ... *Baigneuses au soleil* de Séverac et celui-ci demeurait stupéfait des jaillissements d'eau, des miracles de lumière ... qu'en tirait l'interprète. Séverac éprouvait le même ravissement à l'audition des douze pièces d'*Iberia* ... sept ou huit personnes auxquelles on me présenta et qui se trouvaient être chez Mlle. Selva: Indy, Roussel, Séverac, René et Carlos de Castéra ... J'avais entendu Albéniz jouer inoubliablement le troisième cahier d'*Iberia* et j'emportais la promesse de Roussel et de Séverac de venir entendre leurs oeuvres au Havre."

58 Armengol, "Les pianistes catalans à Paris entre 1875 et 1925," 321. Reprinted from Séverac, "Albéniz", *Le courrier musical* (April 1, 1909), 381–2. "On ne peut pas écouter un morceau d'*Iberia* sans être pris aussitôt d'une sorte de nostalgie de ce si beau pays."

59 A letter from d'Indy to Albéniz dated October 7, 1900 informs us that Albéniz had already presented his resignation to Bordes.

60 Aspry, "Déodat de Séverac," 95. "Votre dévoué et grand admirateur, Séverac." Ibid, 96 (autograph letter, s.d., Bibliotheca de Catalunya, Barcelona). "Cher et idéal ami, Séverac."

61 Blanche Selva, *Déodat de Séverac* (Paris: Librairie Delagrave, 1930), 80. (Reprinted anecdote of Carlos de Castéra) "Albéniz habitait alors aux environs de Nice, au Château Saint-Laurent, spacieuse demeure dans laquelle se trouvait une vaste salle de musique avec un orgue ... C'est Albéniz qui ouvrit lui-même la porte. Comme il demandait à son visiteur ce qu'il désirait, Déodat, tâchant de transformer sa voix, lui répondit: 'Je suis un pauvre musicien sans sou ni logis qui demande l'hospitalité' ... A ce moment, Albéniz le reconnut ... Durant ce séjour ... Albéniz se mettait à l'orgue où il improvisait, et Déodat au piano reprenait son

Séverac also wrote a homage to Albéniz in *Le courrier musical* following the Catalan composer's death in 1909:

> Albéniz was in effect and in all the force of the word, the good man who is devoted, in the shadows, ready to sacrifice himself, and his art is one of the most personal, most refined, and the purest in this epoch ... He felt beauty as do only as those men of our beautiful Midi ... As far as his work, it is that which one can speak only with emotion and enthusiasm! There was so much love in him that his music is the most friendly [that exists]! It is delicate and as seductive as a blossoming orange tree, but it is as ardent as the sun in Spain! ... During the last days of his life, barely a few months ago, a lyrical drama from one of his friends was rehearsed on a Parisian stage. And although tortured by the horrible disease that robbed us of him, he did not cease his passionate interest in this work, forgetting his suffering, forgetting even the death he knew was impending![62]

Because of the importance of Albéniz's music on Séverac's compositional style, Séverac agreed to complete Albéniz's unfinished piano work, *Navarra* (1911), upon Albéniz's death in 1909.[63] Yet, Séverac was initially reluctant, feeling that his own temperament was too Catalan to complete this Andalusian work. In a 1911 letter to Carlos de Castéra, Séverac stated the difficulties in undertaking the project: "As for *Navarra* ... I believe that if you addressed yourself to a composer of a closer temperament to that of dear Albéniz, for example, Granados, he would do it easily."[64] Other musicians also doubted the temperamental match. Writer Henri Collet noted:

> Déodat was too original not to brand [the work] with his charming, but not exuberant personality. He could not feel Navarra ... [He]was too Catalan for [the work] ... Concerned about the balance of the work, he avoided any servile insistence, any useless progression,

---

thème qu'il développait à son tour. Quand l'improvisation de Séverac était heureuse, Albéniz enthousiasmé lâchait son orgue pour aller l'embrasser au piano ... Albéniz l'embrassait ... des larmes coulant de ses yeux."

62 Séverac, "Albéniz", *Le courrier musical*, 12e année, no. 7 (April 1, 1909), 381–2. "Albéniz était en effet et dans toute la force du terme l'homme de bien qui se dévoue dans l'ombre jusqu'au sacrifice et son art est l'un des plus personnels, des plus raffinés et des plus purs qui soient à l'époque actuelle ... Il sentait la beauté comme peuvent seuls la sentir les hommes de notre beau midi ... Quant à son oeuvre, elle est de celles dont on ne peut parler qu'avec émotion et enthousiasme! Il y avait tellement d'amour en lui que sa musique elle-même est la plus amicale qui soit! Elle est délicate et séduisante comme un oranger en fleurs mais elle est aussi ardente que le soleil d'Espagne! ... Dans les derniers temps de sa vie, il y a quelques mois à peine, on répétait sur une scène parisienne un drame lyrique d'un de ses amis et, bien que torturé par l'horrible mal qui devait nous le ravir, il ne cessait de s'intéresser à cette oeuvre avec passion, oubliant ses souffrances, oubliant même la mort qu'il savait prochaine!"

63 Granados was first offered the project; he had turned the offer down and recommended Paul Dukas, who in turn declined. The project was then proposed to Séverac.

64 Aspry, "Déodat de Séverac," 500. "Quant à *Navarra* ... je crois que si vous vous adressiez à un compositeur d'un tempérament plus rapproché de celui du cher Albéniz, par exemple Granados, il vous ferait ça en un tour de main."

he achieved in melancholy and a source of serenity a portrait in which the materials demanded the setting of a dazzling work.[65]

Albéniz's wife was nonetheless appreciative of Séverac's effort, as communicated by her daughter, Laura, in a letter to Séverac:

> I am writing to you on behalf of mother to tell you that she was happy that you have finished Navarra ... Mother found that you have finished the work in a perfect way ... She is very grateful and thanks you from her heart.[66]

Although much has been made of the fact that Albéniz employed mostly Andalusian folk music in his works, it would be a misrepresentation to argue that he avoided Catalan-based works entirely. His Catalan-inspired compositions include his orchestral suite *Catalonia* (1898), a movement entitled "Cataluña" from his *Suite española* for piano (1886), a movement entitled "Capricho catalan," from the piano work *España* (1890), the unpublished composition *Escenas sinfónicas catalanas* (Symphonic Catalan scenes; 1888), retitled *Scènes villageoîses catalanes*, and a lost vocal work with a Catalan text entitled *Tres romanzas catalanas* (1886). In addition, he began a choral-symphonic poem *Lo llascó* written to a text by the Catalan author Apel les Mestres.[67]

The first Catalan-inspired composition by Albéniz was performed in Paris following Séverac's initial enrollment at the Schola Cantorum. It was the orchestral suite *Catalonia* that was inspired by a trip to a small Catalan village where a festival with music and dance had taken place. The work is in a free sonata-allegro form and includes quotations from Catalan folk melodies "El pobre terrisaire" and "La filadora," the latter forming the primary thematic material for the entire work.[68] The composition also includes evocations of the Catalan sardana and the fluviol, which Séverac later included in many of his own compositions.[69]

---

65 Henri Collet, *Albéniz et Granados* (Paris:Alcan, 1926), 159–60. "Déodat était trop original pour ne pas marquer de sa personnalité charmante, mais non exubérante, la *Navarra* qu'au demeurant il ne pouvait sentir ... étant bien trop Catalan pour cela ... Soucieux de l'équilibre de l'oeuvre, (il) se garde de toute complaisance insistante, de toute progression inutile à son sens, et achève dans la mélancolie et la sérénité une fresque dont les matériaux demandaient une mise en oeuvre éclatante."

66 Aspry, "Déodat de Séverac," 501. "Je vous écris de la part de Maman pour vous dire combien elle a été heureuse de ce que vous ayez bien voulu terminer *Navarra* ... Maman trouve que vous avez fini l'oeuvre d'une façon parfaite ... Elle vous en est très reconnaissante et vous remercie de tout son coeur."

67 Only 11 measures of this work exists, however, and it remained unfinished upon the composer's death.

68 This work was conducted by d'Indy for the Société nationale de musique in 1899. It was reviewed in *L'écho de Paris* and again performed at a 1900 event which included works by Catalan composers.

69 The fluviol produces a high-pitched sound which resembles the piccolo. More on this is found in Chapter 3. The score also calls for a group of strolling musicians ("Musiciens ambulants"). Séverac paid homage to Albéniz in dedications, including his piano work *Chant de la terre*, with the inscription "Al car e tant amistous tous musicien Albéniz—Frairalement,

For example, the fluviol is evoked in the initial melodic statement of "La filadora" in Albéniz's *Catalonia*. This is apparent in the melodic construction found in measures 127–159, where perfect fourths and major thirds are prominently displayed within the melody, intervals characteristically found in traditional fluviol introductory passages. In addition, the 3/8 triple meter incorporated in this section reflects the metrical structure found within solo fluviol passages, as found below:

Example 9.3   Isaac Albéniz, *Catalonia*, Measures 127–143

Albéniz's passage can be compared with the opening measures of the sardana section in Séverac's *Sous les lauriers-roses* (1919), where Séverac incorporates a twelve-measure imitation of an introductory fluviol solo.[70] This is incorporated within a 6/8 meter where major third and perfect fourth intervals are prominent. This comparison between the two compositions can be further substantiated by the fact that Séverac dedicated his piano work *Sous les lauriers-roses* to Albéniz.

Ricardo Viñes

A Catalan pianist to have an important influence on Séverac's career and compositional direction was Ricardo Viñes (1875–1943). Viñes participated in the première of several of Séverac's piano compositions and introduced Séverac to many Catalan musicians living in Paris. Originally from Lerida, Viñes left to study at the Paris Conservatoire in 1889, obtaining first prize five years later. As a pupil of Charles Wilfrid de Bériot, the young musician met Ravel in 1888 and subsequently

---

Déodat de Séverac." The French composer's final 1921 piano work, *Sous les lauriers-roses*, is dedicated "to the memory of loved masters Emmanuel Chabrier, Isaac Albéniz, and Charles Bordes." In a letter to Blanche Selva in the same year, Séverac revealed Albéniz' influence: "Among musicians I love the most are Chabrier and Albéniz." See Selva, *Déodat de Séverac*, 80.

70 See Music Example 10.17a.

championed the French composer's works, including his *Menuet antique* at a Société nationale de musique concert in 1898.[71]

Viñes was just establishing his career in 1898 when Séverac was first living in Paris; it is therefore likely that Séverac heard Viñes perform many Catalan works, as he subsequently met the pianist in 1900. One of Viñes's earlier Paris performances was a chamber music event in honor of Spanish composer Enrique Fernández-Arbós. In 1898, Viñes delivered a piano transcription of Chabrier's *España*, and in 1900, he performed a recital that included works by Granados. *Le monde musical* claimed that "[Viñes had an] exquisite charm...[and knew] how to captivate the attention of a large and refined public through a way of playing with color." [72] Within the next five years, Viñes would perform various works by Fernández-Arbós, Ravel, and Séverac.

These include Séverac's *Le chant de la terre*, of which the first edition was dedicated to Viñes with the words "To Ricardo Viñes with all my friendship and admiration, Séverac." In 1902, Viñes performed the première of two movements to Séverac's piano suite *Loin des villes*, later retitled *En Languedoc*. This Brussels performance was soon followed by a Paris concert, and the complete work was performed by Viñes in 1905 at the Schola Cantorum. Séverac subsequently dedicated the first and fourth movements to the pianist.[73]

Viñes was also able to introduce Séverac to various French and Catalan musicians living in Paris because of the pianist's prominence in Parisian social circles. Viñes had established friendships with Maurice Ravel, Albert Roussel, Maurice Delage, painters Pablo Picasso and Georges Braque, as well as many figures in the Paris

---

71 Charles Wilfrid de Bériot (1833–1914) was a professor at the Niedermeyer School, then at the Academy of Paris.

72 Armengol, "Les pianistes catalans à Paris entre 1875 et 1925," 251. Reprinted from *Le monde musical* (April 30, 1900), 130–31. The review is describing a Schola Cantorum concert which took place on December 8. "Il a su néanmoins par un charme exquis et un jeu coloré, captiver l'attention d'un nombreux et élégant public."

73 The two movements were "Vers le mas en fête" and "Coin de cimetière, au printemps." Viñes performed four historic concerts within a three-week period in 1905. The first recital took place on March 27 and was organized into national music styles, especially that of the Spanish and French; the second took place on April 3 and included a traditional program; the third recital took place on April 10 and was dedicated to nineteenth-century composers, including Albéniz and Granados. The final event took place on April 17, was dedicated to French composers, and was divided into three parts: the first concert included works by Franck, d'Indy, Chausson, and Fauré; the second event contained music by Rhené Baton and Samazeuilh Moreau; the third event contained Séverac's "Coin de cimetière, au printemps," Debussy's "L'isle joyeuse," and Chabrier's "Bourrée fantasque."

Ravel's *Miroirs* was first performed for and dedicated to members of the Apaches. Viñes often frequented the salons of Princess de Polignac, Madame de St Marceaux, and Cipa Godebski, where Séverac met Ravel in 1902.

literary community.[74] Viñes also visited Séverac regularly at Séverac's childhood home in Saint-Félix-Caraman between 1906 and 1913.[75]

Joaquín Nin y Castellanos

Séverac also became friends with Catalan pianist Joaquín Nin y Castellanos, a Cuban-born musician who grew up in Catalonia. He arrived in Paris in 1902 and studied harmony and counterpoint at the Schola Cantorum. Nin made his debut as a pianist at the Schola Cantorum in 1903, and within the same year, began giving concerts extensively. Nin eventually became assistant director of the Catalan Institute of Music in 1921.

Séverac and Nin had met in 1902 and soon thereafter frequented concerts together, including a 1902 performance of Debussy's *Pelléas et Mélisande*.[76] Not only was Nin important for Séverac's career at this time because he had performed many of Séverac's piano compositions, but he was also known for performing recitals that included works by Spanish and Catalan contemporaries. In addition, Nin harmonized Catalan folk songs in *Cantilènes lyriques des XVIIème et XVIIIème siècles*.[77] As a result, Séverac was exposed to a plethora of Catalan folk music. Nin was not appreciative of pastiche-like uses of Catalan and Andalusian motifs in works by French composers, however, as he wrote in *Idées et commentaires*:

> Certainly, Debussy and Ravel recently had fun with composing some Spanish pieces, indeed very successfully; but these works here are basically very French. Their content, very freely treated, is invariably French. This is nevertheless a domain which is dangerous to want to exploit beyond certain limits.[78]

---

74 Albert Roussel composed "Four Poems de Henri de Régnier," from *Quatre poèmes*, op. 8 for voice and piano (1907), "dedicated to my comrade and friend Déodat de Séverac with the hope that this music is sympathetic to him." Roussel's *Quatre poèmes*, op. 3 was composed four years earlier.

75 Séverac met de Falla in 1908 and they both saw each other at Apaches meetings. They did not have a close personal relationship, as de Falla was very reserved. Canteloube, who was in the organization, created L'Association des amis de Déodat de Séverac in 1930 and de Falla then enthusiastically accepted the invitation to take part in the Comité d'honneur.

76 Henri Collet, *L'essor de la musique espagnole au Xxème siècle* (Eschig, 1929), 155–6.

77 Armengol, "Les Pianistes catalans à Paris entre 1875 et 1925," 216.

78 Joaquín Nin, *Idées et commentaires* (Paris: Fischbacher, 1912), 207. Cited in François Lesure, "Debussy et le syndrome de Grenade," *Revue de musicologie* (1982), 108. French compositions that contain Spanish elements include Edouard Lalo's *Symphonie espagnole* (1874), Georges Bizet's *Carmen* (1875), Camille Saint-Saëns' *Jota aragonaise* (1880), Emmanuel Chabrier's *España* (1883), Jules Massenet's *Le Cid* (1885), Claude Debussy's *Rodrigue et Chimène* (1890) and *Iberia* (1909), and Maurice Ravel's *Habañera (Site auriculaires)* (1895) and *Rapsodie espagnole* (1907). "Certes, Debussy et Ravel, tout récemment encore, se sont amusés à composer quelques espagnolades d'ailleurs très réussies, mais ces oeuvres-là sont quand même foncièrement françaises. Leur matière—très librement traitée—invariablement française. C'est là, pourtant, un domaine qu'il serait dangereux de vouloir exploiter au-delà de certaines limites."

Although Nin disapproved of French composers exploiting Spanish music elements, his performances of Catalan works and harmonizing of Catalan popular songs exposed Séverac to a greater variety of Catalan compositions.

Catalan Concerts

Séverac was influenced by two important Catalan concerts in Paris in 1900 and 1905 respectively. These were significant for Séverac because they were the first concerts in Paris to highlight Catalan music. The Schola Cantorum organized the 1900 event, which included Catalan interpreters Ricardo Viñes and contralto Maria Gay (1879–1943).[79] The first half of the evening included a performance by Viñes of works by Granados and Albéniz. Gay sang three Catalan melodies—Enric Morera's "Enterro," Juan Gay Planella's "Plor," and Adriá Esquerrá's "Montanya amunt." The second half included five Catalan chansons populaires sung by Gay, a fragment of Pedrell's *Los pirineos* (1890–91), and Ricardo Viñes's performance of a piano transcription of Albéniz's *Catalonia*.[80]

During the 1905 event, Viñes performed two *Danses espagnoles* by Granados, as well as Albéniz's *Sevillanas* (1886), *Torre bermeja* (1889) and *La vega* (1899). Catalan pianist Blanche Selva also performed music by Albéniz, including "Prelude" and "Seguidillas" from *Chants d'Espagne* of 1892, and both Viñes and Selva then performed a two-piano arrangement of Albéniz's *Rapsodie espagnole*. Catalan music was heard when Catalan composer Josep Civil y Castelvi accompanied Maria Gay on piano while performing two of Civil's melodies in a popular style, as well as five popular Catalan chansons—"Canción de susita," "Mes de miag," "Marines filadora,"

---

79 Maria Gay was a Catalan singer born in Barcelona. She studied in Paris before moving to the United States in 1908. She was the sister of painter Ramon Pichot. Gay participated with a group of modern Barcelona artists at the end of the century. She was married to the Catalan musician Juan Gay Planella and adopted his name, having formerly been Maria Pichot. She studied in Brussels and eventually left Juan Gay and married tenor Giovanni Zenatello, subsequently moving to New York and opening an academy of music. After her 1903 concert in Toulouse, Séverac commented on her in a letter to his sister: "Elle est ... une charmante camarade très devouée et je suis sûr qu'elle fera tout son possible pour interpréter quelque chose de moi."

80 Armengol, "Les Pianistes catalans à Paris entre 1875 et 1925," 198. Reprint of a journal of Ricardo Viñes (December 11, 1900), 452. The inclusion of *Catalonia* was a last minute substitution on the part of d'Indy, Bordes, and Albéniz—who decided to eliminate Saint-Saëns' two-piano arrangement of Henri Duparc's *Léonore*, which would have been delivered by Ricardo Viñes and Marcel Labey. Viñes recorded the memories of the event in his journal: "I have been truly satisfied few times in my life ... I played magnificently, I was a formidable success. All of the most demanding musicians were wild with enthusiasm and admiration and they went to tell Bordes, who was still ill. He congratulated me when I went to greet him. Gay sang better than the other day at the Chevillard concert. The Duparcs were there, and they were enchanted." ("J'ai été satisfait comme peu de fois dans ma vie ... J'ai joué magnifiquement, j'eus un succès formidable. Tous les musiciens les plus exigeants étaient fous d'enthousiasme et d'admiration et ils sont montés le dire à Bordes, toujours souffrant, qui m'a félicité lorsque j'entrai le saluer, la Gay a mieux chanté que l'autre jour au concert Chevillard. Il y avait les Duparc, enchantés.")

"Comte l'arnau," and "Cançon de vidal."[81] Gay also sang three harmonized Catalan popular songs accompanied by guitarist Miguel Llobet (1878–1938)—"Le testament d'Amélia," "La filla del marchant," and "Lo pastoreta," while Llobet also delivered Albéniz's *Granada*, Fernando Sor's *Menuet*, and Francisco Tarrega's *Jota*.[82]

Séverac covered the event in *Le mercure musical* under the pseudonym of AC Sever:

> The Schola Cantorum was pleased to host a performance devoted to Catalan musicians. This is the first time, we believe, that Paris had heard them brought together in a single program. This evening was a tremendous success ... It is impossible to express here the charm, intensity, and sonic diversity of Llobet's guitar.
>
> Even if several of the works performed were already known to the public from concerts by Selva, Viñes, and the Société nationale, this evening was, for many, a revelation and we are not at all exaggerating in saying it was a ringing success. There is at this time, if not a real "Catalan school," at least a particular group of musicians, very remarkable, even in this corner of Spain, where artistic and intellectual life seems to be taking flight.
>
> In the course of the evening, Blanche Selva, a great musician and committed Catalan ... gave a colorful interpretation of Chants d'Espagne and the impressive and delightful Vega of Albéniz. Many works by Albéniz have characterized the evolution of talent of this musician who today is certainly one of the greats. In looking back on the epoch when some of his works were written, it is difficult not to admit that Albéniz has surpassed those of us who have the reputation of being the most "modern," the most "Impressionist." In his work, there are very special qualities of color and rhythm, since they are the very expression of the temperament of a race, but always of an unquestionable artistic value. The young composer Granados was represented at this concert by two notable and elegant Danses espagnoles, which Ricardo Viñes played delicately and with great nuance.
>
> After the two delightful dances by Granados, Ricardo Viñes let us hear the Tour vermeille and La sevillane with new ears and this exquisite pianist was wildly applauded. With Blanche Selva, Ricardo Viñes also played Albéniz's Rapsodie espagnole for two pianos. Selva could only have been bested by the great and beautiful Catalan singer Maria Gay. With a sunny spirit, and sometimes with a delightful charm, she sang popular songs and refined and tasteful selections by J. Gay. She then revealed to us the talent of a young, up-and-coming Catalan composer, J. Civil, whose two melodies (the second, especially, so expressive and so intense!) ... were true triumphs. Remember his name: he will be famous one day[83]

---

81 Josep (José) Civil y Castelvi was a pupil of d'Indy between 1909 and 1921. He came to France in 1904, studying organ with Alexandre Guilmant and composition with Vincent d'Indy. He later became a professor of harmony at the Schola Cantorum. His brother, Franciusco Civil i Castellini received a diploma from the Schola Cantorum in 1915.

82 Miguel Llobet (1878–1938) was a friend of Albéniz and appeared on programs playing transcriptions of works by Albéniz and Granados. Llobet was also friends with Viñes and it appears that he had a similar relationship with Séverac, as apparent in a letter dated December 20, 1909. He asked the composer for two tickets to Séverac's opera *Le coeur du moulin*, suggesting a certain familiarity.

83 Séverac, *Le monde musical* (May 5, 1905), 124; Séverac, pseud. AC Sever, "Chronique des concerts: musiciens catalans," *Le mercure musical*, 1e année, no. 2 (June 1, 1905), 90–91. [Conflation of two articles.] "La *Schola Cantorum* a eu l'heureuse initiative de donner une séance consacrée aux musiciens catalans. C'est la première fois, croyons-nous,

Regarding Llobet, Séverac commented:

> Above all, Llobet is a charming musician, of a very delicate taste: the way in which he harmonized *Le testament d'Amélia* proves it. But in addition, he has an extraordinary sense of feel and in his hands the guitar becomes a marvelous instrument capable of translating the most intimate and most intense emotions. His guitar is at times just as emotive as the violin when played by the greatest masters.[84]

These concerts provided Séverac with an opportunity to hear a plethora of Catalan works performed by various Catalan musicians. By 1905, his horizons had widened as a result of his contact with many of these Catalan musicians, as well as with much Catalan art and folk music. As a result, Séverac left Paris permanently in 1907 and moved to the Catalan province of Roussillon two years later.

---

que l'on entendait à Paris, réunies sur un même programme cette soirée a obtenu un trop-beau succès ... Il est impossible d'exprimer ici le charme, l'intensité et la diversité des sonorités de l'instrument du guitariste Llobet.

Bien que plusieurs des oeuvres exécutées soient déjà connues du public des concerts Selva, Viñes et de la Société nationale, cette soirée a été, pour beaucoup, une révélation et nous n'exagérons rien en disant qu'elle a obtenu un succès retentissant. Il y à cette heure, sinon une véritable 'école catalane' du moins un groupe musical très particulier, très remarquable même dans ce coin de L'Espagne, où la vie artistique et intellectuelle semble d'ailleurs, reprendre un nouvel et brillant essor.

Au cours de cette séance, Mlle Blanche Selva, en grande musicienne et en catalane convaincue ... interpréta, avec une intelligence de la couleur, les chants d'Espagne et l'impressionnante *Véga* d'Albéniz. Plusieurs oeuvres d'Albéniz ont bien caractérisé l'evolution du talent de ce musicien délicieux qui est certainement aujourd'hui un grand musicien. Lorsqu'on se rappelle l'époque où certaines de ses oeuvres ont été écrites, on ne peut s'empêcher de reconnaître qu'Albéniz a devancé certains d'entre nous réputés les plus "modernes," les plus "impressionnistes." Il y a dans son oeuvre, des qualités de couleur et de rythme très spéciales certes, puisqu'elles sont l'expression même du tempérament d'une race, mais d'une valeur artistique incontestable. Le jeune compositeur Granados était représenté à ce concert par deux *Danses espagnoles* pleines de distinction et d'élégance, que Ricardo Viñes joua avec un délicatesse de nuances extrêmes.

Ricardo Viñes après les deux délicieuses danses de Granados, nous fit de nouveau entendre *La tour vermeille* et *La sevillane* et l'on fit fête à ce pianiste exquis. Avec Blanche Selva, Ricardo Viñes joua également la *Rapsodie espagnole* d'Albéniz, pour deux pianos: on ne pouvait mieux confier la partie vocale qu'à la grande et belle cantatrice catalane Maria Gay. Elle chanta avec une fougue ensoleillée, parfois avec un charme délicieux, des chants populaires et d'autres, très raffinés et savoureux de J. Gay. elle nous révéla ensuite le talent d'un jeune compositeur catalan d'avenir: J. Civil, dont deux mélodies (la deuxième surtout si expressive et si intense!) ... obtiennent un vrai triomphe. Qu'on retienne ce nom, il sera célèbre un jour."

84 Séverac, *Le monde musical*, 124. "Llobet est d'abord un charmant musicien, d'un goût très délicat (la façon dont il a harmonisé *Le testament d'Amélia* le prouve) mais il est de plus un interprète extraordinaire et la guitare devient sous ses doigts un merveilleux instrument capable de traduire les sentiments les plus intimes comme les plus intenses et aussi émotionnant parfois que le violon lorsqu'il est joué par les plus grands maîtres."

Artists and Poets

Séverac also became friends with Catalan painters and writers in Paris, including the Cubist painter Pablo Picasso, the poet Guilluame Apollinaire, and sculptor Manolo (Manuel Martinez-Hugué).[85] Manolo met Séverac in 1902 and introduced him to Picasso, who later remarked that "Séverac is always one of the best memories in my life of Art, with all the admiration that I have [for him]."[86] Picasso later contributed a sketch of Séverac for a 1951 exhibition in honor of the composer at the Musée d'art in Céret.

Séverac spent evenings socializing with the group at Montmartre cafes, including Au lapin agile, the Bateau lavoir, and Austin's Bar, where the group often spent the entire night discussing art, philosophy, and politics. Séverac's contact with these artists and writers was significant because many of these painters had moved to Rousillon by 1910, and friendships that had developed between Séverac and "La bande à Picasso" helped inspire Séverac to move to French Catalonia.[87]

Picasso appreciated sardana music and the sounds of cobla instruments, and his friendship with Séverac in Paris and Céret helped expose Séverac to conversations about the sardana and cobla instruments. This fact is supported by the poet Max Jacob, who also socialized with Séverac and Picasso in Paris and Céret, and later dedicated his poem "Honneur de la sardane et de la tenora" to Picasso.[88] However, it was not until Séverac moved to Céret that he was able to hear these instruments on a regular basis.

---

85 Guillaume Apollinaire was a poet who later collaborated in articles written for *Revue des revues* and *La revue d'art dramatique et musical*, where he discussed his love for old Christmas songs, music-hall songs, music by Hector Berlioz, and music theater. His interest in chansons populaires rivaled that of Séverac. Manolo was born at Barcelona in 1872 and made a decision early in life to be a sculptor. He knew the young Pablo Picasso during the last decade of the nineteenth century. Manolo was one of the few friends with whom Picasso felt comfortable—especially in receiving professional criticism.

86 Pablo Picasso, "L'hommage à Déodat de Séverac," *Revista musical occitania*, 1952 (special edition). Other members of the "bande à Picasso" included painters Henri Matisse, Georges Braque, Maurice Vlaminck, André Derain, as well as poets Max Jacob and André Salmon. "Séverac est toujours un des meilleurs souvenirs de ma vie d'Art avec toute l'admiration que je lui garde."

87 Jeanine Warnod, *Le bateau-lavoir* (Paris: Mayer, 1986), 75. Manolo's monarchist beliefs were similar to those of Séverac.

88 Max Jacob, *Le laboratoire central* (Paris: Gallimard, 1980), 131.

Chapter 10
Séverac's Catalan Works

Séverac left Paris permanently in 1907 to live briefly in his childhood home in Saint-Félix-Caraman. By 1909, he had settled in the town of Céret, a Catalan town in the Pyrenees mountains in the province of Roussillon.[1] This move was inspired by the desire to live close to French and Catalan friends in Céret's artistic community, including Manuel Hugué y Martinez, Pablo Picasso, Frank Haviland, Max Jacob, Juan Gris, Georges Braque, Moise Kisling, and André Derain. Yet, it was also a decision prompted by the composer's fascination with the land and the music of its people.

Séverac eventually sought to write music that reflected a shift from programmatic piano music of a generally regionalist character to works that contain indigenous Catalan elements. Séverac adopted this regionalist attitude towards a territory in which he had not previously lived. This does not so much demonstrate the flexibility with which Séverac employed his regionalist aesthetic, but reflects the nature in which he employed the term; that a southern French regionalist could live in any of the Mediterranean provinces, and this would reflect Mistral's pan-Latin regional philosophy. However, Séverac quickly became enamored of purely Catalan music and soon composed various Catalan-based compositions. These include the use of the cobla in his tragédie lyrique *Héliogabale* (1910), his cantata *Lo cant del Vallespir* (1911), and incidental music to Emile Verhaeren's *Hélène de Sparte* (1912). Séverac also composed piano and piano-violin compositions that imitate cobla instruments, including *Suite Cerdaña* for piano (1908–11), *Minyoneta: souvenir de Figueras* for violin and piano (1919), and *Sous les lauriers-roses* for piano (1919). Imitation of cobla instruments in these works is achieved through the employment of melodic configurations characteristic of fluviol writing, the use of harmonic intervals that are sounded in cobla ensembles, and the incorporation of rhythmic patterns characteristic of those found in sardanas. Séverac also composed music based on Catalan goigs (hymns), or paid homage to goigs through programmatic references accompanied by hymn-like music.

---

1 Séverac settled in Céret at the end of 1909 and beginning of 1910. After spending several months at the Hotel Armand, he rented a small house on Saint Ferréal Street where he began to compose *Héliogabale*. In 1911, the Catalan press announced Séverac's permanent move to Céret. See Joseph Canteloube, *Déodat de Séverac* [1st Edition, Paris, 1929] (Béziers, France: Société de musicologie de Languedoc, 1984), 24–5.

Héliogabale (1910)
Tragédie Lyrique in Three Acts, Libretto by Emile Sicard

Héliogabale is a three-act tragédie lyrique based on a libretto of Marseille journalist and poet Emile Sicard (1880–1921), directed by Louis Hasselmans (1878-1957), and first performed in the outdoor Théâtre des Arènes in Béziers in 1910.[2] Fifteen thousand spectators attended the event. There were a total of 407 instrumental musicians and solo singers, and 160 chorus members accompanying 60 dancers from the Opéra-Comique and La Scala. The opera contains seven spoken roles, and these actors were from L'Odéon in Paris. There were also three sung roles, two of which were from the Opéra in Paris—soprano Germaine Le Senne, as Cynthia, and the tenor known as Frantz, who played Lucilius. Also singing a solo role was the baritone known as Demangane. The mis-en-scène designer was Eugène Ronsin, who also worked for Debussy in the première of *Pelléas et Mélisande*. The Mattes-Cortie cobla ensemble also performed in the work, providing a Catalan, or southern regional ambiance.

The plot of *Héliogabale* centers around the story of Christianity and Roman decadence during the waning years of the Roman empire, which occurred under the reign of an emperor of Syrian origin, Bassien Flagabal, or Héliogabale. Héliogabale was born in AD 204 in a small town in Phoenicia. When he was very young, he was named "priest of the sun," and in AD 218, rose from private soldier to head of the empire. Although he was a malcontent from childhood to 14 years old, the senate later recognized him as the head of the Western world. He became the High Priest of the phallic cult of the sun and raised his status as sun god above all other Roman gods.

Act I, entitled "La démence" (Insanity), centers around the triumph of Rome and consists of nine scenes as well as five important music numbers. These include an initial prelude for orchestra wherein the Roman fanfare theme enters and is developed within the trumpet section. The second piece is entitled "Cortège des roses" and the third number, "Le cortège d'Héliogabale," consists of dancers and soldiers acclaiming the emperor as trumpets and bugles sound from the wings. A salute to Héliogabale follows as all enter into the room in which a feast takes place, which includes the "Choeur des favoris et des courtisanes" number followed by "Le festin," in which the theme at the beginning of the act serves as the basis of this finale. It ends with majestic and triumphant trumpet and bugle fanfares evoking the glories of Rome.

---

2   The work has often been compared to Debussy's *Le martyre de Saint Sébastien*, Fauré's *Prométhée*, Honegger's *Le roi David: psaume symphonique en trois parties d'après le drame de René Morax* (Lausanne, Switzerland: Edition Foetisch, 1921), as well as Roussel's *Padmâvatî*, op. 18 (Paris: Durand, 1919–23), which was an evocation of the eighteenth-century opera-ballet.

Louis Hasselmans was a conductor and formerly a cellist, who won first prize at the Paris Conservatoire in 1893, played in the Concerts Lamoureux, and was a member of the Quartet Locien Caplet. He was also the grandson of the orchestra director at the conservatory in Strasbourg.

Act II entitled "Les catacombes" contains Christians within the catacombs singing Gregorian chant, followed by an "Offrande des fidèles" (Offering of the Faithful), a second invisible choir of Christians singing in the distance, and an Alleluia sung by women. The acolytes of Callixtus then sing a choral fugue over which the liturgical theme "Fidelis servus et prudens" is sung. After the solemn benediction of water by the deacon and the singing by the Christian choir, there follows a baptism of Claudien and kiss of peace. Meanwhile, a cleric and his acolytes sing the Alleluia "Virgo florens Aaron," which is continued by the Christians. A final chorus, "Voici nos coeurs prêts à souffrir," ensues.

Act III is entitled "La mort d'Héliogabale" and is dedicated almost entirely to dance. The initial music number is the "Danse du soleil" followed by dancers in "La bacchanale" and "La mascarade;" in the latter Séverac incorporated a donkey and a caricature of Pegasus and Bellerophon.[3] A processional "Escorte de l'empereur" then takes place, followed by a final scene consisting of a Ballet-mimodrame by Gabriel Boissy entitled "La résurrection d'Adonis," which is in three parts: "Les funérailles d'Adonis," "La résurrection d'Adonis," and the "Danse de l'adolescent." A Phoenician virgin is then taken to Héliogabale as conspirators suddenly invade and cry "to death" while soldiers rush towards Héliogabale and carry him away. The crowd sings while Christians chant the Alleluia quietly in the background as Héliogabale is thrown into the river.[4] Héligabale dies after chanting a final "Hymne au soleil" as the actual sun sets over the outdoor theater in Béziers and the tragédie lyrique concludes.

The three principal themes in the drama include a fanfare theme sounded by trumpets (allegretto) and somewhat in the style of Wagner, which alludes to the power of the Roman empire, an "oriental scale" representing Héliogabale's theme, and the Christian theme inspired by the hymn "O crux ave spes unica."

Héliogabale *and En Plein Air*

The fact that the première of *Héliogabale* was to be performed en plein air met with resistance from many of Séverac's colleagues and mentors. This was especially the case with Vincent d'Indy and René de Castéra, who both thought that great art could not be performed in outdoor settings. Both expressed disapproval and suggested that the outdoor première of *Héliogabale* would help undermine the legitimacy of the work. Séverac commented on d'Indy's disapproval of the outdoor performance:

> I want to get the maestro [d'Indy] to promise to come to Béziers. ... The maestro has never come to the performances at Béziers. Had he attended, he would have seen that it is possible to do a good thing in this [outdoor] setting. This was Bordes's feeling.... It is not because of the "open air."[5]

---

[3] This section is based on three recurring themes of a folk-like aesthetic depicting the myth of Pegasus and Bellerophon. In Greek mythology, Bellerophon attempted to get into heaven on the back of the horse Pegasus, but the attempt was foiled by Zeus.

[4] See Canteloube, *Déodat de Séverac*, 64-8.

[5] Jean-Bernard Cahours d'Aspry, "Déodat de Séverac" (unpublished manuscript), 43. "Je veux faire promettre au 'maître' de venir à Béziers ... Le maître n'est jamais venu aux

Séverac had to continue to defend en plein air performances because of reprimands by various colleagues, including the skepticism that Séverac encountered from Carlos de Castéra, to whom Séverac replied in a letter:

> My dear friends, I must admit that I don't understand the distrust that you all have of the work that I am creating right now.... As for the question of a lyric tragedy performed outdoors, it seems to me that there is nothing there to offend the sensibilities of "true artists!" One musician, who is clearly a respectable artist, was not averse to writing a work for the arena: Gabriel Fauré.... The opportunity presented itself to me.... I took advantage of it and do not believe that I have in any way betrayed "Art," even with a capital "A."[6]

Séverac would have been alluding here to Fauré's tragédie lyrique *Prométhée*, which also had its première at the Théatre des Arènes in Béziers a decade earlier. Other works performed en plein air include Saint-Saëns' *Déjanire*. It is important to note that neither Saint-Saëns nor Fauré received criticism for performing their works outdoors. There are several reasons for this: because Séverac was criticized by colleagues for leaving Paris and not composing on a regular basis, he was open to indictment from composers in Paris. More importantly, however, was the fact that Séverac's above comments allude to the connection between en plein air performances and so-called popular music, as the latter would have likely been performed outdoors in festivals such as the one in which *Héliogabale* had its première. Séverac was beginning to compose various popular works and orchestrate popular works by other composers in order to earn a living. This combination of creating so-called popular works together with compositions performed en plein air led to fervent criticism from many colleagues in Paris.

This connection between en plein air and popular music implied to the elite that audience members were either peasants or simply those who attended works that appealed to the masses, or as one observer remarked, "[the] earthy and vulgar taste of these people."[7] Therefore this attitude concerning en plein air performances had social implications, as alluded to in an essay by Marcel Pottecher, one of the first authors to promote this phenomenon:

> It is the intention of the people's theater to mix the classes, and far from excluding the elite, it believes that the latter is indispensable for ensuring that the event has an artistic

---

représentations de Béziers. S'il y avait assisté, il aurait vu qu'il est possible de faire une belle chose dans ce cadre. C'était l'avis de Bordes ... Ce n'est pas la faute du 'plein air.'

6   Canteloube, *Déodat de Séverac*, 25. [Letter dated April 3, 1910.] "Je t'avoue ne pas très bien comprendre la méfiance que vous avez tous, braves amis, pour l'oeuvre que je fais en ce moment ... Quant au principe de la tragédie lyrique en plein air, il n'y a rien là qui puisse, me semble-t-il, choquer les sentiments des 'véritables artistes'! Un musicien qui est assez artiste n'a pas dédaigné d'écrire une oeuvre pour les Arènes. Il s'appelle: Gabriel Fauré ... L'occasion s'est offerte à moi ... Je l'ai saisie et ne crois pas en rien avoir trahi 'l'Art' même avec un 'A'."

7   Gabriel Boissy, "Théâtre des arènes de Béziers, *Héliogabale*," *Le théatre*, no. 283 (October, 1910), 17; reprinted in Andrea Musk, "Regionalism, Latinité and the French Musical Tradition: Déodat de Séverac's *Héliogabale*," *Nineteenth Century Music Review* (Aldershot: Ashgate, 2002), 248. "goût un peu truculent et vulgaire de ces populations."

tone, and that it is elevated so as to prevent it from descending into the vulgarity of facile effects, banal melodrama and grotesque farce.[8]

Séverac's viewpoints regarding the social role of en plein air performances were less patriarchal than that of Pottecher, as Séverac commented on the democratic role of en plein air venues in the program to his theater work *La fille de la terre*:

> The open-air theater must be popular or not exist at all. But, in this case, the word popular implies all the masses, the crowd that constitutes the whole city, the crowd where the humble rub shoulders with the elite; a magnificent community that dictated the realization of Greek tragedy. Here, in place of the myth of antiquity, freed and exalted, is the social conflict between town and country, a daily conflict, a conflict that is only too real in our villages.[9]

Séverac's democratic or semi-proletarian ideals were interestingly ironic, considering the fact that he was an aristocrat; yet because of his poetic interest in peasant culture, Séverac was anxious to see various classes within rural areas intermingle.[10] Andrea Musk notes that these proletarian overtones are symbolized in *Héliogabale* through the portrayal of Christians, who are depicted not as glorious heroes, but as ordinary masses who have suffered under stifling Roman rule; that is, a "doctrine of weak and oppressed victims [that] take on the destiny of the Roman world."[11] In a way, Séverac wanted to legitimize peasantry in the eyes of the elite in the same way that he wanted to sanction folk music and pastoral life to the urbane Paris community, which often held a patriarchal view towards rural culture.

Séverac's interest in having *Héliogabale* performed en plein air was initially inspired by Bordes' outdoor performance of works by Monteverdi and Rameau in Montpellier, as evident in a letter from Séverac to René de Castéra:

> As for the orchestration [of Héliogabale], I consider the enormous mass of sound at my disposal to be like a great organ.... As you can see, there isn't any connection between the orchestration [in this work] and my orchestration of "Le coeur du moulin," which is essentially pointillist .... For the dances, I will attempt to achieve a resonant effect, like

---

8   Andrea Musk, "Aspects of Regionalism in French Music during the Third Republic: the Schola Cantorum, d'Indy, Séverac and Canteloube," translated by Musk (PhD Dissertation, Oxford University, 1999), 138.

9   Déodat de Séverac, program to *La fille de la terre*, 13 (Private collection: SS), reprinted in Musk, "Aspects of Regionalism in French Music during the Third Republic: the Schola Cantorum, d'Indy, Séverac and Canteloube," 142.

10   This idealization of the peasant was criticized by some as being socialist, which was also a concern for critics of Millet's Barbizon School paintings heralding peasant culture. Many accused these paintings of inspiring socialism.

11   Musk, "Regionalism, Latinité and the French Musical Tradition: Déodat de Séverac's *Héliogabale*," 241, citing *Album officiel* (Private Collection Sociéte de Séverac), 9. "voici que déjà la doctrine des faibles et des opprimés commence à participer aux destinées du monde romain."

the one Bordes dreamed of for outdoors. ... Do you remember the marvelous effect of the stuff that Bordes had us hear in the villa gardens at Montpellier?!!![12]

Séverac was also inspired by the outdoor performance of Fauré's tragédie lyrique *Prométhée* at the Thèâtre des Arènes in Béziers. In fact, it was upon Fauré's recommendation, that Séverac wrote to Castelborn in order to request the use of the Thèâtre des Arènes for the première of *Héliogabale*:[13]

> I would have liked to have written an outdoor work ..., and certainly for a magnificent theater such as yours. It's a dream I've had for a long time, as I was one of your most faithful admirers ... In any case, it would give me, a man of uncompromising Mediterranean stock, great pleasure to write truly Mediterranean music and to see it performed in the wonderful setting of Béziers.[14]

As observed in Séverac's comments, his interest in outdoor performances is also related to his pan-Latin regionalist affinity for southern France and Mediterranean culture, as further corroborated in an interview in *Excelsior*, where Séverac stated "If I happily created the music of *Héliogabale*, it is because I am decidedly from the South of France. I love outdoor performances."[15] According to Musk, this interest in Latinité implied a return to the Greco-Latin tradition, an important aspect of Mediterranean regionalism. This form of régionalisme within music found its place not only in en plein air venues per se, but also in the physical representations of Greek and Roman culture found in some of the architecture in southern France. For *Héliogabale*, this architectural symbol was the Béziers arena in which the

---

12 Aspry, Déodat de Séverac, 433. [Conflation of two letters, Séverac letter to René de Castéra, 1910, and letter to Jean Poueigh, 1910.] "Quant à l'orchestration, je considère l'énorme masse sonore dont je dispose comme un grand orgue ... Cela n'a, comme tu le vois, aucun rapport avec mon orchestration du 'Coeur' qui est surtout pointilliste ... Pour les danses, je ferai l'essai d'un effet sonore que Bordes rêvait pour le plein air ... Te souviens-tu de l'effet merveilleux des choses que Bordes nous fit entendre à Montpellier dans les jardins de la villa?!!!"

13 Works by other French composers intended for en plein air include Saint-Saëns' *Pallas Aathénée* and *Déjanire*, Gluck's *Armide*, and Spontini's *La vestale*.

The Thèâtre des Arènes in Béziers was developed by the millionaire viticulturer and amateur musician Fernand Castelbon de Beauxhostes, who hosted annual music celebrations during one week every August between the years 1898 and 1914. See Musk, "Regionalism, Latinité and the French Musical Tradition: Déodat de Séverac's *Héliogabale*," 241, 233; most of Musk's article contains information included in her dissertation.

14 Ibid., 427. Recounted by Auguste Sérieyx in *L'action française*. "J'aurais aimé écrire une oeuvre pour le plein air ... et surtout pour un théâtre magnifique comme le vôtre. C'est un rêve que je fais depuis longtemps déjà, car j'ai été un de vos admirateurs les plus fidèles ... Dans tous les cas, ce serait un grand bonheur pour moi méridional intransigeant, que d'écrire la musique d'une oeuvre absolument méridionale pour la voir réaliser dans l'admirable cadre de Béziers."

15 Canteloube, *Déodat de Séverac*, 25–6. "Si j'ai fait avec joie la musique d'*Héliogabale*, c'est que je suis méridional, très méridional. J'aime le spectacle de plein air."

work was performed, which resembles many Roman theaters.[16] Another aspect of Mediterranean regionalism was found in the region's warm climate, often referred to in Séverac's thesis as a relationship between the Midi and the sun, which echoed Mistral's pan-southern regionalist theories.[17]

Despite the massive attendance at the première of *Héliogabale*, some critics, including E.D. in *La revue musicale*, commented on the work and its lack of merit as a national subject treated in the outdoor theater at Béziers:

> In such a grandiose atmosphere at the amphitheater of Béziers—a place as suited to the creation of a national lyric theater through its revival of the great solemnities of antiquity—why put so much effort, money, science, art and other skills to the service of a subject like Héliogabale? In Paris, a work about this pathetic emperor—this "poor young man," to cite Renan's description of Nero—could succeed as a curiosity appealing to a public that is fond of varied shows. But does it merit the honor of being staged in a theater, like the Dionysian at Athens, that affects the periodicity, brilliance and character of an annual festival? I would prefer us to treat national subjects at Béziers. These should be capable of inspiring noble sentiments and encouraging healthy enthusiasm. The resources are not lacking. We have, we French, a wonderful history of unparalleled richness, in a land that has seen a feudal and Christian Middle Ages, a series of magnificent kings and superb knights, Joan of Arc, the Revolution, the epic Imperial epoch, in a word, the most beautiful epic and lyric material imaginable, I regret that energy is channeled into magnifying a ... [Héliogabale].[18]

Héliogabale *and the Cobla*

Another regionalist aspect to *Héliogabale* was Séverac's employment of the Catalan cobla, with which he became enamored upon moving to Roussillon.[19] Several months after his arrival, Séverac heard three cobla ensembles, a music society, a choir, and cabaret music.[20] It was at this time that Séverac often spoke of feeling more Pyrénéen than Toulousain:

---

16 Other Roman towns in southern France in which en plein air performances took place included Arles, Orange, Nîmes, and Carcassone.

17 See Séverac, "La centralisation et les petites chapelles musicales,"*Le courrier musical*, 11e année, no. 1 (January 1, 1908), 5.

18 E.D., "Héliogabale aux arènes de Béziers," *La revue musicale*, 10e année, no. 18 (September 15, 1910), 398; reprinted and translated in Musk, "Aspects of Regionalism in French Music during the Third Republic: the Schola Cantorum, d'Indy, Séverac and Canteloube," 146.

19 Séverac's use of the cobla in *Héliogabale* is based on Mistral's pan-Latin ideals, which associates Roman history with outdoor performances. Roman incursions into what is now the south of France, including Catalonia, explain why Séverac would use Catalan instruments in an opera that does not contain a Catalan story or include Catalan music.

20 Séverac referred to the sardana as a "most noble and most Athenian dance." Pierre Camo recalled that Séverac was "literally haunted by the rhythm of the sardana." Canteloube stated that Séverac's "soul expanded to the rhythm of the sardanas [and] to the expressive timbre of the Catalan cobla." See Aspry, *Déodat de Séverac, 1872–1921: musicien du soleil méditerranéen* (Belgium: Séguier, 2002), 62.

> You ask me my impressions of Roussillon, on the Catalan songs and on cobla music. I respond to you simply that I do not know a country as beautiful as Roussillon and the soul of which is as well expressed and translated in its popular music. The Basque region is the land of Romantics; the classicists certainly would choose Roussillon.[21]

Catalan cubist sculptor Gustave Violet recalled Séverac's reaction at first hearing the cobla in Céret:

> Déodat loved our Roussillon profoundly.... Its landscape and especially its popular music had been a revelation for him. One evening in Céret ... Déodat and I heard the cobla of Peps de Figuères ... Déodat's eyes were filled with tears and he was trembling with emotion. As the music died down, Déodat said to me: "I absolutely must do something with this region and with this music."[22]

The composer himself attested to being inspired by the ensemble upon first hearing it in 1910 after moving to French Catalonia:

> One evening ... for the first time in my life, I heard a Catalan cobla. I can remember it as if it were yesterday.... [The cobla] possesses qualities otherwise unknown to me until now.... The instruments sing with joy ... [and] passion. The Vallespir area has become the land of my dreams! This dream was finally realized ... the moment when I composed Héliogabale.[23]

Séverac was attracted to the Catalan tiple and tenor, in part, because he had been an oboist during his youth and remained attracted to the sounds of shawms. Séverac's appreciation for the timbre of these instruments prompted him to devise notation for the purpose of enabling cobla musicians to perform in his proposed Catalan-based

---

21 Letter to Jean Amade, April, 1912, reprinted in Pierre Guillot, *Déodat de Séverac: écrits sur la musique* (Paris: Pierre Mardaga, 1993), 95. Jean Amade (1878–1949) was a Catalan poet who wrote the words to *Lo cant del Vallespir*. "Vous me demandez mes impressions sur le Roussillon, sur les chants catalans et sur la musique des 'coblas.' Je vous répondrai simplement que je ne connais pas un pays aussi beau que le Roussillon et dont l'âme soit aussi bien exprimée et traduite dans sa musique populaire. Le Pays Basque est la patrie des Romantiques; les classiques choisiraient certainement le Roussillon."

22 Blanche Selva, *Déodat de Séverac* (Paris: Librairie Delagrave, 1930), 22–3. "Déodat aimait profondément notre Roussillon. Ses paysages et surtout sa musique populaire avaient été pour lui une révélation. Un soir à Céret ... Déodat et moi écoutions la cobla de Peps de Figuères ... Les yeux de Déodat étaient remplis de larmes et il était tremblant d'émotion. Lorsque la musique se fut tué, Déodat me dit: 'Il faut absolument que je fasse quelque chose avec ce pays et avec cette musique.'"

23 Vallespir is a region in French Catalonia near the Spanish border, with Céret as the capital. Pierre Guillot, ed., *Déodat de Séverac: la musique et les lettres* (Liège, Belgium: Pierre Mardaga, 2002), 95–6. [Séverac letter to Jean Amade, 1912.] "Un soir ... pour la première fois de ma vie, j'entendis une 'cobla catalana.' L'impression m'en est restée comme si elle était d'hier ... possèdent un ensemble de qualités inconnues jusqu'à ce jour ... Les instruments chantent la joie ... la passion. Le Vallespir devint le pays de mon rêve! Ce rêve put enfin se réaliser ... au moment où je composais *Héliogabale*."

works.[24] This issue of notation illustrates Séverac's early interest in extending the abilities of cobla instruments in order that they received official orchestral status and therefore "legitimized" the instruments in the ears of his audience, thus mixing together so-called "peasant" sounds of the cobla with the elite's appreciation for symphonic instruments. Séverac's interest in notation is supported by comments made by Albert Manyach-Mattes, the leader and first tiple player of the Mattes-Cortie cobla ensemble, a group that performed in the première of *Héliogabale*.[25]

> The Mattes-Cortie cobla played on Barry Square, and from the orchestra, we did not lose sight of the artist [Séverac], who seemed keenly interested in the Catalan instruments. He stood sometimes to the right and sometimes to the left of the cobla, pulled back, moved across, and even going under the instrument pavilion; obviously the young composer was trying to analyze the value of the primas and tenors. After the celebration, Séverac invited the musicians to see him. After having told them of his admiration, he presented to them a penciled sketch intended for the cobla instruments. They did not have the heart to tell him that it was only playable on flutes or clarinets ... Without a doubt, they were clear enough, since the next day, [he] offered them a new arrangement. He asked them to try it on the tenor, which remained, more or less, in the "Mascarade" [from Héliogabale].[26]

Séverac's interest in legitimizing cobla ensembles is also evident in Canteloube's comments:

> We can only second what our friend Déodat de Séverac said and agree with Manyach's desires to see Catalan instruments take their place in the modern orchestra. They would spice up the rhythms lost to the large heavy mass of strings and the flabby sonority of the brass. From a rhythmic point of view, resonant strength, agility, [and] incisive abilities, a cobla "drives" the orchestra. Let an experienced violin-maker study the instruments we are talking about and refine and perfect them: there's quite little to do. Composers would

---

24 See Albert Mattes, *L'independant* (Toulouse: France, March 17, 1955); also see Robert F. Waters, "Regionalism and Catalan Folk Elements in the Compositions of Déodat de Séverac, 1910–1919" (PhD Dissertation, University of Maryland at College Park, 2002). Cobla musicians were accustomed to performing without scores. However, Mattes and his cobla ensemble were able to read music as well as play by ear; this explains why they were able to perform with Séverac's symphony orchestra in *Héliogabale*.

25 The ensemble also included Joseph Cortie, second tenor, and Vincent and Louis Cortie, first and second tiples respectively.

26 *Prima* is the Catalan word for tiple. Albert Manyach-Mattes, "Les catalans et Déodat de Séverac," *Le coq catalan* (June 11, 1921). "La cobla Mattes jouait sur la place du Barry, et de l'orchestre nous ne perdions aucun mouvement de l'artiste qui paraissait s'intéresser vivement aux instruments catalans. Se plaçant tantôt à droite, tantôt à gauche de la cobla, s'éloignant, se portant en face, venant même sous le pavillon des instruments, le jeune compositeur cherchait evidemment à se rendre compte de la valeur des 'primes et des ténors' et peut-être eut-il ce jour-là l'idée de les utiliser. Après les fêtes, Séverac invita les musiciens à venir le voir. Après leur avoir confié son admiration, il leur présenta une notation au crayon destinée aux instruments de la cobla. Ils n'osèrent lui avouer cependant que ce n'était jouable que sur flûtes ou des clarinettes ... Sans doute furent-ils suffisamment subjectifs, puisque le lendemain leur proposant de nouvelles notation. Il les pria d'essayer sur le tenor; ce qui est resté, ou à peu près, de la 'Mascarade.'"

finally have at their disposal rhythms and sounds that no other instrument can give them, and the modern orchestra would see its strength, the firmness of its attacks, and the clarity of its rhythms all grow. We are certain of it, because we have written for primas and tenors. We know that amidst the dull bassoons, horns and saxophones, these [instruments] can bring a hint of the sunny climate from the countries for which they provide a stirring voice.[27]

Séverac's compositions written between 1910 and 1919 demonstrate his stylistic evolution in various ways, including his use of more incisive rhythms, and it is this characteristic enhanced by the cobla that makes Séverac's regionalist transformation in music during this time profound. Other musicians and most of the press found the use of the cobla and its inherent ability to rhythmically enliven *Héliogabale* exciting. Blanche Selva commented that in *Héliogabale*, "His latest style shows a marvelous clarity and incisive neatness."[28] Paris music critic Pierre Lalo of *Le temps* alluded to this use of rhythm in a review of a concert version of the opera presented at the Salle Gaveau in Paris in the winter of 1911. This event helped establish Séverac as a much more important composer within Parisian music circles than he had been previously:[29]

[There was] a group of Catalan musicians whose instruments Séverac hired. [One instrument was] a sort of rustic oboe which sounded harsh and pronounced and was enormously and deservedly successful. Their rhythm had an intense and admirable energy. In Héliogabale, they alternate with ordinary "woodwinds" from the orchestra, playing the same phrases or the same fragments of phrases one after the other. Each time that the Catalan [musicians] played, the rhythm took on a sharp and superb clarity, accent, and bite. Each time that our musicians played, [they sounded] dull, soft, weak, and malleable.

---

27 Canteloube, "La musique populaire, les 'coblas' et les instruments catalans," *Le courrier musical et théatral*, vol. 31, no. 18 (November 1, 1929), 581–2. "Nous ne pouvons que confirmer ce que disait notre ami Déodat de Séverac, et qu'approuver le souhait de Manyach! Celui de voir les instruments catalans prendre leur place dans l'orchestre moderne auquel ils redonneraient le mordant que la trop grande masse des cordes et la sonorité flasque des cuivres leur a fait perdre. Au point de vue rythmique, puissance sonore, agilité faculté incisive, une cobla 'tire' l'orchestre, qu'un luthier avisé étudie les instruments dont nous parlons, les assouplisse et les perfectionne: Il y a bien peu à faire. Les compositeurs auraient enfin à leur disposition des rythmes et des timbres qu'aucun instrument ne peut leur donner, et l'orchestre moderne verrait augmenter singulièrement sa puissance, la fermeté de ses attaques et la netteté et ses rythmes. Nous en sommes certains, car nous avons écrit pour les primes et les tenors et nous savons que ceux-ci peuvent nous apporter, au milieu de la grisaille des bassons, des cors et des saxophones, un peu de soleil des pays dont ils sont l'émouvante voix."

28 Aspry, "Déodat de Séverac", 393. "Son style dernier est d'une merveilleuse clarté, d'une netteté incisive."

29 The composer had already been known in the Parisian music world through the success of various compositions, including the Paris presentation of the opera *Le coeur du moulin* (1909) and the performance of four (out of five) movements to *Cerdaña*, which had its première the same year.

Would the sense of rhythm [from the cobla] be a primitive musical virtue that disappears among the civilized?[30]

Many well-known composers heard *Héliogabale*, either at its première in Béziers, or at the concert performance in Paris one year later These include Camille Saint-Saëns, Gustave Charpentier, Vincent d'Indy, Joseph Canteloube, and Gabriel Fauré. Fauré's reaction to the concert in Paris was recalled by Canteloube:

> Fauré, among others, attentively followed the score. The "Mascarade," with the intervention of cobla instruments, pleased him so much that one truly saw him stamp his feet with enthusiasm and call out "encore, encore." And in the act of the Christians, he cried out "this is admirable! admirable! What true music ... This is delicious! And how simple it is, without all of the pretense that so many others believe is required in art ... [When] Séverac has something to say, he says it simply. Many have nothing to say, and they do all they can to mask the emptiness ... What music! What true music! This flows naturally and without effort ... What an artist and a revelation!"[31]

In this later indoor concert performance of *Héliogabale* at the Salle Gaveau in Paris, the instrumentation was modified, as the small hall lacked the same quality of sound found in the Béziers arena. As a result, only two tiples, two tenors, and a contrabassoon were used, and they were placed offstage as if to sound from a distance.[32] The number of orchestral musicians was reduced from 560 players to 180. Manyach-Mattes described the audience:

> Among the listeners that followed the original score during the performance were the undisputed masters of musical art—Saint Saëns, Charpentier, Fauré, d'Indy, Canteloube.... With a light tingle in our hearts, we heard prolonged waves of unanimous applause for the four [cobla] musicians on stage.[33]

---

30 Pierre Lalo, "La musique: *Héliogabale* aux concerts Hasselmans," *Le temps* (April 18, 1911), 3. "Un groupe de musiciens catalans, dont M. de Séverac a employé les instruments, sorte de hautbois rustiques, au timbre plein, rude et fort, ont eu un succès énorme et mérité. Le rythme à chez eux une intensité et une énergie admirable. Dans *Héliogabale*, ils alternaient avec les 'bois' ordinaires de l'orchestre, les uns et les autres disant tour à tour les mêmes phrases ou les mêmes fragments de phrases. Chaque fois que c'était aux catalans à jouer, le rythme prenait une netteté, un accent, un mordant incisifs et superbes. Chaque fois que c'était à nos instrumentistes, tout s'émoussait, s'amollissait, devenait faible et comme savonneux. Le sens du rythme serait-il une vertu musicale primitive, qui dégénèrè chez les civilisés?"

31 Selva, *Déodat de Séverac*, 64. "Fauré, notamment, suit attentivement sur la partition, et la 'Mascarade,' avec l'intervention des instruments de la cobla, lui plait à tel point qu'on le voit réellement trépigner en réclamant le bis, qui est accordé, puis un second, accordé aussi, et enfin un troisième. Et à l'acte des chrétiens il s'écrie 'c'est admirable! admirable! Que de vraie musique ... C'est délicieux! Et comme c'est simple, sans tout le chiqué que tant d'autres se croient obligés, pour faire de l'art, de mettre autour! ... Séverac a quelque chose à dire, et le dit tout simplement. Beaucoup n'ont rien à dire, alors ils font tout ce qu'ils peuvent pour masquer le vide! ... Cela coule, naturel, et sans effort! ... Quel artiste et une révélation!'"

32 Albert Manyach-Mattes, *L'indépendant* (March 17, 1955).

33 The preparation for this Paris performance contained innumerable problems, including the fact that a page to the orchestral score was lost and Séverac had to recompose this section.

The three primary sections in *Héliogabale* to contain the cobla are found in Act III and include "Danse du soleil," "Mascarade," and "Bacchanale," the latter without sardana rhythms. In "Danse du soleil," the tiples and tenors of the Catalan cobla are sounded as Héliogabale enters, and then the choir sings while the "Danse du soleil" unfolds:[34]

Example 10.1   "Danse du soleil," *Héliogabale*, Act III, no. 1, mm. 1–9 (piano-vocal score)

Séverac orchestrates the melody in this passage with divided tiples and tenors together with flutes, and harmonize with each other in major third and perfect fourth intervals. Séverac, in the score, allowed traditional symphonic instruments to be substituted in place of a cobla ensemble; that is, for oboes and English horns to replace tiples and trumpets and trombones to be substituted in place of tenors. The accompanying bass line is then sounded by bassoons and string bass.

Selva, *Déodat de Séverac*, 64. "La présence parmi les auditeurs qui tous suivaient l'exécution de l'oeuvre sur la partition originale, des maîtres inconstestés de l'art musical! Saint-Saëns, Charpentier, Fauré, d'Indy, Canteloube ... C'est avec un léger picotement au coeur que nous entendîmes alors monter vers l'estrade les applaudissements unanimes et prolongés qui salvaient l'intervention des quatre instrumentistes."

34   Unpublished manuscript, courtesy of Editions Salabert. The score gives the conductor permission to replace Catalan instruments with piccolos, flutes, oboes, and English horns.

Héliogabale *and Legal Matters*

Although there appeared to be many audience members at the première of *Héliogabale* in Béziers, Joseph Charry, the director of the Théâtre des Arènes and one of the organizers of the Béziers performance, handed out free tickets because of many unoccupied seats. Séverac, Sicard, and other participants, including one of the organizers, Charles Guéret, considered themselves therefore to be a financially "injured party," as they incurred financial debt from the Béziers performance.[35] Séverac subsequently threatened legal proceedings by instigating a complaint against Charry under the auspices of the Société des auteurs. As a result, Charry seized the orchestral and choral score and withheld it from Séverac. Séverac attempted several times to recover the material and was finally forced to ask publisher Alexis Rouart to confiscate the score from Charry's home in order to perform the work in Paris. This failed, and a proposal was then offered to Charry that Séverac keep the material, but be obliged to loan it to him upon demand so that he could have the work performed. Charry agreed and the formal complaint was withdrawn; nonetheless, Charry was late in returning the orchestral score, which forced Séverac to postpone the Paris performance.[36]

Other problems arose with regard to the score of *Héliogabale*. Act I of the work is preceded by a prologue entitled "Les deux triomphes," with a poem by Charles Guéret.[37] This opening was scored for orchestra and chorus together with one tenor and soprano soloist singing Guéret's text, in following the tradition of the French eighteenth-century tragédie lyrique. Problems arose following the Paris event in that because of free tickets issued at Béziers, Guéret felt cheated on royalties that were promised him based on a percentage of tickets sold. Guéret therefore refused to allow Séverac permission to continue using the prologue and Séverac then felt it necessary to have the work performed without the text as a result. Librettist Emile Sicard had originally signed an agreement specifying that no performance of *Héliogabale* take place without Guéret's prologue, however, and so further presentations of *Héliogabale* were prevented.

In an article in *Comoedia*, Gabriel Boissy described the dilemma, where he referred a "business partner," implying Charry, and an "organizer," which is a reference to Guéret:

> A struggle between a financial backer of this spectacle and one of the spectacle's organizers led to the former seizing this material. But before belonging to the people who use it, such material first belongs to the composer or, strictly speaking, to the publisher. Now, everybody's dead, or almost everybody. But the financial backer, a self-made man, is still alive. And he won't budge. When we asked him to lend us the Héliogabale orchestral

---

35 Joseph Charry (1870–1932) was an osteopath in southern France. He founded many outdoor theaters between 1907 and 1909 and replaced Fernand de Castelborn as Director of the Théâtre de Béziers in 1910.

36 Séverac had scheduled the performance for February 4 and was forced to reschedule the concert on February 18. See Aspry, Déodat de Séverac, 472.

37 The music to the prologue contained principal motives that would be heard during the ensuing drama.

material, he protested and more or less refused. Because of this guy, only a portion of Séverac's music can be played—a portion that is not sufficient to show Séverac's genius. And all this because a greedy man who had a little tiff with a third party refuses the moral and unalienable rights of a composer. Here has clearly arisen a typical conflict where "copyright" violently overrides the moral and superior rights of an artistic creator.[38]

In 1913, Louis Hasselmans, the conductor of *Héliogabale* at Béziers and friend of Séverac, tried to convince Charles Guéret to change his mind over the performing of *Héliogabale* without the prologue. In a letter to Séverac, Hasselmans wrote:

> I made [Guéret] see that he was obliged to send you the score... [even though] he had prohibited you from performing this material in part or in whole. To this, he responded that he would rather let this music languish or destroy it rather than to cave on his position. Given this state of affairs, there wasn't much more to say. So, I stayed put and told him that I would write you. Furthermore, I must tell you that I basically tried to present myself not as your intermediary but as director of classical concerts in Marseille, which leaves you to do as you see fit.[39]

Although Hasselmans suggested that Séverac might have had some luck receiving permission from Guéret if Séverac approached him personally, there is no evidence to suggest that Séverac tried to contact Guéret following the receipt of this letter; and despite Canteloube's attempts to have the orchestral score to *Héliogabale* released following Séverac's death, the composition remained withheld for several decades.[40] The work continues to be important for its inclusion of cobla instruments

---

38 Gabriel Boissy, *Comoedia* (August 2, 1936). This would not only have been the case with the prologue, but also with the ballet "La resurrection d'Adonis" included in *Héliogabale*. "Un différend d'intérêts entre un commanditaire de ce spectacle et l'un des organisateurs du dit spectacle, permit au premières saisir ce matériel, avant d'appartenir à qui l'utilise, appartient d'abord à l'auteur ou, à la riguer, son éditeur. Tout le monde, ou à peu près, est mort. Mais le commanditaire, qui s'est nanti lui-même, survit. Et celui-là n'a pas désarmé. Quand nous lui avons demandé de nous prêter le matériel d'orchestre d'*Héliogabale*, il a opposé des prétentions qui équivalent à un refus. À cause de ce personnage, une partie seulement de la musique de Séverac pourra être jouée, une partie insuffisante pour donner l'idée du génie qu'il déploya à cette occasion. Cela parce qu'une cupidité privée fondée sur un différend avec un tiers, s'oppose aux droits moraux et imprescriptibles d'un auteur. Voilà nettement posé un conflit caractéristique où le droit 'matériel' barre abusivement le droit moral et supérieur du créateur artistique."

39 Aspry, "Déodat de Séverac", 478–9. [Louis Hasselmans, letter to Séverac, March 11, 1913.] "Je lui ai fait observer qu'il était sujet à se voir contraint de te donner communication de la partition ... et voir interdire par toi toute exécution partielle ou totale avec ce matériel. A cela il m'a répondu qu'il préférait laisser dormir cette musique ou la détruire plutôt que de renoncer à ses conditions. Dans cet état de choses il n'y avait plus rien à dire. J'en suis donc resté là lui disant que je t'écrirais. Je dois d'ailleurs te dire que j'ai essentiellement tenu à exprimer que je venais non pas comme ambassadeur mais comme directeur des concerts classiques de Marseille, ce qui te laisse ainsi le champ libre."

40 The work was later performed in 1936 at the Théâtre antique d'Orange. The orchestral-vocal score of *Héliogabale* presently remains unpublished. The autograph manuscript remains in Saint-Félix de Lauragais (formerly Saint-Félix-Caraman), but there is a version owned by

and later influence on Canteloube, who subsequently composed his own works for the cobla. Canteloube also wrote articles on cobla music and continued to champion the inclusion of these instruments in Western orchestras.

Suite Cerdaña: Souvenir d'un Pèlerinage à Font-Romeu, Suite des Etudes Pittoresques (1908–11)
(Memory of a Pilgrimage to Font-Romeu, Suite of Picturesque Studies)

I. En tartane: l'arrivée en Cerdagne (Arrival in Cerdaña)
II. Les fêtes: souvenir de Puigcerda (The Holidays: Memory of Puigcerda)
III. Ménétriers et glaneuses: souvenir d'un pèlerinage à Font-Romeu (Fiddlers and Gleaners: Memories of a Pilgrimage to Font-Romeu)
IV. Les muletiers devant le Christ de Llivia (The Mule-drivers before the Christ of Llivia)
V. Le retour des muletiers (The Return of the Mule-drivers)

Cerdaña was originally entitled *Etudes pittoresques* and included only three movements.[41] The second movement had already been composed as a separate work in 1908, and the fourth movement ("Les muletiers devant le Christ de Llivia") was completed in 1911, the year when the composition was finished under its current title. Séverac's initial intention was to include his piano work *Baigneuses au soleil* as the fourth movement, but Selva suggested that there needed to be a slow piece as penultimate movement.[42]

Cerdaña depicts a musical journey through the Cerdaña region of Catalonia, which includes Séverac's impressions of his trip to the Catalan Pyrénées-Orientales mountain villages of Puigcerda, Font Romeu, and Llivia, all of which are represented in the movements. Canteloube described how Séverac's impressions were conveyed in Figure 10.1.

Editions Salabert that has been photocopied and rented for performance. It is nonetheless in poor condition.

41 The movements were "En tartane," "Ménétriers et glaneuses," and "Le retour des muletiers," respectively.

42 Most evidence points to the first integral performance of the work, excluding the fourth movement, having taken place at the Société nationale de musique in 1911, with Blanche Selva as performer, though Canteloube claims the performance transpired at the Libre esthétique and only included the first, third, and fifth movements. "Les muletiers devant le Christ de Llivia" had its première in 1911 at the Société nationale de musique, with Alfred Cortot as pianist.

Figure 10.1   Joseph Canteloube's description of the five movements to *Cerdaña*

No. 1 "En tartane" (Arrivée en Cerdagne). The curtain rises to reveal the countryside, signaled by the flute of the Pyrenees goat herders. Then, the Tartan rolls along noisily, to the fast trot of its mules, stopping for an instant ... then starts off again finally stopping in Cerdaña with the reminder of the flute of the goat herders.

No. 2 "Les fêtes" (Souvenir de Puigcerda) evokes holidays in the exquisite little Spanish town of Puigcerda, not far from the French border. People sing and dance there. In the middle of the piece, we have a "charming encounter," which I know to be with Laura Albéniz. One sees also customs officers whose bugle [sounds] clash with the ambient atmosphere.

No. 3 "Ménétriers et glaneuses" (Souvenir d'un pèlerinage à Font-Romeu). The first theme, inspired by a popular sardana theme of the region, and the piano part evoke Catalan coblas. The second theme has the allure and color of a religious pilgrimage chant. The piece ends by alluding to the goat herder's flute [from the first movement].

No. 4 "Les muletiers devant le Christ de Llivia." The sound of bells. The hymn *O crux, ave, spes unica*!

No. 5 "Le retour des muletiers." Quickly, but nervously, mules trot.[43]

Séverac evokes peninsular locales, cities, festivals, songs, and dances in *Cerdaña* in much the same way that Albéniz does in *Iberia* (1905–09), completed the same year in which Séverac began composing his work.[44] Both *Iberia* and *Cerdaña* contain

---

43   Canteloube, *Déodat de Séverac*, 54–5. "No. 1: 'En tartane' (Arrivée en Cerdagne). Un rideau se levait sur le pays, au signal de la flûte des chevriers pyrénéens. Puis la tartane roule bruyamment, au rapide trot de ses mules, s'arrête un instant ... puis repart pour s'arrêter enfin, en Cerdagne, au rappel de flûte des chevriers.

No. 2: 'Les fêtes' (Souvenir de Puigcerda) évoque les fêtes dans l'exquise petite ville espagnole de Puigcerda, non loin de la frontière française. On y chante et l'on danse. Au milieu du morceau, on fait une "charmante rencontre" que je sais être Laura, fille d'Albéniz. On y voit aussi des carabineros dont le clairon d'étonne avec l'atmosphère ambiante.

No. 3: 'Ménétriers et glaneuses' (Souvenir d'un pèlerinage à Font-Romeu). Le premier thème, inspiré d'un thème de sardane populaire de la région, et l'écriture pianistique évoquent très curieusement la sonorité des coblas catalanes. Le second thème à l'allure et la couleur d'un chant religieux de pèlerins. Le morceau se termine par un rappel de la flûte des chevriers.

No. 4: 'Les muletiers devant le Christ de Llivia.' De sons de cloches. L'hymne O crux, ave, spes unica!

No. 5: 'Le retour des muletiers.' Au trot rapide, nerveux, des mules trottent."

44   This was the same time in which Debussy created *Ibéria: images pour orchestre* (1909), and when Turina wrote his piano suite *Sevilla* (1909). Andalusian elements, therefore, were being used in various compositions by numerous French and Spanish contemporaries, including Maurice Ravel; yet, Catalan elements employed in music were rare.

dance rhythms, modal mixtures, Phrygian scales, descending minor tetrachords, and imitations of the flamenco cante jondo and guitar.

"Les fêtes: souvenir de Puigcerda" (1908) was the first of the five movements to be composed and to include Andalusian elements, as well as fandango accents found in imitation of the open strings of the guitar through staccato tones. These are found in the 'carabineros' and 'Où l'on trouve le cher Albéniz' sections, where Séverac includes clear-cut articulation and recurrent ostinato patterns as elements of unification. The 'carabineros' section evokes Catalan carabiniers (customs officers) in the border town of Puigcerda as they participate in the festivities. This movement is analogous to "Le jour des noces" in *Le chant de la terre*, and "Le jour de la foire" in *En Languedoc*, where festivities also take place. Séverac described his experiences in Puigcerda:

> I am troubled by the effects of what we are tragically forced to call the border. Border life fascinates me. In these villages, there are carabineers. These soldiers, peripheral characters, have their function, especially Sunday afternoons when people come to dance. This waltz seems full of deep-seated human anguish. Many things that have moved me are at play here: popular sentimentalism, the provincial sadness, the melancholy of twilight, the tavern and the ball next door, exoticism.[45]

The sounds of the Catalan customs officers are evoked through an imitation of bugle calls occurring at unexpected moments in order to highlight their significance:

---

45 Aspry, "Déodat de Séverac," 636. "Je me trouve sous les effets de ce que fatalement nous devons appeler frontière. La vie d'une frontière me fascine. Dans ces villages, il y a des carabiniers. Ces carabiniers, personnages périphériques, ont leur importance, surtout le dimanche après-midi, à l'heure du bal. Cette valse est pleine, me semble-t-il, de complexes humains et d'angoisses viscérales. S'y donnent la main, me semble-t-il, beaucoup de choses qui m'ont ému: le sentimentalisme populaire, la tristesse de la province, la mélancolie du crépuscule, la taverne et le bal voisin, l'exotisme."

214 Déodat de Séverac

Example 10.2 Bugle Calls of Carabiniers, *Suite Cerdaña*, second movement ("Les fêtes: souvenir de Puigcerda")

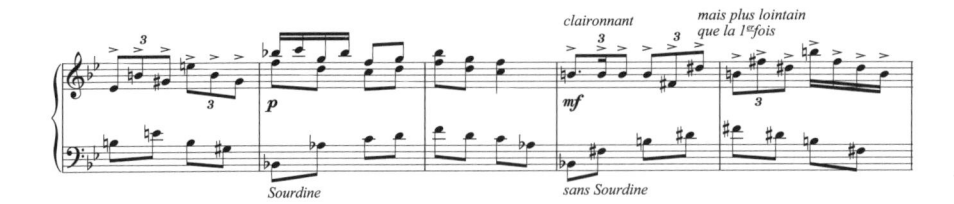

The third movement, "Ménétriers et glaneuses" (Souvenir d'un pèlerinage à Font-Romeu), describes a pilgrimage to an ancient sanctuary of the Virgin Mary in the Catalan mountain village of Font-Romeu. Pianistic passages include fourths and fifths that are common in cobla harmonies. A traditional sardana theme is also embedded in this passage, which is sounded in the double-stemmed eighth-sixteenth notes found in the right-hand piano part.

Example 10.3 Sardana Theme Embedded in Measures 1–6, *Suite Cerdaña*, third movement ("Ménétriers et glaneuses")

A quieter goig theme, evoking the prayers of pilgrims, is also included following the sardana section before again returning to the dance played by the cobla. The goig is a Catalan hymn primarily in honor of the Virgin Mary and was often used in Séverac's later compositions. Goigs often contain an introduction (tornada) followed by couplets and a refrain, and are often related to Catalan folk song, in that both genres contain diatonic scales, are usually syllabic, and maintain a flowing melody and symmetrical phrases. When goigs were composed by Catalan priests from Spain, these works often took on a serious and liturgical character and were generally freer in form than Catalan versions composed in France. The day after Easter, Séverac would often follow goig singers who traveled the roads of Céret. Before sunrise, groups of shepherds would sing the seven beatitudes in the traditional way of their ancestors and would be heard in adjacent valleys.[46] Séverac depicts the ancient custom of uniting dance with Catalan religious traditions in "Ménétriers et glaneuses:"

Example 10.4   Goig Theme Embedded in Measures 64–70, *Suite Cerdaña*, third movement ("Ménétriers et glaneuses")

The fourth movement contains the plainsong melody "O crux ave." Séverac discussed this movement in the following:

> Amigo! You are right to say that between "Ménétriers et glaneuses" and "Le retour des muletiers," a little seriousness is missing ... I tried to compose the small piece that you requested and I'm sending it to you! It is called: "Le Christ espagnol de Llivia." It is a sort of expressive lament on the admirable Christ figure done in the mystical-realist Spanish [style] that is in the old church in Llivia (in Cerdaña).[47]

---

46 Selva, *Déodat de Séverac*, 78.
47 Canteloube, *Déodat de Séverac*, 53. [Séverac letter to René de Castéra, April 21, 1911.] "Amigo! Vous avez eu raison. . . de me dire qu'entre 'Ménétriers et glaneuses' and 'Le retour des muletiers,' il manquait un peu de sérieux. . . J'ai essayé de faire le petit morceau demandé. Je te l'envoie! Ça s'appelle: 'Le Christ espagnol de Llivia.' C'est un sorte de complainte expressive sur cet admirable Christ de l'art mystico-réaliste espagnol qui est dans la vieille église de Llivia (en Cerdagne)."

Séverac again referred to the inspiration for this movement in another letter:

> The old Christ of Llivia, doesn't it remind you of that admirable Spanish Christ that you must have seen once upon a time? It is one of the most moving works of Spanish realism that I know of. To me, it is as beautiful as the one in Perpignan, but less cruelly realist. I tried to get that across in the small piano piece that I sent to René. Tell me if I have succeeded.[48]

This last comment suggests Séverac's insecurity regarding his talent, which began to evolve about the time in which he composed *Cerdaña*, evident in his comments: "In Cerdaña, as in all my works, there are developments that are too long, with useless padding."[49]

Séverac made a decisive break with Impressionism in *Suite Cerdaña*. There are also fewer nonmusical references within each movement, as well as fewer overlapping phrases and imitations of other instruments, including the cobla, than in Séverac's other two piano suites. Séverac began to focus his attention on Catalan music elements, especially rhythm and melody, the former represented by a chord continually repeated, as well as a bass ostinato written under the melody. Also significant are the unbarred passages that return at important points of articulation, as well as the elimination of the glissando, which provided a sense of elasticity in former works. There are also many unresolved chords and delayed cadences, as well as a substantial decrease in the number of metric changes. There is less random harmonic movement between keys in this work, as well as fewer flatted sevenths, seconds, and augmented seconds; Séverac's predilection for flat keys, however, is still prominent.[50] There is occasional polytonality and modality, the latter occurring mostly through raised fourths and sixths.

Sectional divisions and thematic recurrences transpire within the first movement, "En tartane: l'arivée en Cerdagne," which contains irregular phrase lengths and is in the following form: Introduction–A–B–A–B–A–Coda. An initial theme occurs in the opening 'A' section within five different keys and four distinct figurations. The theme then recurs with different patterns within ensuing 'A' sections. A second theme occurs in Section 'B' in the key of C minor in a passage labeled in the score as 'Esperanza', which then recurs in a new key within the second 'B' section. This melody and its recurrences epitomize the spirit and cyclic nature of the suite. Andalusian elements are also written within the 'Esperanza' section, which includes a melody ending in a half cadence in Example 10.5.

---

48 Aspry, "Déodat de Séverac", 332. [Séverac letter to Blanche Selva, 1911.] "Le vieux Christ de Llivia vous souvient-il de cet admirable Christ espagnol que vous avez dû voir jadis? C'est une des oeuvres de réalisme espagnol les plus émouvantes que je connaisse. Il est, pour moi, aussi beau que celui de Perpignan, mais moins cruellement réaliste. J'ai essayé de dire cela dans la petite pièce de piano que j'envoie à René. Vous me direz si j'ai réussi."

49 Ibid., 76. "Dans *Cerdaña*, comme dans toutes mes oeuvres, il y a des développements, trop longs, du délayage inutile."

50 Jan LaRue has stated that Impressionists preferred flat keys because of the relatively veiled character of orchestral sonorities in these keys, owing to the absence of open strings. See Elaine Brody, "The Piano Works of Déodat de Séverac: A Stylistic Analysis" (PhD Dissertation, New York University, 1964), 278–9.

Example 10.5   'Esperanza' Section, *Suite Cerdaña*, first movement ("En tartane: l'arrivée en Cerdagne")

Rhythmic accompaniment presages the upcoming theme as well as a Spanish Phrygian scale in the 'Esperanza' section. This rhythmic motif occurs at measure 1 in the bass clef followed by the Phrygian scale in measure 5.

A tritone relationship between F and B is highlighted in measures 5 and 7 of the aforementioned example, and this is coupled with an underlying diminished chord. This tritone emphasis helps to insure the harmonic and melodic ambiguity of the passage while creating an element of surprise during the next cadence. 'Esperanza' recurs in measure 211, this time a half-step lower, in the key of B minor. However, the rhythm here is syncopated:

Example 10.6   Variation in B minor, 'Esperanza' theme in Measures 211–216, *Suite Cerdaña*, first movement ("En tartane: l'arrivée en Cerdagne")

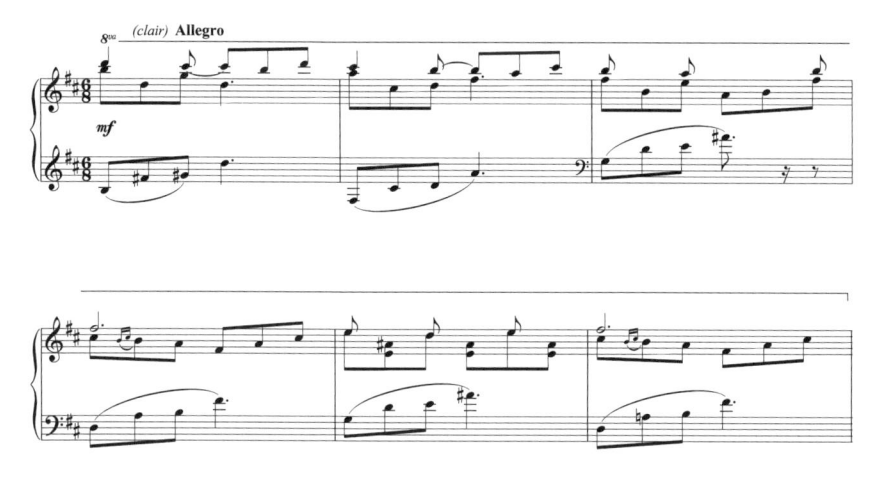

The same melody occurs in the second movement, "Les fêtes: souvenir de Puigcerda," this time in the key of D minor in octaves. Séverac labels this 'A Delightful Encounter':

Example 10.7 'Esperanza' Theme, 'Charmante recontre' section, *Suite Cerdaña*, second movement ("Les fêtes: souvenir de Puigcerda")

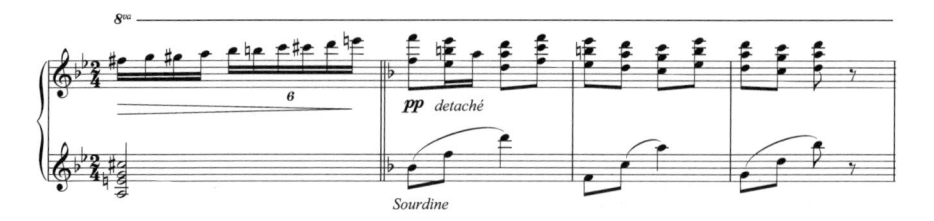

The melody recurs later in the same piece, this time in G minor:

Example 10.8 Variation of 'Esperanza' Theme in G minor, Measures 226–243, *Suite Cerdaña*, second movement ("Les fêtes: souvenir de Puigcerda")

Despite the fact that the 'Esperanza' theme recurs within the second movement, Séverac composed the second movement first; therefore he initially composed the 'Esperanza' within the second movement and later incorporated the theme into the first movement.

In the final movement, "Le retour des muletiers," the motif enters twice in the key of B flat minor, and the measure then shifts to a phrase in which there appears an F sharp seventh chord accompaniment with a flatted ninth, which eventually leads to B minor. Once the new key is sounded, the 'Esperanza' section is stated in full, but with ample inner voices emphasized in order to thicken the texture:

Example 10.9   Stretto-like Variation on 'Esperanza' theme, Measures 46–53, *Suite Cerdaña*, fifth movement ("Le retour des muletiers")

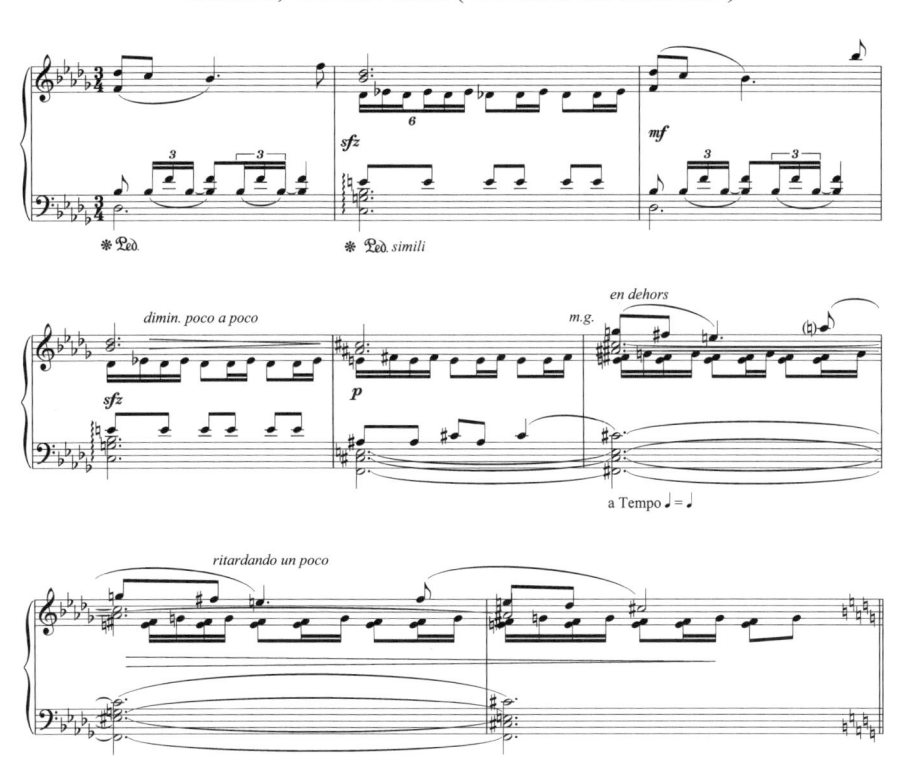

Then, the complete 'Esperanza' theme recurs in B minor:

Example 10.10 'Esperanza' Theme in B minor, Measures 52–63, *Suite Cerdaña*, fifth movement ("Le retour des muletiers")

In measure 79 of the composition, the underlying harmonic structure that supports the opening to the 'Esperanza' section is heard, and this harmonic structure is combined with key pitches taken from the original motive. Now, the recurrence is hidden; yet, there is a programmatic reference in that the section is labeled 'Reminiscence' alluding to the original melody, and accompanied by a descending whole-step pattern and similar rhythmic structure:

Example 10.11   Hidden 'Esperanza' Theme, Measures 79–82, *Suite Cerdaña*, fifth movement ("Le retour des muletiers")

The melody enters again in measure 119 of the composition in the form of a syncopated 6/8 meter. This had occurred in measure 54 in B minor, but in this new section, it enters in F sharp minor:

Example 10.12   Variation of 'Esperanza' Theme in Sextuple Meter, Measures 117–123, *Suite Cerdaña*, fifth movement ("Le retour des muletiers")

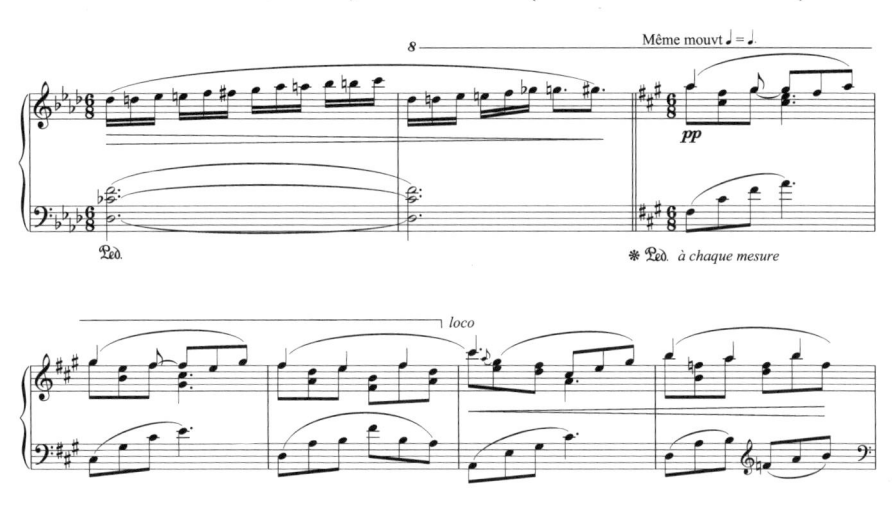

Cerdaña was Séverac's earliest composition to reflect a shift from primarily programmatic piano music of a general regionalist character to works that contain specifically Catalan elements. The work became one of Séverac's most popular piano compositions and was subsequently performed by many pianists, including Blanche Selva and Ricardo Viñes. It would be his last large-scale piano work until after World War I, when he composed his final piano piece, *Sous les lauriers-roses*.

Lo Cant del Vallespir (1911)

Another regionalist work is *Lo cant del Vallespir*, a cantata for soloists, mixed six-part choir, and orchestra. The work is based on a Catalan poem by Joan Amade and was created for a Céret festival. The première consisted of 200 chorus members accompanied by 73 orchestral musicians. Séverac also included in the work baritone and soprano solos, as well as cobla instruments. The poem reflects Amade's Catalan regionalist outlook:

Figure 10.2   Text to *Lo cant del Vallespir*

> Sing of the Catalan homeland,
> Rejoicing earth and homeland of peace,
> The Canigou king of the plain,
> Of the mountain and blue sky:
> Sing of the Vallespir where bumblebees buzz
> Without fear of a freezing wind,
> Where always the partridge
> Can feed their young which chirp nearby;
> Our Vallespir where winter is so beautiful
> That one sees in each branch
> Of covered almond trees which frost up as dust
> To be born soon, under the red sun, a white flower.
> Country of the cherry and beautiful carnation,
> Which the young girl carries
> On her cheek and on her body,
> Let the fruit and let the flower as the most beautiful fruit and flower of
> The garden
> Land of the festive Tech
> Land of Albères,
> Where the sun makes each eye a brother of warmth
> And of the fresh mouth, at the moment when she smiles,
> The sister of cherries.
> O Ancient homeland of the Olive tree,
> O Trees, beloved by our ancestors
> You that give pure and clear oil
> To make our meals better
> And for the light which, by night watches the work of the wise!
> Vallespir of the grapevine and of the reddish oak-cork,
> Of sweet pomegranate agreeable to mouths! ...
> O poetry of the land of Vallespir
> Which makes blossoms of all rocks under the sky!
> Let us sing of what dawn says of our loving heart,
> That which tells the rising star in full bloom;
> Let us sing friends, sing again
> How the tender flower grows by the bank of the river.
> And how do the fledgling birds fall asleep in the nest
> Under the feathers of their mother ...
> Sing that which fills our heart
> Of a pleasure and charm without measure.

Friends, sing, sing of love.
Let us sing, friends, sing of life
Let us sing happily of all good things
Our life which flows with so much sweetness,
As water of the Tech between edges of the meadow
Where freshness reigns!
The word of our ancestors should be spread as other metaphors!
And up to the hour where the sun sets,
Let us sing of the Catalan homeland,
Rejoicing earth and homeland of peace,
The Canigo king of the plain,
Of the mountain and blue sky Let us sing of spring, of laughing summer,
The loving and fresh foliage from the chestnut tree,
And the loving fountains
Where the fairies hide
To charm the young man with their sweet look.
The red barretine and the provocative sandal,
And the belt and the cap
Sing of blooming grace
Of the young girl and the boy!
Let our hearts sing, which sing to our lips,
Nightingales of love launching their trills under a beech tree
As there God's world does on the pasture in the month of May.[51]

---

51 Séverac composed two versions of this work, written after Catalan song themes. The Catalan text to *Lo cant del Vallespir* is as follows:

Cantem la terra catalana,
Terra de l'alegria y terra de la pau,
Lo Canigo rey de la plana,
De la montanya y del cel blau.
Cantem lo Vallespir hont bronzina l'abella
Sens por del vent geliu,
Hont sempre la perdiu
Pot criar sos petits que piulen aprop d'ella;
Lo nostre Vallespir hont l'ivern es tan dols
Qu'hom veu a cada branca
De l'ametller cubert de gibre com un pols
Naixe'aviat, al sol vermell, una flor blanca!
Pais de la cirera y del clavell hermos.
Hont la minyona porta
En sa galta, en son cos.
Com la fruyta y la flor més boniques de l'horta.
Terra del Tech festiu.
Terra de les Alberes.
Hont lo sol fa de l'ull un germa del caliu
Y de la boca fresca, al moment que somriu,
La germana de les cireres.
O terra antigua de l'oliu,
Aybre estimat dels nostres avis

The sardana rhythms incorporated in the opening section of *Lo cant del Vallespir* are different than those used in Séverac's other Catalan-based compositions, in that the work begins in 12/8 meter. The middle section utilizes a more traditional duple meter sardana structure within a percussive section.[52]

    Que donas l'oli pur y clar
    Per fer millor nostre menjar
    Y pel Ilum qui, la nit, vetila el treball dels sabis!
    Vallespir de la vinya y del ciure rojench,
    De la dolsa manglana agradable à les boques!...
    O poesia del pais vallespirench
    Que fas florir sota del cel totes les roques...
    Cantem lo que diu l'alba à nostre cor aymant,
    Lo que li diu l'estela espellida a Llevant;
    Cantem, amichs, cantem encare
    Com creix la tendre flor a la vora del riu,
    Y com los aucellets s'adormen dins del niu,
    Sota les plumes de sa mare...
    Cantem lo qu'umpleix nostre cor
    D'un goig y d'un encant sens mida.
    Amichs, cantem, cantem l'amor;
    Cantem, amichs, cantem la vida;
    Si, cantémla tots de bon grat
    Nostra vida que raja ambe tant de dolsura,
    Com les aygues del Tech entre vores de prat
    ont reina la frescura!
    Cantem la primavera, y l'estiu rialler,
    Lo follatge amoros y fresch del castanyer,
    Y les fonts regalades
    Hont s'amaguen les fades
    Per encisar lo jove amb son mirar dolser...
    La barretina roja y l'espardenya ardida,
    Y la faixa y l'escofflo,
    Cantem la gracia espellida
    De la minyona y del minyo!
    Que canti nostre cor, que cantin nostres llabis,
    Rossinyols de l'amor refilant sus d'un faig:
    Com rajen per l'herbam les deus al mes de maig,
    Que raji lo parlar divi dels nostres avis!...
    Y fins a l'hora hont lo sol cau,
    Cantem la terra catalana
    Terra de l'alegria y terra de la pau.
    Lo Canigo rey de la plana,
    De la montany y del'cel blau!

52 The manuscript of this work exists in Saint-Félix de Lauragais but remains unpublished.

Hélène de Sparte (1912)

Another composition to include the cobla is *Hélène de Sparte*, incidental music to a tragedy written by Emile Verhaeren. What we know of this lost composition comes from letters exchanged between Séverac and the stage director, Alexandre Sanine, about the type of music required.[53] Sanine wrote to Séverac requesting the following:

> I have learned that you have a great desire to write preludes for the four acts of the tragedy. I have nothing against these preludes.... I cannot in any way consent to the performance of orchestral numbers in plain sight. In front of a period curtain from the Trojan War era, such an orchestral group would truly be a sacrilege, a disgrace, a crime. I am of the opinion that we should conceal the orchestra, as in the Wagnerian tradition. We should put the orchestra in the wings or in some sort of pit. No matter what, we should hide the modern orchestra from the audience's eyes. In the parts of the tragedy where the music plays a part in the action on stage, the orchestra will play in the wings, because any appearance of a modern musician would be artistically disharmonious.
>
> Without wanting to impede on your creative freedom and your inspiration, I will simply outline, in very general terms, the general psychological motifs which the themes of the preludes for each of the tragedy's four acts mean to me.... I would never dare to impose the slightest limitation on you, nor give you precise instructions.
>
> I would request that you compose the following numbers: In the first act, whatever sort of savage horn sound signals victory. This is the approach of Helen and Menelaus's victory march. The sounds [should] become more distinct as they approach.
>
> When the nymphs appear, something must change in the offstage orchestration.... A pause for a second, as if the whole earth were silent, and then a complete chaos of crazy sounds. I don't know which instruments to use: an organ, perhaps brass—sounds that Strauss never imagined. A roar, a horror. And after this torrent of sounds, after this total cataclysm, complete silence, a solemn pause. Not a single creature dares to raise his head.
>
> Also for this act, please compose the following: the shepherds welcome Helen with some kind of primitive air played on the clarinet.... Flutes are to accompany Helen's movements through the idyllic scene at the end of the act. I would ask you to compose (always to be played in the wings) a poetic concerto for fifes and a pastoral [cobla].[54]

---

53 A discussion took place between Emile Verhaeren and Alexandre Sanine as to the style of the music. Some claimed that the orchestration to *Hélène de Sparte* was weak.

54 In the final paragraph, Sanine is referring to the fluviol and tenor when he mentions the fifre and chalumeaux pastoraux. Aspry, "Déodat de Séverac," 513–20. "J'ai appris que vous avez grand désir d'écrire préludes aux quatre actes de la tragédie. Je n'ai rien contre ces préludes ... Je ne puis en aucune façon consentir à l'exécution des numéros d'orchestre dans un orchestre découvert. Devant un rideau de style de l'époque de la guerre de Troie, un tel groupe orchestral serait un véritable sacrilège, une honte, un crime. Je serais d'avis de faire couvrir l'orchestre à la Wagner, de créer une sorte de coquille, et en tous cas de dissimuler aux yeux des spectateurs la vue de l'orchestre moderne, et aux passages de la tragédie où la musique, au milieu des actes, entrera en action, l'orchestre jouera dans les coulisses, car toute apparition d'un musicien moderne serait déjà une disharmonie artistique.

Sans vouloir entraver la liberté de votre oeuvre créatrice et l'élan de votre inspiration, je me permettrai seulement de tracer, en lignes très générales, les motifs psychologiques généraux qui m'inspirent des thèmes de préludes pour tous les quatre actes de la tragédie ... Je n'oserai jamais vous imposer la moindre limite, ni vous donner des indications précises.

Séverac commented on Sanine's letter:

> I am more than happy to compose the music for Hélène de Sparte, but on one special condition: that the last scene not be a vulgar melodrama.... The music that [Sanine] requested to ornament his mise en scène is ready, but he sees it interpreted by instruments giving an uncertain evocation of ancient music.
>
> This section of Hélène de Sparte can be beautiful, but the only instruments which can be heard in the scene without offending sensibilities... are Catalan instruments—extraordinarily sonorous coblas which correspond precisely to Sanine's desires.[55]

The première was performed by Ida Rubenstein as Hélène. We understand through letters between Séverac and Alexandre Sanine that the first prelude, "The Return of Helen," reflects commotion in the streets.[56] There is an energetic hymn of joy to Helen's beauty, as water spirits sing of her return. The second prelude, "The Shepherds," is pastoral in spirit, as Helen is in a tranquil and bucolic landscape with small cottages in the background. A passionate prelude to the third act, "Helen's Distress," is followed by the prelude to the fourth act, "The Triumph of Pollux." Here, Helen weeps as she remains in solitude; she then visits her birthplace and finally, there is a cataclysm as a new beautiful world order begins.

Critics were enthusiastic about the work, but many of Séverac's colleagues in Paris, including Ravel, declared that the orchestration was poor and that he was finished as a composer, which helped lead to Séverac's public downfall in Paris. Although the score is missing, Séverac's handwritten opening page does exist:

Je vous demanderais d'écrire encore les numéros suivants: au premier acte, je ne sais quels sons de cors sauvages donnent le signal de la victoire. C'est l'approche de la marche victorieuse d'Hélène et de Ménélas. Ces sons s'approchant deviennent plus distincts.

À l'apparition des naïades quelque chose doit être modifié dans l'orchestration dans la coulisse ... Une pause d'une seconde, comme si toute la terre s'était apaisée, et ensuite je ne sais quel chaos fou de sons. J'ignore quels sont les instruments employés, un orgue, peut-être des sons de cuivres d'un genre spécial, des sons que n'avait jamais imaginés Strauss, un rugissement, une horreur, et après cette débauche de sons, après ce véritable cataclysme, silence complet, pause solennelle. Pas un seul être n'ose lever la tête.

Pour ce même acte, je vous prie d'écrire aussi ceci: les pâtres accueillent Hélène avec quelque air primitif de chalumeau. Ces airs de flûte accompagneront les mouvements d'Hélène jusqu'à la fin de l'acte dans la scène de l'idylle, je vous prierais d'écrire (toujours pour être joué dans la coulisse) un concerto poétique de fifres et chalumeaux pastoraux."

55 Aspry, "Déodat de Séverac," 508. "Je ne demande pas mieux que de faire de la musique pour *Hélène de Sparte* mais à une condition expresse c'est que la dernière scène ne soit pas un vulgaire mélodrame." Aspry, "Déodat de Séverac" (typescript, courtesy of Aspry), 524–5: "La musique qu'il voudrait pour illustrer sa mise en scène est prête mais il la voit interprétée par des instruments donnant une évocation aléatoire (sic) de la musicalité antique.

Cette partie d'Hélène peut être belle mais les seuls instruments qui peuvent être entendus dans cette scene sans choquer ... sont des instruments catalans—des coblas extraordinairement sonores et qui correspondent complètement aux desins de Sanine."

56 Ibid., 515.

Example 10.13   Introduction, *Hélène de Sparte* (Facsimile). Courtesy of Jean-Jacques Cubaynes, director of the Séverac Festival in Toulouse, France

One source of information regarding the 1912 première of *Hélène de Sparte* at the Théâtre du châtelet in Paris is found in the daily republican newspaper *L'indépendant des pyrénées-orientales*, which covered the event favorably:

> Four of our musicians: Albert Manyach, from the Cobla Maties [and the] three Cortie brothers—Louis, Vincent, and Joseph from the Cobla Cortie-Barreil ... will be heard in the incidental music to Hélène de Sparte ... Sanine ... indeed searched for appropriate sonorities to accompany a procession ... all [instruments] were tried—horns, oboes, bassoons, and contra-bassoons ... They immediately chose Catalan instruments very much appreciated in Héliogabale ... This was a dream sound. The music was pastoral. The jubilant music in the first act of Hélène de Sparte was well received, picturesque, and contained a stirring realism. The truly irresistible effect was obtained by the use of the cobla instruments called the prima and the tenor ... The musicians who played them yesterday ... were simply excellent artists.[57]

El Divino de l'Hort (1916)

A composition by Séverac that is influenced by the goig is *El divino de l'hort*. Although this is a lost set of variations for piano (or organ), oboe, violin, and cello based on the Catalan hymn *L'oracio de l'hort*, we do have the first page in Séverac's handwriting:

---

57 Author unknown, *L'indépendant des pyrénées-orientales* (May 17, 1912). "Nous avons annoncé le départ à Paris de quatre de nos musiciens: Albert Manyach, de la Cobla Maties, et des trois frères Cortie Louis, Vincent et Joseph, de la Cobla Cortie-Barreil ... devaient se faire entendre dans la musique de scène de *Hélène de Sparte* ... Sanine ... cherchait, en effet, des sonorités appropriées pour accompagner un cortège ... tout fut essayé, cors, hautbois, bassons, et contrebassons ... Ils eurent recours tout de suite aux instruments Catalans, très appréciés dans *Héliogabale* ... C'était bien la sonorité rêvée. La musique rendait admirablement la grandeur bucolique. La liesse musicale si familièrement populaire qui reçoit *Hélène* au première acte, est d'un pittoresque, d'un réalisme émouvant. L'effet vraiment irrésistible est obtenu ici par l'emploi d'instruments catalans appelés la prima et le tenor ... les musiciens qui ont joué hier ... sont tout simplement, de très sûrs artistes."

Example 10.14 Opening to *El divino de l'hort* (Facsimile). Courtesy of Jean-Jacques Cubaynes, director of the Séverac Festival in Toulouse, France

Josep Pons recalls the origin of Séverac's composition:

> I took him to the church ... and he [Séverac] wanted to play L'oracio de l'hort on the organ. This was such sweet music that it seemed almost hesitant.... among the most natural-sounding music that he has ever played for me. "I think he improvised it," [Gustave] Violet whispered. El divino de l'hort is a song of sorrow, a song of [Christ's] Passion, and Déodat brought out all of its joy.[58]

We also have information as to how the press viewed Séverac's performance of *El divino de l'hort*, as apparent in a review in the journal *Le tanor*:

> He [Séverac] played his admirable El divino de l'hort. A talented violinist accompanied him and an oboe imitated the melodic and sad voice. I felt moved to the bottom of my heart. This ancient melody expressed the very soul of the old mystical and heathen Catalans: mystical in their innocent faith, heathen in their immense love of the Earth.
>
> I thought I heard the voice of ancient races and each harmony was so deep, so natural, that it seemed to come from the faraway lands of those who are no longer among us.... All of the secret emotions that I felt burgeoning inside me emerged through this melody: the sadness of the soul, so weak in the face of an all-powerful God, and love of the fertile land. ... The artist wanted to express... the simple grandeur of nature. He gave his voice to the earth and expressed ... the voice of the Earth ... and ... nature ... appeared before us.[59]

Minyoneta: *Souvenir de Figueras* (1919)

Séverac's *Minyoneta: souvenir de Figueras* for violin and orchestra is a sardana inspired by a voyage to the Spanish Catalan town of Figueras, when the composer commented upon his arrival: "Oh! That I wish that [Blanche] Selva could see a sardana danced like the one danced in Figueras. This is the most plastic dance, the most moving."[60] Séverac employed sardana rhythms within the piano part and this

---

58 Canteloube, 79. "Je le menai à l'église ... et il voulut interpréter *L'oracio de l'hort* à l'orgue. C'était une musique si douce qu'elle paraissait hésitante ... L'une des musiques les plus naturelles qu'il m'ait été donné d'entendre. 'Je crois qu'il improvise,' me soufflait Violet. *El divino de l'hort* est un chant de douleur, un chant de la Passion, et Déodat nous livrait toute sa joie."

59 Aspry, "Déodat de Séverac", 422–3. "Il joue son admirable *El divino de l'hort*. Un violiniste de talent l'accompagnait et un hautbois imitait la voix mélodieuse et triste. Je me sentais ému jusqu'au fond de l'âme. Par cette mélodie antique s'exprimait toute l'âme des vieux Catalans mystiques et païens: mystiques dans leur foi naive, païens dans leur immense amour de la terre.

Je croyais entendre la voix des vieilles races et l'harmonie de chaque phrase était si grave, si naturelle qu'elle paraissait arriver des terres lointaines où vivent ceux qui ne sont plus parmi nous ... tous les sentiments secrets que je sentais vivre en moi s'exprimaient dans cette mélodie: tristesse de l'âme si faible en face de Dieu tout puissant, amour de la terre féconde ... L'artiste avait voulu exprimer ... c'était la simple grandeur de la nature. Il avait prêté sa voix à la terre, il avait exprimé ... voix de la terre ... et ... la nature ... nous apparait."

60 Ibid., 425 –6. [Déodat de Séverac: letter to Blanche Selva, Céret, June 11, 1911.] "Oh que je voudrais que l'amie Blanche puisse voir danser une Sardana comme on la danse à Figuèras! C'est la danse la plus noble, la plus plastique, la plus émouvante qui soit."

underscores the melody played by the violin. The motif alternates with a duple rhythm, thus providing the listener with a typical sardana rhythmic structure. This is further verified by Séverac's instruction that the work includes a 'tempo di sardana':

Example 10.15   *Minyoneta*, Measures 1–14

The sardana is structured within a miniature ABACA rondo form with coda, instead of the more traditional binary structure found in most conventional sardanas. The 'B' and 'C' sections are rhythmically related, and both sections highlight a dominant prolongation with an underlying harmony of diminished chords.

Miscellaneous Works

Tres Recuerdos (1919)
Cortège Catalan (1919)
Souvenirs de Céret (1919)

Tres recuerdos is an Andalusian orchestral work in three movements inspired by Catalan romance novels written in the form of popular poetry. Although this work does not contain Catalan elements, it is Séverac's only published work that contains primarily Andalusian features and is therefore placed within this chapter. This therefore conforms to Séverac's pan-Latin philosophy. The first movement habanera is in C minor in duple meter and entitled "La fenêtre d'amour," or "Bentano de amor" (Lento assai tempo di habanera); the second movement is labeled "Chants de matelots," or "Cantos de marineros" (Andantino), and contains Andalusian Phrygian cadences in G minor in triple meter; the third movement "Lola la délaissée," or "Lola la abandonada" (Sostenuto ma dolce) is a work in F major in 9/8 meter.[61]

---

61 Séverac, *Tres recuerdos* (Paris: Editions Rouart-Lerolle, 1919).

Cortège catalan is a fanfare wedding march for orchestra in ternary form scored for two flutes, two oboes, two clarinets, one bassoon, two French horn, two trumpets, three trombones, drums, and string quintet.[62]

Catalan themes are also incorporated into Séverac's work for violin and piano, *Souvenirs de Céret*. This work adopts a traditional Catalan song, "Lo pardal," which was also used by Joseph Canteloube in an arrangement for cobla composed in 1926. This fact further suggests Séverac's influence on Canteloube with regard to Catalan music.

Sous les Lauriers-roses ou Soir de Carnaval sur la Côte Catalane, Fantasie pour Piano Dédiée à la Mémoire des Maîtres Aimés: E. Chabrier, I. Albéniz et Ch. Bordes (1919)
(Under the Oleander, or Evening at the Carnival at the Catalan Coastline, Fantasy for Piano Dedicated to the Memory of Loved Masters: E. Chabrier, I. Albéniz, and Ch. Bordes)

Sous les lauriers-roses was Séverac's final composition for piano, and one of his last works before he died in 1921. He first entitled the work *Sous les orangers* and began composing it in 1918 when he was a patient in a hospital in Prades during World War I.[63] Although Séverac was released from the hospital following the demobilization of the troops, he sensed irreparable damage to his health.

He was determined to acknowledge a debt to three of his late mentors: Emmanuel Chabrier, Isaac Albéniz, and Charles Bordes.[64] This is accompanied with descriptions of the work in a letter to Blanche Selva revealing the location and specific festivities that inspired the composition:

> This piece is a kind of "suite in one part" ... Here is what I wanted to do ... to give color by means of rhythm rather than harmony ... Among musicians I love the most are Chabrier and Albéniz. This little work is dedicated to them; this is why I have tried to write music that should, it seems to me, have suited them. It is a fantasy where there [is an evocation of] ... a Spanish military band, some dances by the customs officers [at the border], a sardana, a little scherzo in the style of Chabrier, some Basque rhythms for Charles Bordes, some [music in the style of] ... Daquin, and a little "frisky fugue" ... and even a pianola ... I have dreamed of writing this for a long time (twelve years), to be exact, since the time we took a trip with Bordes to Emporda, Figuères, Girona, and Roses, where we attended some festivities of unforgettable color and "Méditerranéanism." It is the atmosphere of one of these festivals that I have tried to depict in [this piece]. If I have not succeeded, it is because I am unable to express what I feel.[65]

---

62 Séverac, *Cortège catalan* (Paris: Editions Rouart-Lerolle, 1919).

63 Aspry, Déodat de Séverac, 422–3, 80.

64 Séverac's indebtedness to Albéniz is suggested by six staccato chords within the piece suggesting Albéniz's *Fête-Dieu à Seville*.

65 Brody, "The Piano Works of Déodat de Séverac: A Stylistic Analysis," 270, 312, translated by author. Séverac's uncertainty about his success in conveying emotion is likely a by-product of the times. Between 1910 and 1920, French composers were often caught between the earlier French Impressionist aesthetic and the later 1920s neo-classical musical style of Les six. As a result, this decrease in emotional expression became part of the transitional

Sous les lauriers-roses depicts a carnival evening in a coastal Catalan town and was first performed by Selva in 1920 at the Société nationale de musique. Séverac first thought of composing the work in 1907 after a trip with Bordes to Catalonia, where he attended festivities that he perceived as possessing "Mediterranean" color. Tempos fluctuate in the piece, as do tonal centers, as there are ten different keys within the piece, beginning in E minor and ending on C major. There is also a slightly irregular formal design within sections, though the entire work is in a modified ternary form. Contrasting textures permeate the work as do chromatic harmonies.

The acknowledgment of a carnival is accomplished in a variety of ways, including allusions to a Spanish military band and a section imitating a pianola, which contains an interpolated bar in altered meter.[66] The composition also includes recurrent rhythmic patterns for unification, especially rhythms extracted from various dances, including not only the sardana, but also a paso doble and scherzo-waltz, the latter containing Basque rhythms dedicated to Bordes. This emphasis on rhythm is increasingly apparent in the 13 metric changes within the piece, which corroborates Séverac's statement about the work: "In this little composition, I have tried something new! To give color through rhythm more than through harmony."[67] This rhythmic interplay is further corroborated in the sardana section, where not only are dance rhythms presented, but there is also an imitation of the Catalan fluviol and drum. Rhapsodic gestures in the work are often dependent on these extra-musical associations.

Figure 10.3   Ten Sections in Séverac's one movement suite, *Sous les lauriers-roses*

Section 1: La banda municipal, tempo di paso doble
Section 2: Petite valse de carabiniers
Section 3: La naïade de Banyuls
Section 4: Quasi sardana
    a) Prélude du fluviol, c'est le prélude obligé de toute sardana
    b) Tempo di sardana, comme un chant populaire
Section 5: Pour Charles Bordes
Section 6: Pour E. Chabrier: scherzo-valse
Section 7: Alla barcarola (un pêcheur fait entendre au loin réminiscence de la sardana)
Section 8: L'ombre charmante du vieux Daquin

---

process, an abatement apparent in Séverac's later compositions. Albert Roussel (1869–1937) is an example of a contemporary and colleague of Séverac at the Schola Cantorum. Although Roussel did not employ Catalan elements, his post-Impressionist compositional style is, in some ways, similar to that of Séverac. Roussel studied composition with Vincent d'Indy and subsequently taught composition at the Schola Cantorum between 1902 and 1914.

66   Ibid., 313.
67   Pierre Guillot, *Déodat de Séverac: la musique et les lettres* (Liège, Belgium: Pierre Mardaga, 2002), 421–2. [Séverac letter to Blanche Selva, 1919]. "Vous verrez que j'ai dans cette petite oeuvre, essayé une chose nouvelle: c'est de donner la couleur par le rythme beaucoup plus que par l'harmonie."

Section 9: "Les coucous," genre cornet à pistons (petite fuguette folichonne)

Section 10: Un piano mécanique lointain fait entendre un dernier de l'air sentimentale

Section 4, "Quasi sardana," is in ternary form and marked 'tempo di sardana comme un chant populaire.'[68] This 'A' section is preceded by a 12-measure fluviol solo beginning on an E flat seventh chord:

Example 10.16   Fluviol Solo Followed by "Quasi sardana," *Sous les lauriers-roses*, Measures 149–211

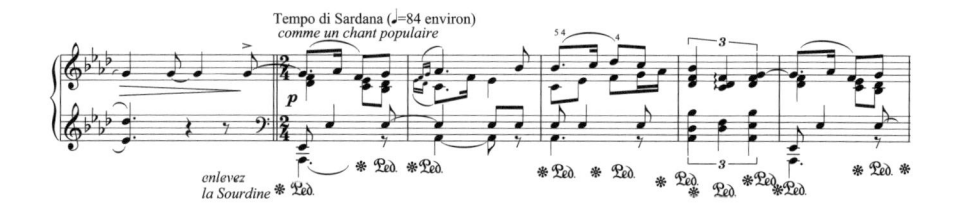

---

68 The idea of including a sardana rhythm that is followed by a section containing a mechanical piano waltz was stimulated by a cacophony of sounds that Séverac had heard in Ampourdan village cafes. Ampoudan is the northeast part of Spain along the coast in Catalonia.

The use of major third and perfect fourth melodic intervals reflect Albéniz's influence, who stressed this interval structure in *Catalonia*. In Albeniz's work, the opening theme of the Catalan folk song "La filadora" is quoted in triple meter.[69] Séverac heard Ricardo Viñes perform a piano transcription of *Catalonia* at the 1900 Schola Cantorum concert which emphasized Catalan works. It is likely that Séverac heard this work for the first time at the concert, which, in turn, had an influence on his fluviol imitation in *Sous les lauriers-roses*.

The 'B' section shown below begins in the relative minor key of F minor as the sardana rhythm sounds in the bass:

---

69 See Chapter 9.

Example 10.17   "Quasi sardana," *Sous les lauriers-roses*, Measures 45–93

This is described by Séverac as the tamborino motif, relating to the use of the drum in ancient cobla ensembles.[70] The 'B' section then switches to the parallel major of F while the rhythmic intensity of the sardana motif builds. Finally, the work returns to the key of F minor and culminates in a stretto-like rhythmic and textural intensification of the original 'B' section motif. The piece then alludes to the 'A' section while in the original key of A flat as the section concludes.

The unconventional key of A flat for a sardana, coupled with the use of ternary form rather than the more traditional binary structure, illustrates the fact that Séverac is paying homage here to the sardana and cobla ensemble within a larger work. Séverac was attempting to do for the sardana what Chopin had done for the mazurka and waltz; to pay tribute to a dance by writing a stylized piece for concert listening rather than a functional piece.[71]

***

---

70 The pipe and tabor were instruments initially used in the Catalan cobla ensemble. Another name for the tabor was the tambourine, or tambourin, a very deep two-headed medieval drum, cylindrical in shape, and with both sides covered with skin. The shell is twice as long as the heads are wide. The instrument was mentioned as early as AD 1080 and was originally of Arabic origin. See Anthony C. Baines, "Pipe and Tabor," *The New Grove Dictionary of Music and Musicians*, second edition, volume 20 (London: Macmillan Publishers Limited, 2001), 764.

71 Another Catalan-based work that does not survive, *Deux paraphrases sur les goigs catalans*, was first performed by Blanche Selva for a benefit concert for war orphans. Selva

Towards the Future: Séverac, Canteloube, and Catalan Music

Séverac's influence on Canteloube with regard to Catalan music is observable in *Sous les lauriers-roses* and Canteloube's *Lo pardal*, where both composers employ fluviol solos.

Example 10.18   Comparison of Fluviol Solos in Séverac's *Sous les lauriers-roses* and Canteloube's *Lo pardal*

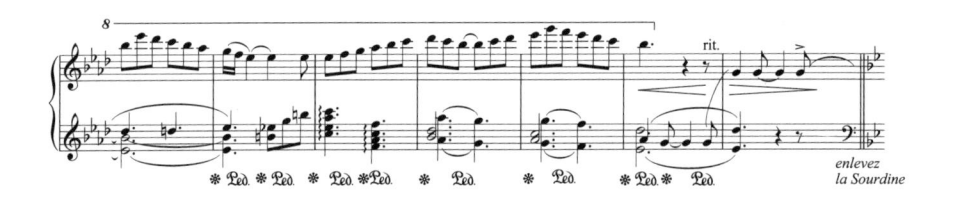

recalls that Séverac improvised goigs: "[Séverac] climbed [up the mountain] ... on a steep footpath which leads to St. Martin-du Canigou ... There was no piano in the abbey, but there was a harmonium ... and bells and organ ... Déodat improvised there on Catalan hymns, on goigs dear to the bishop and to himself, so dear that he declared to his uncle that he would give all of his compositions for the piece." ("Il grimpe ... par l'abrupt sentier qui mène à Saint-Martin-du Canigou ... Il n'y a pas de piano à l'abbaye, mais il y a un harmonium ... en attendant cloches et orgue ... Déodat y improvise sur des cantiques catalans, sur des goigs chers à l'évêque et à lui-même, si chers même qu'il déclare à son oncle qu'il donnerait tout sa musique pour l'air des 'Goigs de la Sanch!'"). See Selva, *Déodat de Séverac*, 77–8.

Measures 1–6 of Canteloube's *Lo pardal* contains a shorter fluviol solo than those found in traditional sardanas and in Séverac's *Sous les lauriers-roses*; yet Canteloube's introduction is in triple meter, which is found in sardana introductions.

The melodic structure in both compositions is comparable, although Canteloube's work includes largely eighth-note and sixteenth-note rhythms. This arrangement therefore appears faster than that found in measures 56 to 67 of Séverac's composition, where dotted quarter note rhythms are largely employed. However, because Canteloube's work is composed specifically for a cobla ensemble, the harmonization of the melody is largely diatonic. Since Séverac reharmonizes the original melody chromatically in measures 56 to 67, this section maintains a quicker harmonic rhythm than that found in Canteloube's work. Séverac's reharmonization includes chords on the dominant at moments when Canteloube resolves on the tonic. As a result, Séverac's version evokes a greater sense of uneasiness, as evident in a comparison of the first beat of measures 58 and 60 of Séverac's work with more traditional sardanas exemplified by *Lo pardal*.

Canteloube also included sardana rhythms in *Lo pardal*:

Example 10.19   Sardana Section of Canteloube's *Lo pardal*, Measures 83–142

Example 10.19   Sardana Section of Canteloube's *Lo pardal*, Measures 83–142, continued

A comparison of the sardana section of Séverac's *Sous les lauriers-roses* to that in Canteloube's *Lo pardal* is found below, and further demonstrates Séverac's regionalist influence on Canteloube's compositions:

Example 10.20   Comparison of Sardana Section in Séverac's *Sous les lauriers-roses* and Canteloube's *Lo pardal*

In a three-movement orchestral work entitled *Lauriers* (1929), Canteloube also used sardana rhythms within the second movement, dedicated "à la mémoire d'un ami," Séverac. The unusual sardana section is in a minor key, and is depicted by Canteloube as 'une sardane funèbre':

Example 10.21   Funeral Sardana in Joseph Canteloube's *Lauriers*, Measures 70–107, second movement ("A la mémoire d'un ami")

Example 10.21   Funeral Sardana in Joseph Canteloube's *Lauriers*, Measures 70–107, second movement ("A la mémoire d'un ami"), continued

Canteloube's *Lauriers* and his other Catalan-based compositions, coupled with specific letters between Canteloube and Séverac, attest to the fact that Séverac had a direct impact on Canteloube's compositional style. Canteloube never forgot Séverac's role as mentor, and later wrote an entire book on Séverac's life and works. This is coupled with various articles Canteloube later wrote on Séverac and Catalan music and musicians.

Chapter 11

Conclusion

Séverac's regionalist philosophy was initially invested in southern French works that, although not Catalan, reflected modes approximating those in folk music from Languedoc. He eventually shifted his attention away from programmatic piano pieces of a general regionalist character to Catalan works that were more specifically regionalist. This was accomplished through the use of sardana rhythms, the employment of the cobla in orchestral works, and through the imitation of cobla instruments and Catalan goigs in piano compositions. His works and philosophy influenced other composers, especially Joseph Canteloube, who then incorporated modes found in French folk music from his own Auvergne region into his music, as well as Catalan rhythms and instrumentation.

Other composers also wrote their own regionalist works after hearing Séverac's Catalan-based compositions. These composers include René de Castéra (1873–1955), a friend and colleague of Séverac at the Schola Cantorum, and Charles Koechlin (1867–1950), who heard the première of *Héliogabale* in Béziers and spoke favorably about the composition.[1] Koechlin's earlier compositions do not include actual folk songs, but instead contain folk-like melodies, including his "Finale" to the *Violin Sonata*, op. 64, of 1916, and *Sonatines* of the same year. However, his later works use actual folk music, including *Vingt chansons bretonnes* for cello and piano, op. 115 (1931), *Les chants de Kervéléan*, op. 197, of 1944, and *Quinze duos pour deux clarinettes* (*Souvenirs de Bretagne*), op. 195, of 1944. All three compositions are of Breton inspiration. *Vingt chansons bretonnes*, op. 115 is a compilation of 20 Breton folk songs arranged for cello and piano, and was Koechlin's first deliberate use of folk song. *Souvenirs de Bretagne* was inspired by Koechlin's 1940 visit to Brittany and includes programmatic movement titles. *Rapsodie sur des chansons françaises*, op. 62 (1915–16, orchestrated 1919) consists of a popular compilation of Breton tunes and legends. While there is no direct evidence to suggest that Koechlin's regionalist compositions were influenced by Séverac's music, when we consider Koechlin's remarks on *Héliogabale*, and his subsequent use of French folk song in his compositions, it seems most likely that Séverac's ideas had some influence on Koechlin's regionalist leanings.[2]

---

1   Castéra's harmonization of folk music is found in *Chansons populaires du Béam*.
2   Séverac's eclectic tastes would explain why Koechlin would take stands against the philosophies held at the Schola Cantorum and yet favor many of Séverac's works. It must nonetheless be stated that additional influence on Koechlin can be found in the Breton compositions of Guy Ropartz. Other musicians later composed works that contained French folk music, including the composer Darius Milhaud in his *Suite provençale*, op. 152 (1936;

Séverac's later regionalist compositions often paid homage to the sardana in much the same way that Chopin incorporated elements of the mazurka. Séverac emphasized the rhythmic elements of the sardana, and occasionally used or referred to cobla instruments in these works. These references include the imitation of the fluviol and drum in *Sous les lauriers-roses*. Because Séverac included innovative harmonies and bold modulations in this composition and in other works, it becomes apparent that Séverac's sardanas are often not created specifically for sardana dancers, but instead illustrate his preference for the sardana as an artistic genre. His sardanas therefore differ from those by contemporaries who created works to accompany local dancers. These compositions often contain simpler and more traditional sardana harmonies and simpler formal structures in order to function more effectively as dance music.

Séverac's affection for the sardana reflected his regionalist outlook—a philosophy that took many forms during the first two decades of the twentieth century. These forms included French, Catalan, and pan-Latin regionalism, all of which were important political, aesthetic, and cultural ideologies. Pan-Latinism was inspired largely by Frédéric Mistral's poetry and his call for a federation among southern French provinces, ideas that inspired a variety of artists, journalists, and musicians from various southern provinces to perceive themselves as different from their northern neighbors.

Advocates of Catalan political regionalism were mostly from northern Spain, because economic disadvantages in Spanish Catalonia were far greater than in the French province of Roussillon. Ironically, this economic situation in French Catalonia was the result of a centralized French political system that provided major communication routes in the form of roads and railways, thus helping to stimulate economic development.

Many Catalans in Spain pleaded for political independence. Yet, various Catalan artists and writers eventually realized the futility of political struggle and began to accord a greater power to the arts, humanities, and sciences to help achieve cultural independence. Catalan regionalism in the late nineteenth century was therefore equated with cultural pride. This cultural emphasis trickled into French Catalonia, where regional patriotism among musicians was highlighted by composing and dancing to sardana music. It was this atmosphere that Séverac encountered during the decade in which he lived in Roussillon, and it became part of his musical life.

Séverac supported French regionalism and its inherent call for administrative reform. He believed that the Paris government was too centralized, and that Paris administrators made too many judgments regarding policies instituted within various provinces—regions about which these administrators often knew little. For Séverac, the musical counterpart to the centralized bureaucracy of the French government was found in the bylaws of the Paris Conservatoire and its relationship with provincial institutions. He argued that the Paris Conservatoire was too authoritarian and its administrators made too many decisions for music schools within various regions. For Séverac, this belief in administrative decentralization had cultural and aesthetic implications. Séverac's proposed decentralized institution would emphasize local

---

Paris: Editions Salabert, 1937) and *Suite française* (New York: MCA Music, 1946) for concert band (1944).

folk songs and encourage composers to incorporate them into their new works.[3] This philosophy was emphasized in Séverac's thesis, where he quoted the philosopher Charles Beauquier (1833–1916):

> Formerly, before the Revolution, a local artistic and literary life existed in each province. Almost every town had glorious children of whom it was proud. Painters, musicians, sculptors, architects decorated their city and didn't dream of asking Paris for her blessing, which would have added nothing to their value. That no longer holds today. Local artists have naught but eagerness to leave their native village, where they do not believe their attainments sufficiently recognized, to run to Paris, where, if they do not have exceptional resistance and even greater luck, they are engulfed in the crowd, they lose their native qualities, become exasperated, and begin to produce some extravagant and unbalanced works in the hope of ultimately enticing the gaze of an indifferent and blasé public. If they had lived at home, going to the very fountainhead of their native soil, many would have developed normally, often in an original fashion, and would have enriched the artistic and intellectual patrimony of their country.[4]

Despite Séverac's involvement with provincial identity, regionalism in France following World War I became a losing proposition. In order to achieve victory during the war, the French government emphasized patriotism and nationalism to muster public support, an emphasis that helped consolidate citizens from various regions into one nation. In addition, easier forms of communication and travel between regions helped bring together people from numerous provinces, thereby unifying the populace from different communities.

In music, this movement simply changed the nature of the regionalist debate. Composers still attempted to foster an interest in French folk song, but no longer

---

3   Séverac promoted régionalisme in his 1907 thesis, where he referred to countless French figures in the name of this regionalism, including Jean Charles-Brun, founder of Federalist régionaliste française, writer-philosopher Maurice Barrès, poet Frédéric Mistral, writer-poet Francis Jammes, publisher Alexis Rouart, folklorist Julien Tiersot, and composers Gabriel Fauré, Georges Bizet, Edouard Lalo, Charles Bordes, and Vincent d'Indy.

4   Charles Beauquier, "Les biens des églises et la décentralisation," *Action régionaliste* (January, 1907). Charles Beauquier was a philosopher and writer on music, as well as one of the chief spokespersons for the regionalist movement. Other publications by Beauquier include a collection of French folk songs entitled *Chansons populaires reçueillies en Franche-Comté* (1894), *La musique et le drame* (1877), and *Philosophie de la musique* (1866). "Autrefois, avant la Révolution, une vie locale artistique et littéraire existait dans chaque province. Chaque ville presque avait des enfants glorieux dont elle s'enorgueillissait. Peintres, musiciens, sculpteurs, architectes ornaient leur cité et ne songeaient pas à demander à Paris une consécration qui n'aurait rien ajouté à leur valeur. Il n'en va plus de même aujourd'hui: les artistes locaux n'ont qu'une hâte: quitter leur ville natale où ils ne croient pas leurs mérites suffisamment reconnus, pour accourir à Paris où, s'ils n'ont pas une force de résistance exceptionnelle et une chance plus exceptionnelle encore, ils sont noyés dans la masse, ils perdent leurs qualités natives, s'exaspèrent, arrivent à produire des choses extravagantes et déséquilibrées dans le but d'attirer enfin les regards d'une foule indifférente et blasée. S'ils étaient demeurés chez eux, puisant aux sources mêmes du sol natal, beaucoup se seraient développés normalement, souvent d'une façon originale et auraient enrichi le patrimoine artistique et intellectuel de leur pays."

as a way of highlighting individual regions within France. Folk music subsequently became a means of emphasizing French nationalist identity to the rest of the Western world. During the war, folk music was no longer emphasized to stress regional identity, but to accent French national identity. *France* now became the new region.

Séverac's departure from Paris in 1907 was in many ways an implementation of his own regionalist philosophy. He returned to Languedoc where he organized a local music society dedicated to improving the level of cultural life in his native village of Saint-Félix-Caraman. He then helped establish the Schola du Lauragais and created a local orphéons organization. Séverac also served for a short time as a council member of his arrondissement. Eventually, he moved to his adopted province of Roussillon. However, Séverac himself indicated the difficulties of escaping Paris, even for the well-intentioned. As he observed:

> All true friends of our national art recognize the fact of centralization's effect on music and lament it, but if they are unanimous in deploring it, alas, they refrain from practicing what they preach. They form leagues; they give lectures; they organize congresses at which the motions of the day unanimously condemn the concept of centralization; but almost immediately afterwards, there they are, returned by the fastest express to the very center of the epidemic they claim to combat. It is so difficult according to them, to live in a provincial town or in the country. "The people there are so uncouth, so ridiculous!" ... Today's musicians, apart from several very rare exceptions, are the prey of this enemy ... They are all, more or less, its benevolent victims.[5]

The question remains: was Séverac a victim of his own regionalist philosophy? His regionalist outlook may have undercut his own advance in music history; in avoiding Paris and its inherent music power structure by moving to Céret, he may have weakened his own career, fame, and eventually, his place for posterity. It is also possible and to be hoped that in this day and age in the new millennium, a time when many artistic voices from the past are gaining an opportunity to be heard through an increasingly wider dissemination of recordings, Séverac may yet have his rightful due in the court of public opinion.

---

5 Séverac, "La centralisation et les petites chapelles musicales," *Le courrier musical*, 11e année, no. 1 (January 1, 1908), 1–2. "Tous les vrais amis de l'Art national reconnaissent le fait et se lamentent, mais s'ils sont unanimes à le déplorer, ils se gardent bien hélas de prêcher l'exemple. Ils fondent des ligues, ils donnent des conférences, ils organisent des congrès où des ordres du jour flétrissent à l'unanimité l'esprit centralisateur; mais aussitôt après les voici revenus, par l'express le plus rapide, au foyer même de l'épidémie qu'ils prétendent combattre. Il est si difficile, à les entendre, de vivre dans une ville de province ou à la campagne: Les gens y ont si vulgaires, si ridicules ... Les musiciens actuels sont, à part quelques très rares exceptions, la proie de cet ennemi ... ils sont tous plus ou moins ses victimes bénévoles."

Appendix

Selective Compilation of Severac's Work List

Organ Music

Suite en mi (1897–99)
Prélude
Choral et variations
Fantaisie pastorale
Fugue

Prélude de quatuor (1898)

Versets pour les vêpres d'un confesseur non pontife (1912)
Domine quinque talenta
Euge serve bone
Fidelis servus et prudens
Beatus IIIe servus
Serve bone fidelis

Petite suite scholastique, sur un thème de carillon languedocien (1912–13)
Prélude (Entrée)
Méditation: pièce chromatique (Offertoire)
Prière-Choral (Chorale Prayer)
Cantilène mélancolique (Communion)
Fanfare fuguée (Sortie)

Lost

Elévation (1890)
Verset (1890)
Verset (or) *Prélude in C* (1892)
Intermède (1897)
Canon par diminution (1898)

Sacred Choral Works

Salve regina for singer and organ (1916)

Lost

Ave verum corpus, motet for two sopranos, two tenors, and organ (1898)
Homo quidam, for three voices, tenors, baritones, and basses (1899)
Sorèze et Lacordaire, cantata for soloists, choir, and orchestra (1911)

Quatre cantiques, for one voice with organ or harmonium accompaniment (1913):
I. Cantique de pénitence; II. Ouvrages du très-haut; III. Cantique pour la communion; IV. Souvenez-vous

Salve regina (second version) for mezzo-soprano, violin, and organ (1917)
O sacrum convivium, motet for four voices and organ (1919)
Tantum ergo for four mixed a capella (1920)
Sainte Jeanne de Lorraine, hymn for one voice with organ accompaniment (1920)

Secular Choral Works

Lo cant del Vallespir, cantata for soloists, chorus, and orchestra (1911) (unpublished but complete facsimile available)

Lost

Chants de vacances, three-part canon (1898)
Saint-Félix, three male voices a capella (1900)
Mignonne allons voir si la rose, four male voices a capella (1901)
Mediterranéenne (1904)
La cité, cantata for soloist, solo vocalists and male chorus (1909)

Musique pour l'inauguration du buste de l'Anton (1913). Cantata for soloist and choir on a sardana rhythm; words by sculptor Gustave Violet for a bust on Anton, who was an old Catalan gardener. The bust was to be erected on a small Catalan holiday given in Prades. Gustave Violet wrote a poem for the occasion.

Perla del Pireneu: conçoneta sur une lleta d'en pere de l'alzina (*La perle des Pyrénées*; 1913). Choral song based on the words of "Pere l'Alzina" and performed in an outdoor theater in the Pyrénées village of Amélie-les-Bains. The poem to this work has been recovered.

Songs

Ritournelle (1896)
Le chevrier (1897–98)
Les cors (1897–98)
Les hiboux (1898)
Renouveau (1898)

L'infidèle (1898)
Les huns [chanson de guerre] (1898)
Aubade à l'étoile (1898)
Paysages tristes: soleils couchants (1898)
L'éveil de Pâques (1899)
Chanson triste (1900) [with violin and piano]
Le chanson de Blaisine (1900)
Le ciel est, par-dessus le toit (1901)
Un rêve (1901)
A l'aube dans la montagne (1903)
Temps de neige (1903)
Chanson de Jacques (1910)
Chanson de la nuit durable (1910)

Flors d'occitania: trois pieces en langue d'oc (1910)
Chanson pour le petit cheval
Aubade
Chant pour Noël

Ma poupée chérie (1914)

Folk Songs, *Chansons du XVIIIe siècle,* 2 collections, for voice and piano (1905, 1907)
Book I:
Ba be bi bo bu!
R'muons le cotillon
Zon, zon, zon!
Le vieil époux
Pour le jour des rois
Le berger indiscret
V'là c'que c'est qu'd'aller au bois
Prière du matin
Ne dérangez pas le monde
Offrande

Book II:
Vaudeville des batelières de St. Cloud
Musette
Le beau Daphnis
L'amour en cage
Le vin de Catherine
Nicodème
L'homme n'est jamais content
La fileuse
Cécilia

Folk Songs, *Les vieilles chansons de France,* for voice and piano (1905)
La semaine de la mariée
La peureuse
La ronde
L'Auvergnat
Le manchon
Ma mère, il me tuera
Les gens qui sont jeunes
Le roi a fait battre tambour
Les belles manières
Le boudoir d'aspasie

Miscellaneous Folk Songs
Philis (1907)

Lost Songs

Folk Songs: *Quatre chansons, anthologie générale des "chansons de France" des origines jusqu'à nos jours,* for voice and piano (1906)
Jean des Grignottes
Le cotillon couleur de rose
Dans les prisons de Nantes
Le roi Renaud

Folk Songs: *Deux chansons du XVIIIe siècle,* for voice and piano (1906)
Cocorico
Le nid

Folk Songs, Miscellaneous, for Voice and Piano (1906–18)
Les housards de la garde, chanson de route (1906)
J'ons eun' joulie maison! chanson picarde (1906)
La mort y la donzella: chanson populaire catalane (1918)

Canzone dans le style néo-javanais: *vocalise-étude dans le mode hypolydien* (1911)

Trois aquarelles (opus posthumous)
Le pêcher rose
La passerelle
Le vieux moulin

Opera

Le coeur du moulin: pièce lyrique in 2 acts, libretto by Maurice Magre (1903–8); première, Opéra-Comique, December 8, 1909, piano-vocal score published

Héliogabale: tragédie lyrique in 3 acts, libretto by Emile Sicard (1910), with prologue—"Les deux triomphes," by Charles Gueret, and Epilogue ballet-mime: "La résurrection d'Adonis," by Gabriel Boissy; première, 1910, piano-vocal score published but complete orchestral facsimile available for rent

Lost

La fille de la terre, tragédie lyrique in 3 acts (1913); première, 1913
Les Antibels (1907–19), no première
Le roi Pinard, operetta (1919); no known première

Incidental Music

Le mirage (1903)

Lost

Mugueto (1911)
Hélène de Sparte (1912)
Les gosses dans les ruines (1918)
Le retour (date unknown)
Victoire de Samothrace (date unknown)

Chamber Music

Sérénade au clair de lune, flute, oboe, 2 cl., bn., 2 horn, percussion, string quartet (1913)
Minyoneta: *souvenir de Figueras,* violin and piano (1919)

Tres recuerdos (1919), arranged for chamber orchestra by Sébastien Chapelier
1) Bentana da amor
2) Cantos de mariñeros
3) Lola la abandonada

Cortège nuptial catalan (1919), piano and violin; arranged for chamber orchestra and violin by Sébastien Chapelier. This is a Catalan wedding march composed for the marriage of Agnes de Monfried and Séverac's former captain in Prades, a physician known as Major Huc.

Souvenirs de Céret, violin and piano (1919)

Lied romantique, violin or cello (opus posthumous, 1929)

Lost

Duo for piano and oboe (or violin) (1890)
Méditation for violin et piano (1897)
Barcarolle for flute and piano (1898)

Parc aux cerfs, chamber suite (1907); suite in an eighteenth-century style in four movements. The work was scored for piano, oboe, and string quartet.

Les muses sylvestres (1907–08)--suite, four parts, wind quintet, string quartet, and piano; rewritten following year for piano and double quintet.

Les nymphes de Nogarède, for violin, cello, and piano (1910)
El divino de l'hort, oboe, violin, cello, and organ (1916)

Elégie héroique (1918) aux morts pour la patrie, with accompanying poem; three versions; a) violin or cello and piano or organ, b) organ, c) song, piano or organ and violin.

Quintet in E for piano and strings (date unknown)
A la font d'en fils—berceuse romantique, string quintet (date unknown)
Berceuse for oboe, violin, and organ (date unknown)
Méditation et musette for violin and organ of the eighteenth century (date unknown)

Orchestral Music

Nymphes au crépuscule, symphonic poem with female chorus offstage (1901–2) (incomplete manuscript, recently completed)

Lost

Poèmes des saisons, symphonic poem (1900)
Didon et Enée, orchestral suite (1901)

Le lac aux ondines (1901) [symphonic poem]—Séverac began composing *Le lac aux ondines* in 1901, a symphonic poem for orchestra or chamber music ensemble. The complete violin part and four pages written for the piano was rediscovered by Canteloube in 1930.

Le triptique, symphonic poem (1903); after a poem by Louis Le Cardonnel (unfinished)
Triptyque (1903–4)

Méditerranéenne, orchestra, began 1904, five movements with songs and dances in the Mediterranean style; unfinished version played for Canteloube in 1906; lost.

Les vendages, piano, orchestra (1906)
Suite no. 1 for orchestra on death of Bordes (1909)
Les grenouilles qui demandent un roi, symphonic poem (1909–21)
L'Enéide, symphonic poem (date unknown)

Piano Music

Scènes des champs (1897)
Impromptu dans le caractère romantique (1898)
Valse métèque (1898)

Sonate (1899)
Adagio-Allegro
Elégie
Allegro-scherzando
Final

Le Vent d'antan: cantilène (1899). The wind to which this composition refers is a southern French wind purported to bring back memories of one's life (unpublished but complete facsimile available)

Le chant de la terre, poème géorgique pour piano (1899–1900)
Prologue
Le labour
Les semailles
Intermezzo: conte à la veillée
La grêle
Les moissons
Epilogue: Le jour des noces

En Languedoc, Suite pour piano (1903–04)
Vers le mas en fête
Sur l'étang, le soir
A cheval dans le prairie
Coin de cimetière, au printemps
Le jour de la foire, au mas

Le soldat de plomb: histoire "vrai" en trois récits, 4 hands (1904)
Stances à Madame de Pompadour (1907)
Pippermint-Get: valse brillante pour le concert (1907)
Danse du "tonneau" et du "bidon" (1907)
Baigneuses au soleil: Souvenir de Banyuls-sur-mer (1908)

Cerdaña: *Etudes pittoresques pour piano* (1908–11)
En tartane: l'arrivée en Cerdagne
Les fêtes: souvenir de Puigcerda
Ménétriers et glaneuses: souvenir d'un pèlerinage à Font-Romeu
Les muletiers devant le Christ de Llivia
Le retour des muletiers

En vacances: Au château dans le parc, petites pièces romantiques de moyenne difficulté pour piano (1911)
Introduction: invocation à Schumann
Les caresses de grand'maman
Les petites voisines en visite
Toto déguisé en Suisse d'église
Mimi se déguise en marquise
Ronde dans le parc
Où l'on entend une vieille boîte à musique
Valse romantique

En vacances II: Petites pièces romantiques de moyenne difficulté pour piano (1911)
La fontaine de Chopin
La vasque aux Colombes
Les deux mousquetaires

Les naïades et le faune indiscret: danse nocturne (1908–19), originally entitled *La nymphe émue du le faune indiscret*

Sous les lauriers-roses ou *Soir de carnaval sur la côte catalane* (1919)

Lost Piano Music

Petite étude in G minor (1886)
P'tit bateau: mélancolie: inspiré à la simple vue d'une certaine cane (1886)
Preludio (1896)
Air de ballet (1896)
Promenade en mer (1896)
Fantine: valse lente, piano (1901)
Le tombeau de Gaugin (1906)

L'encens et la myrrhe (1918–19)—piano suite in four movements evoking the French province of Rousillon; dedicated to Blanche Selva. Movements are "Le cloître d'Elne," "Le frère Eusebius va au moulin," "Communiantes dans un chemin en fleurs au printemps," and "Le frère Eusebius revenant du marché." The work had its première before friends in 1920.

Pavane pour une taupe défunte (date unknown)—piece with humorous title alluding to Ravel's *Pavane pour une infante défunte*

Bibliography

Albéniz, Isaac. *Catalonia*. Paris: Durand et fils, 1908.
—— *La vega*. Paris: Plon, Nourrit et Cie, 1930.
Anderson, Benedict. *Imagined Communities: Reflections on the Origin and Spread of Nationalism*. London and New York: Verso, 1991.
Apel, Willi. "Folk music," *The Harvard Dictionary of Music*, 2nd ed. Cambridge, MA: Belknap Press of Harvard University Press, 1969, 323–6.
Armengol, Montserrat Bergadà. "Les Pianistes catalans à Paris entre 1875 et 1925." PhD Dissertation, Université Rabelais de Tours, France, 1997.
Aspry, Jean-Bernard Cahours, ed. *Le coeur du moulin: bulletin de l'association festival Déodat de Séverac*. No. 1–2, 13 (1988).
—— *Déodat de Séverac*. Biarritz: Atlantica, 2001.
—— *Déodat de Séverac, 1872–1921: musicien du soleil méditerranéen*. Belgium: Séguier, 2002.
—— "Déodat de Séverac" (unpublished manuscript).
Auriol, Henry. *Décentralisation musicale*. Paris: Eugène Figuière et Cie, 1912.
Baines, Anthony C. "Pipe and Tabor," *The New Grove Dictionary of Music and Musicians*, 2nd ed., volume 20. London: Macmillan Publishers Limited, 2001, 762–4.
Balcells, Albert. *Catalan Nationalism*, translated by Jacqueline Hall. New York: St. Martin's Press, 1996.
Barrès, Maurice. *Les déracinés*. Paris: Bibliothèque-Charpentier, 1897.
—— *Appel au soldat*. Paris: F. Juven, 1911.
—— *The Undying Spirit of France*, translated Margaret W.B. Corwin. London: Oxford University Press, 1917.
—— *The Faith of France*, translated Elizabeth Marbury. New York: Houghton Mifflin Co., 1918.
—— *Scènes et doctrines du nationalisme*. [1902] Paris: Plon-Nourrit, 1925.
—— *Mes cahiers* XIII: 25. Paris: Plon, 1929.
—— *Le culte du moi*. [1st ed., 1888] Paris: Plon, 1966.
—— *Un homme libre*. [1888] Paris: Plon, 1966.
Bazin, René. *La terre qui meurt*. Paris: Calmann-Lévy, 1899.
Beauquier, Charles. "Les biens des églises et la décentralisation," *Action régionaliste* (January, 1907).
Bellaigue, Camille. "Revue musicale: *Le coeur du moulin*," *Revue des deux mondes*, 80e année, vol. 55, no. 2 (January 15, 1910), 445–6.
—— "Giovanni Pierluigi a Palestrina," *La tribune de Saint-Gervais*, 1e année, no. 1 (January, 1895), 1–4.
Bernac, Pierre. *The Interpretation of French Song*. New York: Norton, 1978.
Bloom, Harold. *A Map of Misreading*. New York: Oxford University Press, 1975.

—— *The Anxiety of Influence: A Theory of Poetry*. New York: Oxford University Press, 1973.

Boisdeffre, Pierre de. *Métamorphose de la littérature: de Barrès à Malraux*. Paris: Alsatia, 1950.

—— *Barrès parmi nous*. Paris: Dumont, 1952.

Boissy, Gabriel. *Comoedia* (August 2, 1936).

—— "Théâtre des arènes de Béziers, Héliogabale," *Le théâtre*. no. 283 (October, 1910).

Bordes, Charles. "Le Schola de Montpellier: société d'encouragement d'emulation à la musique," *AM Dossier* 1J53.

—— "Le chant populaire," *La tribune de Saint-Gervais* (December, 1896), 183–6.

Bouret, Jean. *The Barbizon School and 19th-century French Landscape Painting*. London: Thames and Hudson, 1973.

Brazes, Edmond. *Céret, musée d'art moderne*. Céret: centenaire Déodat de Séverac (July–August–September 1972).

Brody, Elaine. "The Piano Works of Déodat de Séverac: A Stylistic Analysis." PhD Dissertation, New York University, 1964.

—— "Déodat de Séverac: A Mediterranean Musician," *The Music Review*, vol. 29 (1968), 172–83.

Boussel, Patrick. *L'affaire Dreyfus et la presse*. Paris: A. Colin, 1960.

Bury, Jonathan. *France: 1814–1940*. London: Methuen and Co., 1969.

Caballero, Carlo. Untitled Review, *Journal of the American Musicological Society* (vol. 55, no. 3, 2002), 563–78.

—— "Patriotism or Nationalism? Fauré and the Great War," *Journal of the American Musicological Society* (vol. 52, no. 3, 1999), 593–625.

Caen, A. *Recueil de cantiques spirituels provençaux et français*. [Original publication, 1759] 2nd ed. Paris: P. Chalopin, Imprimeur Librarie, c.1800.

Calvocoressi, Michel Dimitri. "A French Composer of Today—Déodat de Séverac," *The New Music Review* IX (June, 1910), 103.

—— "Déodat de Séverac, auteur du *Coeur du moulin*," *Le gil blas* (November 26, 1910).

Canteloube, Joseph. *Lo pardal: sardane pour "cobla catalane.*" Paris: Heugel, 1926.

—— *Lauriers*. Paris: Au ménestrel, 1929.

—— *Le mas*. Paris: Au Ménestrel, 1929.

—— "La musique populaire, les 'coblas,' et les instruments catalans," *Le courrier musical et théatral*. 31e année, no. 18 (November 1, 1929), 581–2.

—— "Les amis de Déodat de Séverac," *Revue internationale de musique et de danse*, 4e année, no. 33 (May 15, 1930), 187–8.

—— *Vers la princesse lointaine*. Paris: Au ménestrel, 1930.

—— *Les chants des provinces françaises*. Paris: Didier, 1947.

—— *Vincent D'Indy*. Paris: Laurens, 1951.

—— *Anthologie des chants populaires français groupés par provinces*. 4 vols. Paris: Durand et Cie., 1951.

—— *Eaux-vives* (February, 1953).

—— "Comment juger le divorce opposant la musique moderne et le public," *Pour ou contre la musique moderne*, edited by Gavoty, Bernard and Daniel Lesur. Paris: Flammarion, 1957, 80–82.

—— *Déodat de Séverac*. Béziers, France: Société de musicologie de Languedoc, 1984 (1st ed., Paris, 1929).

—— *Déodat de Séverac* [1951]. 2nd ed. Béziers, France: Société de musicologie de Languedoc, 1984.

Capmany, Aureli. *La sardana a Catalunya*. Barcelona: Montaneri i Simón, 1948.

Carbasse, Jean Marie. *Louis-Xavier de Ricard, Félibre rouge*. Paris: Editions Mireille Lacave, 1977.

Carner, Josep Ribalta. *The Catalan Nation and Its People*. Houston, TX: American Institute for Catalan Studies, 1995.

Carraud, Gaston. "Pour le Conservatoire," *Le mercure musical*, 1e année, no. 5 (July 15, 1905), 193–200.

—— "Le coeur du moulin," *La liberté*. (December 10, 1909).

Cavellier, Gabrielle. *Coulisses* (January 1, 1910).

Chanet, Jean-François. "Maîtres d'école et régionalisme en France, sous la troisième republique," *Ethnologie française*, no. 18 (1988), 244–56.

Chapman, Guy. *The Dreyfus Case*. London: R. Hart-Davis, 1955.

Charles-Brun, Jean. *Le régionalisme*. Paris: Bloud et Cie, 1911.

Chase, Gilbert. *The Music of Spain*. New York: Dover Publication, Inc., 1941.

Chateaubriand, François-René de. *Mémoires d'outre-tombe*. Paris: E. et V. Penaud frères, 1849.

Cheydleur, Frédéric Daniel. "Maurice Barrès: Author and Patriot," *The North American Review*. (March–April–May, 1926), 150–56.

Clark, Timothy James. *The Absolute Bourgeois: Artists and Politics in France, 1848–1851*. London: Thames and Hudson, 1973.

Clark, Walter A. *Isaac Albéniz: A Guide to Research*. New York: Garland Publishing, 1998.

—— *Isaac Albéniz*. Oxford: Oxford University Press, 1999.

Colette. *Oeuvres complètes*. Paris: Le Fleuron, se vend chez Flammarion, 1949.

Collet, Henri. *Albéniz et Granados*. Paris: Alcan, 1926.

—— *L'essor de la musique espagnole au Xxième siècle*. Paris: Eschig, 1929.

Combes, Louis. *Le télégramme* (November 30, 1909).

Cortot, Alfred. *La musique française de piano*, vols 1 and 2. Paris: Presses Universitaires de France, 1930.

Cougniaud, Françoise Raginel. *Joseph Canteloube*. Béziers, France: Société de musicologie de Languedoc, 1988.

Curtis, Michael. *Three Against the Republic*. Princeton, NJ: Princeton University Press, 1959.

Dahlhaus, Carl. *Between Romanticism and Modernism: Four Studies in the Music of the Later Nineteenth Century*, translated by Mary Whittall. Los Angeles: University of California Press, 1980.

Dahlhaus, Carl and Rudolf Stephan, ed. *Berliner musikwissenschaftliche Arbeiten*. Munich: Musikverlag Emil Katzbichter, 1974.

Dali, Salvador. *Le mythe tragique de l'angélus de Millet*. Paris: Société nouvelle des éditions Jean-Jacques Pauvert, 1963, 1978.

Davies, John Langdon. *Dancing Catalans*. New York: Harper and Brothers, 1989.

Davray, R. "Héliogabale," *Le courrier musical*, 13e année, nos. 17–18 (September 1, 15, 1910), 594–8.

Demuth, Norman. *Vincent d'Indy*. London: Rockliff, 1951.

Deschanel, Paul. *La décentralisation*. Paris: Berger-Levrault et Cie., 1895.

Driskel, Michael. *Representing Belief: Religion, Art, and Society in 19th Century France*. University Park: Pennsylvania State University Press, 1992.

Dubreuilh, Gaston. *Les nouvelles* (December 9, 1909).

Dumesnil, René. "La Décentralisation musicale en France," *Polyphonie*, cinquième cahier (1950).

E.D., "*Héliogabale* aux arènes de Béziers," *La revue musicale*, 10e année, nos. 17–18 (September 1–15, 1910), 395–9.

Elwitt, Sanford. *The Making of the Third Republic: Class and Politics in France, 1868–1884*. Baton Rouge, LA: Louisiana State University Press, 1975.

Fàbregas i Marcet, Jaume. "The Influence of Spanish Music in *Cerdaña* by Déodat de Séverac." D.M.A., West Virginia University, 2002.

Falla, Manuel de. "Felipe Pedrell," *La revue musicale*, 4e année, no. 4 (February 1, 1923), 1–11.

Fauré, Gabriel. "Les théâtres," *Le figaro* (December 9, 1909), 4–5.

Favre, Georges. *Musiciens méditerranéens oubliés*. Paris: La Pensée universelle, 1985.

Fitzmaurice-Kelly, James. *Lope de Vega and the Spanish Drama*. New York: Haskell House Publishers Ltd., 1971.

Flint de Médicis, Catrina M. "The Schola Cantorum, Early Music, and French Nationalism from 1894 to 1914." PhD, McGill University, 2006.

Forrest, Alan. "Regionalism and Counter-Revolution in France," *Rewriting the French Revolution*. Oxford: Clarendon Press, 1991.

Fraguier, Marguerite Marie de. *Vincent d'Indy*. Paris: Jean Naert, 1934.

Fulcher, Jane. *French Cultural Politics and Music*. Oxford: Oxford University Press, 1999.

——— "The Preparation for Vichy: Anti-Semitism in French Musical Culture Between the Two World Wars," *Musical Quarterly*, vol. 79, no. 3 (Fall, 1995), 458–75.

——— "Vincent d'Indy's 'Drame Anti-Juif' and Its Meaning in Paris, 1920," *Cambridge Opera Journal*, vol. 2, no. 3 (November, 1990), 295–319.

Gastoué, Amédée. "Notes et souvenirs sur Déodat de Séverac," *La tribune de Saint-Gervais* (June, 1921), 199–200.

Geertz, Clifford. *The Interpretation of Cultures*. New York: Basic Books, 1973.

Gellner, Ernest. *Nations and Nationalism*. Oxford: Oxford University Press, 1983.

Gibaldi, Joseph. *MLA Handbook for Writers of Research Papers*, 5th ed. New York: The Modern Language Association of America, 1999.

Gide, André. *Incidences*. Paris: Nouvelle Revue française, 1924.

——— *Prétextes*. Paris: Mercure de France, 1929.

Gildea, Robert. *The Past in French History*. New Haven, CT: Yale University Press, 1994.

Giocanti, Stéphane. "Vincent d'Indy et le régionalisme musical," *La France latine*, vol. 113 (1991).

—— *Charles Maurras: félibre*. Paris: L. de Montalte, 1995.

—— "Vincent d'Indy est-il un compositeur religieux?," in *Vincent d'Indy et son temps*, edited by Manuela Schwartz. Sprimont, Belgium: Mardaga Press, 2006.

Gontier, Augustin. *Metodo ragionato di canto piano: il canto piano nel suo ritmo, nella sua tonalità, nei suoi modi*. Rome: Torre d'Orfeo, 1993.

Gras, Christian, and Georges Livet, eds. *Régions et régionalisme en France du XVIIIe siècle à nos jours*. Paris: Presses Universitaires de France, 1977.

Greaves, Anthony. *Maurice Barrès*. Boston: G.K. Hall and Co., 1978.

Grover, Ralph Scott. "The Influence of Franck, Wagner, and Debussy on Representative Works of Ernest Chausson." PhD Dissertation, University of North Carolina at Chapel Hill, 1966.

Guillot, Pierre, "Claude Debussy and Déodat de Séverac," *Cahiers Debussy*, nouvelle série, no. 10 (1986), 3–16.

—— ed. *Déodat de Séverac: écrits sur la musique*. Liège, Belgium: Pierre Mardaga, 1993.

—— *Déodat de Séverac: la musique et les lettres*. Liège, Belgium: Pierre Mardaga, 2002.

Guilmant, Alexandre. "Du rôle de l'orgue dans les offices liturgiques," *La tribune de Saint-Gervais* (September, 1895), 11–12.

—— Inaugural address for the Schola Cantorum, October 15, 1896, *La tribune de Saint-Gervais* (1901), 52

Gwynn, Denis. *The "Action Française" Condemnation*. London: Burn Oates and Washbourne, 1928.

Halasz, Nicholas. *Captain Dreyfus: The Story of a Mass Hysteria*. New York: Simon and Schuster, 1955.

Hart, Brian Jack. *The Symphony in Theory and Practice in France, 1900–1914*. PhD Dissertation, Indiana University, 1994.

Havart, Max. "Cobles, sardanes, danses, musiques catalanes," *Revista terra nostra* nos. 98–99 (1999), 2–264.

Heartz, Daniel, and Bruce Alan Brown. "Classical," *The New Grove Dictionary of Music and Musicians*, 2nd ed., volume 5. London: Macmillan Publishers Limited (2001), 924–9.

Hitler, Adolf. *Hitler's Secret Conversations 1941–1944*. New York: H. Holt and Co., 1953.

Hobsbawm, Eric. *Nations and Nationalism Since 1780: Programme, Myth, Reality*. Cambridge: Cambridge University Press, 1990.

Honegger, Arthur. *Je suis compositeur*. Paris: Editions du Conquistador, 1951.

Huebner, Steven. *French Opera at the fin de siècle*. Oxford: Oxford University Press, 1999.

—— "Review of *French Cultural Politics of Music from the Dreyfus Affair to the First World War*, by Jane Fulcher," *Music and Letters*, vol. 82, no. 2 (2001).

D'Indy, Vincent. *La tribune de Saint-Gervais: bulletin mensuel de la Schola*, vol. 1 (Paris: Schola Cantorum, 1895).

—— *Chanson populaires du Vivarais*. Paris: A. Durand, 1900.

―― "A propos du Prix de Rome: le régionalisme musical," *La revue musicale*, 2e année, no. 6 (June, 1902).
―― "Pelléas et Mélisande," *L'occident* (June, 1902).
―― *Cours de composition musicale*, 3 vols: vol. 1, 1903, in collaboration with Auguste Sérieyx; vol. 2, 1909, in collaboration with Auguste Sérieyx; vol. 3, 1950, in collaboration with Guy de Lioncourt. Paris: Durand et Cie.
―― *Beethoven*. Paris, 1911.
―― *La Schola Cantorum, son histoire depuis sa fondation jusqu'en 1925*. Paris: Bloud et Gay, 1927.
Instituto de Estudios llerdenses. *Séverac I Viñes: la trobada de dos genis al servei de la música*. Lleida: Institut d'Estudis llerdencs, 1985.
Isherwood, Robert M. "The Centralization of Music in the Reign of Louis XIV," *French Historical Studies*. VI (Fall, 1969), 156–71.
Ivanova, Anna. *The Dance in Spain*. New York: Praeger Publishers, 1970.
Jacob, Max. *Le laboratoire central*. Paris: Gallimard, 1980.
Jankélévitch, Vladimir. *La rhapsodie*. Paris: Flammarion, 1955.
―― *La présence lointaine: Albéniz, Séverac, Mompou*. Paris: Editions du Seuil, 1983.
Jenkins, Robin. *The Sardana Dancers*. London: J. Cape, 1964.
Johnson, Douglas. *France and the Dreyfus Affair*. London: Blandford, 1966.
Johnson, Graham. Program notes to CD, *Songs by Déodat de Séverac*, performed by Graham Johnson, François Le Roux, and Patricia Rozario (Hyperion A66983, 1998).
Kahan, Sylvia. *Music's Modern Muse: A Life of Winnaretta Singer, Princesse de Polignac*. Rochester, NY: University of Rochester Press, 2003.
Kalfa, Jacqueline. "Isaac Albéniz à Paris: une patrie retrouvée 1893–1909," *Revue internationale de musique française*, vol. 9, no. 26 (June, 1988), 19–36.
Kelly, Jane. "The Piano Works of Déodat de Séverac: Technical and Timbral Concerns." Masters of Music Thesis, University of Queensland, Australia, 1994.
Keym, Stefan. "De la 'Divine Bonté' à l' 'Antéchrist?' Jour d'été à la montagne de Vincent d'Indy compare à Eine Alpensinfonie de Richard Strauss," in *Vincent d'Indy et son temps*, edited by Manuela Schwartz. Sprimont, Belgium: Mardaga Press, 2006.
Koechlin, Charles. "Chronique musicale: *L'or du Rhin*," *Gazette des beaux-arts*, 51e année, vol. 2, no. 63 (December, 1909), 492–4.
Korpeles, Maud. "Definition of Folk Music," *Journal of the International Folk Music Council*, vol. 7 (January, 1955), 6–7.
Korsyn, Kevin. "Towards a New Poetics of Musical Influence," *Music Analysis* 10 (1991), 3–72.
Lafargue, Marc. *Le coq catalan* (March 24, 31, 1923).
Lalo, Pierre. "La musique: au Conservatoire—la grande commission de réformes de 1892," *Le temps* (August 8, 1901), 3.
―― "La musique: le nouveau directeur du Conservatoire," *Le temps* (June 20, 1905), 3.
―― "La musique: concerts—à la Schola Cantorum, les oeuvres de Déodat de Séverac, un musicien nouveau," *Le temps* (July 7, 1905), 3.

—— "La musique: le concours de Prix de Rome en 1905," *Le temps* (July 11, 1905), 3.
—— "La musique: à la societé nationale de musique—son rôle ancien et son rôle actuel," *Le temps* (January 30, 1906), 3.
—— "La musique: le concours musical pour le Prix de Rome (I)," *Le temps* (August 20, 1907), 3.
—— "La musique: le concours musical pour le Prix de Rome—la cantata de Rome—son caractère superficial (II)," *Le temps* (August 27, 1907), 3.
—— "La musique: concerts spirituels—proportion des oeuvres Wagnériennes et des autres," *Le temps* (April 13, 1909), 3.
—— "La musique: à l'opera-comique—première representation du *Le coeur du moulin*," *Le temps* (December 14, 1909), 3.
—— "*Le coeur du moulin*," *La grande revue* (December 25, 1909).
—— "*Héliogabale*," *Le théâtre*, no. 283 (October, 1910).
—— "La musique: *Héliogabale* aux concerts Hasselmans," *Le temps* (April 18, 1911), 3.
—— "La musique: les concours du conservatoire," *Le temps*, (July 14, 1915), 3.
—— "La musique: les débuts du nouveau directeur—la direction de M. Fauré," *Le temps* (August 9, 1921), 3.
Laloy, Louis. "Déodat de Séverac," *Le mercure musical*, 11e année, no. 3 (June 15, 1905), 134–5.
—— Le Scandale du Prix de Rome," *Le mercure musical*, 1re année, no. 4 (July 1, 1905), 178–80.
—— "Les Réformes du Conservatoire," *Le mercure musical* 1e année, no. 11 (October 15, 1905), 451–3.
—— "Les Concours du Conservatoire," *Le mercure musical* 2e année, no. 15–16 (August 15, 1906), 154–7.
—— "La musique," *La grande revue* (December 25, 1909).
—— *La musique retrouvée, 1902–1927*. Paris: Plon, 1928.
Landormy, Paul. "Déodat de Séverac," *The Musical Quarterly*, translated by Theodore Baker (April, 1934), 206–12.
Laplane, Gabriel. *Albéniz: 1860–1909*. Geneva: Editions du milieu du monde, 1956.
—— *Lope de Vega (1562–1635)*. Paris: Librairie Hachette, 1963.
Laurencie, Jean de la. "Quelques souvenirs Vivarais," *Revue du Vivarais*, vol. 39 (March–April, 1932).
Lebovics, Herman. *True France: The Wars Over Cultural Identity, 1900–1945*. Ithaca, NY: Cornell University Press, 1992.
Lehning, James R. *Peasant and French: Cultural Contact in Rural France During the Nineteenth Century*. Cambridge: Cambridge University Press, 1995.
Lepage, Jean. *L'univers pictural de Déodat de Séverac: Musée d'art et d'histoire de Narbonne, 5 juillet–30 septembre 1991*. Narbonne, France: La Ville, 1991.
Lespinard, Bernadette. "Vincent d'Indy et la naissance d'un genre nouveau: les chansons populaires françaises arrangées pour choeur mixte a capella," in *Vincent d'Indy et son temps*, edited by Manuela Schwartz. Sprimont, Belgium: Mardaga Press, 2006.

Lesure, François. "Debussy et le syndrome de Grenade," *Revue de musicologie* (1982),101–109.
Lévy, Suzy. *Journal inédit de Ricardo Viñes: Odilon Redon et le milieu occultiste, 1897–1915*. Paris, 1987.
Lindenlaus, Th. "Les concerts: quelques hommes et quelque oeuvres, Canteloube's *Le mas*," *Le temps* (March 7, 1922), 3.
Livermore, Ann. *A Short History of Spanish Music*. New York: Vienna House, 1972.
Llobregat, Lo gayter del. *Poesias catalanas*, vol. 1. Barcelona: Edició Poliglota—Estampa de Jaume Jepus y Roviralta, 1888.
Lockspeiser, Edward. *Debussy*. New York: McGraw-Hill, 1972.
Machabey, Armand. "Le théâtre musical en France," *Le ménestrel*, 95e année, no. 32 (August 11, 1933), 321–3.
Marco, Tomás. *Spanish Music in the Twentieth Century*, translated by Cola Franzen. Cambridge, MA: Harvard University Press, 1993.
Marnat, Marcel. *Maurice Ravel*. Paris: Fayard, 1986.
Marnold, Jean. "Le Conservatoire et la Schola," *Mercure de France*, 3e année, vol. 43, no. 151 (July, 1902), 105–15.
—— "Le scandale du Prix de Rome," *Le mercure musical*, 11e année, no. 3 (June 15, 1905), 129–33.
—— "Le scandale du Prix de Rome, *Le mercure musical*, 11e année, no. 4 (July 1, 1905), 178–80.
—— "Musique*: Le coeur du moulin*," *Mercure de France*, 20e année, vol. 83, no. 301 (January 1, 1910), 150–51.
Marrus, Michael R. "Folklore as an Ethnographic Source: A 'Mis au Point,'" *Popular Culture in France*, edited by Jacques Beauroy, Marc Bertrand, and Edward Gargan. Saratoga, CA: Anma Libri, and Co. (1976), 109–25.
Massenet, Jules. *My Recollections*, translated by H. Villiers Barnett. Freeport, NY: Books for Libraries Press, 1919, reprinted 1970.
Mattes, Albert Manyach. "Les catalans et Déodat de Séverac," *Le coq catalan* (June 11, 1921).
—— *L'indépendant des Pyrénées-Orientales* (January 14, 1924; May 24, August 11, December 12, 1926).
—— *L'indépendant*. Toulouse, France (March 17, 1955).
Mauclair, Camille. "La Musique," *La revue musicale* (November 15, 1906).
Maurat, Edmond. "L'Enseignement de la musique en France et les conservatoires de province," *Encyclopédie de la musique et dictionnaire du conservatoire*, vol. 2., Paris: Librairie Delagrave (1931), 3576–3616.
Maurras, Charles. *L'idée de la décentralisation*. Paris, 1898.
—— *Enquête sur la monarchie*. Paris: Champion, 1915.
—— *Mistral*. Paris: Aubier, Editions Montaigne, 1940.
Maurras, Charles, and Leon Daudet. *Notre Provence*. Paris: Ernest Flammarion, 1933.
Maus, Madeleine Octave. *Trente années de lutte pour l'art, 1894–1914*. Brussels: Librairie l'oiseau bleu, 1926.

Méline, Jules. *Le retour à la terre et la surproduction industrielle*. Paris: Hachette et Cie., 1905.

Merriman, John. *A History of Modern Europe*. New York: W.W. Norton and Company, 1996.

Meyers, Rollo. *Modern French Music: From Fauré to Boulez*. New York: Praeger Publishers, 1971.

Middleton, Richard, and Peter Manuel. "Popular Music," *The New Grove Dictionary of Music and Musicians*, 2nd ed., volume 20. London: Macmillan Publishers Limited (2001), 128–66.

Mistral, Frédéric. *Lou trésor dóu Félibrige ou Dictionnaire provençal-français* 2 vols. Aix-en-Provence, France: Veuve Remondet-Aubin, 1887.

Mistral Frédéric, "Lou pouèmo dóu Rose" ("Le poème du Rhône en XII chants"), Provençal text and French translation by Frédéric Mistral (Paris: A. Lemerre, 1897).

—— "Lettre de Frédéric Mistral," *Les chansons de France* (July 1, 1906).

—— *Memoirs*, translated by Constance Elizabeth Maud. London: Edward Arnold, 1907.

—— *Mirèio, pouèmo provençau*. Paris: H. Piazza, 1923.

—— *Oeuvres poétiques complètes*, ed. Pierre Rollet. Paris: Ramour Berenguié, 1966.

Mocquereau, André. *Paléographie musicale*, 1st series, x, vols. 1–21. Tournai, France: Société Saint Jean l'Evangéliste Desclée et Cie, (1889–1914, 1921–1954).

—— "L'Art Grégorien: son but, ses procédes, ses caractères," *La tribune de Saint-Gervais*, 5 installments: 2e année, no. 11 (November, 1896), 161–4; 2e année, no. 11 (November, 1896), 164–6; 2e année, no. 12 (December, 1896), 177–81; 3e année, no. 1 (January, 1897), 1–4; 3e année, no. 2 (February, 1897), 17–22.

Mollett, John William. *The Painters of Barbizon*. London: Sampson Low, Marston, 1890.

Mondor, Henri. *Le poème du Rhône en XII chants (Lou pouèmo dóu Rose)*. Paris: A. Lemerre, 1897.

—— "La jeunesse de Barrès: premières lectures de Barrès," *La revue de Paris*, 63e année (January 1956), 5–23.

—— Nobel Prize Library: *François Mauriac, Frédéric Mistral, and Theodor Mommsen*, translated by Annie Jackson. New York: Alexis Gregory, 1971.

Moskovitz, Marc. "Pop," *The New Grove Dictionary of Music and Musicians*, 2nd ed., volume 20. London: Macmillan Publishers Limited (2001), 101–28.

Muris, Jean de. "Compte rendu de la séance d'inauguration de l'école, *La tribune de Saint-Gervais*, 2e année, no. 10 (October, 1896), 145–52.

Musk, Andrea, "Aspects of Regionalism in French Music during the Third Republic: the Schola Cantorum, d'Indy, Séverac and Canteloube." PhD Dissertation, Oxford University, 1999.

—— "Regionalism, Latinité and the French Musical Tradition: Déodat de Séverac's *Héliogabale*," *Nineteenth Century Music Review*. Aldershot: Ashgate (2002), 226–49.

Near, John Richard. "The Life and Work of Charles-Marie Widor." DMA Dissertation, Boston University, 1985.

Nelson, Véronique. "Sardana," *The New Grove Dictionary of Music and Musicians, Musical Instruments*, vol. 16. London: Macmillan (2001), 497.

—— "Sardana," *The New Grove Dictionary of Musical Instruments*. London: Macmillan (2001), 284.

Nerval, Gérard de. *Chansons et légendes du Valois*, translated by Lucie Page. Portland, ME: T.B. Moscher, 1896.

Nettl, Bruno. *Folk Music in the United States*. Detroit, MI: Wayne State University Press, 1960.

—— *Folk and Traditional Music of the Western Continents*. Englewood Cliffs, NJ: Prentice Hall, Inc., 1965.

—— "Folk Music," *The New Harvard Dictionary of Music*, edited by Don Michael Randel. Cambridge, MA: Belknap Press of Harvard University Press (1986), 315–19.

Nguyen, Victor. *Aux origins de l'action française: intelligence et politique à l'aube du XXe siècle*. Paris: Fayard, 1991.

Nin, Joaquin. *Idées et commentaires*. Paris: Fischbacher, 1912.

Orenstein, Arbie, ed. *A Ravel Reader*. New York: Columbia University Press, 1990.

Ors, Joaquim Rubio y (Lo Gayter del Llobregat, pseud.). *Poesias catalanas* vols.1–3. Barcelona: Edició Poliglota——Estampa de Jaume Jepus y Roviralta, 1888.

Osgood, Samuel. *French Royalism Since 1870*. The Hague: Martinus Nijhoff, 1970.

Otwell, Margaret. "The Piano Works of Déodat de Séverac: A Complete Recording." DMA Dissertation, University of Maryland at College Park, 1981.

Paquette, Daniel. Program notes to CD, *Déodat de Séverac: l'oeuvre pour orgue*, translated by David Nussenbaum, performed by Pierre Guillot (Erato, STU71224,), 1985.

Paris, Desde F.A. "Des de Paris; el cant popular religiós," *Revista musical cataláña*, vol. 10, no. 120 (December, 1913), 344–7.

Pedrell, Felipe. *Pour notre musique*. Barcelona, Spain: J.B. Pujol, 1893.

—— *Illustracion musical Hispano-Americana* (October 30, 1894), 153–4.

—— *Por nuestra música*. Bellaterra, Spain: Publicacions de la Universitat Autònoma de Barcelona, 1991.

Pegg, Carol. "Folk Music," *The New Grove Dictionary of Music and Musicians*, 2nd ed., volume 9. London: Macmillan Publishers Limited (2001), 63–7.

Peer, Shanny. *France on Display: Peasants, Provincials, and Folklore in the 1937 Paris World's Fair*. New York: State University of New York Press, 1998, 63–7.

Pépratx-Saisset, Henry. *La sardane, la danse des catalans; son symbole, sa magie, ses énigmes*. Perpignan, France: Labau, 1956.

Picasso, Pablo. "L'Hommage à Déodat de Séverac," *Revista musical occitania*, special edition (1952).

Pinchemel, Philippe. *France: A Geographical Survey*, translated by Christine Trollope and Arthur J. Hunt. New York: Frederick A. Praeger, 1964.

Planhol, Xavier de. *An Historical Geography of France*, translated by Janet Lloyd. Cambridge: Cambridge University Press, 1994.

Platoff, John. "Writing About Influences: *Idomeneo*, A Case Study," *Explorations in Music, the Arts, and Ideas: Essays in Honor of Leonard B. Meyer*, edited by

Eugene Narmour and Ruth A. Solie. Stuyvesant, New York: Pendragon Press (1988), 43–65.

Play, F. Le. *La reforme sociale en France*. Paris: E. Dentu, 1866.

Pothier, Joseph. *Mélodies grégoriennes d'après la tradition*. Tournai, France: Société Saint Jean l'Evangéliste Desclée et Cie, 1880.

Pougin, Arthur. "Le concours du Conservatoire," *Le ménestrel*, 72e année, no. 29 (July 22, 1906), 222–5.

—— "Le concours du Conservatoire," *Le ménestrel*, 72e année, no. 30 (July 29, 1906), 229–34.

Prevost-Paradol, L.A. *La France nouvelle*. Paris: Michel Levy, 1868.

Price, Roger. *A Concise History of France*. Cambridge: Cambridge University Press, 1991.

Pujol, F. "Sardana, cançoner popular de catalanya," vol. 1, *Diccionari de la danza*.

Pustet, Friedrich. *Graduale romanum*. Regensburg, Germany: Société St.-Jean l'Evangeliste et Desclée et Cie, 1871.

Ricart, E.C. *El gris I el cadmi*. Barcelona, Spain: Libreria Catalonia, 1926.

Rioux, Jean-Pierre. *Nationalisme et conservatisme: la ligue de la patrie française 1899–1904*. Paris: Editions Beauchesne, 1977.

Rowdybush, James B. *The Hexagon and the Napoleonic State: A Study of Decentralization and Regional Reform in France*. PhD Dissertation. Berkeley: University of California, 1983.

Rolland, Romain. *Jean Christophe*. Paris: P. Ollendorf, 1905; English version, translated Gilbert Cannan. New York: Henry Holt and Co., 1911.

Ross, James. "D'Indy's *Fervaal*: Reconstructing French Identity at the *fin de siècle*," *Music and Letters*, vol. 84, no. 2 (2003), 209–40.

Rouart, Eugène. "Souvenirs sur Déodat de Séverac," *La revue musicale*, 2e année, no. 11 (October 1, 1921), 216–22.

Rousseau, Samuel. *Rapport sur le concours musica, 1900–1903*. Paris: Chaix, 1904.

Sahlins, Peter. *Boundaries: The Making of France and Spain in the Pyrénées*. Berkeley: University of California Press, 1989.

—— "The Nation in the Village: State-Building and Communal Struggles in the Catalan Borderland during the Eighteenth and Nineteenth Centuries," *Journal of Modern History*, vol. 60, no. 2 (June, 1988), 234–63.

Saint-Saëns, Camille. "Germanophilie," *L'echo de Paris* (October 6, 1914), 1.

Saisset, Henry Pépratx. *La sardane*. Perpignan, France: Labau Perpignan, 1956.

Sand, George, *La mare au diable*. Paris: Larousse, 1977.

Sanford, Elwitt. *The Making of the Third Republic*. Baton Rouge, LA: Louisiana State University Press, 1975.

Sarradet, Xavier. *Un grand musicien, un grand Languedocien, Déodat de Séverac*. Paris: Institut de France, 1984.

Schwartz, Manuela, ed. *Vincent d'Indy et son temps*. Sprimont, Belgium: Mardaga, 2006.

Seager, Frederick H. *The Boulanger Affair*. Ithaca, NY: Cornell University Press, 1969.

Selva, Blanche. *Déodat de Séverac*. Paris: Librairie Delagrave, 1930.

Sérieyx, Auguste. *Vincent d'Indy*. Paris: Albert Messein, 1914.

Séverac, Déodat de. "Causerie musicale: a propos de *Tristan et Iseult* de Richard Wagner," *Le messager de Toulouse* (January 1, 1900).

—— "Toulouse et l'évolution musicale contemporaine," *La renaissance latine* (August 15, 1902), 678–82.

—— *Le chant de la terre*. Paris: Editions Mutuelle, 1903.

—— pseud. A.C. Sever. "Chronique des concerts: musiciens catalans," *Le mercure musical*, 1e année, no. 2 (June 1, 1905), 90–91.

—— *Le monde musical* (May 5, 1905), 124.

—— *Chansons du XVIIIème siècle*. Paris: Rouart, Lerolle et Cie, 1906.

—— *Le mistral* (August 8, 1906).

—— *Les vieilles chansons de France*. Paris: Rouart, Lerolle et Cie, 1906.

—— "La centralisation et les petites chapelles musicales," *Le courrier musical*, 11e année, nos. 1, 3, 5 (January 1, 15, March 8, 1908), 1–6, 37-43, 142–44.

—— "Albeniz," *Le courrier musical* (April 1, 1909), 381–2.

—— *Le coeur du moulin: pièce lyrique en deux actes*, piano-vocal score. Paris: Edition Mutuelle, 1909.

—— *Grand revue* (April 10, 1909), 564–5.

—— *Héliogabale*. Paris: Rouart, Lerolle, et Cie, 1910.

—— *Le cant del Vallespir*. Paris: Festival Déodat de Séverac, 1911.

—— "Chansons du Languedoc et du Roussillon," *Musica*, 10e année, no. 111 (December, 1911), 241.

—— "Quelles conséquences aura la Guerre pour l'art musical en France," *Le courrier de l'aude* (September 20, 1915).

—— *Soleil du midi* (November 8, 1915).

—— *Cerdaña*. Paris: Rouart, Lerolle et Cie, 1919.

—— *En Languedoc*. [1905] Paris: Rouart, Lerolle et Cie, 1919.

—— *Minyoneta*. Paris: Rouart, Lerolle et Cie, 1919.

—— *Tres recuerdos*. Paris: Rouart, Lerolle, et Cie, 1919.

—— *Cortège catalan*. [1919] Paris: Rouart, Lerolle et Cie, 1920.

—— *Sous les lauriers-roses*. [1919] Paris: Rouart, Lerolle et Cie, 1920.

—— *Douze mélodies*. Paris: Rouart, Lerolle et Cie, 1924.

—— *Lied romantique pour violoncello (ou violin) et piano*. Paris: Rouart, Lerolle, et Cie, 1929.

—— *Souvenirs de Céret*. Paris: Rouart, Lerolle, et Cie, 1931.

—— *Sonate*, performed by Isabelle Legoux Laboureau, 1984 (Disc Revolum REV 051 RVM 360).

—— *Déodat de Séverac: Piano Album*. Paris: Editions Salabert, 1991.

—— *Orgelmusik der französischen romantik: petite suite scholastique*. Sankt Augustin, Germany: J. Butz, 1991; originally published, 1913.

—— *Sonate pour piano*. [1903] Paris: Edition de Pierre Guillot, 1991.

—— *L'oeuvre pour orgue: suite en mi*. Longchamp: Editions Europart-Music, 1994.

—— *Trois mélodies et quatre pages pianistiques inédites*. Paris: Presses de l'Université de Paris-Sorbonne, 2002.

——— "Déodat de Séverac: oeuvres inédits pour orchestre." Performed by Robert Benzi and L'orchestre de la Suisse Romande (Espace2 RSR6197, 2006).

——— "Le renouveau de la chanson populaire," *L'action régionale de la Schola Cantorum* (date unknown).

Séverine, ed. *Livre d'hommage des lettres françaises à Zola*. Paris: Société des gens de lettres, 1898.

Shenton, Gordon. *The Fictions of the Self: The Early Works of Maurice Barrès*. Chapel Hill, NC: North Carolina Studies in the Romance Languages and Literatures, 1979.

Sherr, Richard. "Plainchant," *The New Grove Dictionary of Music and Musicians*, vol. 19, online edition. Oxford: Oxford University Press (2006).

Sirinelli, Jean-François. *Histoire des droits en France*. Paris: Editions Gallimard, 1992.

Smith, Anthony. *National Identity*. Reno: University of Nevada Press, 1991.

Solench, Josep Maria Mas i. *Diccionari breu de la sardana*. Barcelona: Santa Culom a de Farners-J.M. Mas i Solench, 1981.

——— *La sardana, dansa nacional de Catalunya*. Barcelona: Generalitat de Catalunya, 1993.

Soltau, R.H. *French Political Thought Throughout the Nineteenth Century*. Oxford: Oxford University Press, 1922.

Soucy, Robert. *Fascism in France: The Case of Maurice Barrès*. Berkeley: University of California Press, 1972.

Soula, Camille, and Ismael Girand, ed. *Hommage à Déodat de Séverac*. Paris: Edition de l'institut d'études occitanes, 1952.

Sternay, François. *Le courrier musical* (March, 1907).

Stockhem, Michel. "Vincent d'Indy en Belgique: réseaux et influences," in *Vincent d'Indy et son temps*, edited by Manuela Schwartz. Sprimont, Belgium: Mardaga Press, 2006.

Stoechlin, Paul de. "*Hélène de Sparte*," *Le courrier musical*,15e année, no. 10 (May 15, 1912), 300–302.

Strasser, Michael Creasman. "*Ars Gallica*: The Société Nationale de Musique and Its Role in French Musical Life, 1871–1891." PhD, University of Illinois at Champaign-Urbana, 1998.

Straus, Joseph N. *Remaking the Past: Musical Modernism and the Influence of the Tonal Tradition*. Cambridge, MA, and London: Harvard University Press, 1990.

Taine, Hippolyte. *The Modern Regime*, translated by John Durand. New York: Holt and Co., 1890.

——— *Origines de la France contemporaine*, 6 vols., 1876–93. New York: H. Holt and Co., 1895; French edition. Paris: Hachette et Cie, 1899.

——— *Origins of Contemporary France*, translated by John Durand. New York: Peter Smith, 1931.

Taruskin, Richard. "Nationalism," *The New Grove Dictionary of Music and Musicians*, 2nd ed., volume 17. London: Macmillan Publishers Limited (2001), 689–706.

——— "Revising Revision," *Journal of the American Musicological Society*, vol. 46, no. 1 (Spring, 1993), 114–38.

Terrus, Etienne. "Les catalans à Déodat de Séverac," *Le coq catalan* (1921).
Terry, Arthur. *Catalan Literature*. London: Ernest Benn Limited, 1972.
Tharaud, Jérôme. *Mes années chez Barrès*. Paris: Librairie Plon, 1928.
Thomson, Andrew. *Vincent d'Indy and His World*. Oxford: Clarendon Press, 1996.
Tiersot, Julien. *Musiques pittoresques*. Paris: Librairie Fischbacher, 1889.
—— *Chansons populaires recueillies dans les Alpes françaises*. Paris: Grenoble H. Falque et F. Perrin, 1903.
—— *Un demi-siècle de musique française entre les deux guerres, 1870–1917*. Paris: Paris Librairie, 1918.
—— *La chanson populaire et les écrivains romantiques*. Paris: Librairie Plon, 1931.
Tombs, Robert, ed. *Nationhood and Nationalism from Boulangism to the Great War, 1889–1914*. Cambridge: Cambridge University Press, 1980.
Tocqueville, Alexis, de. *L'ancien régime et la révolution*. [1856] Paris, Gallimard, 1967.
—— *De la démocratie en Amérique*. [1835] Paris, Garnier-Flammarion, 1981.
Trumble, Robert. *Vincent d'Indy: His Greatness and Integrity*. Victoria, Australia: University of Ballarat Press, 1994.
Underhill, John Garrett, ed. *Four Plays by Lope de Vega*. New York: Charles Scribner's Sons, 1936.
Vallas, Leon. *Vincent d'Indy*, 2 vols. Paris: Editions Albin Michel, 1946, 1950.
Vega, Lope de. *El maestro de danzar* (1585).
Ventura, Pep. *Per tu ploro*. New York: Reinbert and Co., 1949.
Vierne, Louis. "Mémoires," *Diapason* 30, no. 2 (January, 1939).
Villemarque, Hersart de la. *Barzaz-Breiz; chants populaires de la Bretagne*. Paris: Perrin et Cie, 1893.
Violet, Gustave. "Hommage à Séverac." Paris, 1952.
Virgil. *Géorgiques*. [29 BCE] Excerpts from *Géorgic I*, translated by John Dryden and J.B. Greenough, www.classics.mit.edu.
Vlach-Magnard, Claire. *Correspondances de Albéric Magnard*. Paris: Société française de musicologie, 1997.
Vuillermoz, Emile. "La Schola et le Conservatoire," *Mercure de France*, 20e année, vol. 81, no. 294 (September 16, 1909), 234–43.
Warnod, Jeanine. *Le bateau-lavoir*. Paris: Mayer, 1986.
Waters, Robert F. "Regionalism and Catalan Folk Elements in the Compositions of Déodat de Séverac, 1910–1919." PhD Dissertation, University of Maryland at College Park, 2002.
Weber, Eugen Joseph. *The Nationalist Revival in France 1905–1914*. Berkeley: University of California Press, 1959.
—— *Action Française: Royalism and Reaction in Twentieth Century France*. Palo Alto, CA: Stanford University Press, 1962.
—— *Peasants Into Frenchmen*. Stanford University Press, 1976.
—— "The Second Republic, Politics, and the Peasant," *French Historical Studies* vol. 11, no. 4 (Fall, 1980), 521–50.
Weil, Simone. *L'enracinement*. Paris: Gallimard, 1949.

Woldu, Gail H. "Gabriel Fauré as Director of the Conservatoire national de musique de déclamation, 1905–1920." PhD Dissertation, Yale University, 1983.

—— "Gabriel Fauré, directeur du Conservatoire: les réformes de 1905," *Revue de musicologie*, 70/2 (Paris, 1984), 199–228.

—— "Au delà du scandale de 1905: propos sur le Prix de Rome au début du XXe siècle," *Revue de musicologie*, 82e, no. 2 (Paris, 1996), 245–67.

Wright, Gordon. *France in Modern Times*. Chicago: Rand McNally College Publishing Co., 1974.

Wright, Julien. *The Regionalist Movement in France, 1890–1914: Jean Charles-Brun and French Political Thought*. Oxford: Oxford University Press, 2003.

Zeldin, Theodore. *France, 1848–1945: Ambition, Love, and Politics*. Oxford: Oxford University Press, 1973.

—— *France, 1848–1945: Intellect and Pride*. Oxford: Oxford University Press, 1980.

—— *France, 1848–1945: Anxiety and Hypocrisy*. Oxford: Oxford University Press, 1981.

Zimmerman, Edward and Lawrence Archbold. "Why Should We Not Do the Same with Our Catholic Melodies?: Guilmant's *L'organiste liturgique*, op. 65," edited by Lawrence Archbold and William J. Peterson. *French Organ Music From the Revolution to Franck and Widor*. Rochester, NY: University of Rochester Press (1995), 201–47.

Index

Action française 46–9, 71, 202
Action régionaliste 44, 67, 245
Albéniz, Isaac 20–21, 26, 28, 32, 72, 114,
    118, 140, 147, 182, 183, 185–7,
    193–4, 212, 235
angélus 75–7, 93, 105, 115–116, 121,
    130–31, 135, 143, 146
Apaches 27, 35, 192

Barrès, Maurice 5–6, 9, 12, 15, 43–6, 49–55,
    57, 63, 78, 81, 144, 180, 245
Bizet, Georges 148, 245
Bordes, Charles 13, 19–22, 26, 28, 30, 33,
    46, 62, 66–8, 72, 83, 85, 87–8, 96,
    100, 104, 110, 121, 147, 180, 182,
    187, 193, 199, 202, 233, 245

Canteloube, Joseph 6–7, 9–11, 17, 24, 28,
    34, 65–7, 70–74, 103, 110–111, 121,
    124, 133, 143–4, 154, 161–2, 186,
    192, 198–9, 202–3, 207, 210–12,
    215, 230, 238–243
    compositions
        Lo pardal 232, 238–40
Carré, Albert 34, 114
Catalan, Catalonia, Catalonian 7–8, 9–10,
    12–15, 36–7, 47, 72, 91–2, 98, 104,
    109, 123, 140, 151, 153–4, 167–9,
    171–5, 177–80, 182–7, 192–6, 198,
    203–8, 211–16, 222–4, 226, 228,
    230–31, 233–4, 235, 238, 242–4
centralist, centralized, centralization 8, 17,
    41–3, 50, 54–7, 59, 61–4, 66, 168,
    244, 246
Chabrier, Emmanuel 26, 29, 123, 144, 147,
    192, 233
Charles-Brun, Jean 9, 15, 30, 34, 43–4, 247
Charry, Joseph 11, 81, 209

Christian, Christianity 82–3, 103, 129, 168,
    199, 203, 207
cobla xiii, 12–14, 90–92, 169, 173, 176–9,
    196, 198, 203–8, 211–12, 214–216,
    222, 225–6, 228, 237, 239, 243–4
Colette 28, 33

Debussy, Claude 10, 14, 24–7, 29, 30–35,
    58, 76, 95–8, 100–101, 104, 106,
    108, 109, 112, 114, 116–18, 121,
    137, 143–4, 147, 150, 156–7, 159,
    192, 212
    compositions
        Pelléas et Mélisande 27, 29, 33,
            97–8, 104, 106, 108, 112,
            115–18, 121, 192
        *Prélude à "L'après-midi d'un
            faune"* 156–7
Dreyfus Affair 12, 43–6, 49, 53–4, 71, 81
Dubois, Théodore 8, 19, 21, 35, 48, 55, 58,
    88, 114
Dukas, Paul 28, 31, 39, 60, 114, 154

Falla, Manuel de 28, 72, 168 179, 184, 192
Fauré, Gabriel 10, 22, 28–31, 56, 58–9, 81,
    88, 103, 110, 150, 202, 207, 245
Fédéralist régionaliste français 43–4, 245
Félibrige 9, 43–4, 64–6, 69–70, 78, 81, 159
Ferry, Jules 8–9
fluviol 14, 90, 144, 176, 177–8, 185, 198,
    225, 233–4, 238–9, 244
Franck, César 21–3, 30, 86, 88, 100, 109,
    125, 154

Gay, Maria 193–4
goig 14, 171, 198, 215, 228, 237–8, 243
Granados, Enrique 193–4
Guéret, Charles 11, 209–10

Guilmant, Alexandre 13, 20–21, 23, 84–7, 89, 93, 96, 182, 194

Impressionism, Impressionist 32–4, 98–9, 103–6, 121, 123, 129, 136–7, 142, 149, 151, 155–9, 216, 232
industrialization, Industrial Revolution 4, 6, 42–3, 50
Indy, Vincent d' 5–6, 10, 13, 15, 20–31, 34, 38–9, 48, 54, 57–8, 67, 70–75, 78, 82–4, 86–8, 95–6, 101, 103, 110–11, 113, 114, 121, 124–6, 130, 132, 148, 155–8, 180, 183–7, 193–4, 199, 203, 207, 233, 245
   compositions
      Jour d'été à la montagne 72–5, 156
      Poème des montagnes 72, 130

Koechlin, Charles 11, 28, 58, 121–2, 243

Legitimism 8–9, 44–5
Libre esthétique 124, 148–9
Ligue de la patrie française 46–7, 49, 54
Ligue nationale pour la defense de la musique française 29, 48
Llobet, Miguel 194–6

Magnard, Albéric 20, 23–4, 28, 46, 95
Manolo (Manuel Martinez-Hugué) 183, 196, 198
Massenet, Jules 26, 35, 57–8, 114, 192
Mattes, Albert 171, 178, 205, 207, 228
Maurras, Charles 15, 43–4, 46–9, 66, 71, 78,
Messager, André 28, 113–114
Milhaud, Darius 11, 243
Millet, Jean-François 75–6
Mistral, Frédéric 9–10, 12, 15, 37, 43–4, 63–7, 69–70, 81, 110, 143, 197, 203, 244–5

national, nationalist, nationalized, nationalism, nationale, nationalisme 6, 9, 12, 20, 32, 45–9, 51, 53–4, 56–7, 59–62, 64, 71–2, 81, 168, 174, 179–80, 245–6

Nin, Joaquin 192–3

Paris Conservatoire 8–11, 19–22, 54–9, 62, 71, 81–2, 85, 87–8, 110, 182, 184–5, 244
patrie 4, 44, 47–8, 72
pays 4, 44–5, 47, 77–8, 115–116, 160
Pedrell, Felipe 168, 179–180, 182–4, 193
Picasso, Pablo 37, 92, 183, 196, 198
Polignac, Princesse de 28–9
Pothier, Joseph 84–5, 87, 133

Prix de Rome 35, 55, 57–9, 71
Ravel, Maurice 14, 27–30, 32, 34–6, 39, 109, 138, 147, 150, 192, 212, 226
   compositions
      Jeux d'eau 29, 34, 147
      Pavane pour une infante défunte 29, 34, 36
Redon, Odilon 28, 30, 104, 161
region, regional, regionalist, regionalism, régionalisme 4–12, 15, 17, 25, 28, 41–4, 46–7, 49–54, 57, 60, 62–7, 70–74, 73, 75, 77–8, 81–2, 90–92, 96–8, 105, 109, 112, 115–16, 118, 123–4, 129–31, 133–4, 138, 142, 144, 167–8, 171, 179–80, 198, 202–4, 205–8, 222, 240, 243–6
Ropartz, Guy 12, 243
Roussel, Albert 28, 43, 104, 187, 192, 233
Royalism, Royalist 44, 46–7, 50

Saint-Félix-Caraman 17, 36, 44, 84, 92, 115, 144, 192, 198, 210, 246
Saint-Félix de Lauragais xiii, 17, 18, 83, 88, 124, 159–60, 210, 224
Saint-Saëns, Camille 23, 26, 48, 87, 90, 100, 192–3, 202, 207
sardana xiii, 8, 12–14, 90, 92, 153, 169–79, 185, 196, 198, 203, 208, 212, 214–15, 224, 230–31, 233–7, 239–43
Schola Cantorum 9–11, 13–15, 19–22, 24–6, 28, 30, 36, 46, 54, 59, 62, 66–7, 71–4, 81–6, 88, 96, 98, 100–101, 103, 110, 113, 123–4, 130–31, 133,

142–3, 148–9, 151, 153, 158–9, 180, 182–6, 192–4, 203, 233, 235, 243
Schumann, Robert 150–51
Selva, Blanche 10, 19, 21, 23, 28, 39, 72, 82, 114, 130, 142, 148–9, 149, 153, 184, 186–7, 193–4, 204, 207–8, 211, 215–16, 221, 230, 233, 237, 238
Séverac, Déodat de
  writings
    "La centralization et les petites chapelles musicales" 55, 61–3, 66, 203, 246
    Écrits sur la musique xiv–xv, 48–9, 67, 83, 134, 204
    La musique et les lettres xiv, 22–3, 30, 33–4, 45–7, 82–3, 85, 113–114, 124, 142, 154–6, 158, 204, 235
  compositions
    Les Antibels 78, 162
    "A l'aube dans la montagne" 76, 105–7, 110
    Bagneuses au soleil 123, 149, 186, 213
    Lo cant del Vallespir 14, 39, 197, 204, 222–4
    "Les caresses de grand'maman" 149–50
    Cerdaña xiii, 14, 74, 75–7, 105, 108–9, 123, 186, 198, 206, 211–21
    "Chanson pour le petit cheval" 76, 109
    Le chant de la terre 7, 27, 28, 32, 74–6, 95, 123, 129–34, 144, 147, 151, 161, 189, 191, 213
    "À cheval dans la prairie" 74, 140, 142, 144, 146–7
    "Le ciel est par-dessus le toit" 25, 27, 76, 103
    Le coeur du moulin xiv, 13, 15, 33–4, 76–7, 93, 99, 113–22, 160, 194, 201, 206
    "Coin de cimetière, au printemps" 76, 95, 134, 140, 142, 191

"Les cors" 25, 27, 95, 99
Danse du "tonneau" et du "bidon" 150–51
"Danse du soleil" 199, 208–9
"Les deux Mousquetaires" 150–51
El divino de l'hort 87, 228–30
"Epilogue: le jour des noces" 76, 95, 129
"Fanfare fuguée" 92–3
"Fantaisie pastorale" 90–91
"Les fêtes: souvenir de Puigcerda" 186, 211–14, 218
La fille de la terre 162, 201
"La fontaine de Chopin" 150–51
"La grêle" 74, 76, 129–30, 137–8
'Halte à la fontaine' 74, 143–6
Hélène de Sparte 34, 225–8
Héliogabale 11, 14, 37, 93, 198–211, 228, 243
"Les hiboux" 98–9
"Le jour de la foire, au mas" 74, 76, 140, 142, 144, 213
"Le jour des noces" 131, 139–40, 213
"Le labour" 129, 131, 133–4, 139
En Languedoc 3, 5, 68, 70, 74–7, 83, 93–5, 123, 134, 140, 143–7, 151, 161, 213
Loin des villes 82, 140–42, 191
"Le mas en fête" 68, 143
"Ménétriers et glaneuses: souvenir d'un pèlerinage à Font-Romeu" 211–12, 214–15
"Mimi se déguisé en marquise" 149–50
Minyoneta: souvenir de Figueras 14, 39, 197, 230–31
"Les moissons" 76, 95, 129, 131, 139
"Les muletiers devant le Christ de Llivia" xiii, 211–12, 215–16
Nymphes au crépuscule 10, 27, 32–3, 155–7
"Où l'on entend une vieille boîte à musique" 149–50

Petite suite scholastique, sur un thème de carillon languedocien 91–3, 96
"Les petites voisines en visite" 149–50
Poèmes des saisons: tableaux symphoniques 157–8
"Prends mon âme" 27, 98
"Le retour des muletiers" 211–12, 215, 219–21
"Ronde dans le parc" 149–50
"Les semailles" 76, 129–130, 132
Sérénade au clair de lune 18, 151
"Soleils couchants" 27, 101–2
Sonate 103, 123–8, 130
Sous les lauriers-roses 14, 39, 123, 186, 190, 197, 221, 232–41, 244
Suite en mi 87–91, 94, 96
"Sur l'étang, le soir" 94–5, 140, 142–4, 146
"En tartane: l'arrivée en Cerdagne" 211–12, 216–17
"Temps de neige" 76, 97, 104
"Toto déguisé en Suisse d'église" 149–50
En vacances 109, 123, 149–51
Valse métèque 150–51
"Valse romantique" 149–50
"La vasque aux colombes" 150–51
"Vers le mas en fête" 76, 93–4, 140, 142–5, 147, 191
Société musicale indépendante 27–8, 34
Société nationale de musique 26, 27–8, 32, 34, 35, 57, 88, 98, 103, 114, 130, 142, 148–9, 185–6, 189, 191, 194–5, 213, 235

tenor 14, 91, 176, 204, 207–8, 225
Third Republic government 11, 41, 44, 53, 59, 64, 66–7, 72–4, 81–2, 203
tiple 14, 91, 176, 204–5, 207–8
La tribune de Saint-Gervais 19, 84, 86, 88

Viñes, Ricardo 27–8, 34–5, 72, 142–4, 161, 183, 186, 192–4, 221, 235
Violet, Gustave 153, 204
Vuillermoz, Émile 71, 81

Wagner, Richard 18, 22, 29–32, 48, 58, 98, 108–9, 116–17, 199, 225